Prepare Your Taxes

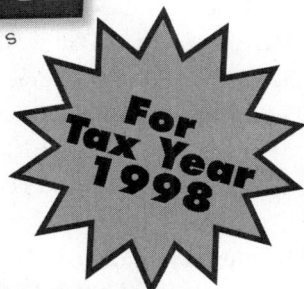

In a Weekend®

Sunrise Midday Sunset

Sunset Evening Sunrise

For Tax Year 1998

with TurboTax® Deluxe

DIANE TINNEY

P

PRIMA TECH

A Division of Prima Publishing

A Division of Prima Publishing

Prima Publishing, In a Weekend, and colophon are registered trademarks of Prima Communications, Inc., Rocklin, California 95677.

Publisher: Matthew H. Carleson
Managing Editor: Dan J. Foster
Senior Acquisitions Editor: Deborah F. Abshier
Senior Editor: Kelli R. Crump
Assistant Project Editor: Kim V. Benbow
Technical Editor: Franni Ferrero
Copy Editor: Laura R. Gabler
Interior Layout: Marian Hartsough
Cover Design: Prima Design Team
Indexer: Katherine Stimson

TurboTax, QuickBooks, and Quicken are registered trademarks of Intuit, Inc. Microsoft is a registered trademark of Microsoft Corporation.

Important: Prima Publishing cannot provide software support. Please contact the appropriate software manufacturer's technical support line or Web site for assistance.

Prima Publishing and the author have attempted throughout this book to distinguish proprietary trademarks from descriptive terms by following the capitalization style used by the manufacturer.

ISBN: 0-7615-1965-3
Library of Congress Catalog Card Number: 98-68115
Printed in the United States of America

99 00 01 02 03 II 10 9 8 7 6 5 4 3 2 1

In loving memory of my father, James Joseph Tinney.

ACKNOWLEDGMENTS

I'd like to thank the folks at PRIMA TECH for providing me with the opportunity to work on this wonderful "In a Weekend" series book. Thanks to Jenny Watson for recommending me for this TurboTax book and doing battle as needed to get this project off the ground. And a special thank you to editors, Kelli Crump, Laura Gabler, and Franni Ferrero for reading the manuscript and finding all my goofs. Your careful review is what gives this book its polish and shine in the end.

Thank you to my friends in the tax community who answered my urgent calls and e-mails when I was researching the new and still changing tax law. Special thanks to Mike Andrew at Super Forms (STF Services) for donating a clean copy of the first tax return form from 1913. Thanks to my husband, Jim, and son, David, for feeding me while I toiled away in the "tower of tax automation."

ABOUT THE AUTHOR

Diane Tinney has authored more than a dozen computer books on topics ranging from setting up a Windows NT server to programming in Visual Basic to organizing your finances with Quicken. When she is not writing, Diane's business, The Software Professional, keeps her busy teaching, creating business applications, and managing Web sites. Her favorite client (other than Prima) is ACT, a nonprofit computer user group for corporate tax accountants.

Prior to becoming an author and business owner, Diane worked at KPMG (one of the big 5 CPA firms) as senior tax manager in their New York City office. Diane's dual career as a tax and software professional has given her a unique perspective on teaching others how to use today's software to complete work more efficiently and effectively.

CONTENTS AT A GLANCE

CONTENTS

INTRODUCTION

Congratulations! Not only have you purchased the best-selling tax-preparation software, but you have also decided to dedicate a weekend to this book so you can learn how to organize your taxes year-round. The tasks of gathering and preparing your tax returns can sometimes seem overwhelming. With this book and TurboTax, you will soon learn how to take the drudgery out of tax preparation and take charge of your tax planning. In one weekend you will learn the most important tax-organization skills and how best to use TurboTax to achieve your goals.

Is This Book for You?

Prepare Your Taxes In a Weekend with TurboTax Deluxe 1998 is for anyone who wants to use TurboTax but needs some help in learning the ropes. Think of this book as a personal tutorial, a one-on-one class with an expert user of TurboTax. What a deal! You get to stay in the comfort of your home and learn how to

✪ Gather your tax data
✪ Get expert advice
✪ Enter your tax data
✪ Find tax deductions
✪ Determine your tax-reporting responsibilities

- Stay informed on tax law changes
- Print and file tax returns
- Develop and monitor a tax-savings plan
- Estimate future tax expenses
- Handle tax audits and inquiries
- Access online tax resources

How Much Time Will This Take?

This book is organized around the normal course of a weekend, from Friday evening to Sunday evening. Each session lasts about three hours, with a break in the middle so you can get a cup of coffee or go for a quick walk. If you have the time, you can cover the entire book in one weekend.

On the other hand, if soccer games, visiting relatives, or work dominate your weekends, you can do the sessions (six in total) one at a time over the course of a week or even several weeks. If today is April 15th, don't worry—extensions are covered in the Sunday Afternoon session, so skip ahead and do that section first. The flexible design permits you to tailor the book to your schedule and preferred learning pace. A sure key to your success!

Some sections, such as dealing with how to electronically file your return, may not interest you at this time. Feel free to skip over these sections, knowing that at any time in the future you can spend just a few moments to learn about the topic when you need it. However, I do recommend that you read the introduction to the sections you skip, if for no other reason than to know the purpose and requirements of the topics covered.

What's Covered in This Book?

- **Friday Evening: Taking Control of Your Taxes** explains your responsibilities as a taxpayer, how to start organizing your tax records, and the resources that you can use to take control of your tax situation. This session provides you with commonsense advice and takes the mystery out of some of the tax law jargon. You will learn about common tax pitfalls and how to avoid them. Other features include step-by-step instructions on how to organize and gather your tax data, as well as information on how to stay current on tax law changes and how they may affect you and your family.

- ✿ **Saturday Morning: Getting Started with TurboTax** introduces you to the core features of TurboTax. If you are new to TurboTax, you will learn how to set up your TurboTax data file. If you've used TurboTax in the past, you will learn how to roll your previous year's data forward into this year's tax file. You will also tour the extensive TurboTax Help files and reference library. In addition, this session shows you how to get expert advice and use the Internet features built into TurboTax. You will learn the difference between the EasyStep Interview and Forms methods and then start filling in basic tax information.

- ✿ **Saturday Afternoon: Starting Your Federal Tax Return** focuses on entering your taxable income. You will enter the amounts from your W-2, 1099s, and Schedule K-1s. You will learn how to navigate the Interview process and tailor the Interview to your tax situation. Also, this session covers Schedule C, sole-proprietor businesses, Schedule E, rent, royalty and supplemental income, and Schedule F, for farming businesses. You will learn about the tax rules surrounding the income you received and determine which amounts are taxable income to you.

- ✿ **Sunday Morning: Finishing Your Federal Tax Return** continues the tax data entry by exploring your adjusted gross income, deductions, additional taxes, and tax credits. You will learn how to identify tax deductions, maintain accurate deduction receipt records to support your claims in the event of an audit, and determine tax credits available to you. This session explains how to compute the underpayment penalty and the safe-harbor rules that might save you money, and it concludes with you finding out the amount of your final tax due or the refund due to you.

- ✿ **Sunday Afternoon: Reviewing and Filing Your Returns** shows you how to use TurboTax to efficiently and thoroughly review your return. You will learn how to find and fix errors, remove forms you no longer need, and override TurboTax computations when necessary. If you are running late and cannot complete your return (if, for example, you are still missing important tax data needed to complete your return), you will find this session useful as it explains how to file for an extension. This session also teaches you how to file your tax return electronically, on paper, or using the 1040PC method. In addition, you will learn how to install the TurboTax state modules. At the end of the session, you'll discover how to print your return for your records, back up your tax data, and organize these tax records for future reference.

✪ **Sunday Evening Bonus Session: Tax Estimates and Planning** explains how to save tax dollars through proper tax estimating and tax planning. You will learn how to use TurboTax to estimate next year's taxes, print and file tax estimate forms, and adjust your estimated taxes for changes in your personal finances during the year. This session covers how to plan for taxable events, find more tax deductions, and track your taxable events through financial software such as Quicken. You will learn how to amend your previous years' returns, and deal with tax audits (including what to do if you are unable to pay your tax liability).

Appendix A discusses how to get forms from the IRS Web site while Appendix B contains a helpful collection of checklists and advice on how to contact tax agencies (complete with addresses, phone numbers, and Web sites).

The Glossary defines the buzzwords in plain English (as edited by my 78-year-old mother, who is not an accountant!).

What Do You Need to Begin?

All you need is TurboTax Deluxe (for 1998 tax returns) installed on your computer and the following personal tax items:

✪ A copy of last year's tax returns (federal and state), including any W-2s or other attachments sent to the IRS or state revenue agencies

✪ Last year's tax source documents such as 1099s, listings of donations to charities, and cancelled checks to prove tax payments

✪ This year's tax source documents (provided you've received them already!) such as 1099s, W-2s, property tax paid receipts, end-of-year bank statements (for interest income), dividend statements from investments, end-of-year pension and retirement account statements, mortgage statements (for interest and taxes paid), and cancelled checks as needed to prove payment

- A financial software program (such as Quicken) and data, so you can extract and examine information as needed; or instead, your cancelled checks, bank statements, and check registers for the year

- Tax records such as automobile mileage logs and receipts that have been kept to support a deduction you plan to take

If you don't have all of the above items, do not despair. The idea is to get you started this weekend with what you have available. As you go along, keep a list of missing items and estimated amounts. When the items come in, you can just fill in the appropriate number and you'll be done, at least until next year!

Special Features of This Book

This book uses a number of special text formats and icons to make your job easier as you work through the sessions. They are used to call your attention to notes, tips, cautions, buzzwords, Web addresses, and tax humor:

NOTE Notes are food for thought as you work through the tutorials. They bring up points of interest or other relevant information you might find useful.

TIP Tips offer helpful hints, tricks, and ideas to apply as you progress through the Interview process.

CAUTION Cautions warn you of possible hazards and point out pitfalls that typically plague beginners.

BUZZ WORD Buzzwords are terms and acronyms that you should be familiar with and keep in mind as you develop and expand your skills with TurboTax.

FIND IT ON ▶ THE WEB Find It on the Webs point out **Web addresses** to which you can go for more information on the current topic.

Tax comic relief boxes brighten your day and help lighten your tax load.

Looking Forward to Taking
Control of Your Taxes

Imagine being able to determine the tax consequences of making an investment or not, to complete and print out your own tax returns, to get expert tax advice from the comfort of your home, to anticipate and meet your tax liabilities on time, and to reduce your tax liability by better understanding the tax law. You're only a weekend away!

Taking Control of Your Taxes

- ✿ Where Do I Start?
- ✿ Types of Individual Income Tax Returns
- ✿ Gathering Source Documents for Taxes
- ✿ Getting Tax Help
- ✿ Key Changes in Tax Laws for 1998

If you're following the "In a Weekend" theme, it's Friday night—the end of a workweek and the beginning of a new skill set. This weekend you will take control of your personal tax situation. You will acquire the skills necessary to understand your rights and responsibilities as a taxpayer; to use TurboTax Deluxe to organize, comply (fill in and print your tax returns), and plan your taxes; and to keep up-to-date on tax law changes and how they affect you.

Please take a moment to read the introduction at the beginning of this book. Aside from providing you with a good overview of how to use the book, the introduction contains a section named "What Do You Need to Begin?" that lists the personal tax information you will need this weekend to prepare your taxes with TurboTax.

So, grab a cup of coffee or a soda and get ready to learn how to

- ✿ Get started
- ✿ Find the right tax advisors and software
- ✿ Avoid common pitfalls
- ✿ Organize your finances for taxes
- ✿ Evaluate your tax situation
- ✿ Understand your taxpayer rights and responsibilities
- ✿ Keep current on tax law changes

Where Do I Start?

The good news is that you've already taken three important steps toward getting started: you bought the leading personal tax-preparation program, TurboTax; you bought this book; and you decided to devote this weekend to learning from both. Experience is sometimes the best teacher you can have. As you work through the book's various topics this weekend, you will accomplish the task of preparing your personal taxes. By the end of the weekend, you will have learned new personal tax organizational skills that will serve you all year-round.

The best place to start is with last year's tax return and records. If you haven't had a chance to dig them up yet (I've been known to label my tax file box "RIP," but you may have your own filing system), please go and pull out this information. If you can, work at the kitchen or dining room table so you can spread out and make piles as needed without running out of room. Give your spouse and the kids some movie money and send them away. (If they won't go quietly, threaten that they will have to do the taxes—works every time!)

TIP

Can't find a copy of last year's return? Try calling your tax preparer from last year (tax professionals always keep client records for a number of years). Or, if all else fails, file Form 4506 with the IRS (for a small fee) and they'll send you a copy in the mail (takes about eight weeks). You can also get a transcript of your return (listing the amounts the IRS recorded from your return for each tax line number) by calling 800-829-1040 (much faster and it's free). If the IRS suggests a 1722 Letter, don't bother requesting one because that only provides a summary of your taxable income and tax paid.

Since people earn income from different sources (wages, rents, royalties, etc.) and have different levels of income, the exact tax forms each person will use differs. In this section you will tour through the most commonly used tax forms and in the process gain a greater understanding of how you need to prepare your taxes. Although you may currently use one tax form (such as a short form 1040A), please read through all the descriptions. Your tax situation may change in the future, in which case you may need to use one of the other forms.

WHY PREPARE MY OWN TAXES?

If you've bought this book and TurboTax, you've probably already found the answer to this question. But for the faint of heart, still unconvinced spouses, or others you may pass this book on to, here is a brief discussion of how you benefit from preparing your own tax return.

When you prepare your own taxes, you become more familiar with why you are taxed, which activities during the year result in taxes being owed, and what documents are important for tax purposes. Armed with a greater understanding of your own tax situation and tax rules in general, you can make better decisions year-round to legally reduce your tax costs. You will also keep more accurate tax records and be more organized because you will better understand which documents and transactions are important from a tax perspective.

You can still use a paid tax preparer to review your tax records and prepared return. The cost will be less, and because you've taken the time to organize your tax records, the tax consultant will be able to give you even better advice on how to reduce taxes and plan appropriately for the future. Most tax preparers today use a program such as TurboTax to prepare your return anyway, so you might even be able to just give the tax consultant your data file along with your tax documents!

Most paid tax preparers are very professional and do an excellent job. But all too often a situation arises where one tax preparer tells you to do X while another tells you to do Y. How can the tax law be applied differently to the same situation? In most cases it cannot. Although gray areas do exist in the tax law, most areas—such as how to treat child support, what moving expenses are deductible, and whether the purchase of a home computer is deductible or not—have been clearly laid out by the IRS. Tax preparers, just like anyone else, can make mistakes and can fail to ask you all the right questions. Currently, no law exists requiring tax return preparers to be certified. For more information on how to select a professional tax preparer, see the section later tonight called "Getting Tax Help."

When you use a computer program such as TurboTax, you gain the expertise of a thousand professional tax preparers. The tax law and computations are checked by tax professionals—and then rechecked again and again before the product ships. (With an installed base of more than 3.3 million users, Intuit, TurboTax's publisher, cannot run the risk of there being any mistakes or missed topics.) TurboTax also comes with a 100% Accurate Guarantee. What this means is that, if you have to pay an IRS or state penalty because of a calculation error in TurboTax, Intuit pays you the penalty plus interest. The TurboTax tax forms are approved as accurate replicas by the IRS and the states.

TurboTax even interviews you, just like a tax preparer, making sure that every important question is asked and that your responses make sense across the board. As an added bonus, TurboTax provides expert video advice from Marshall Loeb, former editor at *Fortune* and *Money* magazines, and Mary Sprouse, former IRS group audit manager and author of *Money* magazine's *Income Tax Handbook.* You'll find a database of tax publications, IRS handbooks, and answers to more than 200 commonly asked tax questions as well. TurboTax guides you and helps you better understand the gray areas of the tax laws.

While it is sensible not to assume you will become a tax law guru, you should not pass up the opportunity to take control of your taxes. In this area, the tax law is clear: taxpayers bear the burden of reporting and proving the accuracy of the information reported. Ignorance of the tax law and how it applies to you is not a valid defense in the eyes of the IRS.

If your tax situation is simple, say just a few Wage and Tax Statements (W-2s) and some interest, dividends, and deductions (such as medical expenses, mortgage interest, and charitable deductions), then you can certainly prepare your own tax return. Even if you contribute to an IRA, have alimony or child support payments, and run a sole proprietorship, you can prepare your own taxes. The more complicated your return gets (such as having rental income from properties you own, gains and losses from sales of securities, and taxable losses), you will need to involve a tax expert to review the tax return that you prepare and guide you in any gray areas unique to your situation. But again, just by preparing your return, you will have a better understanding of your opportunities and responsibilities as a taxpayer. In other words, you have everything to gain and nothing to lose.

Types of Individual Income Tax Returns

Ever since 1913 when the Sixteenth Amendment to our Constitution gave Congress the power to impose and collect income tax, we, the people, have had to file financial reports with the government called *tax returns*. As you can see in Figure 1.1, the original tax return of 1913 was one page long and

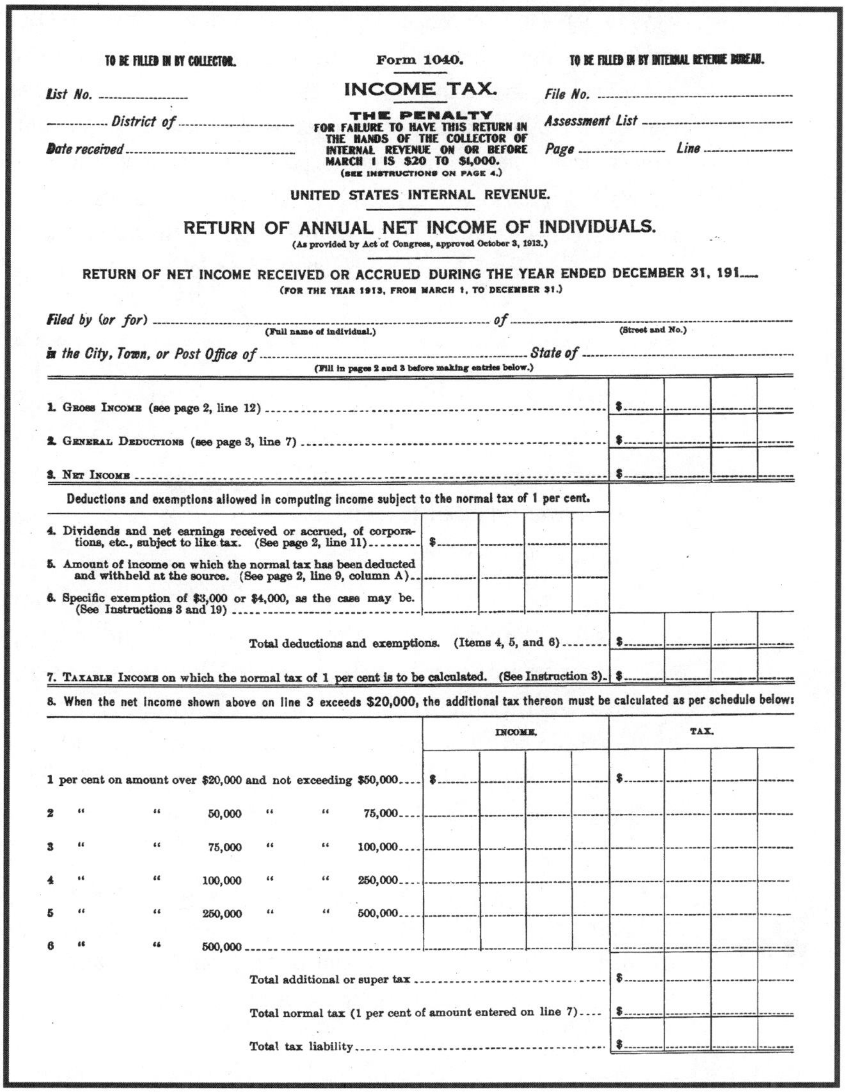

Figure 1.1

Preparing your taxes in 1913 was a breeze!

Figure 1.1

TO BE FILLED IN BY COLLECTOR.

Form 1040.

TO BE FILLED IN BY INTERNAL REVENUE BUREAU.

INCOME TAX.

List No. ....

District of ....

Date received ....

THE PENALTY
FOR FAILURE TO HAVE THIS RETURN IN THE HANDS OF THE COLLECTOR OF INTERNAL REVENUE ON OR BEFORE MARCH 1 IS $20 TO $1,000.
(SEE INSTRUCTIONS ON PAGE 4.)

File No. ....

Assessment List ....

Page .... Line ....

UNITED STATES INTERNAL REVENUE.

RETURN OF ANNUAL NET INCOME OF INDIVIDUALS.
(As provided by Act of Congress, approved October 3, 1913.)

RETURN OF NET INCOME RECEIVED OR ACCRUED DURING THE YEAR ENDED DECEMBER 31, 191.....
(FOR THE YEAR 1913, FROM MARCH 1, TO DECEMBER 31.)

Filed by (or for) .... of ....
(Full name of individual.)   (Street and No.)

In the City, Town, or Post Office of .... State of ....
(Fill in pages 2 and 3 before making entries below.)

1. Gross Income (see page 2, line 12) .... $........

2. General Deductions (see page 3, line 7) .... $........

3. Net Income .... $........

Deductions and exemptions allowed in computing income subject to the normal tax of 1 per cent.

4. Dividends and net earnings received or accrued, of corporations, etc., subject to like tax. (See page 2, line 11) .... $........

5. Amount of income on which the normal tax has been deducted and withheld at the source. (See page 2, line 9, column A) ....

6. Specific exemption of $3,000 or $4,000, as the case may be. (See Instructions 3 and 19) ....

Total deductions and exemptions. (Items 4, 5, and 6) .... $........

7. Taxable Income on which the normal tax of 1 per cent is to be calculated. (See Instruction 3) $........

8. When the net income shown above on line 3 exceeds $20,000, the additional tax thereon must be calculated as per schedule below:

					INCOME.	TAX.
1 per cent on amount over $20,000 and not exceeding $50,000					$........	$........
2	"	"	50,000	"	"	75,000	
3	"	"	75,000	"	"	100,000	
4	"	"	100,000	"	"	250,000	
5	"	"	250,000	"	"	500,000	
6	"	"	500,000			

Total additional or super tax .... $........

Total normal tax (1 per cent of amount entered on line 7) .... $........

Total tax liability .... $........

only asked for a few pieces of information. Additionally, the tax rate was a modest rate of only one percent on net annual incomes of more than $20,000—and most Americans back then made much less than $20,000 per year!

NOTE

• •

Why do we pay taxes? Well, in addition to financing various government projects (from highways to parks to Congress and even to IRS auditors), taxes are used by lawmakers to control the economy and encourage certain behavior. For example, when the economy demands greater buying and selling of securities such as stocks, Congress lowers the capital gains tax rate. On the other hand, if the budget needs a boost, Congress may increase tax rates or remove deductions. To encourage taxpayers to save more money for retirement, Congress invents a special tax-free treatment for certain accounts such as individual retirement accounts. Other examples of behavior tax laws are the new higher-education tax incentives. Sometimes a tax law is just the result of heavy lobbying by a special interest group. But in the end, we still pay taxes.

• •

Since 1913 the IRS has come up with several versions of the basic U.S. Individual Income Tax Return. Don't worry about the details of qualifying for each type of tax return (that will be covered tomorrow morning)—just get a feel for the types of returns available.

✿ **Form 1040EZ.** This is the tax return for you if you are single or married and filing jointly, have no dependents, and have taxable income of less than $50,000. Furthermore, you and your spouse (if married) must be under 65 on January 1, 1998; you cannot receive any advance earned income payments; your income must be only from wages, tips, taxable scholarships/grants, and unemployment compensation; and your total taxable interest income must be less than $400. This basic tax form is only 12 lines long and is as easy as it gets these days!

BUZZ WORD

◀ ◀

IRS (Internal Revenue Service): The administrative arm of the U.S. Treasury Department is charged with the tasks of collecting taxes, creating the tax forms, regulating the tax law passed by Congress, and auditing taxpayers for noncompliance.

Compliance: In the tax world, this term is used to describe the process of properly and completely filling out a tax form and sending it in on time. As a taxpayer, you must understand your responsibilities (and the instructions on the form!) in order to comply.

Taxpayer: U.S. residents and nonresidents who owe taxes are taxpayers.

Taxable Income: Money you receive that Congress says is taxable. Some examples include wages, salaries, rents, royalties, dividends, interest, alimony, state income tax refunds, pensions, trusts, partnerships, and income from a sole proprietorship.

1040: The form number given to the long version of the U.S. Individual Income Tax Return. Many people refer to individual tax returns in general as 1040s.

◄◄◄

✿ **Form 1040A.** This is the "short form" version of the U.S. Individual Income Tax Return. 1040A asks you for 34 lines of information across two pages and has three auxiliary forms associated with it (Schedules 1, 2, and 3). Anyone who is not allowed to file a 1040EZ and not required to fill out the much longer 1040 return can file with Form 1040A.

✿ **Form 1040.** The "long form" version must be filed by all taxpayers with taxable income of $50,000 or more, who want to itemize their deductions, who have adjustments to income other than a basic IRA contribution, or who have tax credits or owe other taxes not listed on Form 1040A. Weighing in at 65 lines of information spanning two pages, backed up by more than 30 associated forms (most called schedules), this is the tax return the majority of Americans file every year. (No wonder you have a headache!)

The good news is that TurboTax contains most of the tax forms you'll need. Moreover, TurboTax uses an interview process to ask you the appropriate questions and helps you determine which tax return you need to file.

TIP Looking for a tax form that you don't have? TurboTax has most of the forms—and you can print them out with their instructions too. You can also get tax forms online from the IRS. Just point your Web browser to **http://www.irs.ustreas.gov/prod/forms_pubs/forms.html** and select the desired tax form(s) and instruction(s). You'll find that the IRS provides forms in Adobe Acrobat PDF, PCL, PostScript, and SGML formats.

Take a look at last year's tax return. Which type did you file: Form 1040EZ, Form 1040A, or Form 1040? Take a moment to refresh your memory on the types of income you had last year, any adjustments or deductions you might have taken, and the tax credits/payments you made. Notice that regardless of which form you used, the information requested on the tax return follows this basic order:

- Your personal information
- Whether you want to give to the presidential election campaign
- Income you received that is taxable
- Adjustments allowed to taxable income (if applicable)
- The option to itemize deductions (if applicable)
- The standard deduction (for those not itemizing)
- The personal exemption amount
- The tax liability as per the tax tables or tax rate computation
- Tax credits (if applicable)
- Other taxes (if applicable)
- Tax payments already made
- The refund due to you, or the amount you owe the IRS
- Signature

When you stop and look at the big picture, even the most complicated return type looks doable. Better yet, the TurboTax interview process takes you through the return following the steps noted above, guiding you all the way with advice and explanations not always found in the tax form instructions.

Never take taxes too seriously. As the weekend progresses, I'll share some tax humor with you to liven things up a bit. Here's your first "tax comic relief" (a bumper sticker I saw on the highway a few weeks ago):

Dear IRS: I would like to cancel my subscription. Please remove my name from your mailing list.

If only it were so easy!

Other Tax Documents

In last year's tax return you may notice some other tax forms, such as Form W-2 and Form 1099. These additional forms are the returns that businesses (for example, banks, employers, and clients of yours) have to file with the IRS. For each employee, an employer must file a W-2 form (see Figure 1.2), which reports to the IRS the salary paid, the taxes withheld, and any contributions to 401(k) pension plans. In other words, the IRS already knows the information on your W-2 long before you ever file your return. Their computer systems double-check to make sure you've reported the same information on your return. You must attach a copy of each of your W-2s to your return.

TIP

■■

Always review the information reported on your W-2 as soon as you receive it. Compare it with your paystubs and immediately report any errors to your employer. Stay on top of the accounting folks and make sure a replacement W-2 is filed on time with the IRS and that you have a copy to send along with your return.

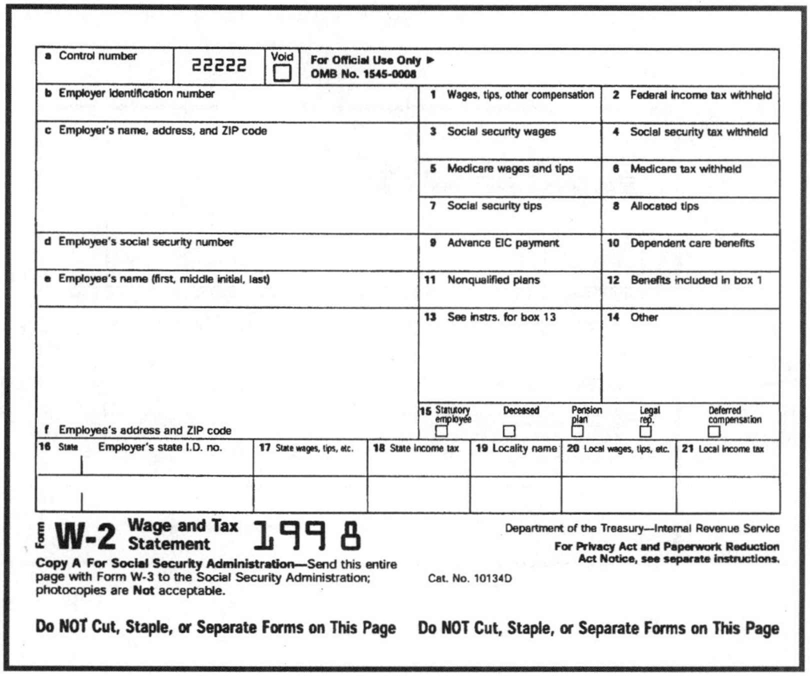

■■

a Control number	22222	Void ☐	For Official Use Only ▶ OMB No. 1545-0008		
b Employer identification number				1 Wages, tips, other compensation	2 Federal income tax withheld
c Employer's name, address, and ZIP code				3 Social security wages	4 Social security tax withheld
				5 Medicare wages and tips	6 Medicare tax withheld
				7 Social security tips	8 Allocated tips
d Employee's social security number				9 Advance EIC payment	10 Dependent care benefits
e Employee's name (first, middle initial, last)				11 Nonqualified plans	12 Benefits included in box 1
				13 See instrs. for box 13	14 Other
f Employee's address and ZIP code				15 Statutory employee ☐ Deceased ☐ Pension plan ☐ Legal rep. ☐ Deferred compensation ☐	
16 State Employer's state I.D. no.	17 State wages, tips, etc.	18 State income tax	19 Locality name	20 Local wages, tips, etc.	21 Local income tax

Form **W-2** Wage and Tax Statement **1998**

Copy A For Social Security Administration—Send this entire page with Form W-3 to the Social Security Administration; photocopies are **Not** acceptable.

Cat. No. 10134D

Department of the Treasury—Internal Revenue Service

For Privacy Act and Paperwork Reduction Act Notice, see separate instructions.

Do NOT Cut, Staple, or Separate Forms on This Page   Do NOT Cut, Staple, or Separate Forms on This Page

Figure 1.2

Form W-2 provides you with the information the IRS has on file for you.

The same is true for Form 1099 (see Figure 1.3). Businesses, organizations, and even individuals who make payments of $600 or more to someone else must report this to the IRS on Form 1099, indicating the type of income (such as interest, nonemployee compensation, and health-care payments). Whereas you need to file a duplicate copy of your W-2 with your federal and state returns, neither the IRS nor the states require you to file copies of 1099s or other informational forms with your return. But again, the IRS knows long before you file your return how much you should be reporting for these items.

Form 1099 comes in many flavors. There are forms for interest income, dividend income, cancellation of a debt, government income, real estate income, medical savings, long-term care/accelerated health, original issue discount, pensions/annuities, miscellaneous income, and income from a broker. In some cases the 1099 reports that you received income net of a tax that was withheld and remitted to the IRS for you. You will want to make sure that any tax already paid to the IRS (from backup withholding) is listed on your tax return (tax payments are on the agenda for the Sunday Morning session). If the 1099 reports tax withheld, it is a good idea to attach a copy of the 1099 to your return for convenient proof of taxes paid.

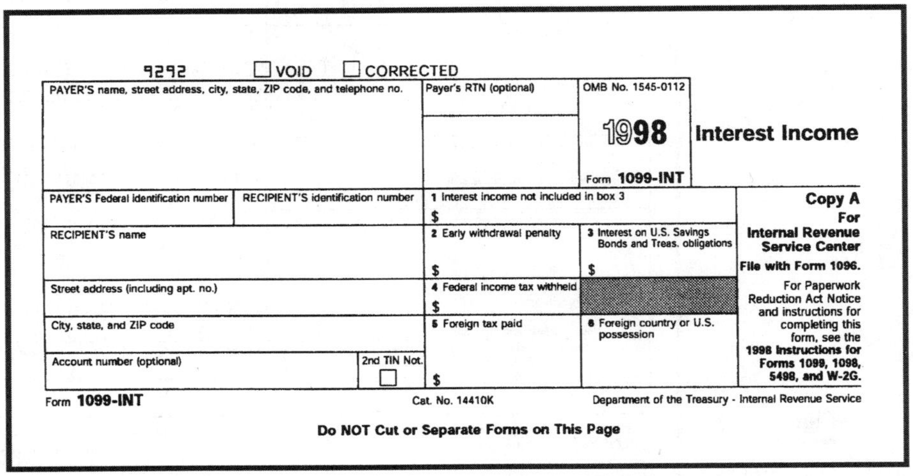

9292 ☐ VOID ☐ CORRECTED

PAYER'S name, street address, city, state, ZIP code, and telephone no.

Payer's RTN (optional)

OMB No. 1545-0112

1998

Form 1099-INT

Interest Income

PAYER'S Federal identification number

RECIPIENT'S identification number

1 Interest income not included in box 3 $

Copy A For Internal Revenue Service Center

File with Form 1096.

RECIPIENT'S name

2 Early withdrawal penalty $

3 Interest on U.S. Savings Bonds and Treas. obligations $

Street address (including apt. no.)

4 Federal income tax withheld $

For Paperwork Reduction Act Notice and instructions for completing this form, see the 1998 Instructions for Forms 1099, 1098, 5498, and W-2G.

City, state, and ZIP code

5 Foreign tax paid $

6 Foreign country or U.S. possession

Account number (optional)

2nd TIN Not. ☐

Form 1099-INT Cat. No. 14410K Department of the Treasury - Internal Revenue Service

Do NOT Cut or Separate Forms on This Page

Figure 1.3

Form 1099-INT is an example of an informational form that you do not need to include with your return.

BUZZ WORD

◄◄

Backup Withholding: Similar to those taxes your employer withholds from your paycheck, but usually only occurring in situations where you failed to provide a social security number. On investment income, backup withholding is 31 percent.

Nonemployee Compensation: A catchall category for any other type of income, such as income from consulting, painting a house, teaching a class, or providing a service for someone other than your employer.

Individual: Generally used to refer to a living, breathing person. Individuals file Form 1040, 1040A, or 1040EZ. Nonresidents file Form 1040NR or 1040NR-EZ.

Sole Proprietor: An individual who is in business independently (having no partners in the business, as well as no shareholders or stock of any kind). Sole proprietors report their income on Schedule C of Form 1040.

Partnership: A group of two or more individuals who are in business together but do not sell shares of stock in the business. Partnerships file Form 1065.

Corporation: A group of individuals who run a business owned by shareholders. The individuals are employees who get a Form W-2. The shareholders get dividend income (Form 1099-DIV) on any corporate profit, along with other types of income like gains from sales of their shares. The corporation files Form 1120.

◄◄◄

TIP

If you know you've received $600 or more from someone but have not yet received your copy of Form 1099, you should call and ask for a copy to be sent to you again. Even if they haven't filed a Form 1099 with the IRS for that amount, the IRS expects you to list that income on your return. In the event of an audit, chances are that an amount of that size will be found. So, avoid the ulcers and file honestly.

In addition to forms that report to the IRS the income you have been paid, the IRS also requires proof of deductions that you might claim. For example, your mortgage company must file Form 1098 (see Figure 1.4) to report to the IRS how much of your mortgage payments were attributable to mortgage interest, points paid on closing, real estate taxes, or if you received a refund for any overpaid interest. Similar information returns are filed for

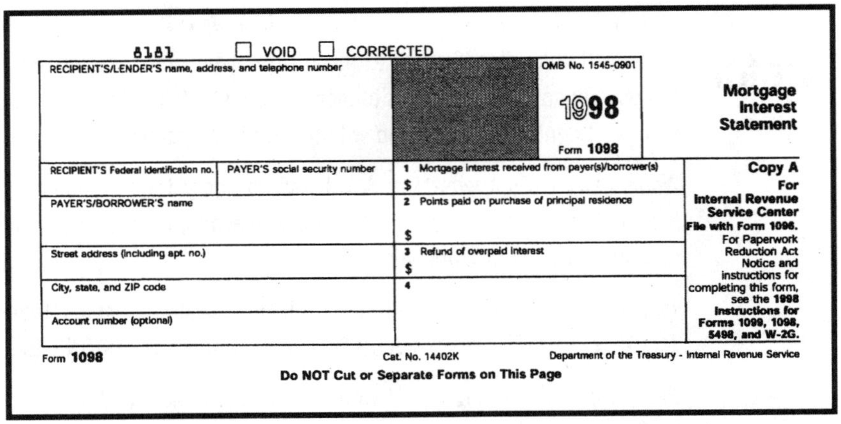

8181 ☐ VOID ☐ CORRECTED

RECIPIENT'S/LENDER'S name, address, and telephone number	OMB No. 1545-0901 1998 Form 1098	Mortgage Interest Statement
RECIPIENT'S Federal identification no. / PAYER'S social security number	1 Mortgage interest received from payer(s)/borrower(s) $	Copy A For Internal Revenue Service Center File with Form 1096. For Paperwork Reduction Act Notice and instructions for completing this form, see the 1998 Instructions for Forms 1099, 1098, 5498, and W-2G.
PAYER'S/BORROWER'S name	2 Points paid on purchase of principal residence $	
Street address (including apt. no.)	3 Refund of overpaid interest $	
City, state, and ZIP code	4	
Account number (optional)		

Form 1098 Cat. No. 14402K Department of the Treasury - Internal Revenue Service

Do NOT Cut or Separate Forms on This Page

Figure 1.4

Form 1098 reports the deductible amounts related to your mortgage.

large charitable contributions, certain medical expenses, moving your primary residence at the request of an employer, student loan interest, and deductible tuition payments.

TIP If you pay your real estate taxes instead of your mortgage company doing so, be sure to keep the cancelled check and property tax bill stamped "paid" by your town clerk with your tax records. And of course be sure to list this as a deductible expense if you decide to itemize your deductions.

Sometimes the other tax documents you receive look like a page out of someone else's return. Figure 1.5 shows Schedule K-1, which is just that—a page out of a partnership's tax return called Form 1065. Don't despair if you have tax documents that look this complex. TurboTax does a wonderful job of walking you through each step for entering the appropriate information for these types of forms so you don't miss anything important.

TIP Pull out a notepad (or open your word processor) and make a list of the source documents for last year's tax return. Then, as you start to receive this year's source documents, you can check off the ones you receive and update the list for new source documents. Figure 1.6 shows you my list for last year's tax return.

SCHEDULE K-1
(Form 1065)
Department of the Treasury
Internal Revenue Service

Partner's Share of Income, Credits, Deductions, etc.
▶ See separate instructions.
For calendar year 1997 or tax year beginning _____ , 1997, and ending _____ , 19 ___

OMB No. 1545-0099

1997

Partner's identifying number ▶

Partnership's identifying number ▶

Partner's name, address, and ZIP code

Partnership's name, address, and ZIP code

A   This partner is a ☐ general partner   ☐ limited partner
    ☐ limited liability company member
B   What type of entity is this partner? ▶ _____
C   Is this partner a ☐ domestic or a ☐ foreign partner?
D   Enter partner's percentage of: (i) Before change or termination   (ii) End of year
    Profit sharing . . . . . . ____ %   ____ %
    Loss sharing . . . . . . ____ %   ____ %
    Ownership of capital . . . ____ %   ____ %
E   IRS Center where partnership filed return: _____

F   Partner's share of liabilities (see instructions):
    Nonrecourse . . . . $ _____
    Qualified nonrecourse financing . $ _____
    Other . . . . $ _____
G   Tax shelter registration number . ▶ _____
H   Check here if this partnership is a publicly traded partnership as defined in section 469(k)(2) . . . . ☐
I   Check applicable boxes: (1) ☐ Final K-1 (2) ☐ Amended K-1

J   **Analysis of partner's capital account:**

(a) Capital account at beginning of year	(b) Capital contributed during year	(c) Partner's share of lines 3, 4, and 7, Form 1065, Schedule M-2	(d) Withdrawals and distributions	(e) Capital account at end of year (combine columns (a) through (d))
			( )	

	(a) Distributive share item		(b) Amount	(c) 1040 filers enter the amount in column (b) on:
Income (Loss)	1	Ordinary income (loss) from trade or business activities . . .	1		See page 6 of Partner's Instructions for Schedule K-1 (Form 1065).
	2	Net income (loss) from rental real estate activities	2		
	3	Net income (loss) from other rental activities	3		
	4	Portfolio income (loss):			
	a	Interest	4a		Sch. B, Part I, line 1
	b	Dividends	4b		Sch. B, Part II, line 5
	c	Royalties	4c		Sch. E, Part I, line 4
	d	Net short-term capital gain (loss)	4d		Sch. D, line 5, col. (f)
	e	Net long-term capital gain (loss):			
		(1) 28% rate gain (loss)	e(1)		Sch. D, line 12, col. (g)
		(2) Total for year	e(2)		Sch. D, line 12, col. (f)
	f	Other portfolio income (loss) (attach schedule)	4f		Enter on applicable line of your return.
	5	Guaranteed payments to partner	5		See page 6 of Partner's Instructions for Schedule K-1 (Form 1065).
	6	Net section 1231 gain (loss) (other than due to casualty or theft):			
	a	28% rate gain (loss)	6a		
	b	Total for year	6b		
	7	Other income (loss) (attach schedule)	7		Enter on applicable line of your return.
Deductions	8	Charitable contributions (see instructions) (attach schedule) . .	8		Sch. A, line 15 or 16
	9	Section 179 expense deduction	9		See page 7 of Partner's Instructions for Schedule K-1 (Form 1065).
	10	Deductions related to portfolio income (attach schedule) . . .	10		
	11	Other deductions (attach schedule)	11		
Credits	12a	Low-income housing credit:			
		(1) From section 42(j)(5) partnerships for property placed in service before 1990	a(1)		Form 8586, line 5
		(2) Other than on line 12a(1) for property placed in service before 1990	a(2)		
		(3) From section 42(j)(5) partnerships for property placed in service after 1989	a(3)		
		(4) Other than on line 12a(3) for property placed in service after 1989	a(4)		
	b	Qualified rehabilitation expenditures related to rental real estate activities	12b		See page 8 of Partner's Instructions for Schedule K-1 (Form 1065).
	c	Credits (other than credits shown on lines 12a and 12b) related to rental real estate activities	12c		
	d	Credits related to other rental activities	12d		
	13	Other credits	13		

For Paperwork Reduction Act Notice, see Instructions for Form 1065.   Cat. No. 11394R   Schedule K-1 (Form 1065) 1997

Figure 1.5

Schedule K-1 reports to the IRS the income you received from a partnership.

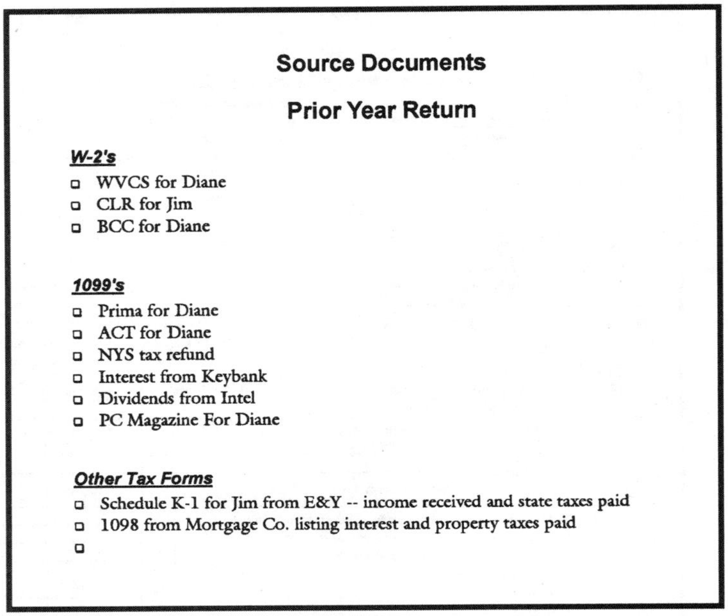

Source Documents

Prior Year Return

W-2's
- ❏ WVCS for Diane
- ❏ CLR for Jim
- ❏ BCC for Diane

1099's
- ❏ Prima for Diane
- ❏ ACT for Diane
- ❏ NYS tax refund
- ❏ Interest from Keybank
- ❏ Dividends from Intel
- ❏ PC Magazine For Diane

Other Tax Forms
- ❏ Schedule K-1 for Jim from E&Y -- income received and state taxes paid
- ❏ 1098 from Mortgage Co. listing interest and property taxes paid
- ❏

Figure 1.6

Making a checklist of source documents from last year's return is a good way to start preparing your taxes.

Using Your Financial Records

In addition to the tax return forms and documents, you will need your own financial records. If you use Quicken or QuickBooks, you may already be tracking taxable transactions throughout the year. In fact, you can transfer your financial information automatically from Quicken or QuickBooks (or any other program that supports the tax exchange format TXF) directly into TurboTax (what a time saver!). I'll explain how to do this tomorrow morning.

NOTE If you want to learn more about using Quicken to organize your tax and financial records, please refer to Prima Publishing's *Organize Your Finances In a Weekend with Quicken Deluxe 99.* You will learn how Quicken helps you reduce the time you spend each month paying bills and makes short work of your tax-preparation and planning needs at the same time.

If your finances are kept in a computer program that does not support the TurboTax TXF file-importing format, you will need to print a year-end report or multiple reports to extract the tax information as needed.

CAUTION

Just because your records print out nice and neat from a computer program doesn't mean that they are correct. The old adage "to err is human" applies to computer programs as well, which can result in reports that do not correctly reflect your finances. The solution is to always print out a full-detail, itemized report for the entire year and review each category for mispostings or omissions. In Quicken, the Itemized Category Report for the full year with Split detail checked will give you the totals that you need for your tax return. By reviewing for missing check numbers, mispostings, and omissions of key items for 1998, you will save yourself a lot of heartache—and maybe some tax dollars too!

If you don't have your checkbook automated, you will need to review it and your cancelled checks to verify amounts and total up deductions. For example, if you get a 1099 that claims someone paid you $900 for services rendered, you should verify that the amount was received and deposited in your bank account. In the case of deductions you plan to take, you will need to prove payment as well as show a receipt of goods. The IRS loves receipts. For example, if you have a small business that you run as a sole proprietorship and you want to deduct office supplies, you will need to show the cancelled check used to pay for the supplies as well as the receipts that detail all the items you purchased.

Speaking of receipts—these are very important tax documents. Always save your receipts, especially for any cash transactions, as this is your only proof that you really purchased what you say you purchased. Get into the habit of filing your receipts by topic, especially ones you know are deductible. For example, you could set up separate files for office supplies for your business, for nonreimbursed employee expenses (such as a computer that you bought for your employer's benefit), and for medical costs (such as doctor's visits and prescriptions).

Gathering Source Documents for Taxes

So far in this session I have discussed many important source documents that you will need in order to prepare your tax return and organize your taxes. Table 1.1 lists the receipts and other tax documents you need to get started.

TABLE 1.1   SOURCE DOCUMENTS FOR YOUR TAXES

Documents	Used for Reporting	Recd.?	Used?	Question?
Last year's tax returns and records	Last year's amounts and carryovers			
W-2s	Wages, tips, salary, and other income from an employer			
Form 4070 or other statements on cash tips received	Tip income			
1099s	Income from interest, dividends, royalties, state tax refunds, and other types of income			
Year-end bank statements	Interest earned for the year			
Year-end investment and broker statements	Interest, dividends, gains, and losses on your investments			
Deposit slips for alimony or child support received and copies of divorce, separation, or custody agreements	Alimony or child support income			
Sole-proprietor business records including but not limited to 1099s, business bank accounts, deposit slips, cancelled checks, invoices, income statements, balance sheets, inventory records, receipts, ledgers, and client and employee records	Business income from cash received (if cash basis) or accrued (if accrual basis), returns and allowances, cost of goods sold, plus any other business income; and business expenses			

TABLE 1.1 SOURCE DOCUMENTS FOR YOUR TAXES

Documents	Used for Reporting	Recd.?	Used?	Question?
Auto mileage log and maintenance log, along with receipts for expenses and checks to prove payment	Deductible auto expenses for work or business use			
K-1 forms from partnerships, S-corps, trusts, or estates	Proof of income and deductible expenses from partnerships, S-corps, trusts, and estates			
Rental property records	Rental income and expenses attributable to rental properties			
Form W-2G, personal diary, stubs, or other records of gambling winnings	Gambling and certain other winnings income (no loss allowed)			
Employee benefit statements	Proof of exclusion or inclusion in taxable wage income			
Closing statement for the sale of your personal residence and records of purchase and/or improvements, etc.	Gain or loss on sale of personal residence; loss carryover to new home			
Investment closing statement for the sale of real estate, and records of purchase and/or improvements, etc.	Gain or loss on investment			
Form 1099-R	Taxability of retirement, pension, or annuity lump sum distributions received			
Form 1099G	Taxability of unemployment compensation income received			

TABLE 1.1   SOURCE DOCUMENTS FOR YOUR TAXES

Documents	Used for Reporting	Recd.?	Used?	Question?
Social security income statements	Taxability of social security income			
Trust statement and proof of contributions to retirement plans such as 401(k) plans, IRAs, IRA-SEPs, Roth IRAs, and Keoghs	Taxability of retirement contributions			
Moving receipts and cancelled checks, reimbruse- ments from employer, mileage log, and distance to and from new and old job	Deductibility of moving expenses			
Self-employed health insurance policy and cancelled checks to prove payment	Deductibility of health insurance cost for self-employed taxpayers			
Home office expense receipts, allocation, and proof of business use	Home office deductions			
Medical, pharmaceutical, and dental expense receipts and cancelled checks	Medical and dental expense deductions			
Cancelled checks for taxes paid during the tax year, tax returns filed, receipts for taxes withheld, W-2s, 1099s, Form 1098, and real estate tax bill marked "paid" by town clerk	State and local income tax, personal property tax, and real estate tax deductions			

TABLE 1.1 SOURCE DOCUMENTS FOR YOUR TAXES

Documents	Used for Reporting	Recd.?	Used?	Question?
Form 1098 or year-end mortgage statement, along with cancelled checks	Mortgage interest deduction, points deduction, and property tax deduction			
Contribution recognition letters, receipts, and cancelled checks; appraisals on property donated along with original cost	Contributions deduction			
Police records, witness accounts, newspaper articles, and insurance papers on losses from theft or casualty	Deductible expenses owing to a casualty or theft loss			
Membership card, dues invoice, and cancelled checks or paystubs	Deductible dues for a union or other recognized organization			
Unreimbursed employee expense receipts, proof of employer request to incur expense, and cancelled checks	Deductible employee expenses			
Bank statement or receipt for bank deposit box rental	Bank deposit box deduction			
Cancelled checks and invoices for tax-preparation fees and/or tax software cost	Tax-preparation expenses			
Cancelled checks and invoices for child or dependent care expenses and taxpayer ID for caregiver	Child or dependent care deductions			

NOTE The IRS has the right to disallow any deductions that you cannot prove, so be sure to have such items as cancelled checks, receipts, account statements, and relevant logs before you take any deduction.

If you're missing a receipt, contact the seller. Businesses must keep records of their sales for five to seven years, so they should be able to provide you with a copy or replacement receipt. If you are missing a cancelled check, contact your bank. For a small fee, they will send you a copy of your cancelled check. If you paid for the item by credit card but cannot find your receipt, the credit card statement and your cancelled check paying that credit card bill may be enough documentation. When you make multiple purchases from a vendor selling many types of products, your best documentation is a receipt that itemizes the name and cost of each item individually.

Keeping Tax Records

Now that you've looked through last year's tax return and records, you have a good idea of the types of information you need to prepare this year's tax return—and the types of information you need to keep to prove income and expenses in the event of an audit. As you begin to receive tax documents for this coming tax return, check off the item received and file it away. If you don't have a filing system set up yet, consider the following list of suggested names for file folder tabs:

- **1998 Tax Return—Income.** In this folder, file the W-2s sent by employers; any 1099 forms for interest, dividends, or other income received; and any K-1s received from partnership income. As soon as you receive these documents, compare them with your records and immediately notify the issuer in writing of any errors and request corrected copies. (Keep any such letter in this file too.)

- **1998 Tax Return—Deductions.** In this folder, file all receipts and cancelled checks that prove you paid for any item you intend to deduct from your taxable income. Letters from charities, appraisals for donations, and insurance papers that prove a casualty or theft loss all go here. In some cases, such as the sale of a residence or a move made at the request of an employer, the documents surrounding the event(s)

are so voluminous that they won't all fit in one folder. That's fine—just label each additional folder appropriately (for example, "Move to Memphis") and keep it with your main deductions folder. When you print a copy of your final return for your records, you can always cross-reference the deducted amount to a file name so that three or four years from now you can find where your numbers came from.

✿ **1998 Tax Return—Business 1.** For each type of business you run as a sole proprietor, set up a summary folder in addition to your business records (see the sidebar, "Business Records"). File here any 1099s you receive for work you did in the business and for interest that the business bank account earned, your log for any business-related car expenses, and the summary reports (end-of-year income and expenses) for your business. Depending on how large the business is, this summary folder may be backed up by a box or several boxes of receipts, cancelled checks, bank statements, ledgers, and asset depreciation records. The purpose of the summary files is to bridge the gap between your detailed business records and your tax return.

✿ **1998 Tax Return—Tax Credits.** In this folder, you would place proof of any tax credits (such as for child or dependent care) that you intend to take.

✿ **1998 Tax Return—Tax Payments.** If you made any estimated tax payments during the year, this folder would contain the cancelled checks, copies of the estimated tax forms filed, and any proof of mailing in the tax payment (U.S. Postal Service registered receipt or certified mail receipt). If you have an overpayment based on last year's tax return, to be applied to this year's, put a copy of that tax return page in this folder, or simply make a note here of the amount. Any 1099s or W-2s that show tax payments should be copied or noted in this folder too.

✿ **1998 Tax Return—Questions/Issues.** Use this file as your catchall for any questions, ideas, or issues that you want to address at tax time. Add other folders as needed to store documents pertaining to any major issues, such as medical costs related to an illness, casualty losses, rental properties, and changes in filing status (single to married, married to widow, etc.).

✪ **1999 Tax Return—Estimated Tax Payments.** This folder will contain the estimated tax forms and calculations for 1999. One of the last steps of completing your 1998 tax return will be to estimate how much you will owe for 1999 and prepare the federal and state Estimated Tax Returns for 1999 (if applicable to you). This is your first step in creating a tax plan for 1999.

When you finish your tax return, do yourself a favor and set up the file folder tabs for next year before you go out to celebrate!

TIP

Another great tax organizing tip is to establish a tax calendar. You'll know exactly when your return, estimate, and extension deadlines are. Also, you need to know the last dates on which you can make contributions to tax-related accounts, such as retirement accounts, or make elections for special tax treatments. Both Quicken and TurboTax can help you create and maintain a tax calendar. As an added bonus, they both have an alert feature that will remind you "X" number of days (which you can determine) prior to a tax deadline.

BUSINESS RECORDS

The IRS doesn't specify the record-keeping format that you must use, but you are required by law to retain permanent, accurate, and complete records that clearly present your earnings, deductions, and credits. Computer programs such as QuickBooks help you maintain proper records while giving you a great tool for measuring and enhancing profitability. Paper-based record-keeping systems can be purchased at office supply stores. You can also hire an accountant to set up and/or maintain your records for you. In any event, your business records should include the following:

✪ **Cash Disbursements (CD) Journal.** All expenditures for the business should be recorded in a cash disbursements journal (this is similar to a checkbook register). The CD journal lists the date, check number (or cash withdrawal), payer name, expense description, and expense category. For each expense category,

you should have folders or envelopes set up so you can file away the receipt (if needed, write on or number your receipts to make it easier later to match up receipts with CD entries). If you use a petty cash fund, be sure to set up a petty cash journal and keep track of the inflows and outflows too.

✪ **Sales or Accounts Receivable (AR) Journal.** All cash register totals should be recorded on a daily basis in a sales journal. If you invoice clients for services or products, then you might prefer to use an accounts receivable journal. In either case, the journal lists what you sold, who bought it and when, how much you were paid for it, and any sales tax you collected on it.

✪ **General Ledger (GL).** Think of the general ledger as a combination of your balance sheet and income statement, albeit in greater detail. The balance sheet section lists all your assets (such as cash on hand, cash in banks, accounts receivable, and equipment), your liabilities (such as loans, accounts payable, and sales tax collected but not yet remitted to the state), and equity (such as the owner's investment account). The income statement lists all the current income and expenses for the year.

If you use this type of record-keeping system, you will manage your day-to-day business better and you will save time in the long run. However, in the event of an audit, the IRS will want to see the original source documents (cancelled checks, bank statements, cash register receipts, sales tax remittances, mileage logs, expense receipts, etc.), so be certain to create a clear path from the source document to the accounting system and back again so you can easily put your fingers on the right document whenever you need it.

Storing Tax Records

The IRS has three years from the due date of your return in which to examine it. So, at the very least you should keep your tax records for three years after you file your return. For example, if you file your return on February 15, 1999, you should keep all the related tax records until April 15, 2002

(April 15 being the due date of the return). If you carry forward any tax information from one tax year to another (such as a loss carryover), then you need to keep records from the prior year(s) for the same length of time as needed for the year in which you used the carryover amount.

You should also keep any records of transactions relating to the basis of a property (such as a house) for as long as they are important in figuring out the basis of the original or replacement property. Likewise, records of contributions to IRAs, retirement plans, and other such investments should be kept indefinitely.

Since the IRS can go back as far as six years in cases where more than 25 percent of your gross income has not been reported, many tax consultants advise that you keep records for at least six years. Personally, I like the number seven. You never know when you've accidentally filed something in the wrong year, and that extra year always helps me sleep better.

Keep in mind that if fraud is involved, or if you fail to file a return, then the IRS has no time limits.

> Why do sharks not attack IRS auditors?
>
> Professional courtesy.

Getting Tax Help

At some point you may decide that you need to find a tax professional to help you sort through your tax records, review your TurboTax-prepared tax return, or give you advice on tax-planning opportunities. As mentioned earlier in the sidebar, "Why Prepare My Own Taxes," tax preparers and consultants come with a variety of skills and many significant differences in background, education, and certification.

✿ **Certified Public Accountant (CPA).** A CPA is certified by a state (ask which state their certificate is from) after attaining a college education, passing a rigorous national exam, and usually completing a specified number of hours of accounting work. Basic federal tax law is covered as part of a CPA's training. In order to keep their certificate, CPAs must complete continuing-education classes dealing with accounting and tax topics every year (the number of required hours varies state to state, ranging from 40 to 120 hours). A CPA can specialize in taxes, and within the tax field can further specialize in individual taxes. Some CPAs work in the tax department of a large CPA firm year-round, while others only help out on basic returns during tax season. Look for a CPA who specializes in individual taxes and works year-round in the tax department of a medium to large-size firm. This person is the best tax preparer/advisor money can buy—and unfortunately, the most expensive. Hourly rates for such experts go from $100 to $300 per hour, based on years of experience. Actual costs per tax return are usually predetermined and, depending on complexity, can run from $500 to several thousand dollars per return.

TIP The top CPA firms in the world are referred to as the "Big Five": Arthur Andersen, Deloitte & Touche, Ernst & Young, KPMG, and PricewaterhouseCoopers. Try to get your tax advisor from one of these firms to be assured world-class service.

- **Public Accountant (PA).** A PA is a state-licensed accountant who meets the annual continuing-education requirements of that state but who did not pass the CPA exam. Fees are usually lower, but again be sure that the PA works mainly in the tax area year-round, not just during tax season.

- **Tax Attorney (TA).** A TA is a lawyer who specializes in tax law year-round. TAs usually do not do any type of tax-preparation work, but they are highly knowledgeable in the gray areas of tax law and are usually very well versed in tax-planning opportunities. Large CPA firms usually employ TAs who are also CPAs—this is who you'll want by your side if you ever need to go to tax court. Rates are, as you probably guessed, very high ($200 per hour and up).

- **Accountant.** Accountants are not held up to any standards or continuing education requirements like CPAs, PAs, and TAs. Anyone can claim to be an accountant, so be sure to ask about relevant tax-preparation education and experience before you hire someone to prepare your return.

○ **Enrolled Agent (EA).** An enrolled agent is someone who has passed an exam given by the IRS and received a license from the IRS to prepare tax returns. EAs do not necessarily have any accounting background, a college education, or relevant work experience. But on the plus side, the IRS EA exam is thorough in covering the most common individual tax laws, and EAs must complete continuing-education classes each year. Moreover, an EA works in taxes exclusively. EAs charge less than CPAs but provide you with more tax expertise than a general PA or an accountant.

○ **Preparers.** Anyone can be self-described as a tax preparer, but that doesn't mean the individual has the appropriate training, experience, or resources to properly advise you on your tax situation. To bring in a few extra bucks, financial advisors, insurance salespeople, and bookkeepers sometimes moonlight as tax preparers during tax season. Fees for tax preparers are relatively low, but unless your situation is very basic, a tax preparer is usually not going to be the best tax advisor.

Always get personal recommendations from other clients of the tax expert you choose. Check references and compare hourly fees based on the complexity of your tax situation. Ask how many years the person has worked in taxes and if they like the tax area. Find out if they work only in individual taxes or if their true specialty is another area, such as corporate tax law. If you've decided to go with a large firm, ask if you will meet with the same tax advisor throughout the year. Larger firms seem to have more turnover, and having an ongoing relationship with one individual can be very beneficial over the years.

Ask what percentage of the tax advisor's returns get audited, how those audits went, and what the predominant key issues were. Also find out if the advisor (working as a tax preparer or advisor) has ever been fined by the state or the IRS.

In the area of costs, find out the fees required to prepare your return, to review a return that you have prepared, to get planning advice, and to represent you before the IRS and/or state authorities. Compare these figures with those of the other tax advisors you are interviewing. Weigh the costs against the feedback from other clients, as well as against your own gut reaction to each tax advisor. If you feel more comfortable with one over another, you

may be more apt to use that person's services and in the end have a better tax plan for your future.

Take a Break

Okay, so your head is spinning and you're just about to turn on a movie. Don't do it! Instead, go out for a walk, make some popcorn, or grab a soda. After you've had a break, you'll review the new tax laws that were enacted in 1998, determine what new data you'll need to collect, and explore last minute steps you can take to reduce your taxes.

Key Changes in Tax Laws for 1998

Between the *Taxpayer Relief Act of 1997* (which became law in the summer of 1997) and the *IRS Restructuring and Reform Act of 1998* (which became law in the summer of 1998), there are many new tax laws that will affect your 1998 tax return. The good news is that TurboTax knows about these new rules and will prompt you during the interview process to provide the appropriate information. TurboTax also contains text, instructions, and video discussion of each new tax rule for 1998.

Since the focus of this session is to gather your tax data, I've included in this section a brief overview of the new tax rules so you can gather the appropriate information. Some rules actually went into effect in 1997, but changed slightly in 1998. Be sure to read through this section in case there is an opportunity for you to save taxes or avoid paying a penalty. Don't worry about the details and calculations—I'll get into that tomorrow as you enter your data.

Saving Taxes with a Child Care Credit

Who said the kids can't save you money? In 1998 you can get up to a $400 credit (that's dollar-for-dollar tax money saved) for each child under age 17. The exact amount of the credit reduces on a sliding scale to zero based on your adjusted gross income (AGI). For single taxpayers, the credit goes to zero for an AGI over $82,000, and for joint returns, an AGI over $118,000. So, as long as your AGI is less than that, the kids can save you money in 1998!

Tax data you need:

✿ Birth certificate to prove the age and relationship of each child and social security number for each child. (This information is needed anyway to claim a child as a dependent.)

Reducing Taxes on Higher Education

Education is perhaps one of our nation's greatest assets. Congress has recognized this and provided several tax credits and beneficial tax treatments for the money you and your employer spend on higher education.

First, you may elect to take either the Hope Scholarship Tax Credit or a Lifetime Learning Credit (but not both). Each credit is for expenses paid during the taxable year or within the first three months following the tax year (that would be until March 31, 1999, for the 1998 tax year). In other words, the credits do not allow you to prepay education expenses. As with the Child Tax Credit, the benefits phase out to zero based on your AGI.

Other tax benefits include an exclusion for employer-provided education, expansion of the state-sponsored tuition plan benefits, deductibility of student loan interest, and education IRAs.

Tax data you need:

✿ Proof of payment, such as cancelled checks.

✿ Proof of enrollment in a qualified higher-education program (such as a report card with credit hours listed or an enrollment form that lists credit hours).

✿ Proof of attendance on at least a half-time basis as part of a degree or certification program; or proof that attendance for any credit hour(s) was to improve job skills.

✿ Proof of qualified amounts, such as an itemized invoice that shows qualified tuition payments separate from ineligible amounts (books, room and board, etc.).

Hope Tax Credit

Higher-education tuition and related expenses (but not room and board or books) that you pay for yourself, your spouse, or your dependents may qualify for the nonrefundable Hope Tax Credit. The credit is equal to 100 percent of the first $1,000 and 50 percent of the next $1,000 of qualified expenses. That's a maximum of a $1,500 tax credit against taxes that you owe (but not beyond the taxes that you owe). The Hope Tax Credit is available for just the first two years of higher education and can only be taken for two tax years. Only expenses paid after January 1, 1998, qualify.

Life-Time Learning Credit

On the other hand, you may prefer to take the Life-Time Learning Credit (you can't take both Hope and Life-Time). The Life-Time Learning Credit is not limited to two years and doesn't change based on the number of students in a family.

The Life-Time Learning Credit is equal to 20 percent of qualified tuition and fees up to $5,000, which results in a maximum credit of $1,000 per tax return. For years beginning after December 31, 2002, the limit goes to $10,000, which is a maximum credit of $2,000 per return. Only expenses paid after June 30, 1998, qualify for the Life-Time Learning Credit.

Exclusion for Employer-Provided Education

Undergraduate courses that your employer pays for can be excluded from taxable income for courses beginning before June 1, 2000, up to a maximum amount of $5,250. Exclusion means that if the amount is included in your W-2 or if you received a 1099 that includes undergraduate education amounts paid for you by your employer, you can reduce the taxable wage or 1099 amount by up to $5,250. This exclusion does not apply to graduate level courses.

Tax data you need:

⚙ Proof that the employer paid your tuition.

⚙ Proof of the amount the employer paid.

⚙ Proof of enrollment in a qualified undergraduate course.

⚙ Proof that the qualified amount was included in the W-2 or 1099 you received; or proof of how you excluded it from your taxable income.

◆ ◆

CAUTION When dealing with IRS rules that say you can "exclude" something from your taxable income, you need to be careful not to double-dip. For example, if your employer already excluded a $2,000 tuition payment that they made on your behalf from your W-2, you would be wrong to subtract another $2,000 from your W-2 salary amount. On the other hand, if your employer had included that payment in your taxable wages on Form W-2, then you would need to subtract $2,000 from your wages to arrive at the correct taxable wage amount.

◆ ◆

State-Sponsored Tuition Plans

If someone in your family has a state-sponsored tuition plan, you might enjoy more tax savings this year. The Taxpayer Relief Act of 1997 expanded several definitions used to qualify for tax benefits. Beginning August 20, 1996, the term "qualified higher education" was expanded to include more educational programs. In 1998 qualified payments now include room and board. Furthermore, the term "member of the family" has been expanded to allow more tax-free transfers, rollovers of credits, and balances in tuition programs. All good news for those with state-sponsored tuition plans.

Tax data you need:

⚙ Proof of state-sponsored tuition plan.

⚙ Proof of enrollment in qualified education programs.

⚙ Proof of the amount paid, along with an itemized list of qualified expenses paid.

Student Loan Interest

Finally! Some relief for those of us who take out loans to pay for our own education! For qualified education loan payments that are due and paid beginning January 1, 1998, you can deduct the interest. Loans can be for you, your spouse, or any dependent.

However, only the first 60 months of interest qualifies, and then only up to $1,000 in 1998; $1,500 in 1999; $2,000 in 2000; and $2,500 in 2001. The allowable deduction reduces to zero on a sliding scale, reaching zero at a modified AGI of $55,000 for single taxpayers, or $75,000 for joint returns.

Tax data you need:

- ✪ Loan statement that lists the total interest paid for 1998.
- ✪ Cancelled checks to prove payment.
- ✪ Proof of enrollment in a qualified education program.

Education IRAs

Beginning in 1998 annual contributions to an individual retirement account (IRA) that was set up for the specific purpose of funding education can reduce your gross income up to $500 per beneficiary. As with any IRA, the benefit reduces to zero based on a sliding scale, reaching zero for single taxpayers with an AGI of $110,000, or $160,000 for joint returns.

Distributions from an education IRA are excludable from income up to the qualified education expense amount. So, if you only paid $200 for qualified education, you can only exclude $200. Rollovers and transfers to other family members for the same purpose are tax-free, which helps families with two or more children in college.

Tax data you need:

- ✪ Proof that the IRA was set up solely to fund educational expenses.
- ✪ Proof of payment.
- ✪ Proof of qualified amounts paid, such as an itemized invoice.
- ✪ Proof of enrollment, such as a class syllabus or report card.

Making a Tax-Free Profit on Your Home

In the old days, Americans bought one home and lived there most of their lives. Nowadays, many Americans own several homes during their lifetime, perhaps because of job changes or other economic opportunities. Congress has recognized this change and modernized the tax rules so that Americans are not penalized for realizing multiple gains on the ownership of multiple primary residences during a lifetime.

For sales of a primary residence after May 6, 1997, you can exclude from your income any gain on the sale up to $250,000 for single taxpayers, or up to $500,000 for joint returns. (Wow, what a house to have such a gain, huh?) In order to qualify for this hefty exclusion, you must have owned the home and used it as your primary residence for two of the five years prior to the sale date. This exclusion is available to taxpayers every two years. So, if you sell your New York home, move to Los Angeles to take a new job, and decide after a few years to move elsewhere, any gain on either sale (up to the maximum allowable) is tax-free. And in two years, you can move somewhere else and enjoy the tax-free gain rule again. So, the only thing you need to determine is how to sell your house at a gain—not always easy to do in today's market.

Saving Taxes on Capital Gains and Losses

In 1998 gains on sales of investments (such as stocks and bonds that you owned for more than one year) qualify for a new, lower capital gains tax rate of 20 percent (or 10 percent for taxpayers in the 15 percent tax bracket). However, gains on the sale of collectibles will still be taxed at the higher 28 percent. Too bad for all of those Beanie Baby collectors!

Tax data you need:

✪ Proof of purchase date and amount.

✪ Proof of sale date and amount.

✪ Proof of any other related transaction expenses, such as a broker fee. Note that if the broker withheld taxes on the gain, it was probably at the higher rate, and you will get that money back when you file your return.

Escaping Tax with IRAs

Individual retirement accounts (IRAs) have been around for many years, but the rules and regulations surrounding IRAs have been a sore point for numerous taxpayers. In the last two recent tax acts, Congress tried to smooth over some of these issues and give taxpayers more flexibility in using IRA funds.

Unfortunately, the result is more complicated rules, which can frustrate even the most experienced tax accountant. When you enter your IRA data Sunday morning, you will explore the nuances of the various IRA plans into which you can enter. For now, here is an overview of the new rules and the highlights of how they might affect your 1998 return.

Roth IRA

The Roth IRA, named after U.S. Senator Bill Roth (who thought it all up), has sparked a lot of interest and confusion over the past year. In case you haven't heard, the Roth IRA allows you to boost your retirement income while helping with your estate planning. First, unlike regular IRAs, you don't have to withdraw money from your Roth IRA when you reach age 70½. Upon your death, the Roth IRA passes to your beneficiaries, largely tax-free, and continues to grow tax-free under rules similar to those governing regular IRAs. Any money withdrawn by your beneficiaries is tax-free, whereas money drawn from a regular IRA would be taxable to the beneficiary. Furthermore, as long as you and/or your spouse have taxable income, you can continue to make contributions to a Roth IRA (in regular IRAs this is not permitted after age 70½).

Another key advantage of a Roth IRA is that you can withdraw any part of your annual contribution to the IRA (but not the income earned in the IRA) at any time for anything without incurring a penalty or tax. If you're over 59½, you can also withdraw the earnings tax- and penalty-free (provided the Roth IRA account is at least five years old). Regular IRAs do not permit any premature withdrawals without inflicting stiff penalties and taxes unless you meet specific exceptions (such as first-time home buyers, qualified education expenses, or disabilities and certain medical expenses).

The annual nondeductible Roth IRA contribution amount is limited to $2,000, provided you have taxable income of at least that amount. Furthermore, the allowable contribution is reduced to zero based on a sliding scale, reaching zero for single taxpayers with a modified AGI of $110,000, or $160,000 for joint returns.

If you want, you can convert a regular IRA to a Roth IRA—but only if your modified AGI is less than $100,000. The part of the roll over amount which was deducted from your gross income in prior years is taxable. If the rollover is completed by January 1, 1999, you can spread the tax out over four years. Otherwise, the entire tax must be paid to avoid the penalties for early withdrawal. If you roll over a regular IRA to a Roth IRA and then change your mind, you can revert back to the regular IRA, provided you complete the transfer back to a regular IRA by the due date of your return (April 15, 1999, for 1998 returns).

Tax data you need:

⚙ Proof of contribution amount made by due date of return (April 15, 1999, for 1998 returns).

⚙ Proof of newly opened Roth IRA.

⚙ Proof of any conversion from a regular IRA to a Roth IRA, if applicable. (Be sure to keep all prior account statements for the old IRA so you can prove which portions were deducted—and which were not deducted—from your gross income in prior years.)

Expanded Regular IRAs

Beginning in 1998 the AGI limits on the amounts that you can contribute to regular IRAs have been expanded. Also in 1998 the regular IRA contribution has been reduced to zero for single taxpayers with an AGI of $40,000, or $60,000 for joint filers. These amounts will continue to expand over the years until 2007, when the contribution amount goes to zero for single taxpayers with an AGI of $60,000, or $100,000 for joint returns.

Furthermore, if you cannot or do not make contributions to a deductible IRA or Roth IRA, you can make contributions to a nondeductible IRA. However, in total, your contributions to all IRAs in a taxable year cannot exceed $2,000 plus a similar amount for your spouse.

Another new rule has to do with the restrictions on participation in employer-sponsored retirement plans. In 1998 if your spouse participates in an employer-sponsored retirement plan, you are no longer considered an active participant yourself. So, you can contribute up to the $2,000 limit to your IRA even though your spouse is barred from making such contributions.

Tax data you need:

♻ Proof of payment to an IRA plan by due date of return (April 15, 1999, for the 1998 tax year).

♻ Proof of total contributions to all IRA types not exceeding $2,000.

♻ Proof that the taxpayer making contributions has not participated in an employer-sponsored retirement plan.

Miscellaneous Tax Tidbits

In addition to these sweeping changes in categories that affect most taxpayers, Congress added a few minor changes that may or may not affect you. Table 1.2 outlines the changes and describes the key data you need to gather.

TABLE 1.2 MISCELLANEOUS NEW TAX RULES		
Tax Area	**Description of New Rule**	**Tax Data You Need**
Estimated taxes	In 1998 no underpayment penalty will be imposed provided the tax due (less withholding tax) is under $1,000 or if you have paid in at least 100 percent of last year's tax due. In 1999 this safe harbor increases to 105 percent of the prior year's tax.	Proof of tax withheld (W–2s and 1099s), taxes paid (cancelled checks), tax payment carryovers (prior year's return), and prior year's tax liability (prior year's return).
Standard deductions	For dependents with earned income, you can use the higher of the standard deduction or the earned income plus $250.	Proof of dependent's earned income. Dependent must meet other requirements, which you will learn about tomorrow.

TABLE 1.2 MISCELLANEOUS NEW TAX RULES

Tax Area	Description of New Rule	Tax Data You Need
Charitable	Beginning in 1998 the deduction for miles you drive for charity is increased from 12 to 14 cents per mile.	Proof of mileage driven and purpose as charitable (usually a mileage log with purpose clearly stated and verified by a charitable organization).
Paying tax due	As of May 5, 1998, the IRS began accepting credit card payments. (Great, you can earn air miles on your taxes now!) You can pay your taxes using MasterCard, American Express, Discover, and possibly Visa (details were still being worked out at the time this book was printed). Downside: taxpayers—not the IRS—must pay the merchant fee (usually between three and six percent of the transaction amount).	Just your credit card with a sufficient credit limit.
Farm income	For 1998, 1999, and 2000, farmers can elect to average their income over the current and prior three years.	Proof of taxable farm income over the years being averaged (books and records of farming business).
Foreign income	In 1998 you can exclude up to $72,000 of foreign earned income.	Proof of qualified income earned in a foreign country including tax returns filed in that country.
Parking benefits	Employer-provided parking benefits qualifying for the monthly exclusion ($170 plus inflation adjustment) may be offered in lieu of taxable cash compensation.	Proof of parking benefit and amount included in gross income (W-2).
Home office deductions	No change made for 1998 returns. A beneficial rule change was postponed to the 1999 tax year that would allow home offices to qualify if used to conduct administrative or management activities (not done anywhere else) for the benefit of the employer.	None.

What You Can Do Now to Save Taxes

It's never too late to start saving money, especially when it comes to the taxes you pay. This section will focus on what you may be able to control at the last minute. I'll explain various tax-planning strategies that you can implement by December 31—and other things that you can do by April 15—to reduce your tax costs. Toward the end of this book, in the Sunday Evening Bonus Session, you'll learn how to put together a formal tax plan.

Controlling Time

Depending on the type of tax year you've had—and what you expect to happen in the next year—you may want to accelerate taxable income or postpone income into the next year. The same can be said of deductions, such as charitable contributions. In some cases you have no control over when you receive or spend money, but to whatever extent you can time your income and/or expenses, it's all that much better for you.

Suppose that 1998 has been a lean year and you expect to get a new job or client in 1999, which will earn you more money and put you into a higher tax bracket. You would benefit from pulling in as much income as possible in 1998 and postponing deductible expenses to 1999. For example, you could bill clients early in December instead of waiting until the end of December. You could also wait to buy new equipment until 1999 or postpone donations to charities.

On the other hand, if 1998 has been a high-income year, you might want to postpone billing clients until the last moment and not sell any property at a gain in 1998. You would want to increase your deductions and look for ways to reduce your gross income, such as by opening a medical savings account or contributing to a retirement plan. By the time you complete your tax return tomorrow, you will learn more about these items. In the Sunday Evening session, you will also learn how to plan for 1999 and beyond.

> **TIP** Timing the sale of property can help you control the flow of taxable income across years. A sale is generally taxable in the year in which the title passes to the buyer.

Year-End Tax-Planning Ideas

Here is a handy list of some items for which you might be able to control the timing between December and January:

- Mortgage payment (interest deduction)

- Donations of money or property (charitable deduction)

- Visits to the doctor and/or dentist, as well as prescription costs (medical deduction)

- Self-employed business income/expenses (Schedule C income)

- Contributions to 401(k) plans (20 percent of wages up to $10,000 excluded from your income)

- Contributions to IRAs, Keoghs, and other retirement plans (subject to limitations and excluded income)

- Year-end bonus (taxable when received)

- Fourth-quarter state tax payments (deductible in the year paid; if you pay by December 31, 1998, the estimate is not due until January 15, 1999, so you can deduct it in 1998)

- Sale of capital property such as stocks and bonds held for more than 12 months to take advantage of the lower capital gains tax rate

- Shift income to your children under age 14 to get a lower tax rate on the earnings

- Deductible subscriptions and dues (miscellaneous deductions)

NOTE
You have until April 15 to contribute to such retirement accounts as IRAs, IRA-SEPs, Keoghs, and Roth IRAs. However, contributions to 401(k) plans must be completed by year-end (December 31).

What's Next?

The most time-consuming part of preparing your own tax return is gathering the data and determining which tax law changes affect you. And that's exactly what you accomplished tonight. When you return in the morning, you will start up TurboTax and explore its key features. You will familiarize yourself with the Help system, tax library, expert advice, and video clips that explain everything in plain English. Then, you will learn how to create your tax data file, import last year's data (if you used tax software), and import any 1998 data from other financial systems you may use, such as Quicken.

So, get a good night's sleep—the fun with TurboTax will begin in the morning!

Getting Started with TurboTax

- ✿ Exploring TurboTax
- ✿ Getting Expert Advice
- ✿ Importing Data
- ✿ Setting Up Tax Links
- ✿ Using TurboTax with Quicken and QuickBooks

Good morning! If you're following the "In a Weekend" theme, it's Saturday morning and you had no tax nightmares last night. Because, of course, you knew that today you would be completing your federal tax return with the help of TurboTax. TurboTax has been around for more than a decade and continues to be the leading individual tax-preparation software on the market. You can be confident in the tax law, tax advice, and tax calculations you'll find here. And in my personal opinion, the software always seems so much more reliable than other software. (I have yet to encounter a bug that prevented me from completing a tax return.)

This morning you will learn how to

- Create a tax file
- Use key features in TurboTax
- Navigate between features
- Get expert advice
- Research tax questions
- Import last year's data
- Import this year's data
- Select a data entry method
- Customize your data entry method
- Enter basic tax information
- Save your tax data file

TurboTax to the Rescue!

Last night's section probably raised more questions than answers. You took a good look at your tax return data from last year and began to organize this year's tax data. And in doing so, you may have recognized some areas where you could save taxes or at least reduce the tax cost—provided you qualify under the various tax rules. TurboTax helps you take control of your taxes by helping you to further organize your tax records and in explaining the consequences of that data. The nuances of the tax rules are explained as you enter your data and discover which tax rules apply to your situation. In some cases qualifying means that you save tax dollars; in other cases it may mean that you owe more taxes and/or need to maintain more complete tax records. In either case it is always better to know your tax opportunities and responsibilities before a tax auditor appears at your door!

TurboTax Deluxe provides you with the following key features:

- All the tax forms and instructions you could ever want (okay, make that all you could ever need)

- The option to enter data directly on forms (tax pros love this) or enter data in response to questions (which explain what, why, and how—useful for everyone, even tax pros)

- The ability to roll over last year's TurboTax data (which saves you time from having to reenter data and ensures that you won't miss a tax carryover amount)

- The ability to import data from Quicken, QuickBooks, and other financial software that supports the TXF format (which saves you time from having to reenter this year's amounts and ensures that you won't miss taxable income or tax deductions you've previously flagged)

- On-screen tax reference books, tax advice, IRS publications, tax form instructions, and even video tax advice on key areas—all context-sensitive and tied in with where you are in the program

- Online support for tax law and program updates, additional Web resources, and tax news alert services

- Free electronic filing (regularly $9.95)

- Integration with and support for state income tax return software (which must be purchased separately), which saves you time from having to reenter data and ensures that you won't miss taxable income or state deductions and/or adjustments

☼ A built-in review process that checks your final return for omissions, errors, inconsistencies, and potential tax audit issues

☼ Tax-planning calculations, ideas for next year based on this year's data, and tax deadline reminders

☼ Quicken's Financial Planner QuickPlan edition, which allows you to plan financially for more than just taxes

About now you're probably wondering why you've been paying someone else to do your return. Just think of the money you're going to save this weekend.

> While I was reviewing a prior year's return with a client, the client turned to me and said that he had lied on his return last year. Being immediately concerned, I asked him to explain further. He said that he had listed himself as the "Head of the Household."

Opening TurboTax

If you haven't had a chance yet to install TurboTax, open the box and read over the QuickStart card included with your software. Convenient having the installation instructions on such a small card, isn't it? Follow the steps to install TurboTax on your computer. After installation is complete, your computer will restart, after which you will see the TurboTax program icon on your desktop (see Figure 2.1). Double-click on the TurboTax icon to start TurboTax, or from the Start menu choose Programs, TurboTax Deluxe 1998, 1998 TurboTax Deluxe.

Exploring TurboTax

When TurboTax opens, a bit of music plays, and then TurboTax reminds you to register your copy if you haven't done so yet. The online registration requires a modem. However, you can instead use the registration card included in the TurboTax box and mail in the card the old-fashioned way.

TurboTax Icon —————

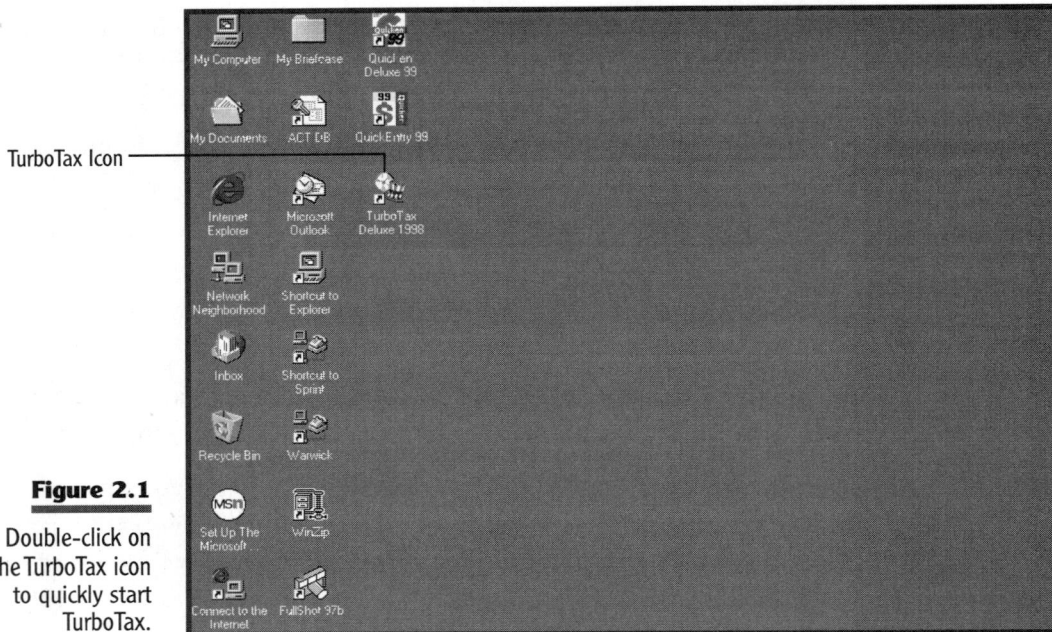

Figure 2.1

Double-click on
the TurboTax icon
to quickly start
TurboTax.

Just be sure to register so you'll get free software updates, free technical support, and the free TurboTax newsletter.

Once you get past the registration dialog boxes, your screen should look like Figure 2.2. Review the components of the screen from top to bottom now so you can become familiar with the screen elements and their names.

At the top of the screen, there is a menu system commonly referred to as the menu bar. As you click on a menu name (such as File), a longer menu of choices appears, with some choices (such as TaxLink) unfolding into submenus. To display other menus, just point to the menu name. Take a minute to explore the menus. As you study each aspect of TurboTax, you will learn the corresponding menu items.

To leave the menu system, just press the Esc (escape) key on your keyboard. Below the menu bar, you see numbered folder tabs labeled as follows:

1. Start

2. Import

Folders

FAQ Links

Menu bar

Navigator

Video Player

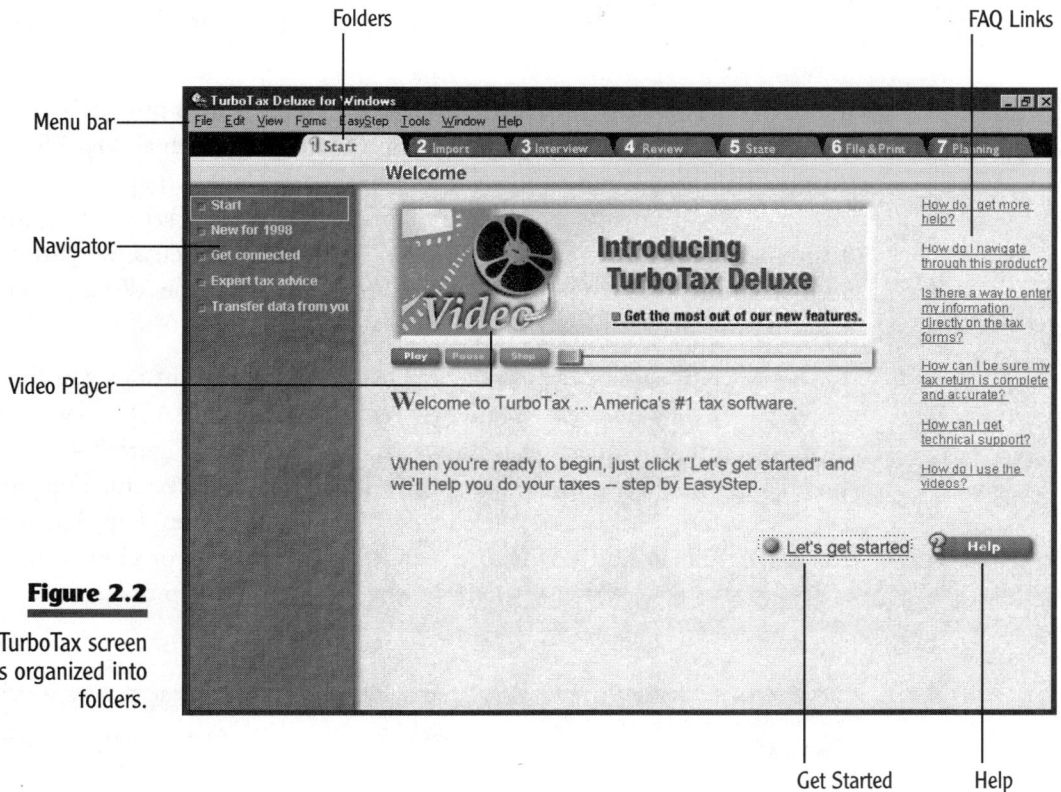

Figure 2.2

The TurboTax screen is organized into folders.

Get Started

Help

3. Interview

4. Review

5. State

6. File & Print

7. Planning

This is the order in which you will use TurboTax to complete your tax returns, do tax planning, and organize your tax records. Take a moment now to click on each tab and see how the screen changes when you do. Notice that some things stay the same, although the exact words and pictures may change. On the far left is a blue navigation bar, which lists the steps to be completed within that folder. This is called the Interview Navigator. Later in this session you will learn how to use the Navigator for your particular tax return needs.

In the middle of most folders will be a Video Player, which provides you with personal assistance throughout TurboTax. Tax experts such as Mary Sprouse (former IRS group audit manager and author of *Money* magazine's *Income Tax Handbook*) and Marshall Loeb (former editor at *Fortune* and *Money* magazines) explain the tax laws in plain English and discuss the issues you need to know about. Figure 2.3 shows one clip from the Welcome video. Click on the Play button to look at the Welcome video.

To the far right side in each folder is a list of hyperlinks (just as you find on a Web page). The links are Frequently Asked Questions (FAQs)—when you click on a link, the question is answered. As you see in Figure 2.4, the Frequently Asked Questions are part of the TurboTax Help system. The answer to the question (link) that you clicked on appears in the Help dialog box. You can scroll up and down to review the other FAQs, or choose another Help topic to read. When you are finished, close the Help dialog box.

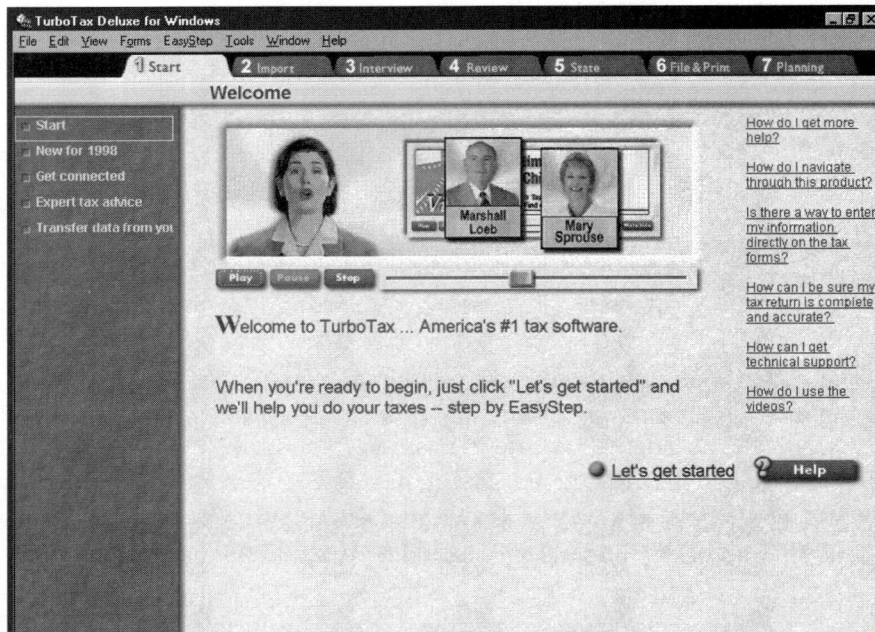

Figure 2.3

Sit back and listen as tax experts explain the tax rules to you.

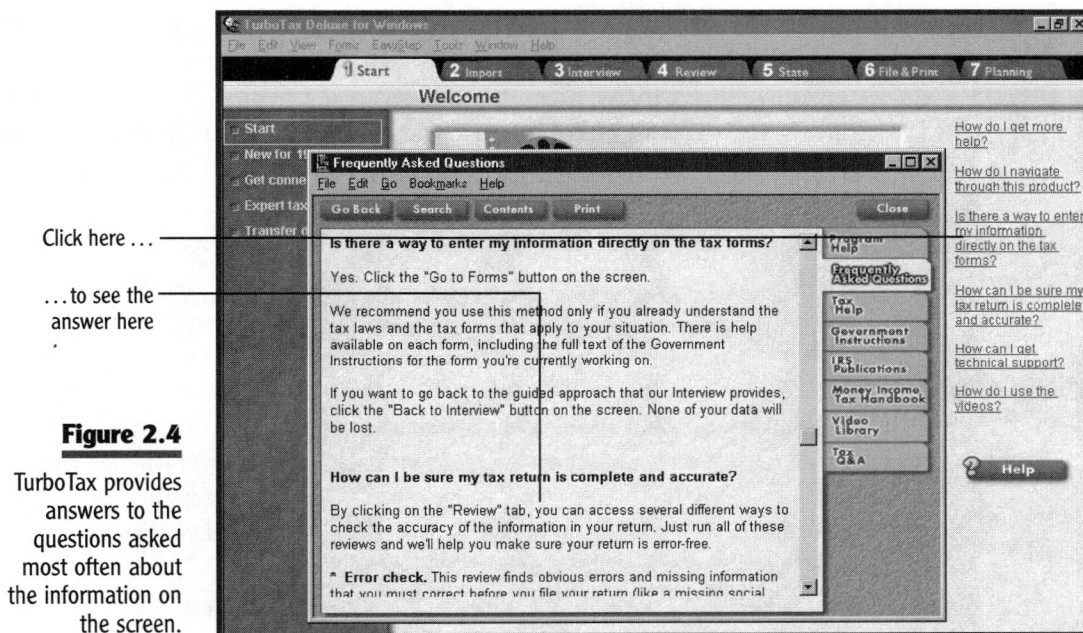

Click here ...

...to see the
answer here

Figure 2.4

TurboTax provides
answers to the
questions asked
most often about
the information on
the screen.

TIP

Reading over the FAQs is a great way to learn more about TurboTax and the tax law. Chances are that someone else has had the same question you have—and that TurboTax has the answer spelled out in clear language.

Below the FAQ links is a Help button, which opens the Help dialog box with the Program Help tab (as opposed to the FAQ tab) selected. The Help system provides you with instructions on how to use TurboTax, the FAQs, Tax Help, Government Instructions, IRS Publications, *Money* magazine's *Income Tax Handbook,* a Video Library, and a Tax Q&A filled with expert advice from tax professionals across the country.

The remaining elements on the screen vary from folder to folder. For example, in the Start folder, you can click on a couple of bullet points to learn more about the new features in TurboTax, the new Tax Laws for 1998, or just get started using TurboTax. In the Interview folder, the buttons allow you to move backward (to step 2), learn how to organize your paperwork, learn more about the new tax laws, or start entering data into your return. In some folders you will need to complete just a few steps, in others (for example, Interview) you will have many, many steps. You can at any time click on a previous or future tab, and within that folder a prior or future step. This allows you the freedom to enter the data you have now and return later to fill in the missing items once you have them. You can also move back and forth as needed to review your return and refresh your memory on how you've answered various questions.

◆ ◆

CAUTION In some cases you will not be allowed to advance to or access a feature until you've provided the necessary data or updated your software. For example, you won't be able to work on a state return until you purchase and add that state to your copy of TurboTax (yes, you can do that online). The Review folder is another area that won't work fully until you've entered most of your data. If you've only entered a few items of information, the Review folder will list almost the whole return as being omitted!

◆ ◆

Let's Get Started

Enough with the tour! Choose the Start tab and click on <u>Let's Get Started</u>. The Start folder's Welcome page changes to the New for 1998 page. You can click on <u>New Features</u> or <u>Tax Law Changes</u> to view Help system text on the new features in TurboTax this year or the new tax laws Congress passed for 1998. The <u>Back</u> bullet takes you to the prior page (Welcome) whereas the <u>Continue</u> bullet takes you to the next page. Take a moment to try each option out. When you are finished, click on <u>Continue</u> to move on to the next topic.

As you can see in Figure 2.5, your next step is to get connected—that is, to connect to the TurboTax Web site for a free update. This is an important step, since Congress is famous for last-minute tax law changes that could impact your return. Intuit also uses this update process to distribute any program changes (for example, bug fixes). In order to update online, you need to have access to the Internet. If you don't, you can call 800-264-5943 to get update disks sent to you.

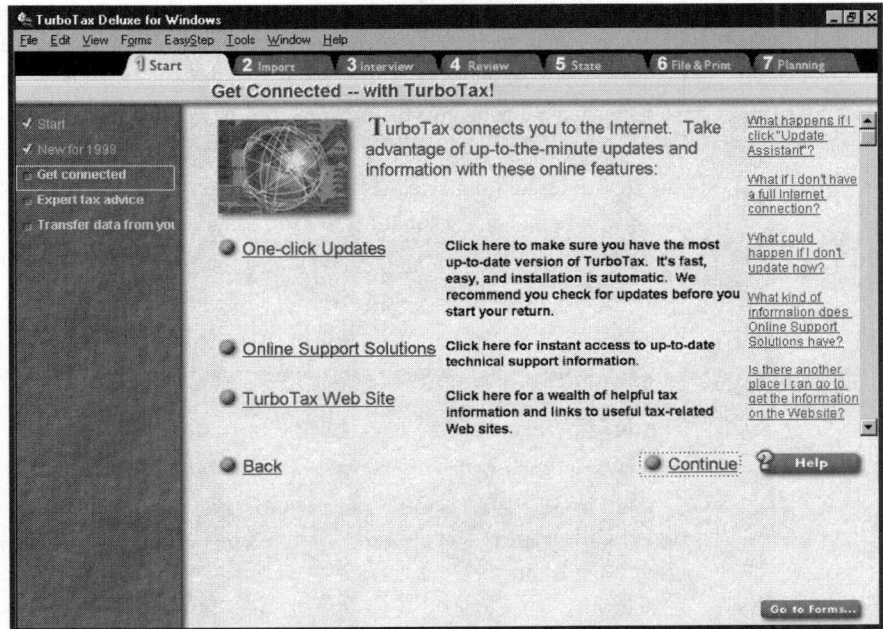

Figure 2.5

Online updates ensure that you are using the most up-to-date software.

TIP

If a few years from now you need to file an amended return or use TurboTax to investigate the source of a number or calculation, you will need your data file, the TurboTax CD, and any updates you downloaded. The updates are downloaded under a file name and in a directory that you specify. You should copy that file to a disk or order the update disks from Intuit and keep them with your tax records.

Periodically, TurboTax will prompt you to check for updates while you work (especially if you are working on this process over the span of a week or more). Alternatively, you can at any time request that TurboTax check for updates by choosing Help, Product Updates from the menu bar. TurboTax will find your Internet dial-up connection and log you on to find any updates. Any data that you have already entered will be transferred into the new forms and then recalculated according to the newest tax law changes.

■■

TIP Unless you have a burning need to get your tax refund as soon as possible, wait until March to work on your tax return. By then, all of your tax documents (such as W-2s and 1099s) should have arrived. The final tax law changes, new tax forms, and program changes should be completed and posted on TurboTax's Web site. In addition, the state tax modules are usually not available until late January—sometimes not even until February for states with tremendous changes (you can download these too at a fee per state). Lastly, by March thousands of folks will have been using TurboTax for a few months and will have found any program operability problems (which Intuit by then would have fixed and included in the updates).

■■

While you're connected to get the update, you might want to check out the TurboTax Support Network and the rest of the TurboTax Web site. The TurboTax Support Network (see Figure 2.6) gives you 24-hour access to technical support via e-mail, online discussion groups, FAQs, and a knowledge base of expert tax advice.

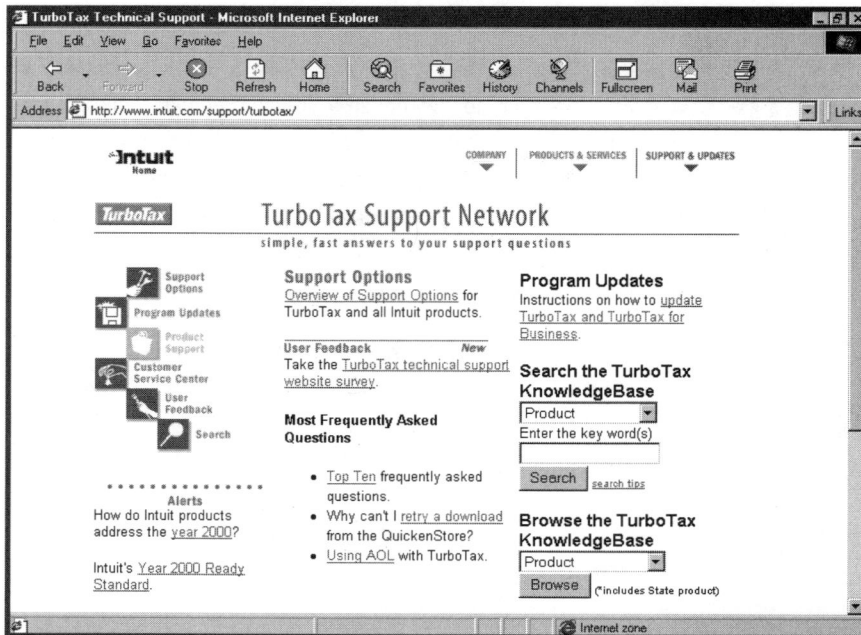

Figure 2.6

The TurboTax Online Support Solutions Center provides quick answers to your questions.

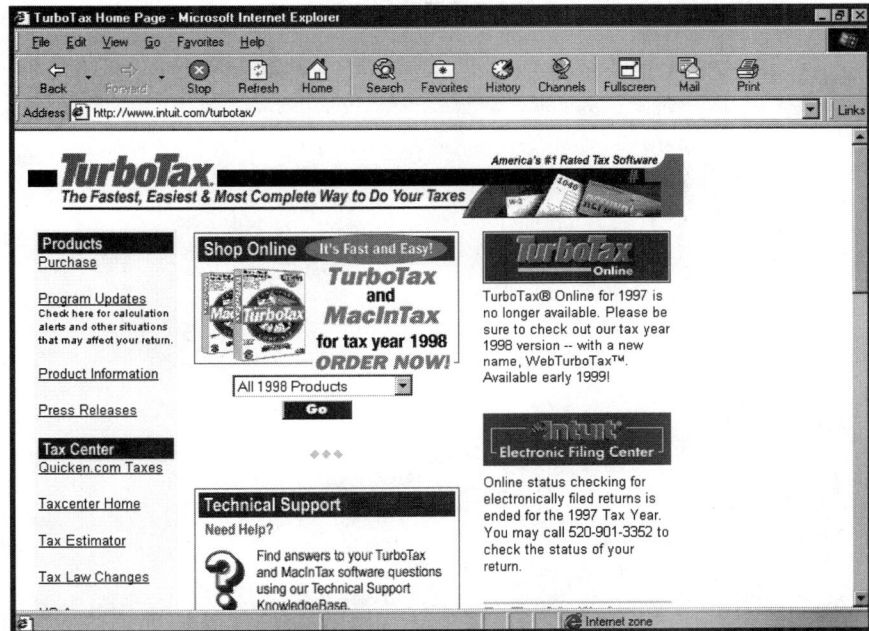

Figure 2.7

The TurboTax Web site even allows you to file online.

The TurboTax Web site (see Figure 2.7) provides you with access to program updates, state downloads, technical support, electronic filing, online filing, online tax calculators, and tax tips from experts.

If you don't have access to the Internet, or if you decide to update later, click on Continue at the bottom right corner of your screen.

Getting Expert Tax Advice

After the update step, TurboTax introduces you to the on-screen guides included on the CD: IRS Publications, *Money* magazine's *Income Tax Handbook,* and Tax Q&A (see Figure 2.8).

To open an on-screen book, click on the book name, or from the menu bar choose Help and the desired publication. Figure 2.9 shows you the IRS Publications List. You can scroll down through the list until you find the exact publication you want and just click on the publication name.

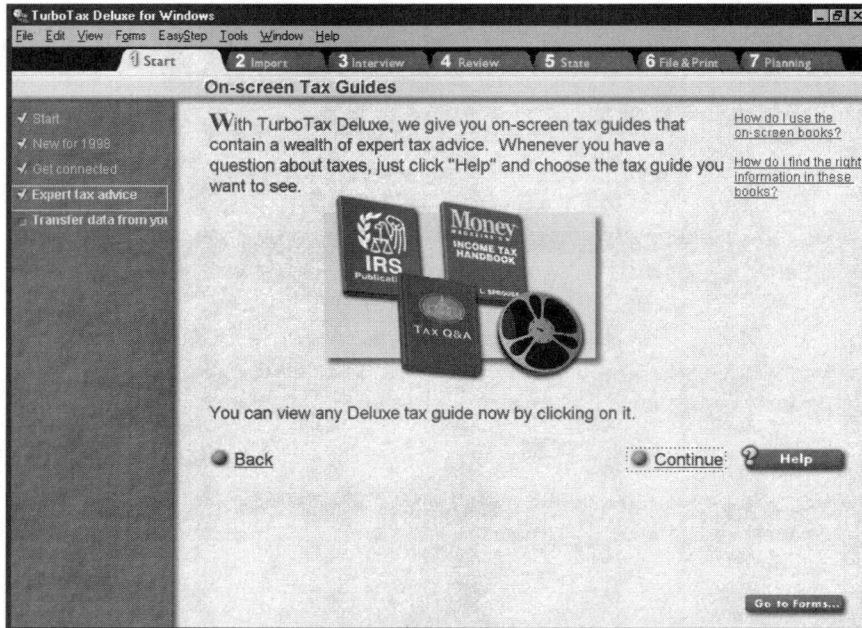

Figure 2.8

TurboTax comes with a complete set of on-screen tax books to help you get control of your taxes.

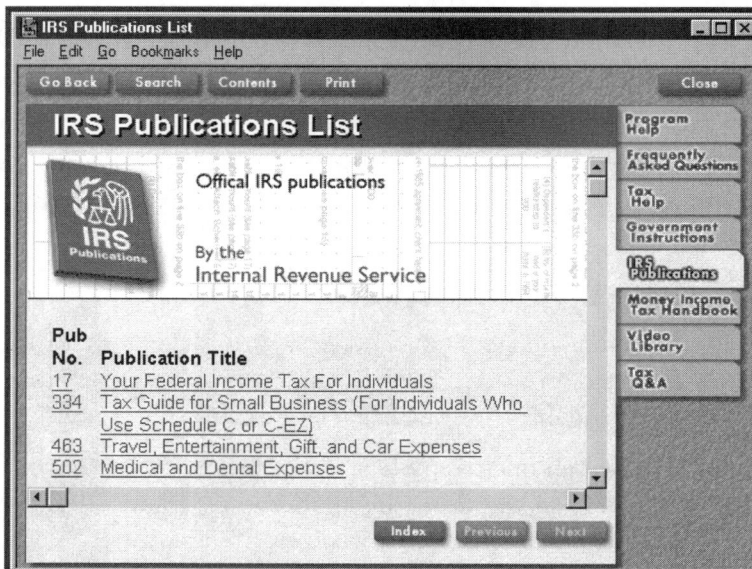

Figure 2.9

The IRS Publications List includes explanations of the tax rules and requirements on a variety of topics.

NOTE The CD must be in the CD-ROM drive in order for you to access books, videos, and certain other storage-intensive resources that would take up too much room on your hard disk. Unlike other computer programs where you only use the CD to install the program once, TurboTax installs just the nuts and bolts of the program on your hard disk. The other, larger portions are kept on the CD. If TurboTax can't find the CD and needs information on the CD, it will just ask you to insert the CD. But this will slow you down a bit, so it is usually a good idea to just leave the CD in the drive while working with TurboTax.

Finding Information

Once you have a publication open, you can read through it just like a printed book. But unlike a printed book, TurboTax's on-screen books provide you with automated Search and Index features.

To find a specific topic, click on the Search button, type in the words that describe what you are looking for (in this example, Roth IRA), and then click on Find Topics. TurboTax will list all matches found within the open publication (see Figure 2.10). If TurboTax finds more than 50 matches to your search criteria, a message displays explaining that only the first 50 will be listed.

Figure 2.10

Use the Search feature to find your way through the numerous pages within a publication.

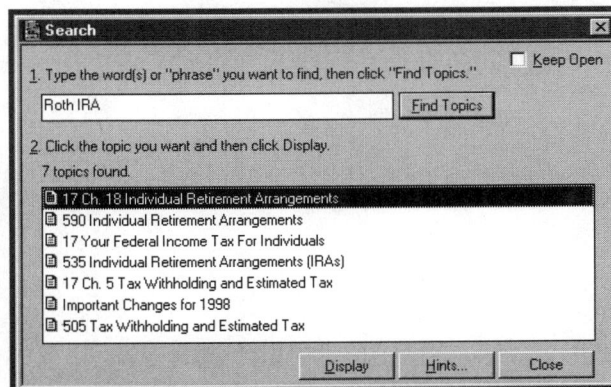

To narrow down your search, click on the Hints button, which suggests that you

- Use more than one word to describe the topic, for example use *Roth IRA* instead of just *IRA*.

- Use the keyword *or* to broaden the topic, such as *Roth or IRA*.

- Use the keyword *near* to find sections which discuss one word/phrase within 8 words of another word/phrase, for example *Roth near IRA*.

- Use quotes around words to find only an exact match of that phrase, such as "Roth IRA" would only find sections where the phrase *Roth IRA* is used (would not find *IRA Roth* or *Roth* followed by some other words and then *IRA*).

If you want to keep the search results on the screen while you view a few of the matches, click on the Keep Open check box in the top right corner. To view a match, select the topic and then click on Display to read that section (see Figure 2.11).

Use the Index button to view the Tax Library Index. Each index entry is a hyperlink, which when clicked takes you directly to the topic page in the

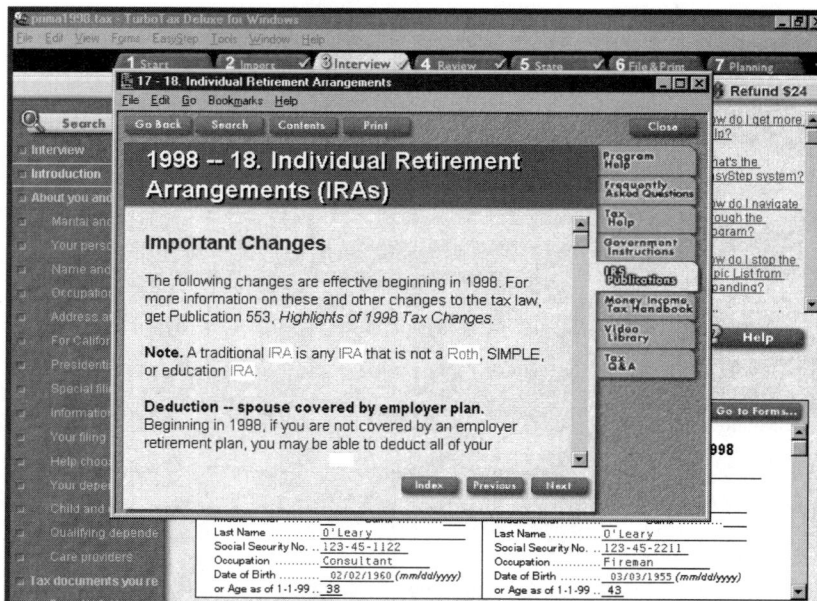

Figure 2.11

Use the Previous and Next buttons to page up and down within a book.

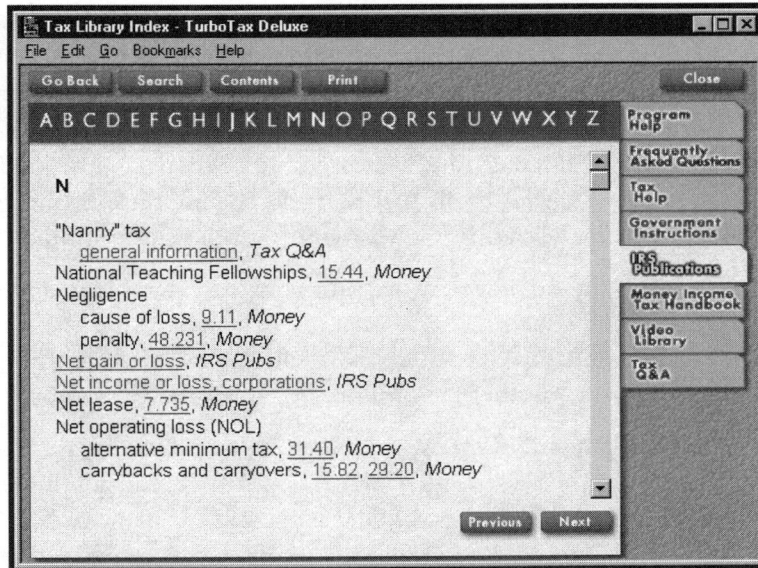

Figure 2.12

Use the tax library index to find information by topic name.

appropriate publication. As you can see in Figure 2.12, the Tax Library Index is organized alphabetically. Just click on a letter and scroll down through the entries until you find the desired item.

TIP Click on the Go Back button to return to the previous book or page, wherever you were last.

Transferring Last Year's Data

Close any publications that you have open and return to the Start folder screen. Click on the <u>Next</u> bullet to complete the Expert Tax Advice step. Notice that this step is now checked off in the Navigator column to the left. TurboTax helps you keep track of where you've been and what you've accomplished by checking off steps (in the Navigator column) as you complete them. To quickly return to a prior step, just click on that step in the Navigator. To move back one step at a time and retrace each step you've taken, use the <u>Back</u> bullet. With TurboTax you are always in control.

If you used TurboTax to prepare your tax return last year, you can transfer your previous year's tax data into this year's tax file. Transferring data saves you the time you would have to spend reentering any data from the prior year that is needed again this year (such as your social security number, address, and tax carryover amounts). To begin the transfer, click on the option Transfer From Last Year. TurboTax prompts (see Figure 2.13) you to select the tax return file that you want to transfer from.

Select the drive letter you want to check, the folder, and the file name that contains your previous year's tax data. Note that the transfer feature only works for TurboTax data files. You cannot roll over the previous year's tax data from another tax product (for example, TaxCut or Personal Tax Edge).

This standard Windows Explorer dialog box will search your hard disk and look for the prior year's data file. If it is not found automatically, you will need to specify the directory, folder path, and file name. If you kept the data on a disk (it's always a good idea to keep your tax data disk with your tax records), put the disk in the drive and let TurboTax know the drive letter and file name. TurboTax does the rest and let's you know when the process is complete.

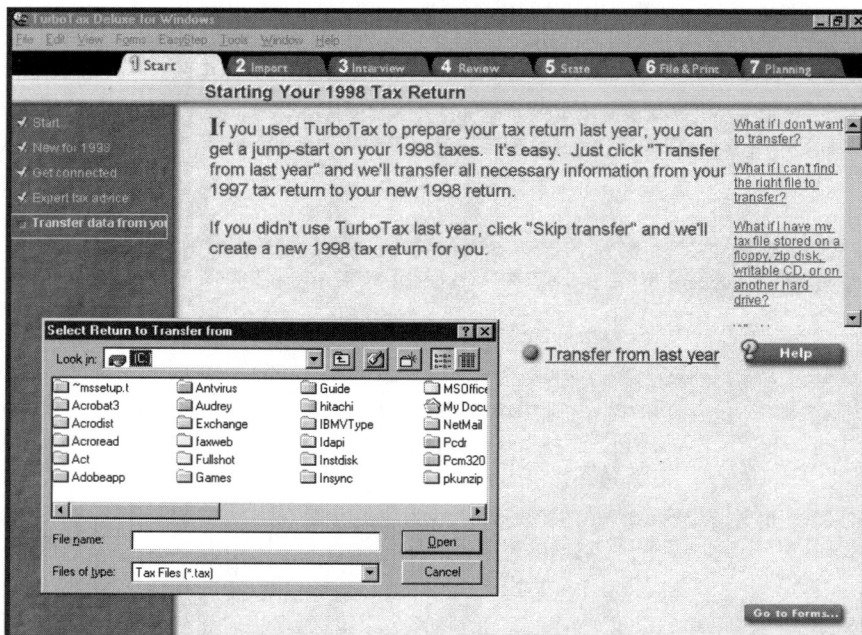

Figure 2.13

Use the standard Windows Explorer dialog box to tell TurboTax where your previous year's tax file is located.

If you didn't use TurboTax last year, just click on the <u>Skip Transfer</u> option and keep in mind the time you will save next year when you get to transfer in your data!

NOTE If your tax return changed since you used TurboTax last year (for example, if you later filed an amended return), you can still transfer the data file to this year's tax return. Just be sure to locate the amounts that changed and carry the adjustments to this year's data file. For example, suppose last year you claimed a charitable contribution of $1,000, which was disallowed and deleted from an amended return for last year. The amended return would show your itemized deduction amount reduced by $1,000, and consequently your tax liability would go up based on the additional taxable net income. On your 1998 tax return you would need to enter the new tax amount on Form 2210 for any current underpayment penalty or exception to be properly computed.

Saving Your Tax File

While you work, TurboTax will periodically prompt you to save your tax data file. At any time, you can save your tax data by doing the following:

1. Press Ctrl+S, or from the menu bar choose File, Save.

2. Type in a file name (such as Brown Tax Return 1998), being as descriptive as you like.

3. Click on the Save button.

Once you have saved your data file with a specific name, you can just press Ctrl+S or choose File, Save to periodically resave your data under the same name. To choose a different name, just use the File, Save As option and type in a new name.

NOTE Separate data file names are usually only necessary when you are preparing separate returns (for example, in case you need to do a parent's or child's tax return in addition to your own).

Creating Other Tax Files

If you need to work on more than one tax return, you will need to create separate tax data files for each return. To do so, follow the steps below:

1. Press Ctrl+N, or from the menu bar choose File, New Tax Return. If you haven't saved the currently opened tax file, TurboTax prompts you to save that first.

2. The new tax data file appears with the first folder, Start, set at the first step.

3. Press Ctrl+S, or from the menu bar choose File, Save to save the new tax data file to a unique name.

4. Repeat steps 1–3 as needed for each tax return that you need to complete.

NOTE   In TurboTax, unlike some software programs that you may be familiar with, only one data file can be open at a time. After you save a data file, the name of the data file currently being used appears in the TurboTax title bar at the top of your screen (just to the left of the program name, TurboTax Deluxe for Windows). When you open another data file, even a new data file, the prior data file is closed first.

If the IRS was run like Microsoft...

The IRS would reject your late or amended tax return based on the grounds that the prior year is no longer being supported.

Importing Financial Data

Regardless of whether you file your tax return yourself or have someone else do the preparation for you, the end product is only as good as the quality of the source data. I cannot emphasize enough the time, heartache, and complications that you will avoid by automating your financial records. Programs such as Quicken, QuickBooks, and Microsoft Money help you automate your financial records by putting your various bank, credit card, and investment accounts on the computer. Once you have everything set up, you merely select bills for payment and print the checks or send the payments online. And balancing your checkbook is a breeze! Better yet, when it comes to tax time, your financial data for the year automatically imports into TurboTax (provided the financial program supports the TXF file format). Importing your financial data directly from a financial program saves you time and reduces the risk of entering the wrong amount into TurboTax.

NOTE
If you want to learn more about what Quicken Deluxe can do for you, before you invest the time, pick up Prima Publishing's *Organize Your Finances In a Weekend with Quicken Deluxe 99*. I've heard that the author adds humor to that process too!

In the second folder, Import (see Figure 2.14), TurboTax gives you the option of importing your financial information from Quicken, QuickBooks, or other financial software packages that support the tax-related data format called TXF.

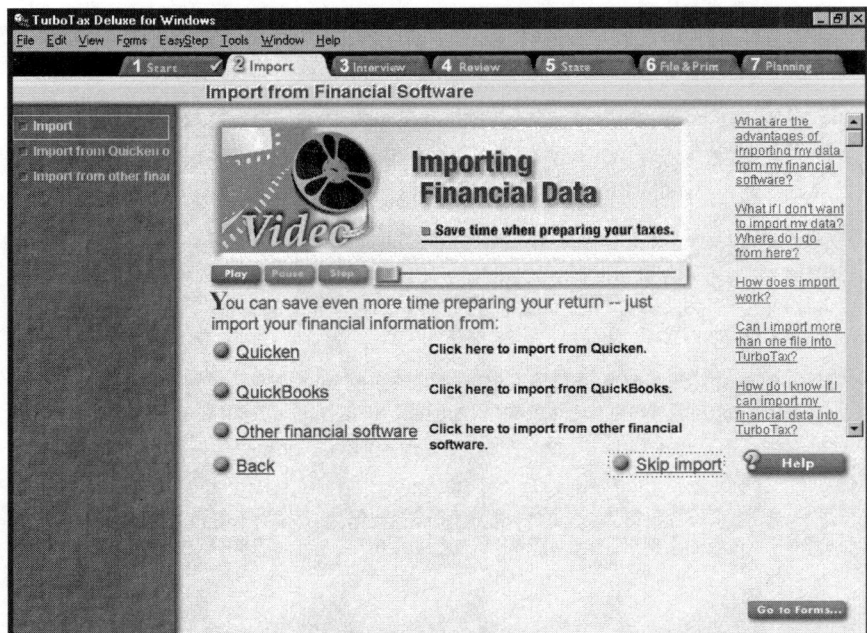

Figure 2.14

Why reenter data? Instead, save time by importing your financial data.

CAUTION

◆ ◆

Be sure to roll over your prior year's TurboTax data *before* you start importing the current year's data. This is the best way to be sure that your amounts post to the correct place in TurboTax.

◆ ◆

Importing from Quicken

You can import from Quicken using either the TXF transfer file method or the more convenient TaxLink method. The key difference is that the TaxLink method assumes that you are a calendar-year taxpayer. If you have a short year return or an odd tax year that is not a full calendar year, then you must use the TXF transfer file method, which allows you to specify the tax year beginning and ending dates. In addition, if your version of Quicken is older (Quicken 5 or earlier), you will need to use the TXF transfer file method.

BUZZ WORD

◀ ◀

Tax Year: The time period from the beginning to the end of a taxable year for which the tax return is being filed.

Calendar Year: A tax year that begins January 1 and ends December 31. Most individual tax returns are filed on a calendar year basis.

Fiscal Year: A tax year that begins on any day and continues for a full 12 months (for example, from July 1, 1997, to June 30, 1998). Fiscal years are usually used by businesses to reflect their accounting year.

Short Year: A tax year that is less than a full 12 months, usually occurring when businesses change their accounting year (such as from fiscal to calendar).

◀ ◀

TIP

■ ■

Although computers can help you track and manage your finances, they cannot do what humans do best: review for reasonableness. Never take a computer printout as absolute truth. Always review the reports for omissions and errors. At tax time I always print a full-year all-account Itemized Categories Report from Quicken with full details. Although it runs 60 or so pages, this becomes an invaluable record of everything I entered into Quicken, thereby providing a complete listing of all my financial transactions. I then review the print-out looking for odd items, such as uncategorized transactions, items in the wrong category, and mystery transfers between accounts. I then compare any tax forms (1099s, charitable receipts, estimated tax payments, etc.) with the printout. I circle and make notes on tax-related categories, such as salary, medical expenses, and specific categories that enter into my home office and Schedule C computations. In a few hours (yes, it *is* worth the few hours), I have complete confidence in the financial data and its validity on my tax return.

Setting Up Tax Links in Quicken

Prior to importing data into TurboTax, you need to set up your tax-related categories in Quicken and point them to the appropriate tax form lines. Categories that were automatically set up by Quicken (such as interest income) are set up as tax-related and point to the correct tax form (Schedule B, for reporting interest income). For new categories that you created, you will need to specify the tax-related nature and point to the appropriate tax form line.

TIP

Get into the habit of assigning a tax-related status and tax links when you set up a new category in order to minimize your work at year-end. If your Category Setup and Edit dialog boxes do not show the tax-related information, choose Edit, Options, Quicken Program and select the General tab. Check the Use Tax Schedules with Categories box and click on OK. You will now be able to set the tax-related nature of categories and assign tax form links in the Category Set Up and Edit dialog boxes.

NOTE

If you have more than one copy of a form, such as two Schedule Cs, you'll need to set up a class for each form in Quicken. For example, if you and your spouse each have a business for which you file a Schedule C, you could create two classes named "His" and "Hers" and then categorize all transactions accordingly (such as "Supplies/His" and "Supplies/Hers"). When you transfer the data to TurboTax, each business will list the appropriate data on its own Schedule C.

To review the tax links for categories, follow these steps:

1. In Quicken Deluxe 99, choose Features, Taxes, Set Up Taxes to open the Tax Link Assistant (see Figure 2.15).

2. Scroll down the Category list box on the left side (listing all active categories). Categories defined as tax-related will have a tax line assignment.

3. For categories that do not have a tax line assignment, but which should, select the appropriate tax form line item from the list on the far right. When you click on a tax line item, Quicken displays a description of the tax form or line across the bottom of the dialog box.

● ●

NOTE   If you are unsure about whether an item is tax-related or not, write it down on a list (do not link the item yet) or press Ctrl+C to view your Category list (which notes items as tax-related or not). You can print the Category list by pressing Ctrl+P. As you continue through the process of organizing your taxes this weekend, refer to the list and make notes on the categories as taxable income, deductible expense, or source data for a tax adjustment or credit. Note the tax form and line number where the item is reported on your tax return. Then return to Quicken and set up the tax links for next year's tax return.

Once this is set up, you will not have to redo this every year, unless the tax forms change. Throughout the year it is always a good idea to periodically print your tax reports and update category settings as needed.

● ●

4. To set a tax link, select the category on the left, choose the appropriate tax form line item on the right, and click on the Assign Line Item to Category button.

5. To remove a tax link, select the category on the left and click on the Clear Assignment button.

6. To remove all tax links, click on the Clear All Assignments button.

7. When you are finished, click on OK to save your changes, or on Cancel to exit without saving (Quicken will prompt you to verify the cancellation).

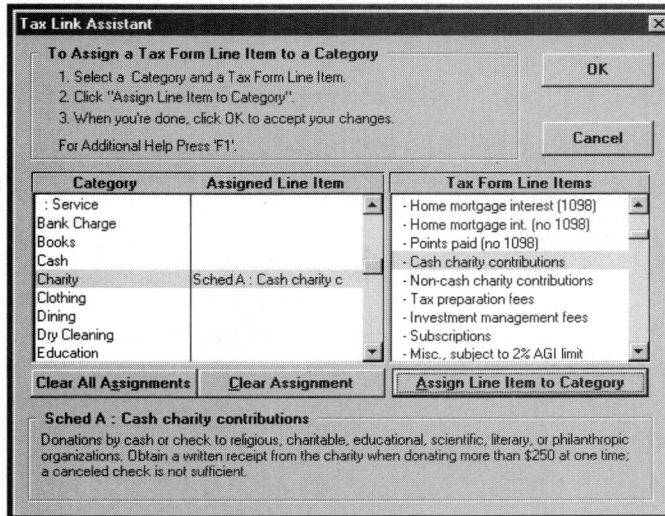

Figure 2.15

In Quicken you can use the Tax Link Assistant to assign tax links to categories.

TIP

Each time you enter a transaction, you must ask yourself a question: "Does this transaction generate taxable income or a potential tax deduction?" If the answer is yes, then you must assign it the appropriate tax-related category. For example, if you get a bonus check from your boss, you need to classify that deposit as a taxable receipt of income in a category such as salary or bonus (which would be reported on the salary and wages [W-2] line of Form 1040). If by accident you classify that deposit to the wrong category, such as cash, which is not tax-related, your tax reports (and consequently your tax return) would be incorrect.

Periodically throughout the year, review your categories for tax-related items. Run the tax reports (Tax Summary, Capital Gains, and Tax Schedule reports) and review the information contained on these reports, checking for errors or omissions. Then when tax time rolls around, you will have all your ducks in a row and be able to automatically import accurate data into TurboTax!

Importing Data into TurboTax Using Quicken Tax Links

To start the Import procedure from TurboTax, click on <u>Quicken</u> (the first bullet point listed in the TurboTax Import folder), which takes you to an explanation of how easy it is to import your data from Quicken into Turbo-Tax. Select the Import Now option. TurboTax searches your computer and locates the most recently used Quicken data file (see Figure 2.16).

If this isn't the Quicken data file that you want to import from, click on the Browse button to specify a different data file. Otherwise, click on Continue to view the TaxLink Instructions dialog box (see Figure 2.17).

TIP

You can import multiple Quicken data files into TurboTax. To do so, import the first data file as described here using the TaxLink method. Then for the remaining data files, use the TXF method (see the next section). The additional imported data is added on to your TurboTax data.

Figure 2.16

TurboTax finds your Quicken data file.

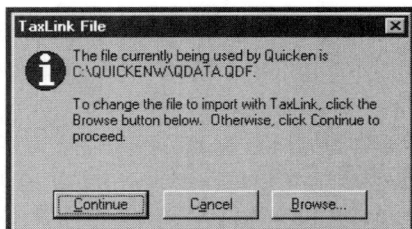

Figure 2.17

In three quick steps, you'll be done importing!

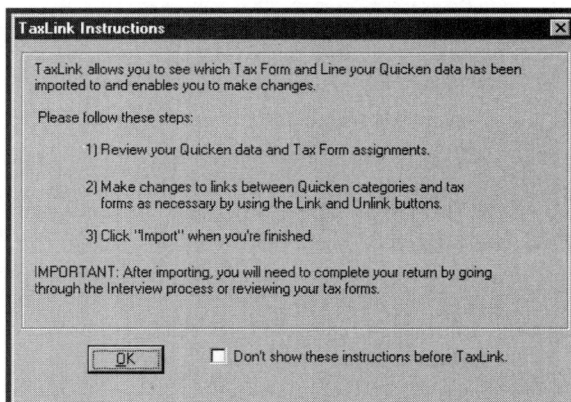

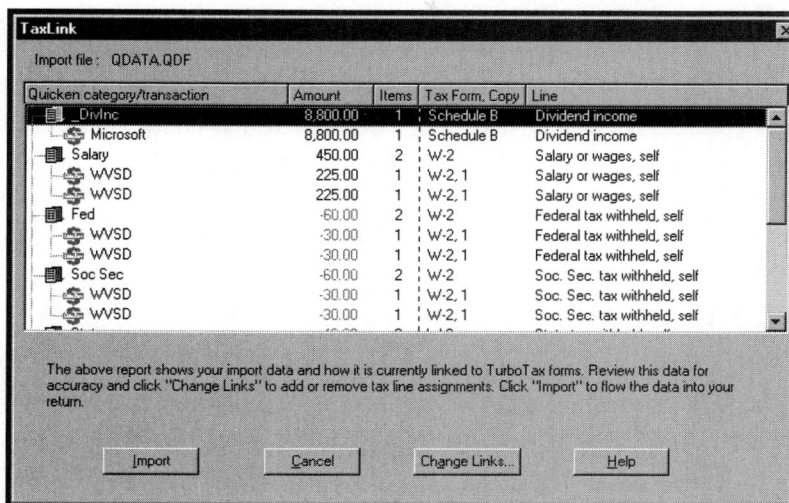

Figure 2.18

TurboTax allows you to review your Quicken data before importing.

The instructions explain that you will be able to review and change Quicken tax links in the next step before actually importing. Click on OK to view the TaxLink dialog box (see Figure 2.18).

Review the tax form and line assignments for the categories listed. To change a tax link, select the category and then click on the Change Links button. The Change Links button displays the details so you can change the tax link and even provides a Zoom to Quicken button in case you have to change an amount. Note that the Zoom to Quicken button becomes active only when you have an item selected.

◆ ◆

CAUTION Do not close Quicken while you are working on the TurboTax TaxLinks Import.

◆ ◆

When you are satisfied with the tax link settings, click on the Import button to transfer that data from Quicken into your TurboTax data file. After importing, TurboTax reports that the import was successful and prompts you to click on Next to continue to folder tab 3, Interview.

TIP

After the import completes, you can review your imported data in TurboTax by choosing Tools, My Tax Data. The imported data is flagged with the label "Import." If you want to see the data on the form, click on the data item and then the Go to Form button. If the data item appears to be on the wrong form, choose Interview, and EasyStep will walk you through the process of correcting the posting. When you are finished viewing the form, click on the Close Form button to return to the Import tab. If you don't want to keep the data that was just imported, choose File, Remove Imported Data.

Importing Data from QuickBooks

QuickBooks cannot generate a TXF file, so the TaxLink method described above for Quicken is the only method available to you. As with Quicken, be sure to have your tax links set up in QuickBooks and periodically review the tax links and reports in order to reduce your end-of-year work.

CAUTION

Since QuickBooks cannot generate a TXF file, TurboTax's ability to import fiscal year and short year data from QuickBooks is limited.

Note that you cannot import data into TurboTax that comes from older versions of Quick-Books (Windows version 3 or earlier and all DOS versions).

In TurboTax's Import folder, choose the QuickBooks option and follow the on-screen instructions. The TaxLink screens and procedures are the same as described above for Quicken.

NOTE

In QuickBooks, only accounts and subaccounts assigned to tax form lines import. Further-more, QuickBooks data imports to only one copy of each tax form. For example, one Quick-Books data file can only post to one Schedule C. If you have multiple businesses, you should keep separate books for each business and set up separate QuickBooks data files for each. You cannot import from multiple QuickBooks data files to a single TurboTax file. You will have to manually enter data for the other businesses into TurboTax. You can, however, import one QuickBooks file using the TaxLink method and then import multiple Quicken data files using the TXF method described in the next section.

Importing with a TXF File

If you have more than one Quicken data file, if you have a fiscal or short tax year, or if you are using another financial software package, you will need to use the TXF method. Basically, Quicken or the other financial software package exports your tax data to a tax exchange format (TXF) file. TurboTax then imports that file into your current tax file.

To import TXF files from Quicken, follow these steps:

1. Set up Quicken to use tax schedules with categories by choosing Edit, Options, Quicken Program. In the General folder, check the box for Use Tax Schedules with Categories.

2. Review your categories list for the appropriate tax-related assignments.

3. Create a Tax Schedule Report or a Capital Gains Report, as needed.

4. Review the report(s) for errors. Make sure the report covers the correct time period (the full tax year) and that the information in the report is accurate, complete, and up-to-date.

5. After correcting any errors or omissions, with the report displayed, click on the Export button and enter a name for the file (Quicken automatically adds the TXF file extension). Pay special attention to the file name and the location where the file is saved on your hard disk, so that when you are prompted, you can tell TurboTax where it is.

6. If necessary, repeat steps 1–5 for each Quicken data file and tax report that you need to transfer to TurboTax.

7. In the second TurboTax folder (Import), click on the <u>Other Financial Software</u> option and then the <u>Import Now</u> option. TurboTax prompts you for the TXF file name and location of your saved Quicken data file (see step 5 above).

8. If necessary, change to the correct drive and folder location. Select the file name to be imported and click on Open. Confirm your wish to import that data now. TurboTax adds that data to your tax file.

After importing, TurboTax reports that the import was successful and prompts you to click on <u>Next</u> to continue to folder tab 3, Interview.

To import data from other financial programs, follow these steps:

1. Consult the documentation or Help files for the financial program (look in the index for the topic "Export" or "Tax Return").

2. Review any assignment of data to tax-specific categories or tax form lines. Print any reports that you can to verify the tax information that will be exported.

3. Follow your program's instructions on how to create the TXF file (note that some programs use a different file extension even though they support exporting in a TurboTax format). Pay special attention to the file name and location where the file is saved on your hard disk, so that when you are prompted, you can tell TurboTax where it is.

4. If necessary, repeat steps 1–3 for making multiple file Imports.

5. In the second TurboTax folder (Import), click on the <u>Other Financial Software</u> option and then the <u>Import Now</u> option. TurboTax prompts you for the TXF file name and location (see step 3 above).

6. If necessary, change to the correct drive and folder location. If your exported file does not have the TXF file name extension (for example, a CheckFree file has a TAX file name extension), choose to view Files of Type: All Files (*.*). Select the file name to be imported and click on Open. Confirm your wish to import that data now. TurboTax adds that data to your tax file.

After importing, TurboTax reports that the import was successful and prompts you to click on <u>Next</u> to continue to folder tab 3, Interview.

Take a Break

Well, depending on whether you used TurboTax last year, and whether this year you're using a financial software program that you can import into TurboTax, you may or may not need a break at this point. Regardless, take a moment to stretch and refill your coffee cup. When you return, you'll advance to the Interview tab and start entering the current year's data.

To Interview or Not to Interview

The next tab after Import is the Interview folder tab. You'll notice that the fourth tab is entitled "Review," so you can deduce that the Interview tab is where the entire tax return is done. TurboTax allows you to enter your remaining tax data either through an Interview process or directly into the tax forms.

You should use the Interview method (also known as the EasyStep Interview method) unless you are very familiar with tax law and tax forms—and even then you can benefit from using the Interview method as a built-in reviewer that oversees your work as you go and suggests options and opportunities. Even more important is that the Interview method provides a good double-check to be sure that you haven't forgotten a tax rule, missed a new tax line, or used the wrong tax form. TurboTax even allows you to tailor the Interview process to better meet your needs. For example, if you know you don't have any farm income or loss to report, you can skip right past that part of the Interview.

If you're a pro, you can at any time go right to the electronic forms and fill them out as you would your paper forms. Just choose Forms, Open a Form or the Go to Forms button and select the forms with which you want to work. Enter your data, use the Edit, Add Supporting Details menu option to create backup schedules as needed, and use QuickZoom to drill down or up through a return.

TIP If you decide to use the Forms method but later want to switch to the Interview method, just go to the Interview folder and select the topic on the left that you want to start with. In fact, you can switch between the Interview folder and your tax forms as often as you need. While in the Interview method, the Go to Forms button in the bottom right corner takes you to your tax forms. While in the Forms method, the button in the top right corner of your screen reads "Back to Interview."

CAUTION

When using the Forms method, be sure to complete the Federal Information Worksheet. Also, do not enter a zero in blank fields. Leave the blank fields blank unless you want to put a dollar amount in the field. Zero amounts indicate to the TurboTax Review program that you meant to enter a dollar amount and will result in many Review form errors.

The EasyStep Interview method assumes that you have no tax background and leads you through the process of filling out the forms by asking you questions. When you supply the answers to those questions, EasyStep posts the answers to the appropriate tax forms (behind the scenes) and performs the calculations before asking you the next set of questions. Throughout the Interview process, TurboTax prompts you to periodically save your data. When you finish, the EasyStep Interview automatically leads you to the fourth tab folder, Review, where your return is checked for errors, omissions, audit flags, and tax savings opportunities.

NOTE

This book uses the EasyStep Interview method to organize the tax law by topic. If as a tax expert you decide to use the Forms method, you will be able to follow along on your form as I go through the Interview questions.

Entering Personal Information

Whether you use the EasyStep Interview method or the Forms method, the first task you must complete is to enter your personal information (such as your name, address, and social security number) and answer some personal questions about your marital status and any dependents that you support. TurboTax stores this basic information on a form it calls the Federal Information Worksheet. Based on this personal information, TurboTax determines your filing status and the type of federal tax return you might need to file (1040EZ, 1040A, or 1040). This determination (as you might expect from last night's session) sets the stage for the type of questions the Interview process will ask you. If you have to fill out the "easy" 1040EZ, you will be done much sooner than you would be if you had to fill out the 1040!

NOTE For some parts of this Interview, a fictitious family of two working adults with three children (two school-aged and one in college) is used to illustrate the majority of the Interview questions. Your own situation will differ, and based on your responses, some of the Interview questions that you get will be different than the ones presented here in this session. For example, if you are single and have no dependents, you will not be prompted to enter any dependent names, ages, or social security numbers. On the other hand, if you own a farm you will be prompted to provide information on the profit or loss from your farm (Schedule F), an area my fictitious family will not be asked about. You will probably prefer to enter your own data, so that you can get your tax return done while you organize your tax records. In either case, you will learn what you need to know in order to prepare your tax returns using TurboTax.

Take a moment now to play the Tips on the Interview video to learn more about the TurboTax Interview process. Then, review the FAQ's on the far right side. Click on any that interest you and read over the Help text answers provided. When you are finished, click on <u>Continue</u> to start entering your personal information (see Figure 2.19).

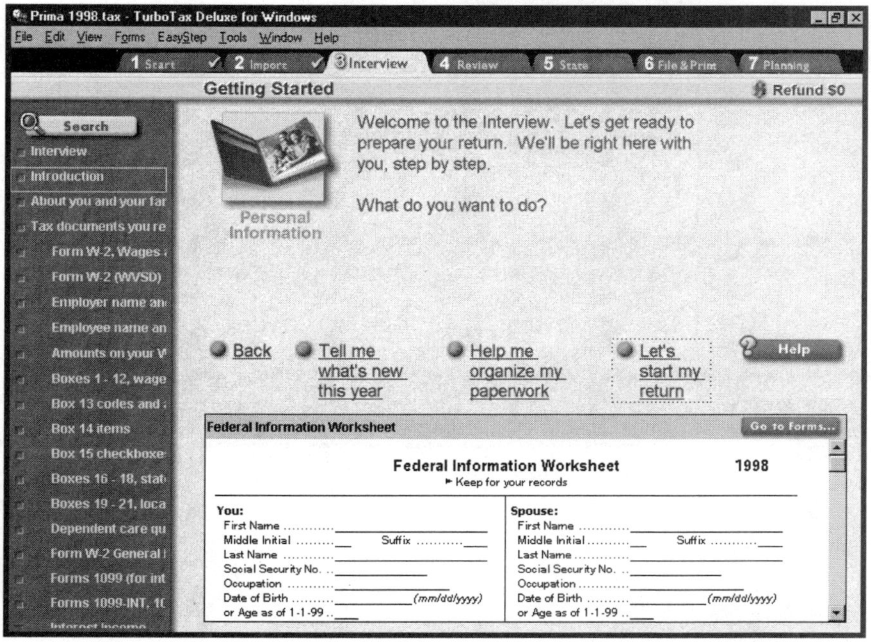

Figure 2.19

The first step is to enter some personal information.

NOTE

If you are using the Forms method, choose Forms, Open A Form and select the Federal Information Worksheet. If you rolled over your previous year's TurboTax data to this year, most of this information will be pulled in already. The Interview process will just ask you to confirm that the data has not changed (for example, if you moved to a new home or are supporting a new dependent).

When you are ready, click on <u>Let's Start My Return</u>. The TurboTax Interview begins with the questions outlined in Figure 2.20.

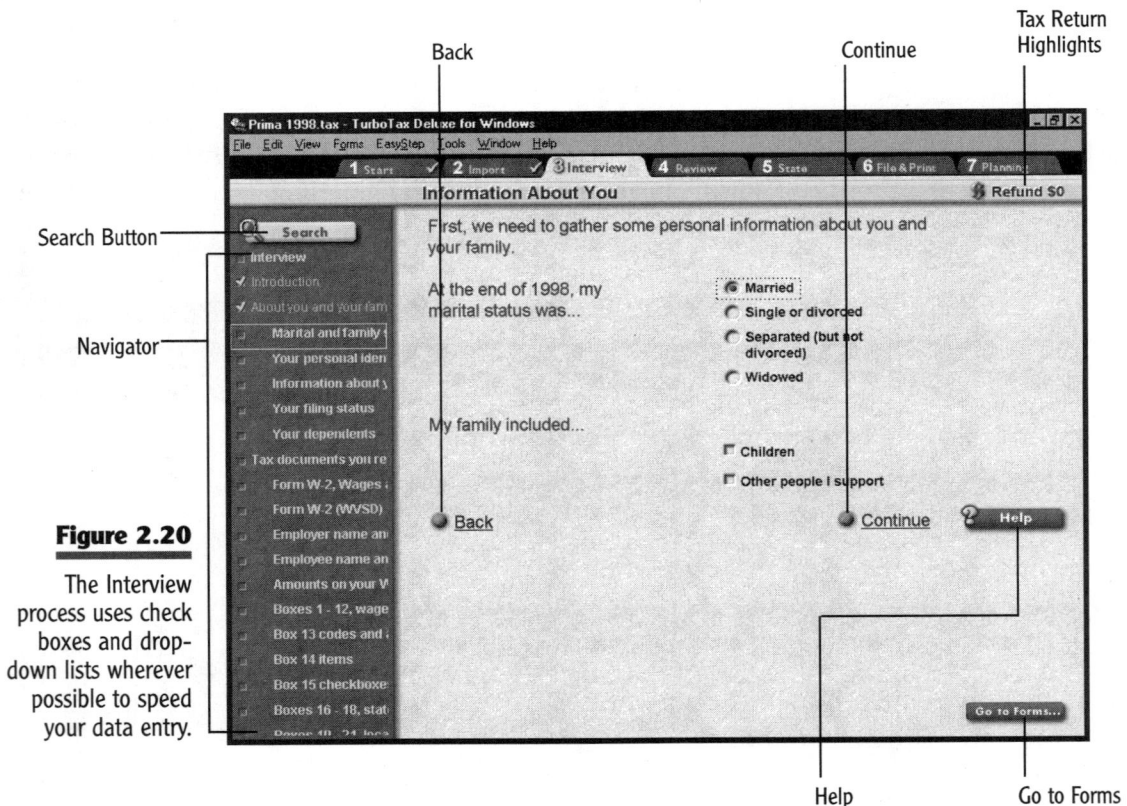

Figure 2.20

The Interview process uses check boxes and drop-down lists wherever possible to speed your data entry.

Marital Status

Tax rates are based on your filing status, which in most cases reflects your marital status as

- Married
- Single or divorced
- Separated (but not divorced)
- Widowed

This is the first Interview question. Note that you should answer based on your status as of December 31, 1998, regardless of how your status might have changed during the year. Later in this session, TurboTax will guide you through selecting the proper filing status.

TIP Single tax rates are generally higher than most of the other types of filing status tax rates. On the other hand, much has been written about the *marriage tax,* which results when each spouse contributes equally to the joint taxable income. When this occurs, the tax due is higher than it would be if the two individuals were still single. For several years, lawmakers have been trying to correct this situation; but alas, at the time of this writing, the marriage tax has not yet been alleviated.

BUZZ WORD *Filing Status:* Describes the household for which a particular tax return is being filed. Tax rates and other tax rules (such as taxation of social security income and the Earned Income Credit) are calculated based on your filing status. The types of filing statuses are Single, Married Filing Joint, Married Filing Separate, Head of Household, and Qualifying Widow(er).

Innocent Spouse: Used by a spouse to claim no responsibility for a broken dish. No, seriously, the Innocent Spouse rule is a tax law that protects spouses who are not liable (in the eyes of the IRS) for taxes due on a jointly filed tax return. The Innocent Spouse rule is usually used in situations where a spouse who makes a high income has provided misinformation in a tax return and then skipped town without paying the additional tax due of $500 or more (assuming the innocent spouse had no knowledge of the misinformation).

Select the marital status that best reflects your situation on December 31, 1998. Then indicate whether your family (household) included children or other people that you support (such as an elderly parent, even if they don't live with you). Click on <u>Continue</u> to see the next Interview question.

TIP You can claim as a dependent a relative you support (that is, you pay more than 50 percent of that person's living expenses) even if the person does not live with you. You can also claim someone who lives with you but is not related to you, provided that person lived in your home for the entire year. Later in this session, TurboTax will review the dependency rules and determine if such dependents qualify.

Entering Taxpayer Information

Next, TurboTax asks you to fill in some basic information that will go on the first page of your tax return (see Figure 2.21). Go ahead and fill in your name

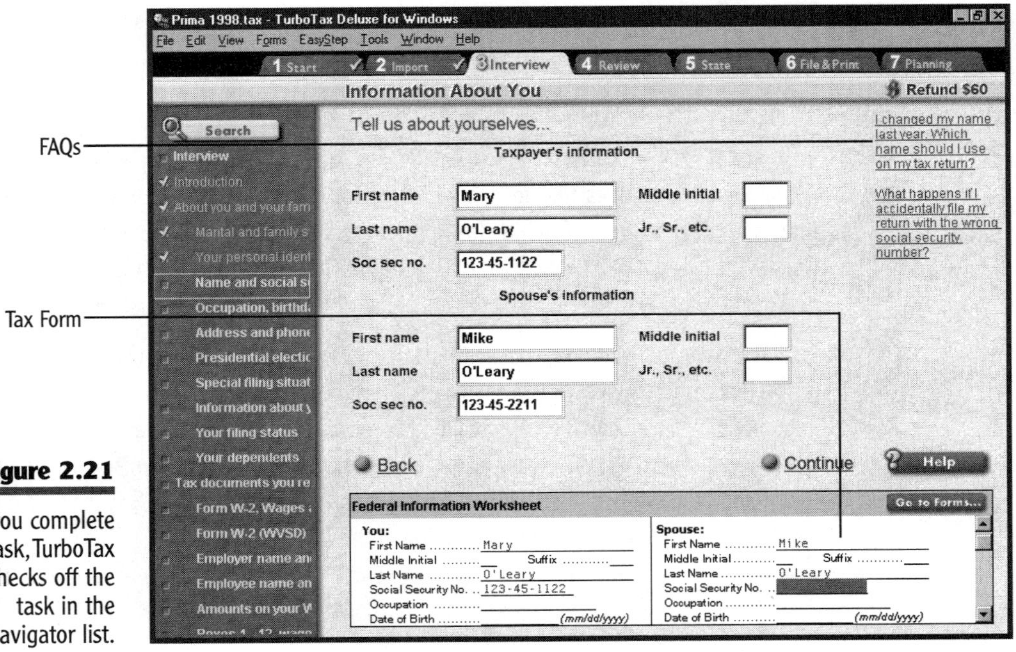

Figure 2.21

As you complete a task, TurboTax checks off the task in the Navigator list.

and social security number. Notice the Help text links to Frequently Asked Questions (FAQs) on the right side of the screen. If your name changed or if you had previously filed a tax return using the wrong social security number, go ahead and click on the appropriate FAQ to learn what to do.

At the bottom of the screen, TurboTax displays the tax form or schedule on which you are working. As you enter data in the Interview section above and move off that field, the data is automatically entered in the tax form below. At any time, you can click on the Go to Forms button and view the entire form or look at other forms.

Click on Continue to move on to the next Interview question. Notice that the Federal Information Worksheet at the bottom of your screen contains the data you entered so far and has scrolled down to reveal the next set of information fields that you will be filling in (see Figure 2.22).

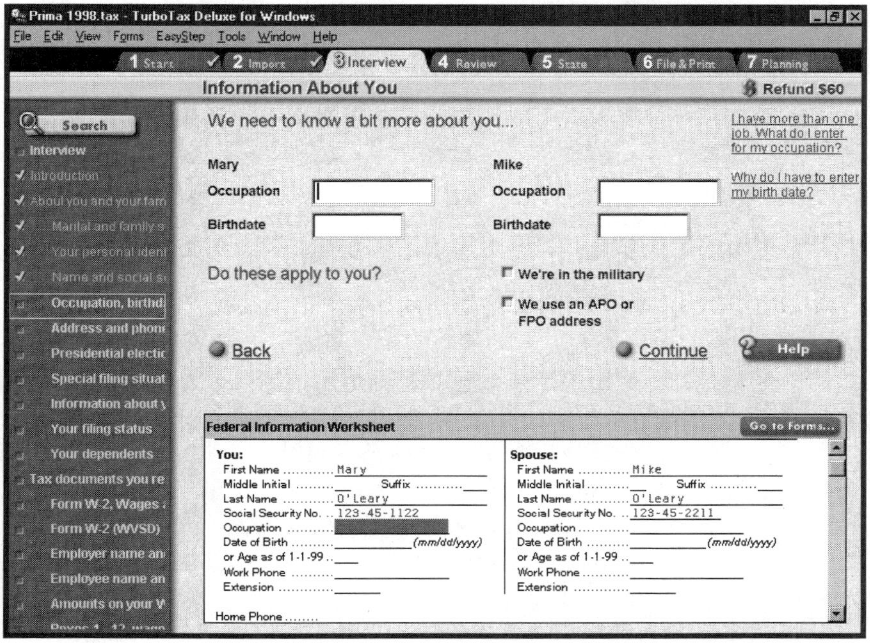

Figure 2.22

Some information (such as your date of birth and military status) is used only by TurboTax to see if you qualify for a tax benefit.

TIP

Navigating back and forth between Interview screens is easy. You can use the Back and Continue buttons to move backward or forward, one screen at a time. Or click on the Interview topic listed in the Interview Navigator to go directly to that topic (click once to activate the Navigator, and then click once on the topic name to go to that topic). Notice that when you click on the Navigator, it expands to show you the full topic name.

The next set of information requested concerns your occupation, birth date, and military status. Although your occupation goes on your tax return, the other information does not. TurboTax needs to know your age and your military status to determine if you qualify for any beneficial tax treatment. Go ahead and answer these questions and click on Continue when you are ready.

NOTE

Good news for our armed forces personnel. Combat pay for active services in a combat zone or for a person while hospitalized to treat a combat wound is excluded from taxable income. Bosnia, Herzegovina, Croatia, and Macedonia are qualified hazardous duty areas and qualify as combat zones for tax purposes. If you indicate here that you are in the military, TurboTax will guide you through the process of entering your combat pay and determining the other tax savings for members of the armed forces.

Although kids can sometimes make you feel as though you have served in a combat zone, for purposes of my fictitious family, I'll give the parents civilian occupations.

The next set of Interview questions prompts you to enter your mailing address. If you received a preprinted label with your federal tax forms package, compare that preprinted label with last year's tax return. If the address is incorrect, or if you've moved during the year, you will need to complete Form 8822 (Change of Address) and file it with this return. TurboTax will help you complete Form 8822 a little later in the Interview process. Enter your mailing address now.

TIP

Only use a post office box address if the post office won't deliver to your home address.

The home phone and work phone numbers are only needed on some state tax returns, not the federal tax return.

When you are ready, click on <u>Continue</u> to go to the next topic, which is only for residents of California and New York—states that have multiple IRS return-processing centers. Figure 2.23 shows you what you're missing if you don't live in New York (in addition to some beautiful lakes and mountains!).

The next Interview question asks if you and/or your spouse want to contribute $3 of the IRS's money (not yours) to the Presidential Election Campaign Fund. Depending on how you feel about the president, the IRS, and your hard-earned tax dollars, you may or may not want to contribute. In any event, this question has no bearing on your final tax bill.

TurboTax lists several special filing situations, which may or may not apply to you and your spouse. If applicable, check the corresponding box to indicate if you or your spouse is legally blind, can be claimed as a dependent on someone else's tax return, or passed away before filing this tax return. When ready, click on <u>Continue</u>.

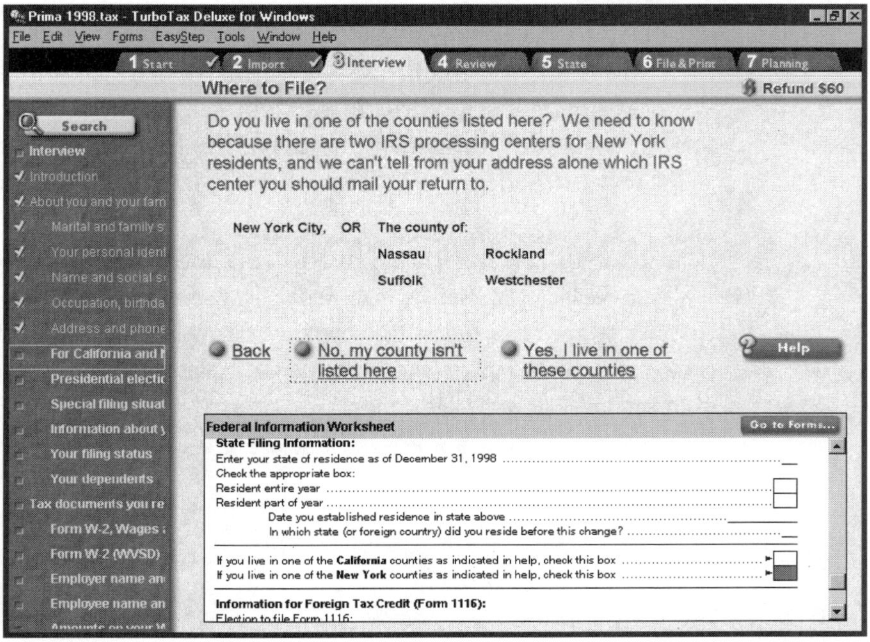

Figure 2.23

TurboTax needs to know where you live so it can print the mailing label for you!

Using TurboTax for State Tax Returns

A great side benefit of using TurboTax to complete your federal tax return is that it automatically posts your federal tax data to the state tax data file. This means that 80 percent or more of your work is automatically completed for your state tax return. Depending on the tax rules in your state, you may or may not need to enter additional information. Some states use your federal AGI as a starting point and then add and subtract based on state tax rules. Other states start with your gross income and allow no adjustments other than a few state tax adjustments (such as for property taxes paid). In any event, I highly recommend that you purchase and use the TurboTax state tax module for your state.

NOTE You can purchase the state tax modules over the phone (800-4-INTUIT) or online (**www.turbotax.com**) for about $27.95 per state. Note that while TurboTax Deluxe ships in mid-December, the state tax modules don't become available until mid-January to mid-February, depending on the state and how long it takes the state to release its final tax forms and rules. In most cases, the states wait for the federal forms to be released, which causes the delay.

If you think you might use the TurboTax state tax modules, go ahead and answer the questions posed (see Figure 2.24). Otherwise, click on <u>Continue</u> to move ahead to the next topic. For my fictitious family, I'll enter them as New York residents as of December 31, 1998, and for the full year of 1998.

TIP If you lived in more than one state during the year, or if you earned income in another state, you may need to file more than one state tax return. The TurboTax state tax modules walk you through the process of determining which states you must file in and what type of tax return to file in each state.

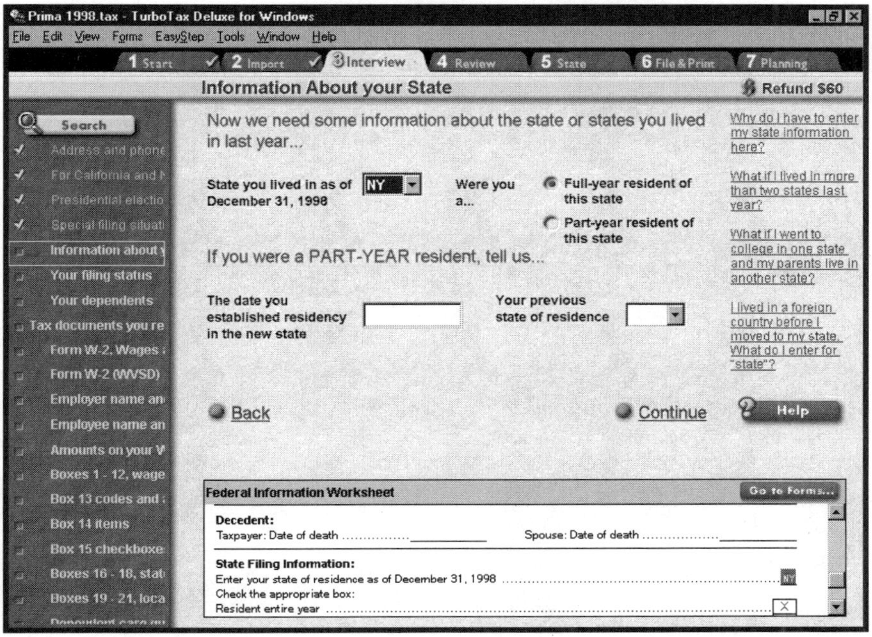

Figure 2.24

Your state tax return obligations depend on your residency status.

Choosing Your Filing Status and Using the Guide Me Feature

A critical decision in preparing and planning for your taxes is which filing status you should file under. As you can see in Figure 2.25, TurboTax guesses at your filing status based on the marital status you indicated in the beginning of this Interview. But what if your status changed during the year? What if you want to file under a different status this year? To explore your options, use the Guide Me bullet (see Figure 2.25).

The Guide Me feature of TurboTax takes you into a mini-interview. If you are a tax expert or you know your filing status for sure, go ahead and make that selection and move on. But if you are unsure of your filing status, go through the Guide Me mini-interview to determine if you qualify for a more beneficial tax status (see Figure 2.26). You will find Guide Me bullets on similar topics throughout the Interview process.

Guide Me bullet

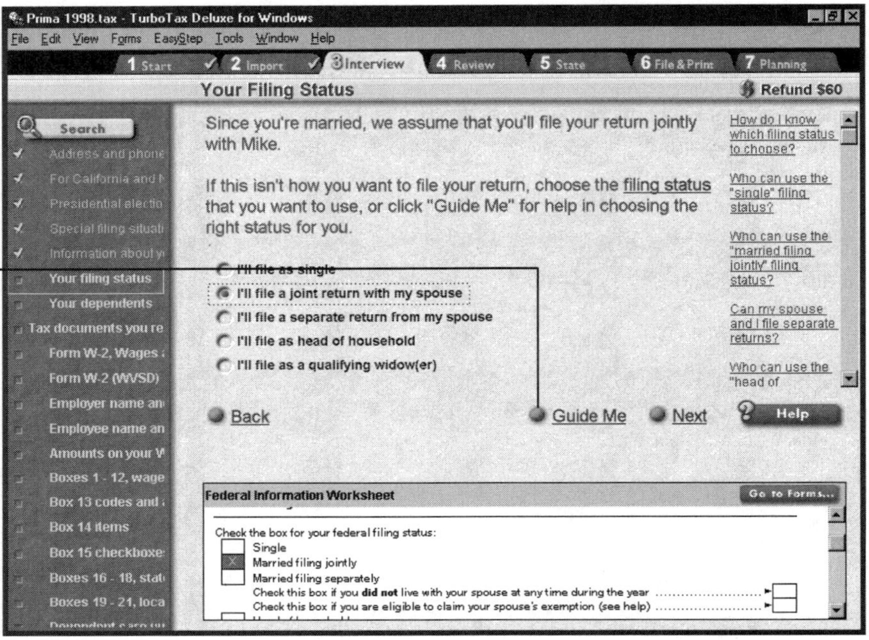

Figure 2.25

Choose your filing status wisely.

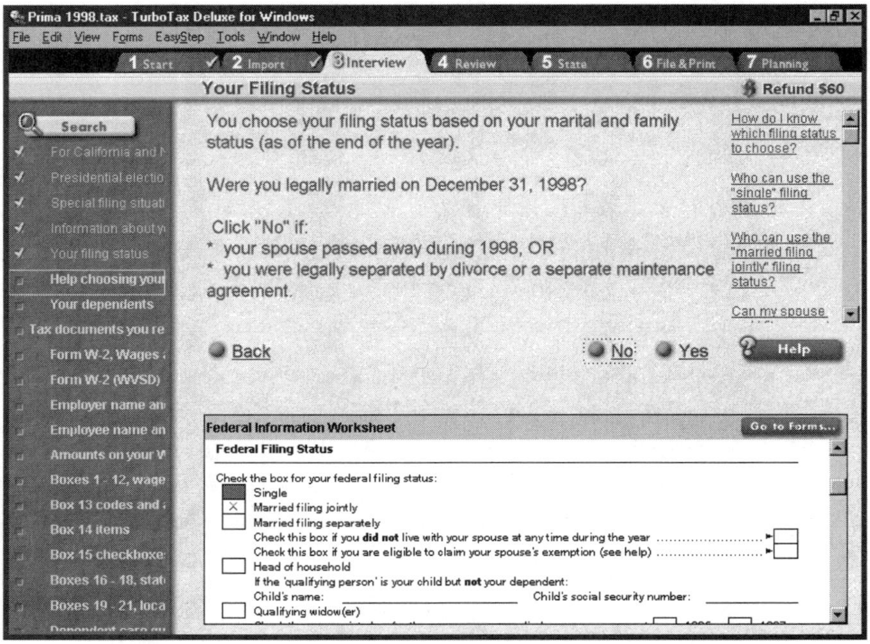

Figure 2.26

The Guide Me mini-interview helps you explore your options.

Here is a brief overview of each filing status. For a more in-depth discussion, consult TurboTax's Help screens or use the <u>Guide Me</u> bullet.

- **Single.** Select this filing status if you are unmarried and you have no children or have children and do not qualify for the more beneficial Head of Household filing status (see below).

- **Married Filing Joint (MFJ).** Select this filing status if you are married as of December 31, 1998, or if you were widowed in 1998 but living together as of the date of death. If at the end of the year you live together in a common-law marriage that is recognized by the state you live in or were married in, the IRS considers you to be married. If you were widowed in either of the two most recent years and maintain a household for yourself and a child, you may qualify for the more beneficial Qualifying Widow(er) rates (see below).

- **Married Filing Separate (MFS).** Select this filing status if you are married and qualified to file a joint return, but instead both you and your spouse decide to file separately. This status is usually used by separated couples or by couples with significantly different levels of income and expenses that result in a tax savings by using the MFS tax rates. TurboTax keeps an eye on this issue and advises you during the Review process if you would benefit from MFS or MFJ tax rates.

◆◆

CAUTION Married Filing Separate taxpayers have more rules to contend with than those having other filing statuses. For example, both taxpayers filing MFS must use the same type of deduction: itemized or standard. Also, there are several tax credits, such as the Earned Income Credit and Child and Dependent Care Tax Credit, that MFS taxpayers are not permitted to use. Before changing your filing status to MFS, double-check your facts and consult with a tax expert if you have any doubts or questions.

◆◆

- **Head of Household (HOH).** Select this status if you are unmarried on December 31, 1998, and you maintain a household for a child, parent, or other relative. You can also qualify as being "unmarried" for HOH filing status if you lived apart from your spouse for at least the last six months of 1998 and your spouse files separately. A final court decree (but not an order or provisional decree) of separation or divorce by December 31, 1998, would also qualify you as "unmarried" for HOH. The HOH tax rates and rules are more beneficial than the Single tax rates and rules.

CAUTION

The dependency rules for Head of Household are very strict. Be sure to go through the Guide Me mini-interview to be sure that you qualify. For example, even though you are allowed to claim a tax exemption under a multiple support agreement for a child, this does not mean that the child is your dependent. You must maintain the household for that dependent.

✿ **Qualifying Widow(er).** In the year that your spouse dies, you can file a joint return if you did not remarry during that year. If in the two years that follow your spouse's death you do not remarry, you can file as a Single, or if you qualify, as a Widow(er). To use the Qualifying Widow(er) tax rates (same rates as MFJ), you must have a dependent child who lived in your home for the entire year (except time spent away at school or on holidays) and you must pay for more than half of the cost of maintaining the home.

Select the appropriate filing status and click on Continue to move on to the next topic.

> How do you know you have a good tax advisor?
>
> There's a loophole named after her.

Claiming Dependents

Each person who qualifies as your dependent reduces your tax bill by $2,700 per dependent. Hmm, makes you want to have more kids, right? Well, maybe not. Anyway, dependents can be children, parents, grandparents, or unrelated friends that you care for during the year. The IRS determines who qualifies as a dependent based on the following criteria. To qualify as a dependent, the person must meet all five.

✿ **Relationship or Member of Household Test.** The person must be your relative (regardless of whether they lived with you or not), a foster child (who must live with you for the full year), or an unrelated person who is a member of your household for the full year.

○ **Gross Income Test.** Children aged 19–23 who were not full-time students or who are 24 or older by December 31, 1998, cannot be claimed as dependents if their gross income is $2,700 or more. Other relatives or unrelated persons cannot be claimed if their gross income is $2,700 or more.

○ **Support Test.** You must show that you paid for more than half of the dependent's living expenses (support) or, if you are sharing the support with others, that you contributed more than 10 percent of the more than half support.

TIP

Here's how to figure out if your dependent meets the support test. Total up the dependent's own income plus income received from you and others (if any). If you provide more than 50 percent, you get the exemption. If you and others together provide more than 50 percent, you all must decide who will get the exemption. The person who gets the exemption must attach to their return the Form 2120 (Multiple Support Declaration), which must be signed by each person who contributes more than 10 percent. TurboTax provides Form 2120, if you need it.

○ **Citizenship or Resident Test.** In order to qualify as a dependent, this person must be a citizen of the United States, a national, or a resident of the United States, Canada, or Mexico.

○ **Joint Return Test.** In order to qualify as a dependent on your return, the person cannot file a joint return with his or her spouse (unless the joint return being filed is under the income threshold and is filed merely to claim a refund of withholding tax).

BUZZ WORD

Personal Exemption: An amount set by Congress that reduces your tax liability. In 1998 the amount is $2,700 for you, your spouse, and each of your qualifying dependents.

NOTE

• •

The total personal exemption amount for you, your spouse, and your dependents is phased out if your AGI is more than $186,800 (MFJ), $155,650 (HOH), $124,500 (Single), or $93,400 (MFS). TurboTax will take care of this reduction if you fall into this situation.

• •

As with any tax topic, the rules have various exceptions and nuances that you should investigate if your situation warrants. For example, the IRS defines relatives as "blood relatives." This means that while your mother's brother or sister qualify as a relative, their spouses do not. The TurboTax Help files provide basic dependency test information in the FAQs area. For more in-depth coverage, consult the Tax Help tab in the Help dialog box. If your question is still unanswered, consult your tax advisor.

Once you have determined who qualifies as a dependent, enter the relevant information into the Interview area (see Figure 2.27). For each dependent, you'll need to provide their name, social security number, and year of birth.

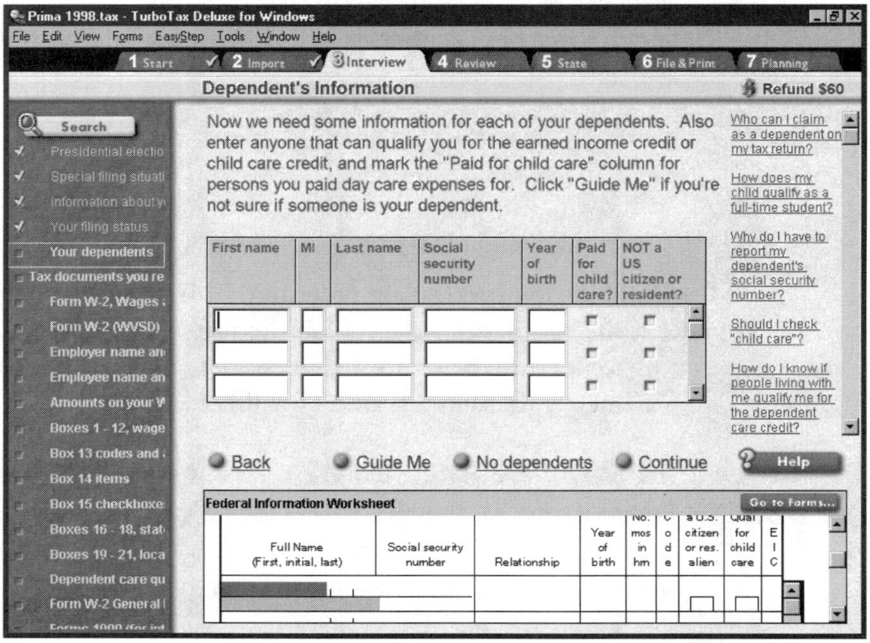

Figure 2.27

You can get tax benefits for each qualifying dependent.

In the last column, indicate whether you pay any day-care expenses (these may qualify for the Earned Income Credit or Child and Dependent Care Tax Credit).

NOTE

You must supply a social security number (SSN) for each and every dependent, even that cute new baby! To get an SSN, file Form SS-5 with the Social Security Administration or Form W-7 with the IRS as soon as possible, so that you get the number before the April 15, 1999, filing deadline. If you still haven't received the SSN by the time you need to file, write "Applied For" in the space provided and attach a copy of the application to your return. You can call the IRS at 800-TAX-FORM to get a copy of Form SS-5 sent to you. Or go online to

FIND IT ON ▶
THE WEB

download a copy of Form W-7 from the IRS's Web site at **www.irs.ustreas.gov/prod/ forms_pubs/forms.html**. Now, if only we could apply for an SSN over the Web…maybe next year.

If you have no dependents, click on <u>I Have No Dependents</u> and skip the remainder of this section. If you have dependents, you have more work to do (isn't that always the case!).

When you finish entering all the information for each dependent, click on <u>Continue</u> to move on to the next set of questions. For each dependent, TurboTax asks you to describe the type of dependent (such as those living with you or not), the number of months the dependent lived with you, and the relationship (if any) of the dependent to you. This process double-checks that the dependent qualifies for your tax return. When you are done with this section, click on <u>Continue</u>.

TurboTax alerts you to the new rules for the Child and Dependent Care Tax Credit, available for each dependent child under age 17. Take a moment now to play the video on tax credits for children. When you are finished, click on <u>Continue</u> to move to the next topic, Child and Dependent Care Expenses. At the top of the screen (see Figure 2.28), TurboTax provides a link to the IRS publication on what qualifies as creditable day-care expenses. If you have time, click on the <u>IRS Publications</u> link to review the rules and tests for the child and dependent care credit.

IRS Publications Link

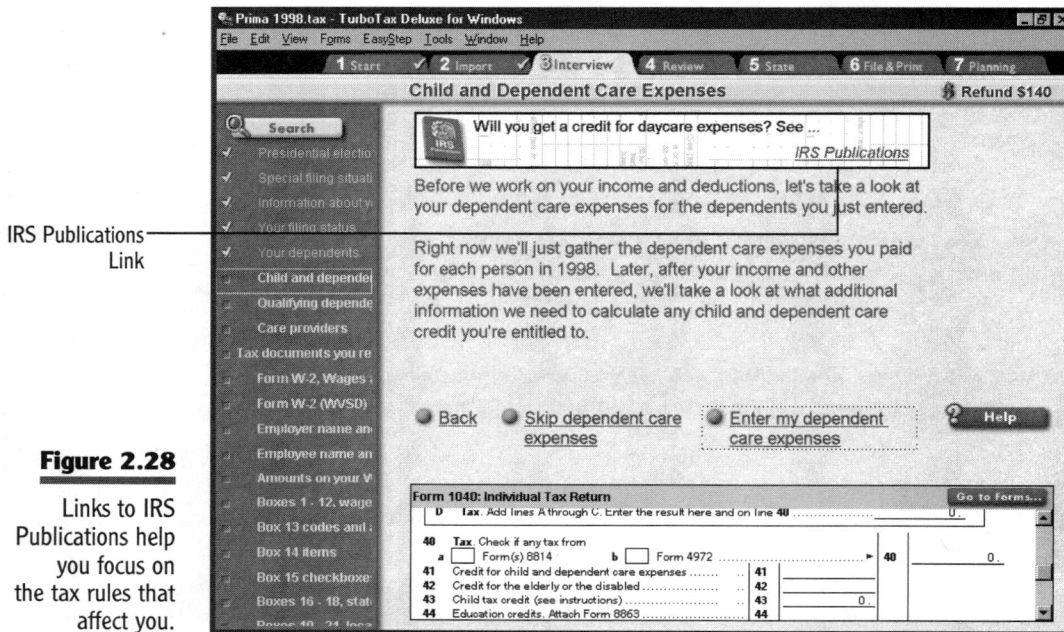

Figure 2.28

Links to IRS Publications help you focus on the tax rules that affect you.

When ready, click on <u>Enter My Dependent Care Expenses</u> or <u>Skip Dependent Care Expenses</u>, as applicable. If you qualify, you will need to enter your qualified expenses for each dependent (see Figure 2.29). Use the FAQ Help links on the right or click on the hypertext <u>Qualified Dependent Care Expenses</u> to find out which expenses qualify for the credit.

NOTE

Note that overnight camps do not qualify for the Child and Dependent Care Tax Credit, but day-camp programs do qualify. See the FAQs for more examples of what qualifies and what does not.

Click on <u>Continue</u>. TurboTax then prompts you to provide information on each care provider (such as name, address, taxpayer identification number (TIN), Social Security Number (SSN), or Employer Identification Number (EIN). Complete this information and click on <u>Continue</u> to move ahead.

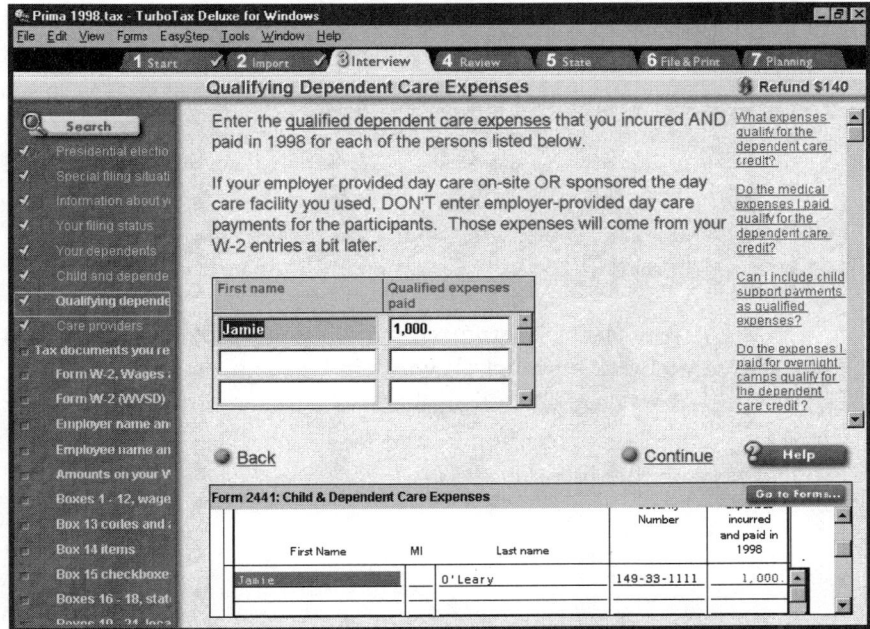

Figure 2.29

The qualified dependent care expenses may save you tax dollars in the form of a tax credit.

If you paid qualified medical expenses, employment taxes (such as for at-home care nurses), or other qualified dependent care amounts, enter these amounts in the spaces provided. When you are done, click on Continue to access the last Interview question.

TIP

If you or your spouse were disabled or a full-time student at any time during the tax year, you may be eligible for special tax treatment. For more information on the tax benefits, click on the Help button.

When you are done, click on Continue to complete this section and move on to the next topic, entering your gross income.

◆ ◆

CAUTION Periodically, you should save your tax file. TurboTax does a great job of saving now and then while you work, but it's a good idea to save on your own too. To save your data file, press Ctrl+S.

◆ ◆

What's Next?

Was that your stomach growling or mine? Well, this would be a good time to break for lunch. If you're in Chicago, do me a favor and order one of those deep dish pizzas from Nancy's. When you come back, you'll enter your taxable income amounts and see what adjustments you can make to lower your taxable income.

Starting Your Federal Tax Return

- ✪ Entering Wages, Salary, and Other W-2 Data
- ✪ Entering Schedule K-1 Information
- ✪ Reporting Business Income
- ✪ Reporting Rents, Royalties, and Supplemental Income
- ✪ Reporting Farm Income

Each year, the organization Americans for Fair Taxation (**www.fair-tax.org**) calculates the day on which most U.S. citizens will have earned enough to pay their taxes (in 1998 it was May 8). The organization declares this day to be Tax Freedom Day and reminds us all to celebrate it in style. But your own personal tax freedom day may be sooner or later than the national holiday. One way you can control your tax freedom day is by having a better understanding of which financial transactions create taxable income for you.

Determining your taxable income, identifying income that is exempt from taxation, and adjusting your taxable income for special tax treatments is the focus of this afternoon's session. You will find out

- ✿ What to do with all the numbers on your W-2
- ✿ How to enter 1099 information
- ✿ Tax issues on a K-1 form
- ✿ How to enter business income
- ✿ Tax issues surrounding rental income
- ✿ What other income is taxable

Entering Wages, Salary, and Other W-2 Data

The most common tax form that Americans receive is the W-2. Just like that first paycheck you received as a kid, the first W-2 you got was amazing. Unless you had tracked your gross income and the amounts withheld from each paycheck, you were probably stunned to find out how much you made compared with what you received cash-wise in your paycheck. If I'm not mistaken, this "amazement" continues to this day.

Now you can start unraveling the mystery concerning your paycheck. Your employer hires you to do work at a certain salary (annual amount) or hourly wage. This amount is your *gross income*. The federal government and the state(s) in which you work require that employers withhold taxes from your paycheck. The rate of withholding is determined by you when you fill out Form W-4 (usually required on the first day you work). Figure 3.1 shows you what Form W-4 looks like. TurboTax provides you with this form, and during Sunday's tax-planning session, you will learn how to better manage your withholding rate.

Notice that you must select a filing status (Single, Married, or Married at the Higher Single Rate), indicate how many allowances (dependents) you can claim, and optionally designate any additional tax amount that you want withheld. If you meet certain criteria, you could be exempt from withholding, and in that case no amount would be withheld. States, of course, have their own set of rules. It is possible to be in a situation where you have tax being withheld for federal but no tax being withheld for state tax purposes.

TIP

If one spouse works for an employer and the other has a business for which quarterly estimates must be paid, you could elect to pay the additional tax due weekly on the first spouse's paycheck instead of filing quarterly estimates. For example, suppose the additional tax estimated to be due is $8,000. Instead of filing quarterly estimates of $2,000 each quarter, you could ask the employer to withhold $154 per week (which totals to just over $8,000 in 52 weeks).

Form W-4 (1999)

Purpose. Complete Form W-4 so your employer can withhold the correct Federal income tax from your pay. Because your tax situation may change, you may want to refigure your withholding each year.

Exemption from withholding. If you are exempt, complete only lines 1, 2, 3, 4, and 7, and sign the form to validate it. Your exemption for 1999 expires February 16, 2000.

Note: *You cannot claim exemption from withholding if (1) your income exceeds $700 and includes more than $250 of unearned income (e.g., interest and dividends) and (2) another person can claim you as a dependent on their tax return.*

Basic instructions. If you are not exempt, complete the Personal Allowances Worksheet. The worksheets on page 2 adjust your withholding allowances based on itemized deductions, adjustments to income, or two-earner/two-job situations. Complete all worksheets that apply. They will help you figure the number of withholding allowances you are entitled to claim. **However, you may claim fewer allowances.**

Child tax and higher education credits. For details on adjusting withholding for these and other credits, see **Pub. 919,** Is My Withholding Correct for 1999?

Head of household. Generally, you may claim head of household filing status on your tax return only if you are unmarried and pay more than 50% of the costs of keeping up a home for yourself and your dependent(s) or other qualifying individuals. See line **E** below.

Nonwage income. If you have a large amount of nonwage income, such as interest or dividends, you should consider making estimated tax payments using Form 1040-ES. Otherwise, you may owe additional tax.

Two earners/two jobs. If you have a working spouse or more than one job, figure the total number of allowances you are entitled to claim on all jobs using worksheets from only one Form W-4. Your withholding will usually be most accurate when all allowances are claimed on the Form W-4 prepared for the highest paying job and zero allowances are claimed for the others.

Check your withholding. After your Form W-4 takes effect, use Pub. 919 to see how the dollar amount you are having withheld compares to your estimated total annual tax. Get Pub. 919 especially if you used the Two-Earner/Two-Job Worksheet and your earnings exceed $150,000 (Single) or $200,000 (Married).

Recent name change? If your name on line 1 differs from that shown on your social security card, call 1-800-772-1213 for a new social security card.

Personal Allowances Worksheet

A   Enter "1" for **yourself** if no one else can claim you as a dependent . . . .   A _____

B   Enter "1" if:
- You are single and have only one job; or
- You are married, have only one job, and your spouse does not work; or
- Your wages from a second job or your spouse's wages (or the total of both) are $1,000 or less.   B _____

C   Enter "1" for your **spouse**. But, you may choose to enter -0- if you are married and have either a working spouse or more than one job. (This may help you avoid having too little tax withheld.). . . . .   C _____

D   Enter number of **dependents** (other than your spouse or yourself) you will claim on your tax return . . . .   D _____

E   Enter "1" if you will file as **head of household** on your tax return (see conditions under **Head of household** above) .   E _____

F   Enter "1" if you have at least $1,500 of **child or dependent care expenses** for which you plan to claim a credit . . .   F _____

G   **Child Tax Credit:**
- If your total income will be between $20,000 and $50,000 ($23,000 and $63,000 if married), enter "1" for each eligible child.
- If your total income will be between $50,000 and $80,000 ($63,000 and $115,000 if married), enter "1" if you have two eligible children, enter "2" if you have three or four eligible children, or enter "3" if you have five or more eligible children . . .   G _____

H   Add lines A through G and enter total here. **Note:** This amount may be different from the number of exemptions you claim on your return. ▶   H _____

For accuracy, complete all worksheets that apply.
- If you plan to **itemize or claim adjustments to income** and want to reduce your withholding, see the Deductions and Adjustments Worksheet on page 2.
- If you are **single**, have **more than one job** and your combined earnings from all jobs exceed $32,000, OR if you are **married** and have a **working spouse or more than one job** and the combined earnings from all jobs exceed $55,000, see the Two-Earner/Two-Job Worksheet on page 2 to avoid having too little tax withheld.
- If **neither** of the above situations applies, **stop here** and enter the number from line H on line 5 of Form W-4 below.

- - - - - - - - - - - - - - - - - - -   **Cut here and give the certificate to your employer. Keep the top part for your records.**   - - - - - - - - - - - - - - - - - - -

Form **W-4** Department of the Treasury Internal Revenue Service	**Employee's Withholding Allowance Certificate** ▶ **For Privacy Act and Paperwork Reduction Act Notice, see page 2.**	OMB No. 1545-0010 **19**99

1 Type or print your first name and middle initial Last name	2 Your social security number

Home address (number and street or rural route)	3 ☐ Single ☐ Married ☐ Married, but withhold at higher Single rate. **Note:** *If married, but legally separated, or spouse is a nonresident alien, check the Single box.*
City or town, state, and ZIP code	4 If your last name differs from that on your social security card, check here. **You** must call 1-800-772-1213 for a new card . . . ▶ ☐

5   Total number of allowances you are claiming (from line H above or from the worksheets on page 2 if they apply) .   **5**

6   Additional amount, if any, you want withheld from each paycheck . . . .   **6** $

7   I claim exemption from withholding for 1999, and I certify that I meet **BOTH** of the following conditions for exemption:
- Last year I had a right to a refund of **ALL** Federal income tax withheld because I had **NO** tax liability **AND**
- This year I expect a refund of **ALL** Federal income tax withheld because I expect to have **NO** tax liability.

If you meet both conditions, write "EXEMPT" here . . . . ▶   **7**

Under penalties of perjury, I certify that I am entitled to the number of withholding allowances claimed on this certificate, or I am entitled to claim exempt status.

Employee's signature (Form is not valid unless you sign it) ▶ _____   **Date** ▶ _____

8 Employer's name and address (Employer: Complete 8 and 10 only if sending to the IRS)	9 Office code (optional)	10 Employer identification number

Cat. No. 10220Q

Figure 3.1

Form W-4 tells the IRS and your employer how much to withhold from your paycheck.

Here's a listing of the information contained on a typical worker's pay stub:

Weekly Salary	$500
Federal Taxes Withheld	(100)
State Taxes Withheld	(50)
Medical Benefits	(10)
401(k) Contribution	(20)
FICA	(30)
State Unemployment	(5)
Net Pay	285

So, throughout the year you have been paying federal and state taxes. When you file your returns on April 15, you provide the tax authorities with your additional tax information and you get credit for the taxes you've already paid. Most pay stubs include a running total (year-to-date) amount for each item. You should be able to add up each pay stub or use the year-to-date totals and compare those items with your W-2. If the two are not identical, call the employer's payroll department and ask about the discrepancy. The employer may need to file a new, corrected W-2 with the IRS and the state tax authorities. If this is the case, make sure you get a copy for yourself too.

NOTE   If you didn't receive a W-2 form from one of your employers, call the employer's payroll department and ask for a copy (a regular photocopy will do). If the employer won't send you a W-2, call the IRS at 800-829-1040 and provide them with the employer's name, address, and employer or taxpayer identification number (EIN or TIN) if known. The IRS will contact the employer and straighten them out for you. This might be one instance where you actually like the IRS!

W-2s usually come as multipage forms (for example, Copy B for your federal tax return, Copy C is for employee's records; Copy 2 is for state, city, or local; and Copy D is for the employer). If you lose one of the pages of your W-2, don't despair. Just make a photocopy of another page or use one of the extra pages (such as an extra copy for a local tax return that you don't need).

◄◄◄

BUZZ WORD

Gross Income: In tax lingo, gross income refers to your total income before any exclusions, deductions, or adjustments.

Withholding Tax: Tax from your earned income that is withheld by the payer, who remits it to the taxing authority for you. Commonly withheld taxes include federal and state income taxes, social security tax (FICA), and Medicare tax.

Estimated Tax: Tax you pay in advance, usually on a quarterly basis, that is determined according to your best estimate of how much tax you will owe for the current tax year. Estimated taxes are usually paid by people (such as sole proprietors) who earn money from which no withholding tax is taken.

◄◄◄

Customizing Your Interview

The first screen in the TurboTax Interview (see Figure 3.2) asks you to identify the tax forms that you received, such as W-2s, 1099s, and Schedule K-1s.

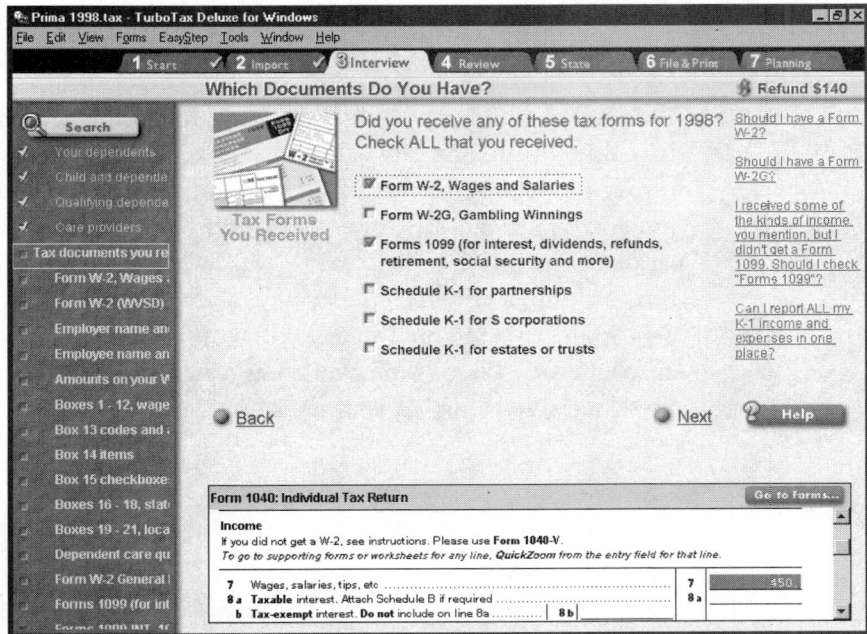

Figure 3.2

Check off the tax forms that you have received.

When you check off the box for each tax form you've received, TurboTax will know which questions to ask you. This is how you customize your Interview process to meet your needs.

NOTE Depending on the tax forms you receive, which boxes you check off, and what data you enter, your TurboTax Interview process may lead to questions that won't be encountered in this session. No matter what your circumstances are, the process of using TurboTax and the skills you learn about organizing your taxes will be the same—it's only the exact Interview questions that may vary depending on your circumstances. When in doubt, use the Help system, listen to the expert advice on the videos, and consult your tax advisor as needed.

Look over the tax forms that you've received, and check off the applicable boxes. If you are expecting a tax form but have not received it yet, you can check the box and fill in the name as a reminder. Later, when the form comes in, just click on the form topic in the Navigator (or on the Forms if you prefer), and enter the remaining data. Click on the <u>Next</u> bullet to start entering data from your tax forms.

Making Sense of Your W-2s

Although you may not be able to make sense of the net pay you receive, with the help of TurboTax you can make sense of all those numbers on the W-2 forms. If you used TurboTax last year and rolled over your prior year's data into this year's data file, or if you imported data from a financial software package (such as Quicken), TurboTax will begin the process by collecting data for known employers. As you can see in Figure 3.3, the data imported from Quicken contained wage and tax information for an employer named WVSD. TurboTax fills in as much as it can and then prompts you to fill in the remaining data from your W-2.

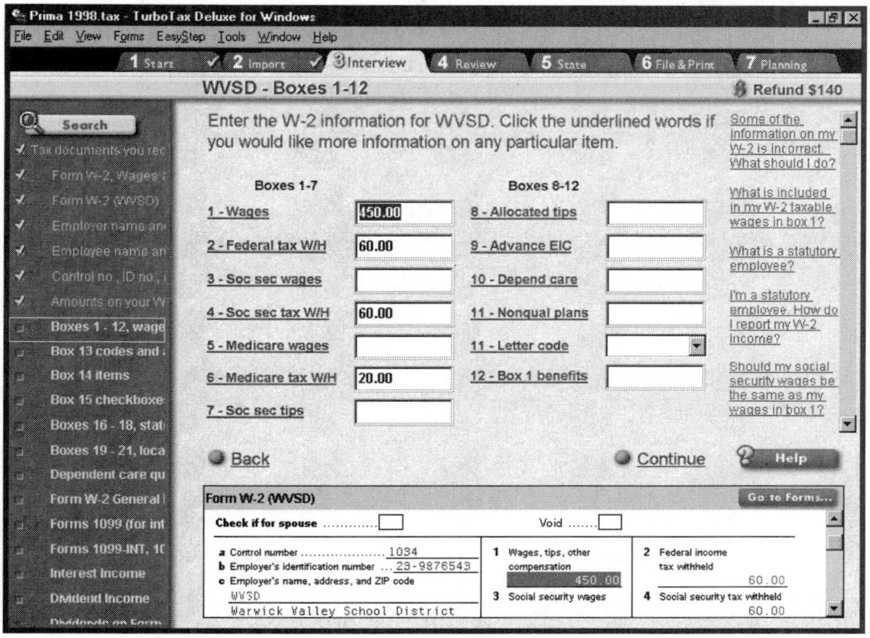

Figure 3.3

TurboTax saves you time by entering your data from the prior and current year as applicable.

NOTE

. . . .

If you imported data from a financial application (such as Quicken), the amounts reported are from the data that you entered during the year. Compare the amounts with your W-2. If the amounts are different, check your pay stubs to see if you made a data entry error in your financial software. If the W-2 doesn't jive with your pay stubs, then see my note earlier on how to contact your employer and the IRS. If the W-2 amounts match your pay stubs, go ahead and enter your W-2 amounts (just type right over any incorrect imported data).

. . . .

If you changed employers during the year, TurboTax asks you for some basic information, such as the new employer's name, address, and identification number (EIN, located in box b of the W-2). Then TurboTax prompts you to fill in the W-2 data by box number, starting with boxes 1–12. At any time, you can learn more about the data in each box by clicking on the box name. Figure 3.4 shows you the Help text for Box 3 - Soc Sec Wages.

CAUTION

◆ ◆

If you plan to file your return electronically, you must enter all of the data from your W-2 into TurboTax, including the control number (box a), the EIN (box b), and the employer's name and address (box c). This version of your W-2 is sent electronically in lieu of the hard copy you would normally send in with your return.

◆ ◆

If there is no amount in a particular box, just skip right to the next box. Click on <u>Continue</u> as needed to move ahead to other boxes. If you no longer work for an employer for which TurboTax shows a W-2, click on <u>Delete This W-2</u> in order to remove the data and the W-2 from your current tax data file. (This will not affect your prior year's data or current year's financial software data.)

Click here . . .

. . . to get Tax Help

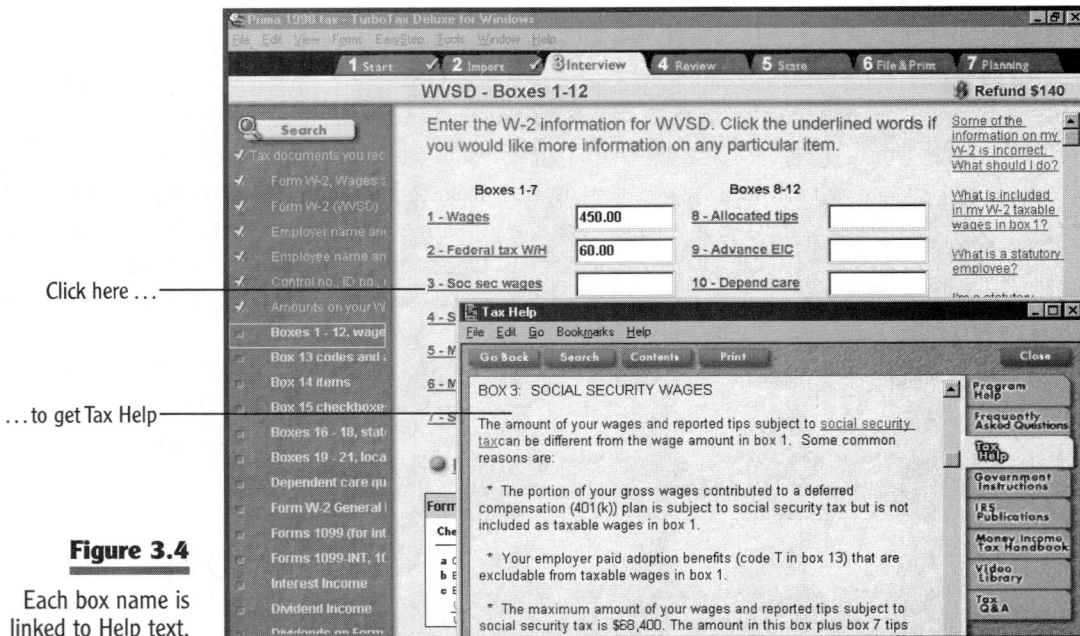

Figure 3.4

Each box name is linked to Help text.

> **TIP**
>
> Unless specifically exempt from tax by law, everything you receive from your employer is taxable, whether paid in cash, property, or services. Employers should list all of your taxable income on your W-2, but occasionally their accounting systems will falter and you'll be left with money in the bank that doesn't match your tax return. Save yourself the hassle by going over your deposits during the year, looking at any amounts from your employer. Items such as sick pay, vacation pay, severance pay, jury fees, and bonuses are all taxable wage income. Property received as payment for your services is taxable at its fair market value. Such property might be company stock or prize points redeemable for merchandise. When in doubt, call your employer's payroll or employee benefits department or your tax advisor for guidance.

Exploring the W-2 Boxes

Although the TurboTax Help system does a great job of explaining the nuances of each box on your W-2, sometimes it's beneficial to just get the big picture. Table 3.1 provides you with a brief description of each box and why the information is important.

TABLE 3.1 W-2 BOXES		
Box Letter or Number	**Name**	**Description**
a	Control number	Used by some employers to identify individual W-2 forms. TurboTax only needs this information if you are filing your return electronically.
b	Employer's ID number	Used by the IRS to identify employers. TurboTax only needs this information if you are filing your return electronically.
c	Employer's name and address	Used by the IRS if there's a need to contact your employer. TurboTax only needs this information if you are filing your return electronically.

TABLE 3.1 W-2 BOXES (CONTINUED)

Box Letter or Number	Name	Description
d	Employee's SSN	Used by the IRS to identify you! Make sure that the number on the W-2 is correct and that you enter your SSN correctly into TurboTax. Many problems with the IRS stem from incorrect SSNs being used. Make sure your employer voids the incorrect W-2 and files a new, correct W-2 with the IRS.
e, f	Employee's name and address	Used by the IRS to communicate with you. You should make sure that the address on the W-2 matches the address on your return (and of course is where you actually live). When addresses don't match, the IRS may decide to investigate. Or, the IRS may change your mailing address to an incorrect one. Make sure your employer files a corrected W-2 with the IRS.
1	Taxable wages and tips	Includes wages, tips, and other compensation (gross amount paid).
2	Federal tax withholdings	Amount of federal tax withheld from your gross wages and submitted to the IRS by your employer on your behalf.
3, 4, 7	Social security wages, tax withholdings, and tips	In 1998 you pay social security taxes (FICA) at the rate of 6.2 percent only on wages up to $68,400. If you made more than $68,400, box 4 should show $4,240.80. If you worked for more than one employer, and more than $4,240.80 was withheld, you can claim the excess as additional taxes paid on this return and get a refund (or use the excess toward decreasing the amount of federal tax you need to pay).
5, 6	Medicare wages and tips and tax withholding	Wages, salary, etc., that are subject to the 1.45 percent Medicare tax (no threshold or limit applies) and the Medicare tax withheld.
8	Allocated tips	Restaurants employing 10 or more people must report your share of 8 percent of gross receipts as your tip income, unless you reported to your employer an amount of that or higher as tip income.

TABLE 3.1 W-2 BOXES (CONTINUED)

Box Letter or Number	Name	Description
9	Advance EIC payment	Taxpayers filing a Form W-5 asking for an advance on Earned Income Credit (EIC) from their employers have the amount received reported here. TurboTax will help you apply this amount when you learn about the Earned Income Credit.
10	Dependent care benefits	Reimbursements from your employer for dependent care expenses in excess of $5,000 are generally included in your taxable income. If you enter an amount here, TurboTax will help you fill out Form 2441 and determine the ultimate tax effect on your return.
11	Nonqualified plans	Money you have contributed to a nonqualified deferred compensation plan or a Section 457 plan (see TurboTax Help for more information). This amount is included in your box 1 gross income and is shown separately here simply so you can see how much you gave to the plan. In other words, you pay tax now on the money you put into the plan so you don't have to pay taxes later when you take money out of the plan.
12	Benefits included in box 1	The amount you received in taxable fringe benefits (such as use of a company car, reimbursed education, or membership dues). This amount is already included in box 1 and is listed here simply for your information.
13	See instructions	Can be used by an employer to report any number of items, each coded by a letter. See TurboTax Help for a complete listing of the codes (A–R) and what they mean.
14	Other	Can be used by an employer to report any other payments (such as health insurance premiums) or other benefits not reportable in the other boxes. Ask your employer for a breakdown of the amounts reported in this box.

TABLE 3.1 W-2 BOXES (CONTINUED)

Box Letter or Number	Name	Description
15	Taxpayer status	Lists check boxes for various taxpayer statuses or elections: statutory employee, deceased, pension plan, legal representative, household employee, subtotal, and deferred compensation. If subtotal is checked, your employer made a mistake—you need a new W-2. Check any of the other boxes as noted on your W-2, and TurboTax will prompt you for any additional information as needed.
16–21	State tax information	Information recorded here is for state and local tax authorities and includes state name, state employer ID, your state wages, state tax withheld, locality name, local wages, and local tax withheld. If you had wages and tax withheld from several states, you may have several W-2s to handle the overflow.

NOTE If your employer withheld too much FICA, you will need to get a refund from the employer. The maximum 1998 liability for Social Security (FICA) tax is $4,240.80, which is 6.2 percent on the first $68,400 of salary income. Note that the IRS only refunds excess FICA withholding via your tax return when it's collected from more than one employer.

There is only one thing worse than flu season: tax season. You can recover from the flu!

Entering More W-2s

Once you finish entering the information from the first W-2, TurboTax provides you with the option of entering another W-2, updating an existing W-2, or ending the W-2 data entry session and moving on to the next topic (see Figure 3.5). If you decide to enter a new W-2, TurboTax asks you who the W-2 is for (you or your spouse) and the name of the employer. TurboTax

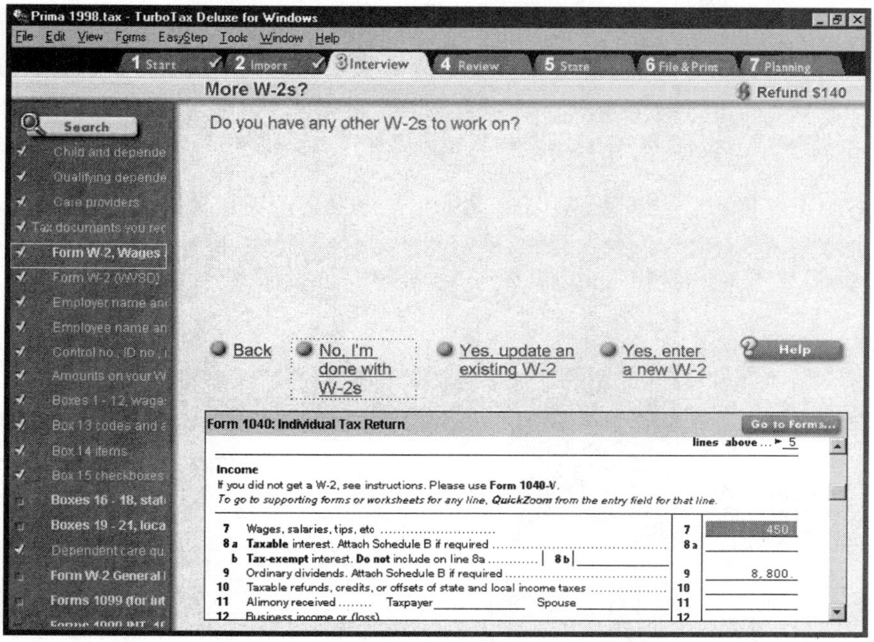

Figure 3.5

You can enter more than one W-2.

then runs through basically the same set of screens, although you may be asked new Interview questions based on the data you enter for the new W-2.

When you are finished, click on <u>No, I'm Done with W-2s</u> in order to move ahead to the next taxable income topic.

Checking on Your Refund or Tax Due

You may have noticed the animated dollar sign in the yellow bar at the top right corner of the Interview folder. In Figure 3.5 it says Refund $140. While you work in TurboTax, this amount changes to reflect your current tax due to the IRS or refund due to you. You can also point anywhere in the area of the "Refund $X,XXX" to see the highlights of your return. Figure 3.6 shows you the highlights of the return for my fictitious family. Notice that since I imported the family's data from Quicken and rolled data over from a prior year's return, TurboTax already includes deduction amounts and tax payment information that I haven't even gotten to yet! TurboTax saves you time *and* taxes. What a deal.

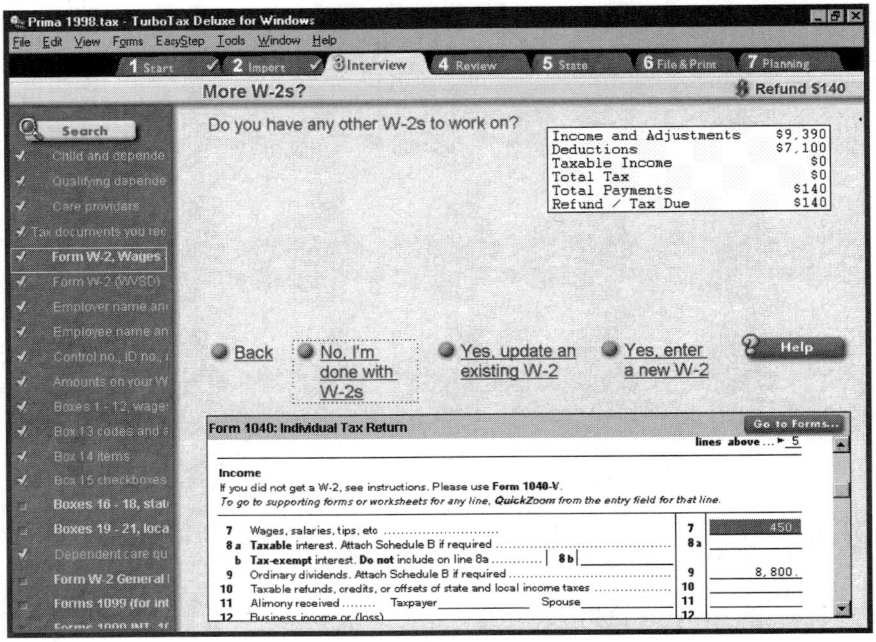

Figure 3.6

Point at the dollar sign to get an instant summary of your tax return.

Entering 1099 Income

As you learned last night, the IRS requires businesses, employers, financial institutions, and yes, even individuals to file a Form 1099 to report who you paid, how much they were paid, and why they were paid. The IRS uses this information as a double-check to make sure that the proper tax is paid on taxable transactions. For example, when you deposit money in a savings account and the bank pays you interest, that interest is taxable income to you. The bank must file with the IRS a Form 1099 (for amounts over $10) that states the amount of interest paid to you, your name, your address, and most important, your taxpayer identification number (for individuals, the TIN is your social security number). The IRS then uses this information to make sure you report that income on your Form 1040 tax return.

In certain cases the IRS requires you the taxpayer to withhold taxes from your income and remit the tax amount directly to the IRS. This is called *backup withholding*. Payment transactions subject to backup withholding include interest payments, dividends, royalties, rents, consulting fees, commissions, broker payments, and gains on the sale of property.

The backup withholding rate is huge, a flat 31 percent rate. So it behooves you to know this area of tax law and prevent backup withholding whenever possible.

In most cases you can avoid backup withholding by providing the payer with your TIN or SSN. This is usually done on Form W-9 or a similar custom form, such as an application for a bank account. On the form, you provide your TIN and certify (under penalties of perjury) that your TIN is correct and that you are not subject to backup withholding.

TIP

TurboTax doesn't include a Form W-9, but you can call the IRS at 800-TAX-FORM or get one from their Web site at **www.irs.ustreas.gov/prod/forms_pubs/forms.html**. Or your payer should be able to give you a Form W-9 or the substitute W-9 that they are currently using.

For miscellaneous payments reported on Form 1099-MISC (other than royalty and fishing boat payments), backup withholding doesn't apply unless

- ✪ You received $600 or more from one payer this year
- ✪ The payer had to give you a Form 1099 last year
- ✪ You were subject to backup withholding last year

CAUTION

The penalties for giving false information with the intent to avoid backup withholding are severe: a civil penalty of $500 and a criminal penalty of up to $1,000 or one year in jail, or both.

Don't ignore notices from the IRS explaining that you provided an incorrect TIN to a payer or notices from a payer asking for your TIN. Be sure to file a Form W-9 with the payer and send the IRS a copy too.

So, gather together your 1099 forms and substitute statements so you can start entering your information. TurboTax provides you with a handy checklist of 1099 forms (see Figure 3.7) and asks you to check the boxes for the 1099s that you have received for 1998. By doing so, you customize the Interview process and tailor TurboTax to better meet your needs.

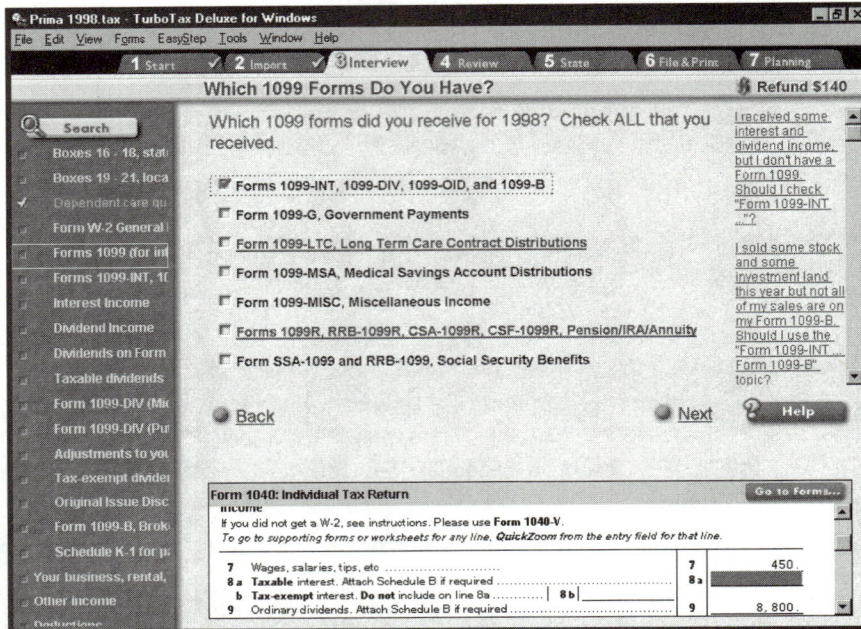

Figure 3.7

Tell TurboTax which types of 1099s you've received.

Remember that some 1099 forms are substitute 1099s and may look different than the standard Form 1099. Figure 3.8 shows you a standard 1099-INT. It is easy to overlook substitute 1099s, so be sure to check all bank account and year-end statements for the 1099 information you have received.

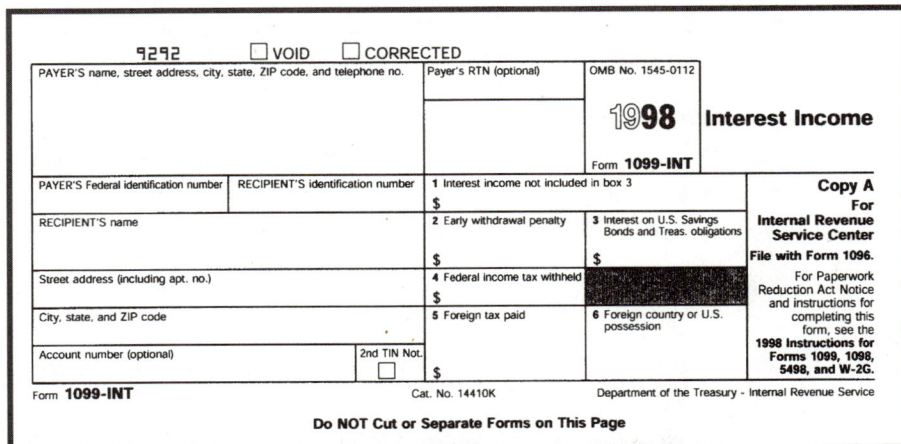

Figure 3.8

The official IRS 1099-INT form

Entering Investment Income

If you received a 1099 for interest, dividends, OID (original issue discount), or broker transactions, TurboTax displays the Interview menu in Figure 3.9 After you complete entering a 1099 for this category, you will be returned to this screen so you can choose to enter another 1099. When you are done entering 1099s for this category, click on Done with These Forms 1099 in order to move on to the next category of 1099s.

Interest Income

If you have a 1099-INT, received tax-exempt income, or interest from mortgages that you lent, click on Interest Income and then begin entering the information for that interest income. First, you will be asked the type of interest you are reporting. If you are reporting interest from someone who made mortgage payments to you, be sure to check the applicable box.

As you can see in Figure 3.10, you can enter just one 1099-INT at a time. The data entry fields are set up by box number, in rows and columns. Once

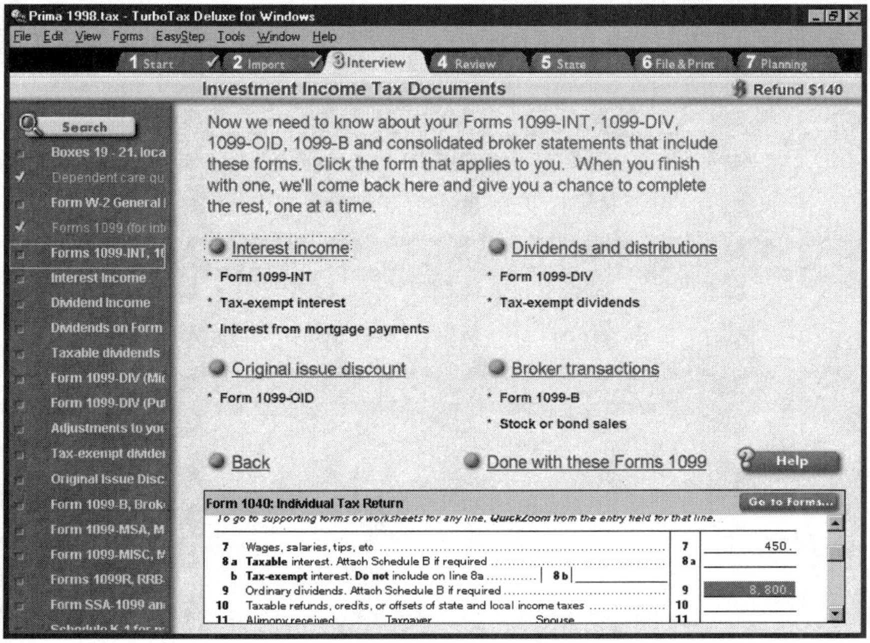

Figure 3.9

Most taxpayers receive 1099s for income earned from investments.

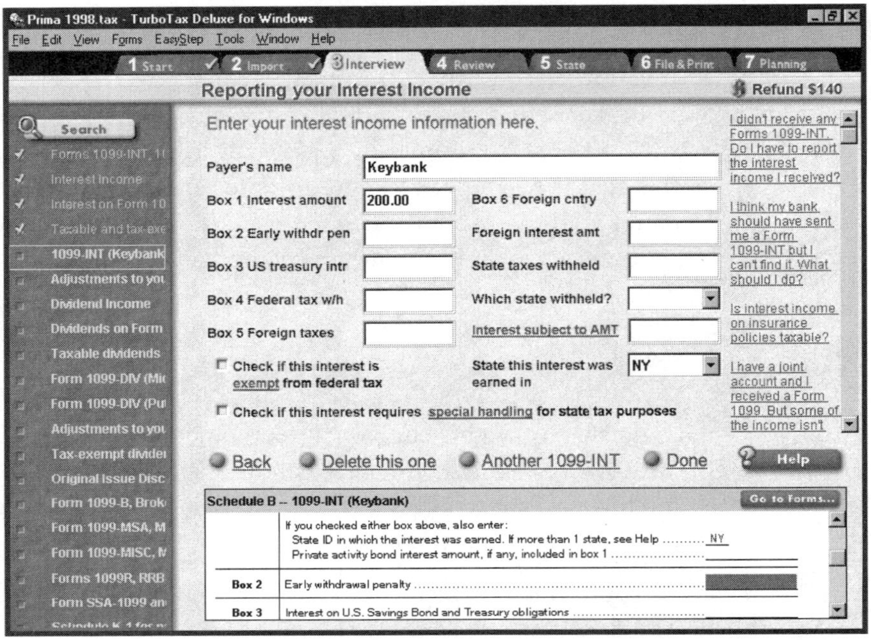

Figure 3.10

As with other areas of the Interview, the form you are filling out appears at the bottom of the screen.

you enter the data for a Form 1099, click on <u>Another 1099-Int</u> to enter data for another 1099, or click on <u>Done</u> if you have no more 1099-INTs to enter.

TIP

Review the FAQ Help links listed on the far right of your screen. If any apply to you, click on the FAQ to learn about the tax issues.

Form 1099s are similar to W-2s in that they have boxes of data. TurboTax makes it easy for you to enter data by listing the box number from the 1099-INT tax form. If the interest is exempt from Federal taxation, be sure to check the box below Box 5. To learn more about tax exempt interest, click on <u>Exempt</u> (see Figure 3.11).

NOTE

Interest that you earn on tax-deferred accounts (such as an IRA, a retirement fund, or an annuity) is not taxed until you take money out of the account.

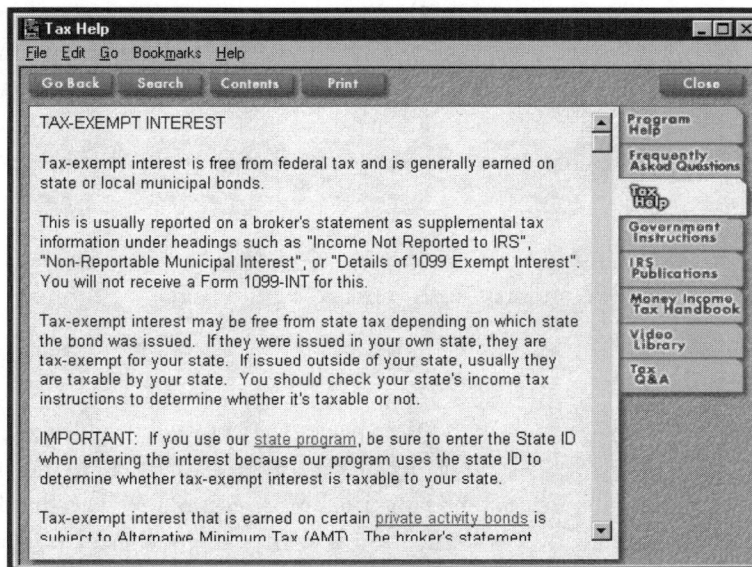

Figure 3.11

Tax-exempt interest is free from Federal tax and usually earned from state or local municipal bonds.

TIP

Click on the Help button at any time to get a complete description of every box on your 1099.

When you cash in government bonds, you receive interest income that is taxable to you in the year in which you receive the interest. A special tax incentive applies to Series EE bonds issued after December 31, 1989, where the bond proceeds are used to pay for higher education. The interest income is not taxable, provided you meet certain qualifications. If you check this box, TurboTax will walk you through the qualification tests and assist you in filling out Form 8815 (Exclusion of Interest from Series EE U.S. Savings Bonds).

NOTE

Not all interest you earn is taxable. For example, interest on state and local municipal bonds is exempt from federal income tax and in most cases is exempt from state income taxes too. Interest from investments in U.S. Treasury bills, bonds, notes, and zero coupon bonds is exempt from state income tax but is taxable on your federal tax return.

NOTE   TurboTax will prompt you to enter information for the tax-exempt items. You should enter this information, even though you know the amount is exempt from taxation. Tax-exempt amounts are used by the IRS to determine other tax effects, such as the amount of taxable social security income and whether or not you can take an IRA deduction.

When you are ready, click on Continue to return to the Investment Income Tax Documents screen (refer to Figure 3.9).

Dividend Income

If you have a 1099-DIV or received tax exempt dividends, click on Dividends and Distributions in the Investment Income Tax Documents screen and then begin entering the information for that dividend income. The Interview on dividends begins with a video that introduces you to how dividends are taxed (see Figure 3.12).

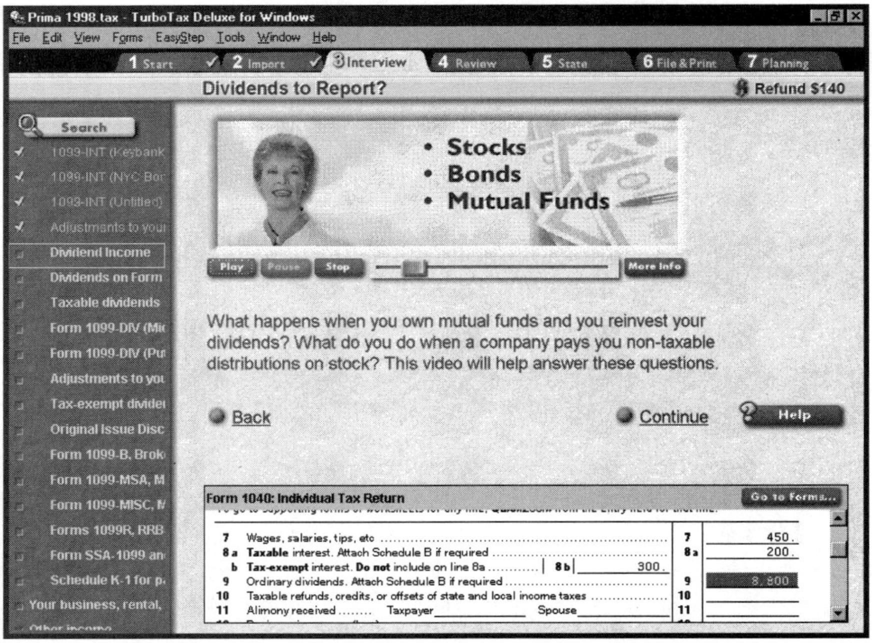

Figure 3.12

Dividend income comes from investments in stocks, bonds, or mutual funds.

Take a moment to view the video. Click on the More Info button on the Video Player to open the Help screen and see a list of related topics. Then review the FAQ items listed down the right side of the Interview folder to see if any of these questions apply to you.

TIP
■ ■
Just because the statement says that a financial institution is paying you dividends, it's not always considered dividend income in the eyes of Uncle Sam. For example, dividends from credit unions, co-ops, money-market accounts, savings and loan associations, mutual savings banks, and building and loan associations are actually interest paid to you and reported on Form 1099-INT.
■ ■

When you are ready, click on <u>Continue</u> so you can get started. First, you will be asked to identify the types of dividends that you received. If you received tax-exempt dividends, be sure to check the applicable box. As you can see in Figure 3.13, the dividend data entry is similar to that used in the 1099-INT and W-2 Interview. Each line corresponds to a box on Form 1099-DIV.

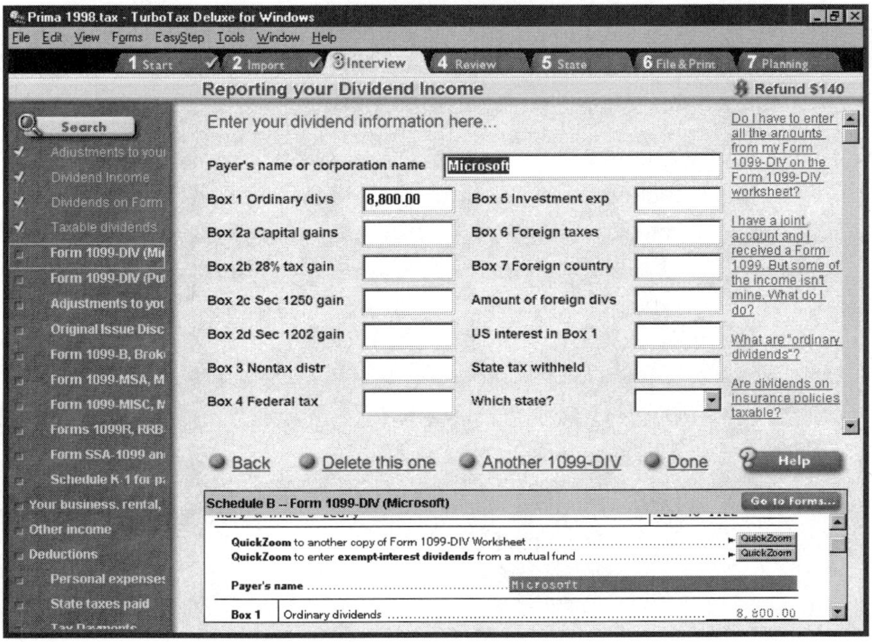

Figure 3.13

TurboTax provides you with a consistent interface wherever possible.

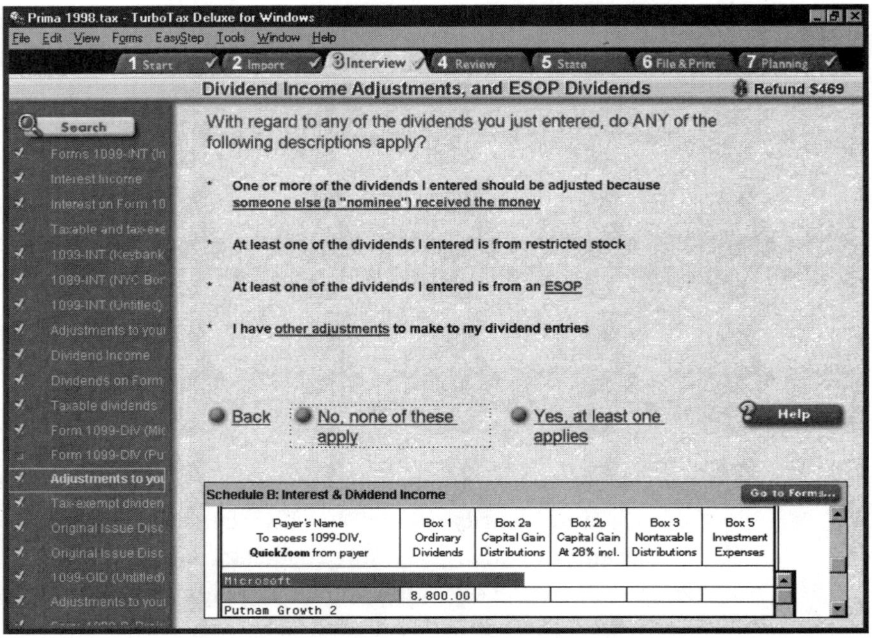

Figure 3.14

Some dividends require special treatment.

Go ahead and enter the information for the 1099-DIVs you have. Click on Another 1099-DIV to enter more 1099-DIVs. Click on Done when you have entered all of your 1099-DIVs.

The next Interview question (see Figure 3.14) asks if any of your dividends include U.S. government interest, are shared with someone else, are from restricted stock, or are from an employee stock ownership plan (ESOP). If any of these apply to you, click on Help to get a full description of these unusual types of dividends. When you are ready, click Yes or No as applicable.

◄◄

BUZZ WORD

Dividend: Money or property (such as stock) distributed to the shareholders of a company, usually out of current earnings.

Ordinary Income: Money earned during the regular course of business (for example, income from selling a product).

Capital Gain: Money earned on the sale of a capital asset.

Capital Loss: Money lost on the sale of a capital asset.

Capital Asset: Personal or investment property. Property you use in your business or property that is allowed a tax deduction for depreciation is not a capital asset. All other items are considered capital assets.

Capital: Generally refers to the excess of your assets over your liabilities.

Return of Capital: Money paid to an investor out of capital instead of earnings. In essence, the company is returning part of your initial investment. Return of capital amounts reduce your cost basis in the company and are not taxable. If your cost basis reduces to zero, any further return of capital results in taxable capital gains.

Stock Split: A situation where your shares in the company increase, but the cost basis does not. In effect, you don't earn any money. For example, if you bought 100 shares of XYZ at $10 per share last year, and this year the company did a 2-for-1 stock split, you would now have 200 shares of XYZ costing $5 per share.

◀◀◀

NOTE Just because you reinvested your dividends doesn't mean that the earnings are tax-free. You still need to report the earnings and pay tax on the amount reinvested.

While I'm on the topic, stock dividends are taxable, but stock splits are not. In a stock split you do not receive anything of value. Companies usually do a stock split to reduce the cost of a single share of stock, hoping to make their price more appealing in the marketplace.

As with interest, some dividends are tax-exempt, such as dividends from mutual funds that invest in tax-free municipal bonds. The next Interview question (see Figure 3.15) asks you to list any tax-exempt dividends that you received from mutual funds. If you plan to use the TurboTax state module, be sure to note the state in column three. In column four, list any dividend amounts that were from private activity bonds (see your mutual

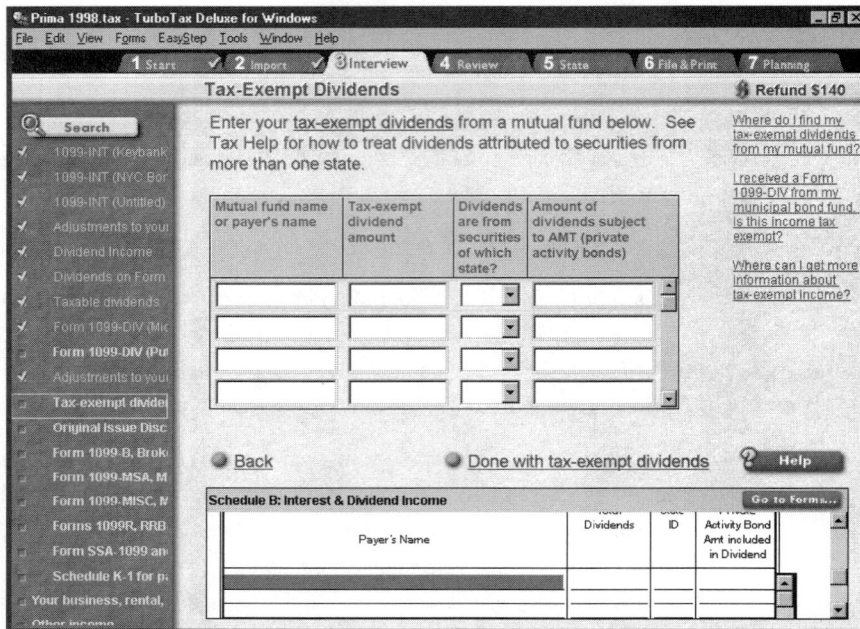

Figure 3.15

Tax-exempt dividends from mutual funds save you tax dollars.

fund statement for this designation, sometimes listed as the AMT amount). Some private activity bonds are subject to alternative minimum tax (AMT).

◆ ◆

CAUTION Be careful of 1099-DIVs you receive from seemingly tax-exempt sources. If the payer went to the trouble of filling out and filing a 1099-DIV for you, chances are that the dividend income reported therein is taxable as noted. For example, although dividends from a municipal bond fund are usually tax-exempt, if the bond fund sells the assets and realizes a gain, the gain is taxable to you as a dividend (and is reported on form 1099-DIV).

◆ ◆

When you finish, click on <u>Done with Tax-Exempt Dividends</u>. TurboTax returns you to the Interview menu dealing with investment income so you can enter another type of 1099.

A friend of mine, who is a CPA specializing in taxes, read the story of Cinderella to her toddler for the first time. The little girl was fascinated by the story, especially when the pumpkin turned into a golden coach. Suddenly she piped up, "Mommy, when the pumpkin turned into a golden coach, would that be classed as a short-term or long-term capital gain?" This year I'm hiring her daughter to enter my data into TurboTax!

Original Issue Discount Income

You know, I thought computer folks were, well, a bit nerdy—until I had to learn all about original issue discount for the CPA exam (refer to Figure 3.9). No one should have to learn about OID, let alone its tax effects, which is probably why the IRS created 1099-OID. The issuer of the bond must make the OID calculation and report it to you and the IRS on form 1099-OID.

BUZZ WORD

◄◄◄

Original Issue Discount (OID): The amount that results when a bond is sold for a price less that its face amount. For example, suppose XYZ prints up 100 bonds with a face value of $1,000 each. You decide to buy the bond for $900. The $100 difference is the "interest" you will earn over the life of the bond. This interest is called OID.

◄◄◄

Basically, for each year that you hold the bond, you must include in your taxable income the part of OID that you earned that year, whether or not the bond issuer paid you in cash. The OID rules apply to other long-term deposits (such as CDs) held for more than a year. However, the OID rules do not apply to

- Cash-basis taxpayers with obligations of a year or less
- U.S. savings bonds
- Tax-exempt obligations
- Loans of $10,000 or less from individuals after March 1, 1984
- Obligations from individuals before March 2, 1984

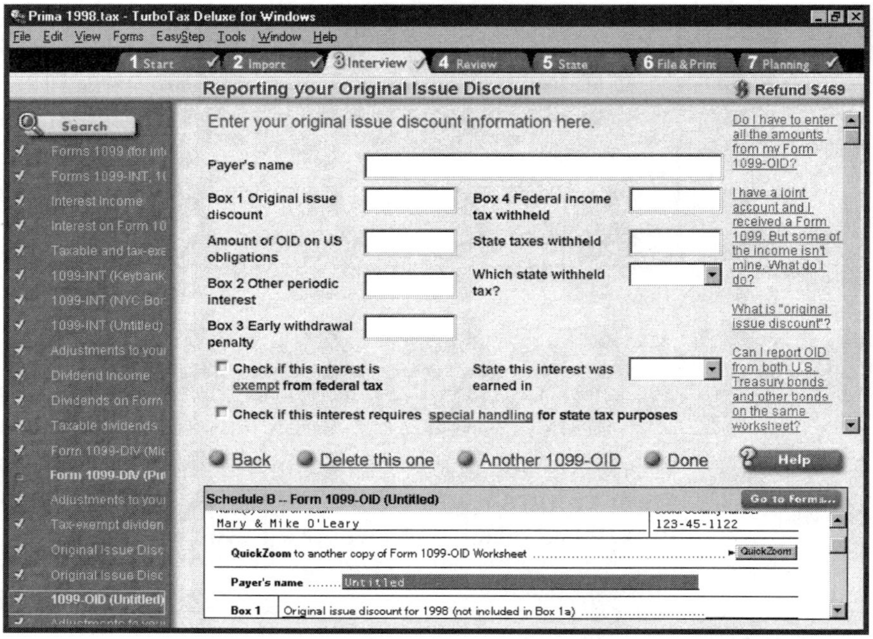

Figure 3.16

You must pay tax
on original issue
discount interest as
it is earned.

If you have a 1099-OID, go ahead and click on <u>Original Issue Discount</u> and enter the amounts, box by box as you did with the other 1099s (see Figure 3.16).

CAUTION If your 1099-OID statement reports OID from U.S. Treasury bonds on the same statement as OID from other bonds, you need to enter the amounts on two separate lines, as if you had received two separate 1099s.

Broker Transaction Income

Broker transactions—that is, the transactions surrounding the purchase and sale of investment property (also known as capital property)—can be very complicated (refer to Figure 3.9, the Investment Income Tax Documents screen). If you buy and sell capital property on a regular basis, you should consult with your broker, your financial advisor, or a tax expert to be sure that you are reporting the transactions appropriately.

On the other hand, if you just sold a few shares of stock or had a gain on the sale of your Beanie Baby collection from 1995, TurboTax can help you sort through the complicated rules and get your tax return done.

Form 1099-B (Proceeds from Broker and Barter Exchange Transactions) is used to report the proceeds from the sale or redemption of securities, commodities, broker transactions, and barter exchanges of goods and services. Proceeds from real estate transactions (including sales and exchanges of stock in a cooperative housing corporation) are reported on Form 1099-S.

NOTE Capital assets include all personal or investment property except for property you use in your business or property that is entitled a tax deduction for depreciation. The distinction is important because tax reporting and your tax due will be different based on whether an item you sold is a capital asset or not. For example, the delivery truck that you use in your business is not a capital asset because it is an expense of your business, which you depreciate over time. On the other hand, your personal car that you drive the kids around in is a capital asset. Stock that you invest in is a capital asset, but if you are a stockbroker and your business is to sell stock, the assets are inventory, not capital assets.

The first screen in the Form 1099-B, Broker Transactions Interview provides you with a video (see Figure 3.17). Take a moment to play the video. Then click on the More Info button and review the publications available online for this topic. Next, glance through the FAQs to see if any apply to you. When you are ready to start, click on Continue.

TIP If you imported data from Quicken using TaxLink, you can at any time return to Quicken and edit the source data as needed. For example, suppose you realize that you incorrectly entered the purchase date for a security. Simply minimize TurboTax, open Quicken, enter the changes, and close Quicken. In TurboTax choose File, TaxLink, Quicken TaxLink (click on OK if the instruction box reappears). Review the data in the TaxLink dialog box, and click on Import when you are ready to import the data into TurboTax. TurboTax will overwrite all TaxLink data with the new data (you will not end up with duplicate data). If the form with the old data is still open, close and reopen the form (or in the Interview, click on Back and then Continue). The screen will now display your updated data!

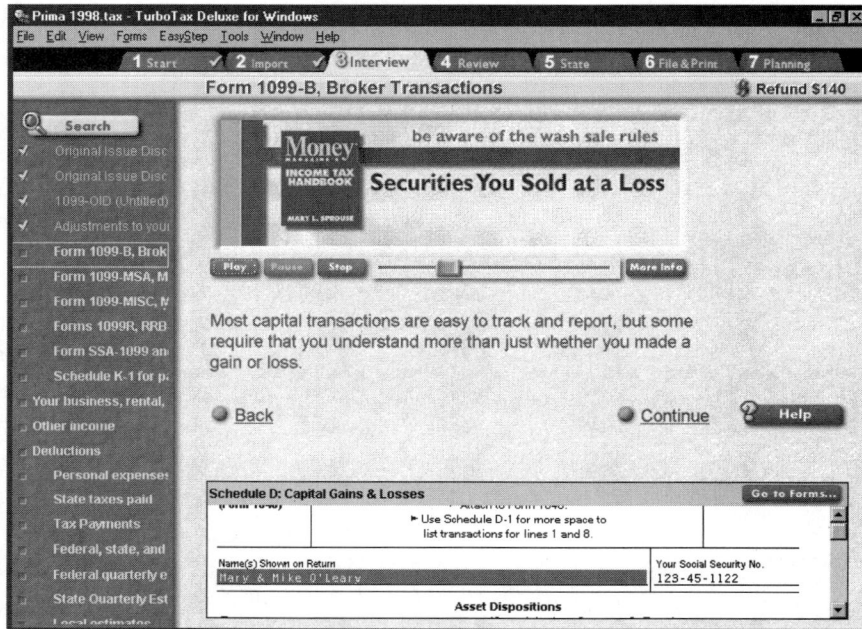

Figure 3.17

Capital transactions can be either very easy or very complicated.

The first thing you notice about the data entry grid for broker transactions is that the columns and rows are switched (see Figure 3.18). Each column is a separate sales transaction. You can use the scroll bar across the bottom of the grid to move over and see more columns. Click on the Help button to see detailed descriptions of each item being requested. Glance through the FAQs to see if there are answers for your own questions.

The information you enter into the grid mentioned above is at the same time placed into the form at the bottom of your screen, Schedule D: Capital Gains and Losses, which goes with your return to the IRS. To see the entire Schedule D form, click on the Go to Forms button. When you are finished, use the Back button on the Form to return to the Interview.

Be sure to provide the IRS with an accurate description, such as "100 shares of XYZ stock." In the event of an audit, it may dispel the mystery and help the agent match up 1099-Bs with your return.

The date bought and sold are important because they determine how long you held the investment. Tax rules and ultimately your tax due rides on whether

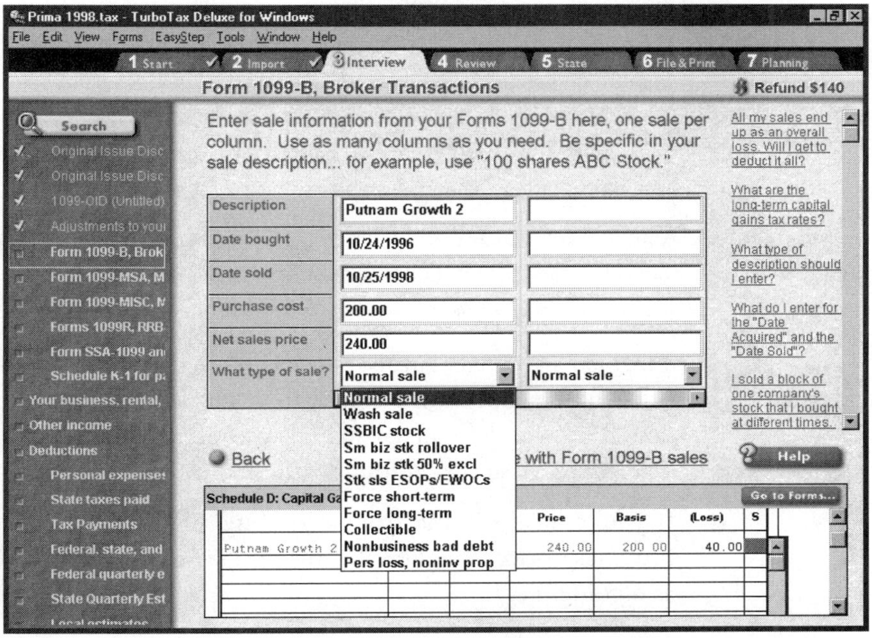

Figure 3.18

Capital gains and losses are reported on Schedule D.

you held the asset for less than one year (short-term) or more than one year (long-term). The good news is that you just enter the dates—TurboTax will do the math for you in order to properly classify your capital sales.

Here is the "long" and the "short" of it:

- Short-term gains and losses are netted against each other.
  - A net gain is taxed at regular tax rates.
  - A net loss reduces your long-term gain if you have one. Otherwise, the short-term loss is carried over to next year's tax return.
- Long-term gains and losses are netted against each other.
  - Any net short-term loss reduces the long-term gain.
  - A net long-term loss can be used to reduce other income up to a maximum of $3,000 (or $1,500 for Married Filing Separate). The remainder is carried over to next year's tax return.
  - A net long-term gain is generally taxed at the lower 20 percent capital gains tax rate (or 10 percent if you are in the 15 percent tax bracket). Long-term gains on collectibles are taxed at 28 percent.

NOTE

The new tax law eliminates the more-than-18-month holding period that caused taxpayers so much grief in preparing their 1997 tax returns. In 1998 gains on sales of investments such as stocks and bonds that you owned for more than one year qualify for a new, lower capital gains tax rate of 20 percent (or 10 percent for taxpayers in the 15 percent tax bracket). However, gains on the sale of collectibles will still be taxed at the higher 28 percent.

Note that the benefits of the lower capital gains tax rate only applies if you realize a net long-term capital gain. Congress wants to reward people who invest for the long haul.

The next two items TurboTax asks for are the purchase price and the net sales price. These amounts are used to calculate the taxable gain or loss. If your tax records and financial records are organized correctly, you'll be able to determine these two amounts quickly.

If you're having some trouble finding all the data to determine your basis (purchase price), Table 3.2 provides you with a worksheet that you can use as a guideline.

CAUTION

Box 2 of Form 1099-B shows either the gross sales price or the net sales price of your asset. The broker may not have known about all of your expenses surrounding the sale. If the amount you report on your tax return differs from the amount shown on Form 1099-B, attach a statement that explains the difference and reconciles the amounts. If the 1099-B is in error—for example, if it reports a gain that didn't occur or an incorrect Taxpayer Identification Number (TIN)—be sure to ask the broker to reissue the 1099-B.

The last item you need to complete for each sale is the type of sale. As you can see in the drop-down list box in Figure 3.18, TurboTax provides you with choices of normal and special sale types. In most cases you will have a normal sale. To learn about the other types of sales, click on the Help button.

Continue entering sales into the various columns. Make notes as you go concerning questions you have for your broker or tax advisor. When you finish, click on <u>Done with Form 1099-B Sales</u>. TurboTax returns you to the Investment Income Interview menu. Unless you have other 1099s to enter here, click on <u>Done with These Forms 1099</u>. TurboTax asks you some last questions about Foreign bank accounts and trusts. Answer Yes or No as applicable. When finished, Click on <u>Done</u>.

TABLE 3.2 CALCULATING YOUR CAPITAL GAIN OR LOSS

Step	Item	Description	Amount
1	Net sales price	Total amount for which the asset was sold, less expenses of sale (such as commissions, fees, and taxes)	
2	Purchase price	Original amount you paid for the asset	
3	Purchase expenses	Amounts you paid in addition to the purchase price, which were required aspects of the purchase (such as recording fees, broker fees, and certain legal fees)	
4	Improvement costs	Amounts you've paid over the life of the asset to prolong its life, adapt it to new uses, or in any way add value to it	
5	Reductions	Amounts that account for depreciation, casualty losses, and return of capital	
6	Purchase cost (adjusted basis)	Total of amounts in steps 2, 3, and 4 together, less the amount in step 5	
7	Gain (or loss)	Step 1 less step 6	

NOTE If you have other types of 1099 income (such as government payments, long-term care contracts, medical savings accounts, retirement benefits, or social security income), go ahead and enter that information now. The next topic in the Interview for my fictitious family is 1099-MISC.

Other Types of 1099 Income

Form 1099-MISC is used to report a variety of miscellaneous income that you might receive, such as royalties, consulting fees, and prizes. If you received any 1099-MISC forms and checked the corresponding box in Figure 3.7, TurboTax will display Figure 3.19. If you forgot to check the 1099 box, use the Navigator to move back to the Interview topic "Forms 1099 (for interest, dividends, refunds, etc.)" and check the 1099-MISC box. Click on <u>Next</u> and skip ahead to the 1099-MISC Interview, as shown in Figure 3.19. To get a quick overview of the types of income reported on a 1099-MISC, play the video.

Click on <u>Continue</u> so you can get started. The 1099-MISC Interview works pretty much the same way as the other Interviews. First, TurboTax asks you to enter the payer's name as it appears on the 1099-MISC. The next screen (see Figure 3.20) displays a list of the boxes, by number with brief descriptions. For a more in-depth description of each box item, click on the box number or name. At the top of the Interview page, be sure to specify who the 1099-MISC was issued for—you or possibly your spouse.

NOTE

If you receive one 1099-MISC form that reports amounts for several Schedule Cs, or amounts for a Schedule C and some other tax form, you should enter each amount as a separate 1099-MISC so that you can later link the individual amounts to different tax forms.

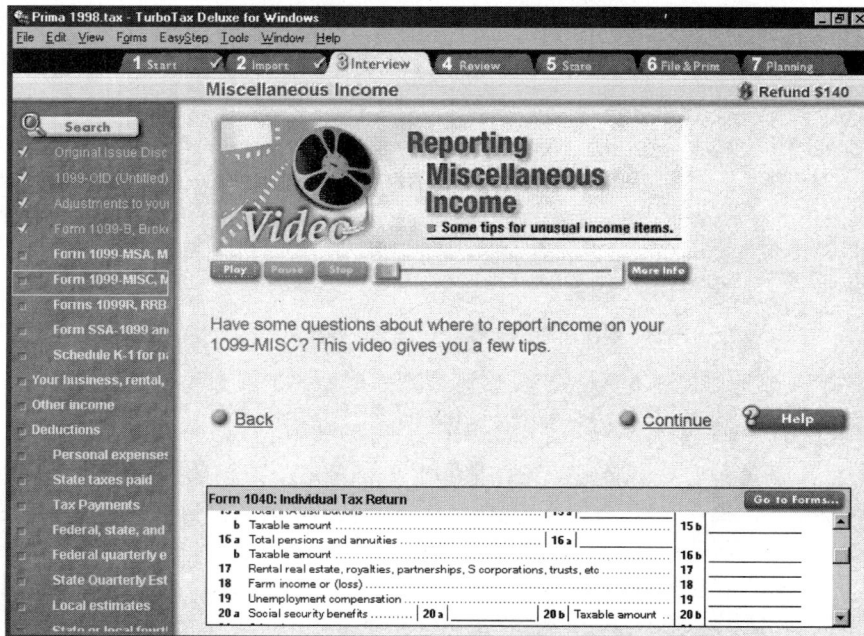

Figure 3.19

TurboTax will help you determine where to report your 1099-MISC income.

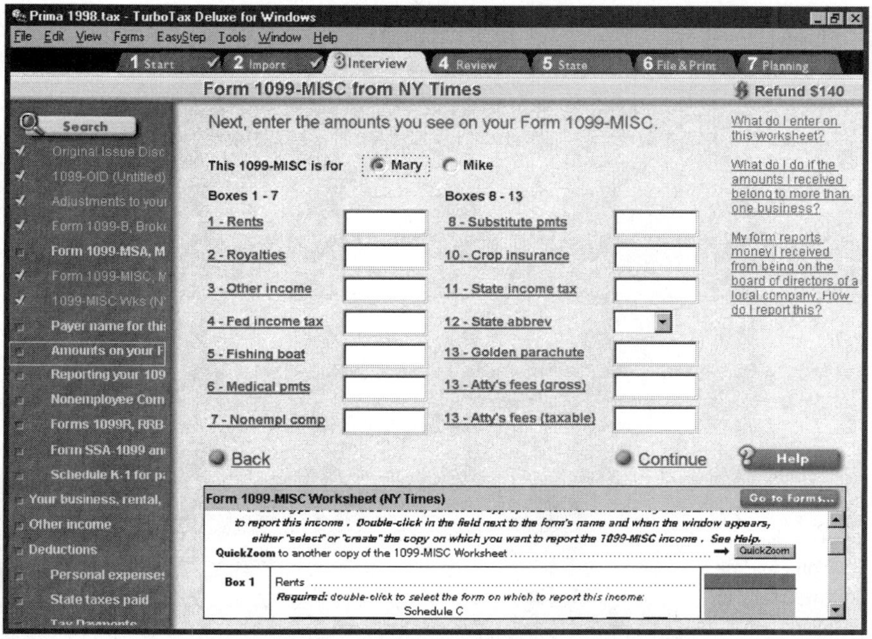

Figure 3.20

Click on the FAQs at any time to get answers to your questions.

When you have completed entering the 1099-MISC information, click on Continue. Depending on the box in which you entered an amount, Turbo-Tax may ask you to select where you want to report the amount. For example, Figure 3.21 shows the Interview question that comes up when an amount has been entered for nonemployee compensation. Depending on your situation, this amount might be taxable as wages (like your W-2 amount), and belong on Schedule C (if earned as part of a sole proprietorship), or belong on Schedule F (if earned as part of running a farm). If you select Schedule C or Schedule F, the TurboTax Interview will ask you to select an existing business (from the prior year's data that you rolled over) or create a new business. If you select Wages, the Interview will ask if you have any other 1099-MISC forms to enter.

Continue entering 1099-MISC forms as needed. When you are finished, click on No, I'm Done with 1099-MISCs when the More 1099-MISC screen appears.

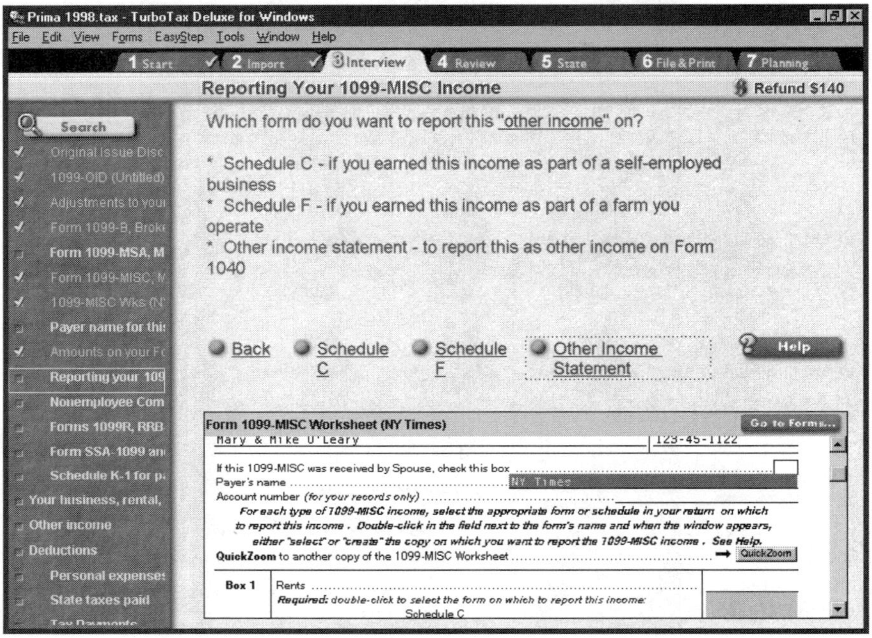

Figure 3.21

You can link your tax data to specific forms.

Take a Break

Bet you thought the break would never come! Well, you deserve a vacation on a cruise ship somewhere, but a walk and a snack will have to do for now. Go outside and make a snowman or throw a snowball at your tax return. (If you're lucky enough to live in the South, you can work on your tan.) Do whatever you need to do to clear your mind. When you return, you'll learn how to enter income from a partnership K-1, complete your self-employment Schedule C, and enter any additional taxable income that you may have.

Entering Schedule K-1 Information

Partnerships, S-corps (small corporations), trusts, and estates file tax returns that report the activities of the organization and transactions with the partners, shareholders, or beneficiaries. Like a W-2 and a 1099, partnership, S-corp, trust, and estate tax returns are filed for informational purposes only—no tax is computed on the tax return. Instead, the tax is paid by the partners, shareholders, or beneficiaries who received income from the organization. Each return contains a Schedule K-1, which provides the partner, shareholder, or beneficiary with a breakdown of the earnings and tax treatment.

The good news is that the organization is responsible for keeping track of all the nuances of the tax law and computing the taxable amounts. When you receive your K-1, in most cases you can just transfer the amounts to your tax return. As a bonus, the K-1 does a good job of explaining where to report the various amounts on your tax return. TurboTax helps you transfer the amounts and alerts you to any additional nuances that you might need to investigate.

NOTE You need Schedule K-1 to properly report your share of partnership, S-corp, trust, and estate income or loss. As with Form 1099, you do not need to attach a copy of the K-1 to your federal tax return. However, some states do require that you attach a copy of the K-1 along with a schedule that lists the taxes paid in other states for which you are claiming a credit. If you are using the TurboTax state module, the Review process will alert you to this need. If in doubt, contact the issuing organization.

Setting Up the K-1

The first screen on Partnership Issues provides you with a video on the tax treatment of general and limited partners. Take a moment now to play the video. When finished, click on <u>Continue</u>. Next, TurboTax prompts you to enter the name of the organization, a partnership in this case (see Figure 3.22).

NOTE My fictitious family has a partnership K-1, so the Interview questions here will cover partnerships. The process is the same for other types of K-1s, although the exact questions being asked will differ based on the type of organization and income.

When you are ready, click on <u>Continue</u> in order to move on to the next set of Interview questions. As you can see in Figure 3.23, TurboTax needs to know who the K-1 is for (you or your spouse), the partnership ID number

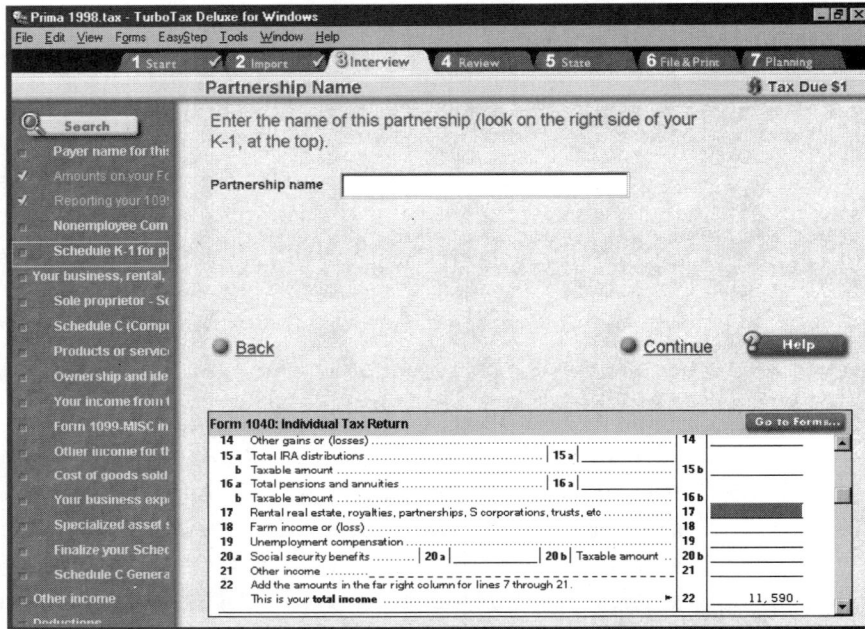

Figure 3.22

TurboTax helps you transfer your K-1 amounts to the proper section of your tax return.

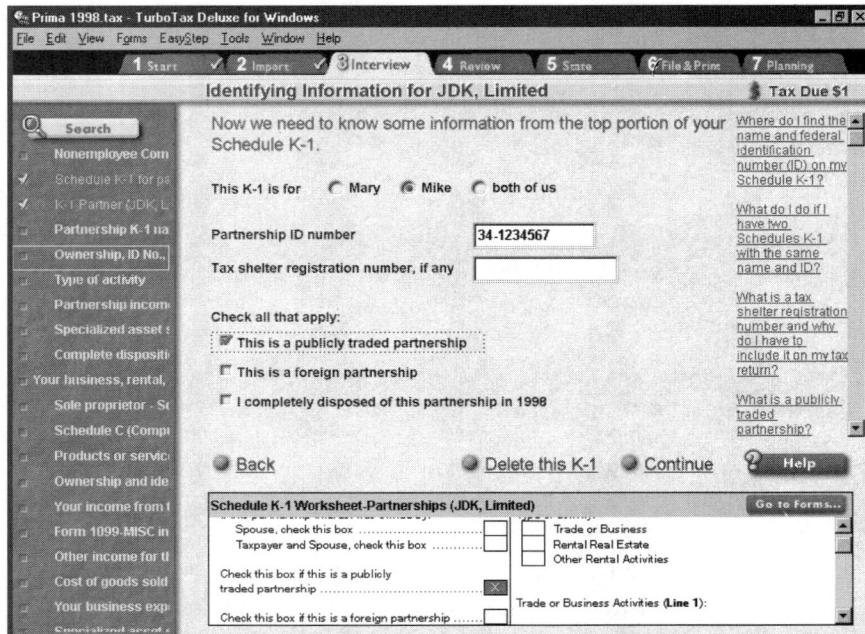

Figure 3.23

The type of partnership determines many tax effects on you the recipient.

(the partnership's TIN), the tax shelter registration number (if applicable), and the type of partnership (publicly traded, foreign, or if you sold your partnership shares this year). You will find the partnership's TIN at the top of the K-1, usually above the partnership's name and address. The tax shelter ID (if applicable) is listed on line G of your K-1. If the partnership is publicly traded, the box on line H will be checked. Line C of your K-1 explains whether the partnership is domestic or foreign.

TIP Are you unsure of what a publicly traded partnership is? Click on the corresponding FAQ to learn more about partnership types.

After you have filled in the required information, click on Continue in order to move ahead.

The next Interview question (see Figure 3.24) asks if the partnership is involved in a trade or business, real estate rental, or the rental of other property. You can determine this by looking at lines 1, 2, and 3 of your

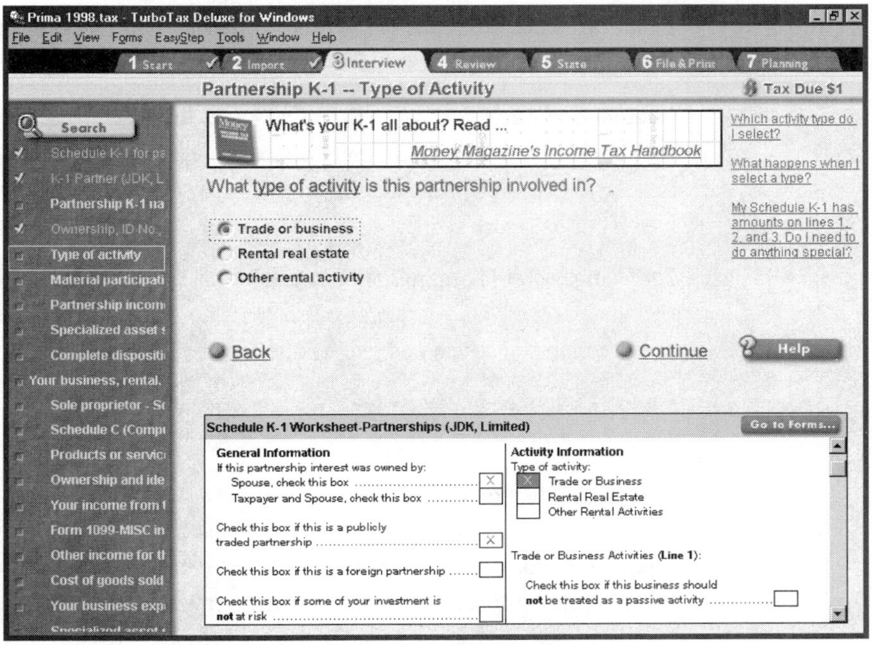

Figure 3.24

The IRS taxes you based on what the partnership did.

K-1, which reports the income that you have earned. The type of income that the partnership earns determines the type of income that you have earned. And each of these three income types is handled differently on your tax return.

If you only have one amount on line 1, 2, or 3, go ahead and select the corresponding activity type. If no amount appears on line 1, 2, or 3, select the activity Trade or Business.

If, however, you have two or three amounts on lines 1, 2, or 3, you will need to split your one K-1 into two or three K-1s. This is necessary so that Turbo-Tax can properly classify and report your tax data. If you were doing the return manually, you would need to do the same additional work. Click on the FAQ regarding multiple-activity K-1s to get specific instructions on how to split your K-1 amounts. This is not a difficult task, but you will have to do it offline. Consult your partnership's tax department or your tax advisor if you need more information or an explanation of the multiple activities.

NOTE

Most partnerships are formed to conduct a trade or business, which results in ordinary income. Sometimes partnerships engage in sidelines that are not part of their business, called passive activities. Passive activities include investing in rental operations or other businesses in which you do not materially participate.

Noticing that many taxpayers were using losses from passive activities to lower their ordinary taxable income, the IRS created the passive-activity loss rules to close the loophole. The intent was to prevent taxpayers from deducting losses on their returns for activities that they weren't actually involved in.

Portfolio gains or losses from investments of stocks, dividends, and interest, although passive in nature, are not considered passive income for this purpose. And if the partnership is in the business of selling and renting real estate, then the activity is not passive.

For more information, review the FAQs, Tax Help, and IRS Publication 541 on partnerships.

When you are ready, click on Continue. TurboTax asks if you materially participate in the partnership's business (see Figure 3.25). If you are unsure, click on the Guide Me bullet, and TurboTax will walk you through the rules and general guidelines (such as number of hours worked, type of work you did, and so on). This issue is important, because if you did not materially

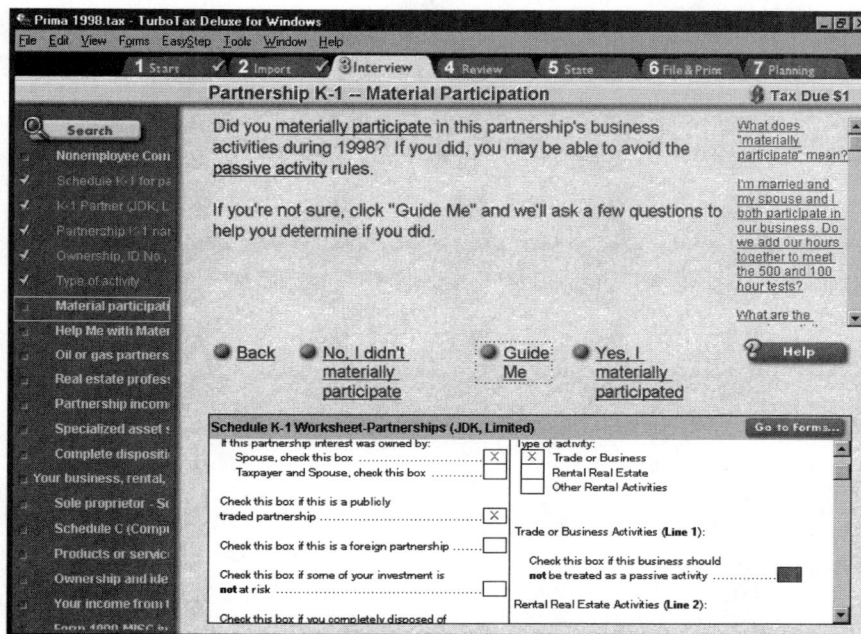

Figure 3.25

The FAQs provide you with new issues to consider.

participate in the business, you may be limited by the passive-activity loss rules (see the previous Note).

After you determine your participation status, go ahead and click on the appropriate response.

Entering K-1 Distributions

Now that your K-1 is set up, you can enter the distribution amounts. Lines 1–25 report your share of the income, payments, deductions, and credits experienced by the partnership. As you can see in Figure 3.26, TurboTax provides you with a list of check boxes for various line numbers so you can limit your Interview to the applicable topics.

Check off the line numbers that have amounts, and then click on Continue so you can begin entering the amounts. As you move through the K-1 and enter amounts, be sure to read over the FAQs, click on hyperlinks in the Interview question, and use the Help system to learn more about the information requested.

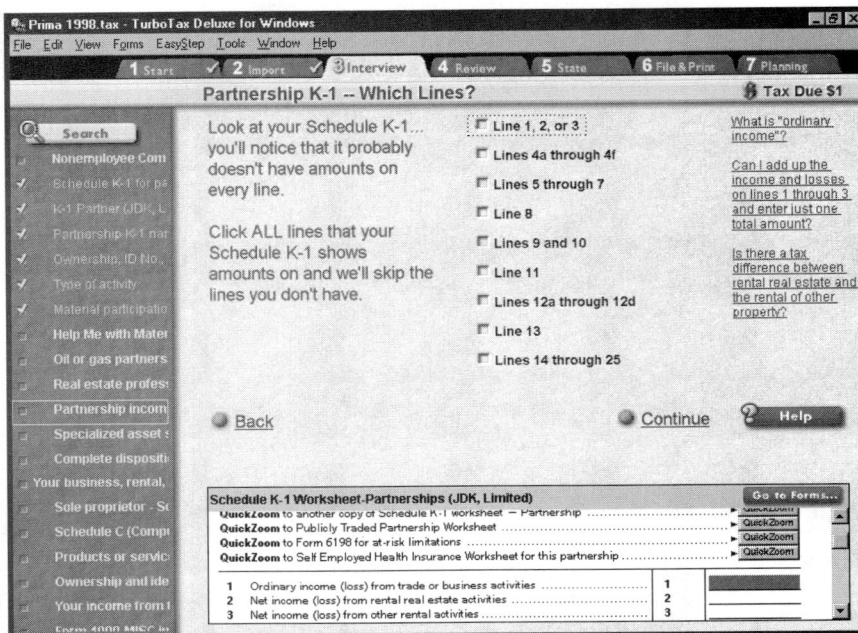

Figure 3.26

Save time by checking off the line numbers that have amounts.

Other Partnership Information

After you have entered your K-1 distributions, TurboTax checks on a few less-common situations (see Figure 3.27). The first question asks if you have a passive-activity loss carryover from last year. You can find that amount on Form 8582, worksheets 5 and 6. (If you used TurboTax last year and rolled in amounts from the prior year, these amounts will have already been posted to your current tax return.)

The second check box refers to the "at-risk" rules, which limit your loss in a business activity to the lesser of the loss or the amount you have at risk. If you are not at risk, TurboTax will walk you through the process of computing the limitations and reporting the deductible loss on Form 6198.

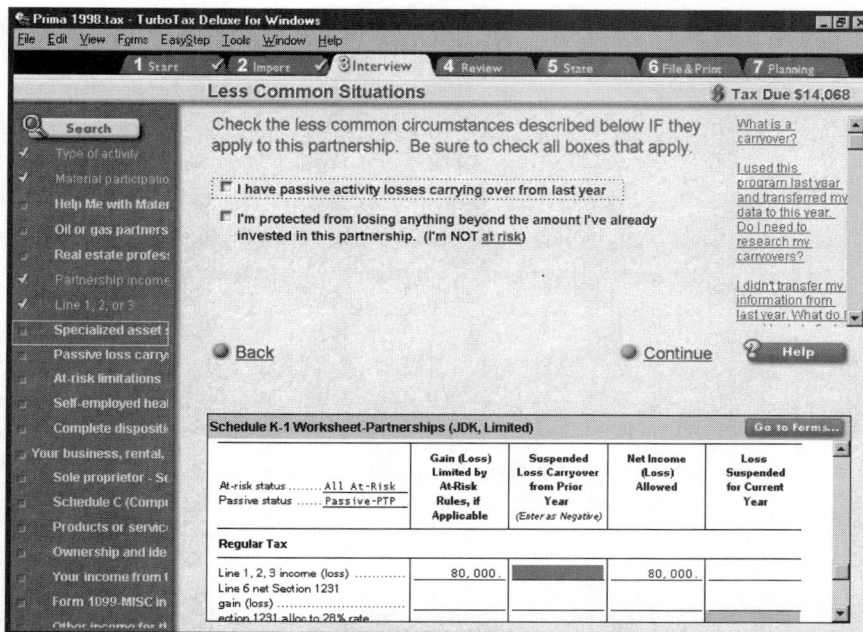

Figure 3.27

You may be able to reduce your tax liability if you have a loss carryover or paid health insurance.

NOTE

If you or your spouse qualifies for health insurance that is partially paid for by an employer, the health insurance you paid for through your own business does not qualify as a business expense. Instead, combine the cost of your health insurance through your business with that from the employer-provided plan, and report the total as a medical deduction.

Check the applicable boxes and click on <u>Continue</u> in order to move on to the next Interview question. Enter any additional K-1s and save your data file (File, Save). When you have completed your K-1 entries, you need to click on No, Done with Partnership K1s to display the next interview topic.

Reporting Business Income

Reporting your business activities is the next Interview topic (see Figure 3.28). If you own a small business that is not incorporated or run as a partnership, then use Schedule C to report your business income as coming from a sole proprietorship. If you operate a farm (lucky you!), report your income and expenses on Schedule F, but if you rent the farm out to someone else to run, use Form 4835. Schedule E is used to report income from rents, royalties, and other supplemental income.

Check the boxes for the business types that you have income or expenses for this year. If you rolled over your prior year's data, TurboTax will know about last year's business activities and prompt you to fill in this year's amounts or remove the business profile, if you are no longer in that business. Then click on Next when you are ready to start the next Interview topic.

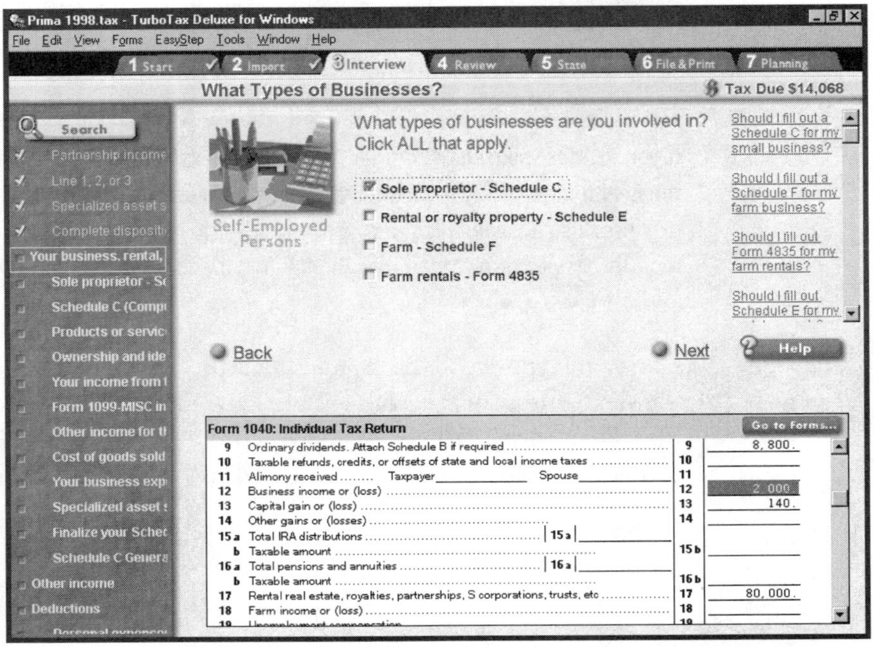

Figure 3.28

Customize the Interview process by checking the business types you are involved in.

Setting Up Your Sole Proprietorship

Working for yourself can be hectic at times, but the rewards in pride of ownership usually outweigh the downsides. Whether your business is a full-time or part-time enterprise, the IRS wants to know all about it. TurboTax helps you file your business tax return forms while walking you through some of the traps and pitfalls to avoid.

The Interview begins with a video which gives you tips on reporting your business income. View the video and click on <u>Continue</u>. TurboTax asks you to briefly describe the business (such as Service: Consulting). Click on <u>Continue</u> again and TurboTax alerts you to the IRS's new system of Principal Business Activity Codes for 1998. Click on <u>Business Code</u> to learn more about the new system. When you are ready, click on <u>Continue</u> to move forward.

Next, the Interview asks you for some basic identifying information for your business (see Figure 3.29). Go ahead and complete this section. Use the FAQs and hyperlinks as needed to get more explanation on the information requested.

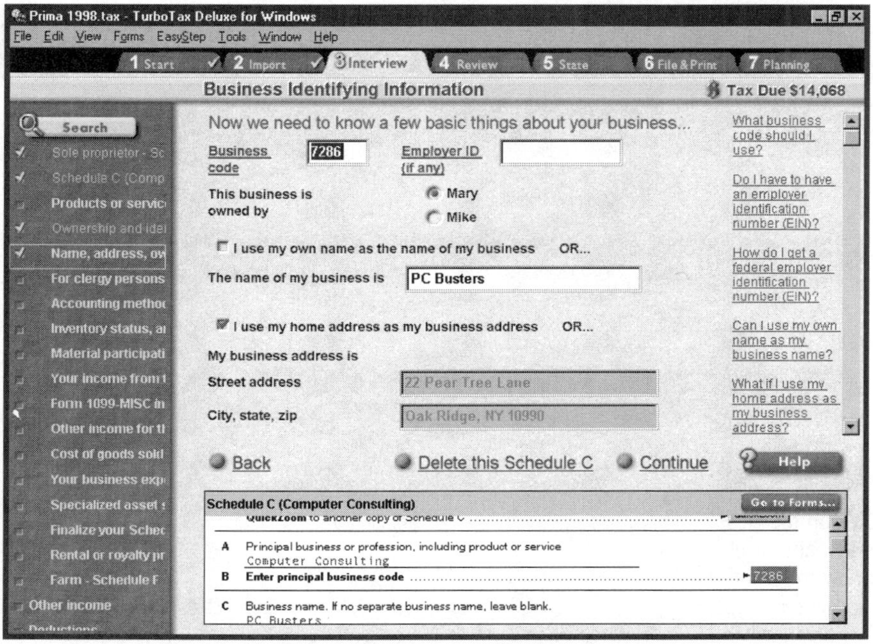

Figure 3.29

First, you need to provide basic information about the business.

TIP

Click on <u>Business Code</u> to get a list of code numbers and descriptions. Choose the code that most closely matches your business activity. The IRS uses this code for demographics and to determine audit issues.

CAUTION

Don't enter your social security number in the Employer ID field. If you don't have an employer identification number (EIN), just leave the field blank.

The third set of Interview questions (see Figure 3.30) asks you how you keep your books and for some other information about your business. Your accounting method (how you keep your books) is important because it determines the timing of when you recognize income and expense.

When you first start up your business, take some time to determine which accounting method is most suitable. If you sell goods and keep an inventory of the goods you sell, you *must* use the accrual method. In certain cases a

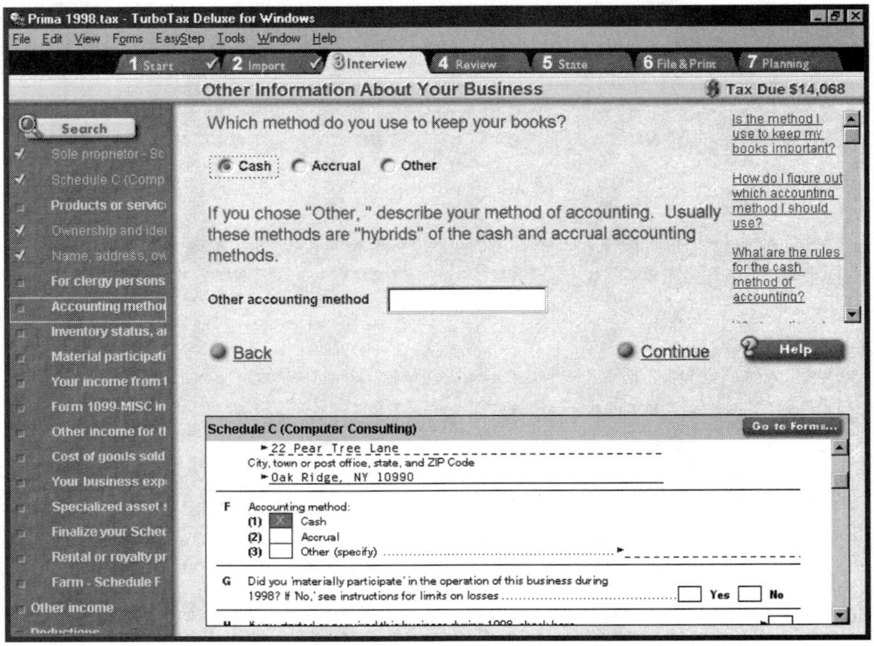

Figure 3.30

Click on the FAQs if you are unsure of how to respond to the questions being asked.

combination method of accrual basis for inventory and cash basis for the remainder of the transactions can be used. When in doubt, consult your accountant. In fact, while you're at it, consider using a computer program such as QuickBooks to maintain your business records. In addition to helping you manage your business, you'll be able to import your business income and expense directly into TurboTax!

BUZZ WORD

◄ ◄

Accounting Method: Rules that guide you when to recognize (record) income and expense.
Cash Basis: A method that recognizes income when you receive payment and expense when you make the payment.
Accrual Basis: A method that recognizes income when you earn the income (regardless of when you receive the cash) and expense when you incur the expense (regardless of when the expense is paid).

◄ ◄

TIP

■ ■

To change your accounting method, you must first file Form 3115 with the IRS and ask for permission. If your application is approved, there may be an additional amount of income that you need to report in your tax return and on your books that represents the difference amount between cash and accrual methods. Be aware of the financial and tax effects the change will have on your business income before you ask the IRS for permission to change.

■ ■

First, indicate your accounting method. Then check off the additional boxes as applicable. Notice that the last check box brings up that issue of whether or not you materially participate in the business, which you just read about in the discussion dealing with partnerships.

Valuing Inventory

If your business has inventory, you will need to select a method to account for the value of that inventory. The IRS recognizes three basic methods:

- ✪ **Cost.** Inventory is valued at what you actually paid for each item.
- ✪ **Lower of Cost or Market.** Inventory is valued at the lower of what you originally paid or the current market value. This is a more conservative method.

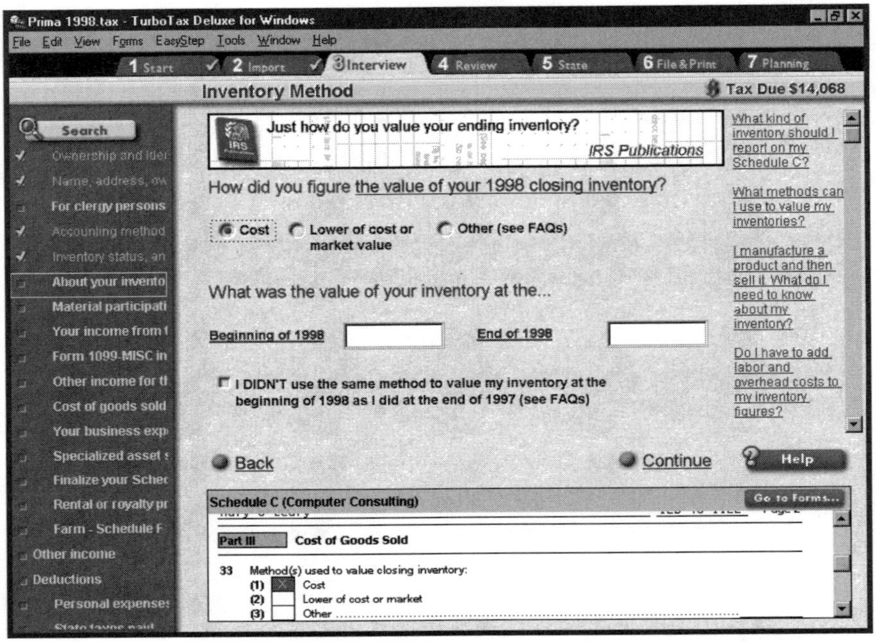

Figure 3.31

How you value your inventory affects your taxable income.

○ **Retail.** Inventory is valued at retail value less the average markup. This method is available only to retailers.

For more information on the different inventory methods, click on IRS Publications at the top of the Interview page (see Figure 3.31) or consult with your accountant.

Select your inventory method and enter the value of your inventory at the beginning and the end of the year. After you do this, click on Continue.

Entering Business Income

Once you finish describing your business and the accounting methods used, the TurboTax Interview moves into the income area. TurboTax will walk you through the Material Participation rules (similar to those covered under Partnership K-1s above). Next, you'll be prompted to enter business income from Form 1099-MISC (see Figure 3.32). Toward the top of the screen, you'll see a link to IRS Publications, which will take you to an explanation of the types

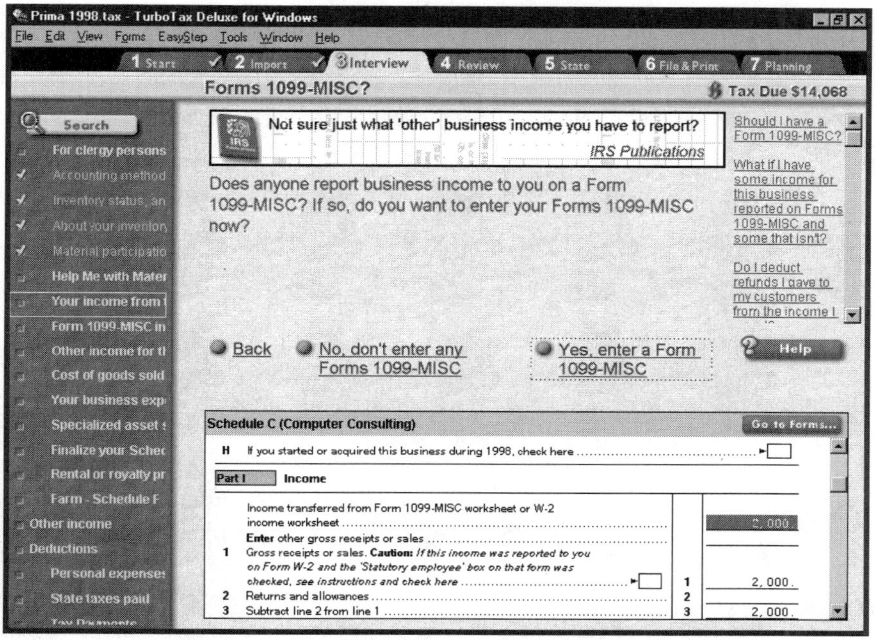

Figure 3.32

Businesses can receive 1099 forms too.

of business income that you need to report (IRS Publication 334). I highly recommend that you order this publication from the IRS (800-TAX-FORM) so that you have it in hard copy. You should definitely read this publication. (Yes, I know how dry this reading assignment will be!) Although much of what is discussed in the publication may not yet apply to you, you will learn about the issues confronting sole proprietors, some of which you may face as your business grows.

If you already entered a 1099 and told TurboTax that it was related to this business, the amount would be posted here already. If you need to enter additional 1099s, or if you need to edit the 1099 already posted to this business, click on Yes, Enter a Form 1099-MISC. If not, click on No, Don't Enter Any Forms 1099-MISC.

The Interview continues by asking you to enter your business income from gross receipts or sales and from any returns or allowances, as well as other business income you received (such as interest on business bank accounts or income from sales of scrap material).

> ### TIP
> Unless you have a financial report that lists the components of "other" income, it is always a good idea to create your own supporting schedule. That way, years from now you will know how you arrived at that number. See the next section for information on how to create a supporting schedule in TurboTax.

Creating Supporting Schedules

TurboTax allows you to create supporting schedules for any line item. Just right-click in the field, then choose Add Supporting Details (see Figure 3.33). Or press Ctrl+I in any field to display the Supporting Details dialog box (see Figure 3.34).

Each Supporting Details dialog box includes a header named according to the relevant IRS schedule or form and the specific line number wherever

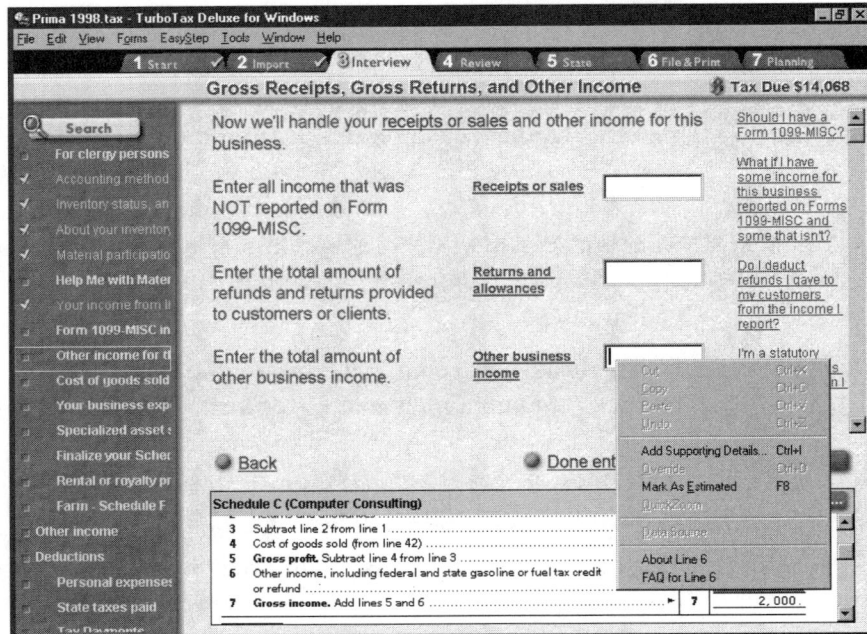

Figure 3.33

A shortcut menu gives you quick access to TurboTax features.

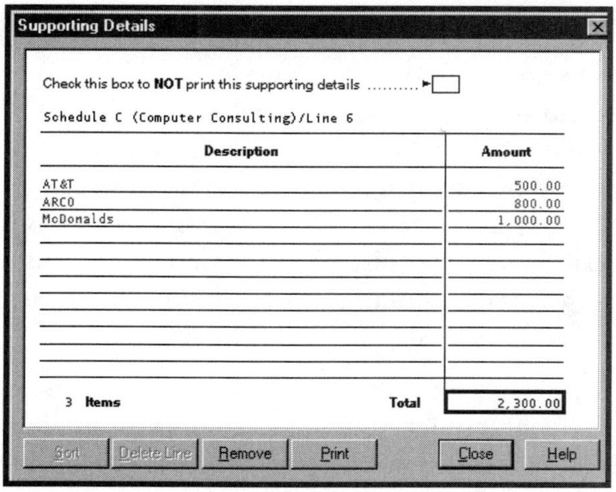

Figure 3.34

Use supporting schedules to document the details behind your tax return amounts.

possible. Enter a full description (up to 256 characters) for each item, along with an amount. The amounts are automatically totaled at the bottom. Additionally, the Supporting Details dialog box allows you to

- Sort items alphabetically by clicking on the Sort button.
- Delete a line by clicking on the Delete Line button.
- Remove the supporting schedule from your tax file by clicking on the Remove button.
- Print the supporting schedule by clicking on the Print button. Note that at any time, you can use the File, Print feature to print all supporting schedules with or without your forms.

While the IRS does not require you to file supporting detail schedules, you should nevertheless print a copy for your records. There is a check box at the top if you decide you don't want to print a copy.

When you finish entering your Schedule C income, click on Done Entering Income.

Entering Business Expenses

If you have cost of goods sold, TurboTax will prompt you to enter those amounts and then move on to several screens that ask about your business expense amounts (see Figure 3.35). It is important to choose the proper category in which to report your business expenses. Some items, such as advertising and legal fees, are self-explanatory. But areas such as depreciation and car expenses may require a bit more thought because the rules for tax are different than the accounting rules. Be sure to use the Supporting Detail schedule feature as needed to list specific items.

Table 3.3 provides you with a handy list of the expense categories on Schedule C. As you transfer your data from your accounting system (which undoubtedly has different names for these expenses), be sure to create a supporting schedule that shows the trail from accounting to tax books. For more information on the tax expense categories, click on the hyperlinked expense name, review the FAQs, or consult IRS Publication 334. If in doubt, consult with your accountant or tax advisor.

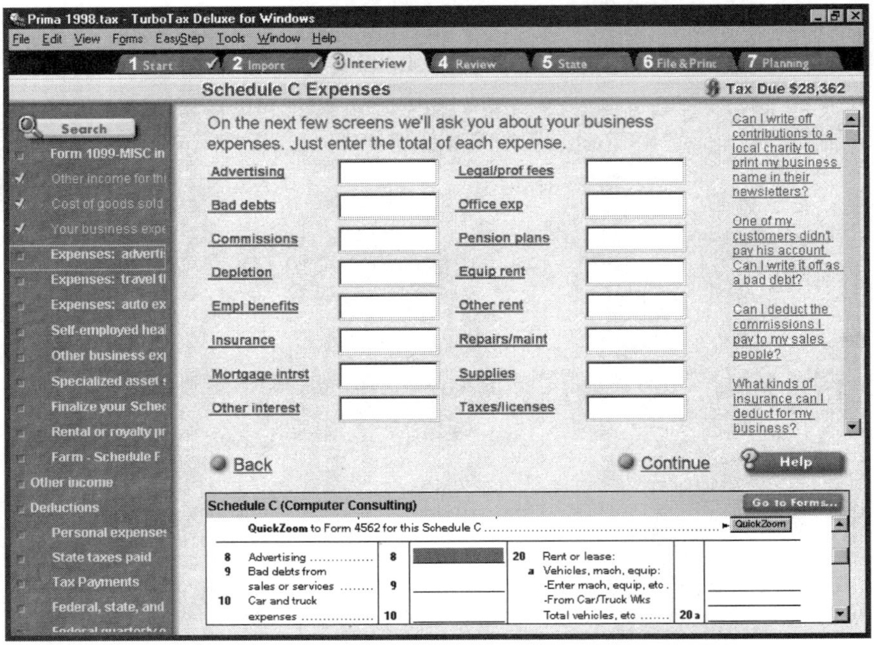

Figure 3.35

Some business expenses are not deductible in the year paid.

TABLE 3.3 SCHEDULE C BUSINESS EXPENSES

Expense Category	Description	Examples/Issues
Advertising	Costs of promoting your business.	Newspaper ads, sponsorship of little league teams, and radio and billboard advertising.
Bad debts	For accrual-basis taxpayers, the amount of accounts receivable that you realize you will never collect. In order to claim a deduction for bad debts, you must have already reported the amount as income or be able to show an actual loss of money.	Unpaid invoices; overdue accounts; and loans to employees, suppliers, or clients.
Car and truck expenses	The use of vehicles for business may be deducted at a standard mileage rate (32.5 cents per mile in 1998) or by keeping a record of actual auto expenses and calculating depreciation.	You must have proof of the business use and keep a record of your mileage, regardless of the expense method chosen.
Commissions and fees	Amounts you paid for commissions and fees.	If you paid someone more than $600 during the year, you must file Form 1099-MISC by February 1, 1999.
Depletion	The amount of wear and tear on a natural resource such as oil, gas, timber, or minerals.	Issues are similar to those for depreciation, but instead pertain to natural resources.
Depreciation	Business assets that last longer than one year, required to be expensed over time as the asset deteriorates, based on approved tax-depreciation methods.	You can take a Section 179 deduction of up to $18,500 in 1998 for business assets that you decide not to depreciate. An advantage of depreciation is that it matches the expense with the earning of income over time (reducing the taxable income accordingly).

TABLE 3.3   SCHEDULE C BUSINESS EXPENSES (CONTINUED)

Expense Category	Description	Examples/Issues
Employee benefit programs	Amounts paid for fringe benefits for your employees. Do not include amounts you paid for your own benefits here—TurboTax will ask for that separately.	Programs dealing with education, counseling, child care, medical, accident counseling (but not retirement plans, which fall under a separate category, see below).
Insurance	Deductible insurance premiums.	Insurance for fire, theft, flood, casualty, and inventory.
Mortgage interest	Interest paid on a mortgage held on real property for the business, for which you received Form 1098. If you paid interest but didn't receive a 1098, check with the mortgage holder. If none was filed, list the interest on the line for other interest (below).	Includes mortgage interest paid on a warehouse, an office, or a factory.
Other interest	Interest paid on a mortgage with no Form 1098, or other business interest.	Includes interest paid on business loans and credit card accounts.
Legal and other professional fees	Fees paid for accountants, lawyers, financial advisors, or other professionals who guide you in running your business.	Start-up expenses are capitalized, not expensed, in the first year.
Office expenses	Expenses of running the office or maintaining the facilities.	Includes supplies, letterhead, business cards, ink cartridges, cleaning products, pens, and paper.
Pension plans	Contributions to retirement plans and profit-sharing plans made by the business on behalf of an employee. Payments made on your own behalf will be entered on the IRA/KEOGH/SEP worksheet later in the Interview.	Includes qualified retirement plans, profit-sharing plans, stock bonus programs, annuities, or SEPs.

TABLE 3.3 SCHEDULE C BUSINESS EXPENSES (CONTINUED)

Expense Category	Description	Examples/Issues
Equipment rental	Rent paid on machinery and vehicles used in the business.	Do not include office or building rent on this line. If your rent over time is actually going toward buying the equipment, then you will need to depreciate the asset rather than expense the rent. Includes car leases (see limitations in Help screen), postage machine rental, and copier rental.
Other rent	Rent paid on real estate.	Includes rental costs for the office, warehouse, factory, or plant.
Repairs and maintenance	Regular maintenance of property used in business. Do not include costs that add to the value of the property. Such amounts (called capital expenditures) add to the basis of the property and are depreciated over time.	Includes the cost of repairing a leaky roof, fixing a broken copier, or replacing light bulbs or tubes in light fixtures. Excluded are the costs of putting on a new roof or installing new (permanent) walls.
Supplies	Miscellaneous small expenses for items needed to operate your business (similar to office expenses).	Includes pens, pencils, shipping boxes, packing material, and coffee.
Taxes and licenses	Deductible taxes paid by the business.	Includes real estate taxes, payroll taxes, franchise taxes, licenses, and permits.
Travel	Ordinary and necessary travel expenses incurred (while away from home) solely for the business. See Help for limitations on meals, entertainment, and travel outside the United States.	Includes the cost of airfare, hotel, cabs, shipping, car rental, food, dry cleaning, phone, passport, and visa, as well as tips and taxes on these items.

TABLE 3.3 SCHEDULE C BUSINESS EXPENSES (CONTINUED)

Expense Category	Description	Examples/Issues
Meals and entertainment	Meals and entertainment for business, whether traveling or not. See Tax Help for limitations on meals and entertainment (generally limited to 50 percent).	Enter in TurboTax the total amount subject to the 50 percent limitation separate from those expenses not limited. TurboTax will do the math for you. See Help and IRS Publication 463 for specific requirements.
Utilities	Utility expenses for your business.	Includes gas, oil, electric, water, and telephone.
Wages	Wages and salaries paid to business employees. Do not include amounts paid to you or your spouse.	Includes wages, salaries, and other amounts (such as child care, moving expenses, grants, and scholarships) paid for on behalf of employees.
Work Opportunity Credit	Form 5884 (Work Opportunity Credit is not included in TurboTax, but you can get it from the IRS by phone or from its Web site.	Enter the amount from Form 5884 here, and TurboTax will handle appropriately.

NOTE If you operate your business from your home, you may be able to take a special home office deduction. If you want to explore the potential deduction, do not enter your "shared" expenses here. Examples of shared expenses eligible for the home office deduction include insurance, mortgage, electricity, rent, cleaning, property tax, repairs, water, and gas. TurboTax will recognize that your business and home address are the same and prompt you for this information a bit later in the Interview.

Go ahead and enter your business expenses into the categories listed. Later on, TurboTax will ask you for your home office expense amounts and give you an opportunity to enter "other" expenses, a catch-all category. When you

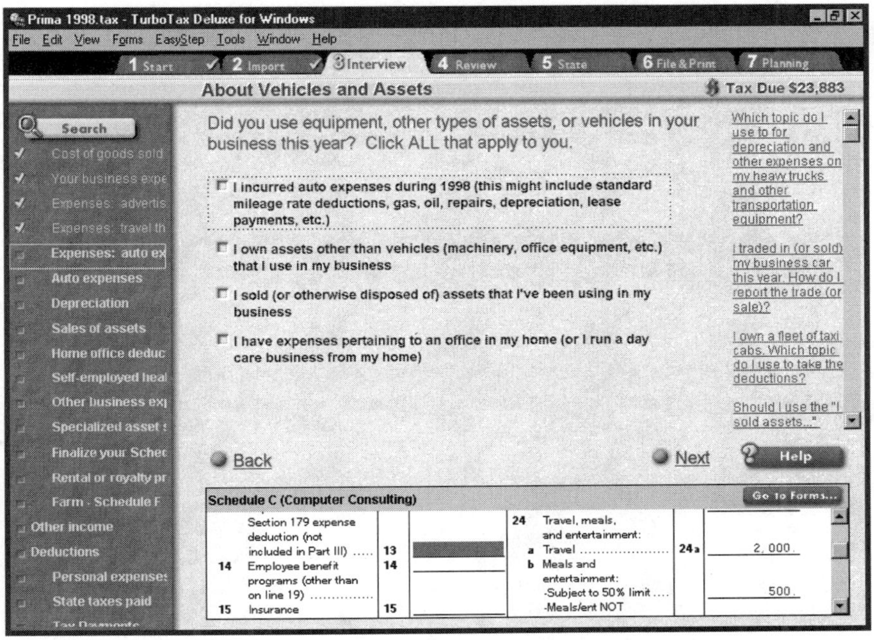

Figure 3.36

Let TurboTax know how you used vehicles and assets in your business.

are ready, click on <u>Continue</u> in order to move on to the next set of Interview questions (see Figure 3.36).

Check off the statements that best describe your additional business expenses. Then click on <u>Next</u> to continue.

Expensing Your Auto

Take a moment to play the video, Recording Vehicle Expenses. It provides you with a good overview of your options on deducting business use of your vehicle. Click on the More Info button to access the additional Help text on this topic. When ready, click on <u>Continue</u> to begin the interview.

If you use a vehicle for business purposes, TurboTax prompts you to enter the make and model of the vehicle (such as Mercury Sable or Jeep Cherokee). Next, enter the date the vehicle was placed into service and the type of vehicle (based on pounds or tractor trailer). The third Interview screen (see Figure 3.37) asks if you used the vehicle for the entire year or not. Be sure to read over the FAQs, because in some cases you will need to answer Yes even

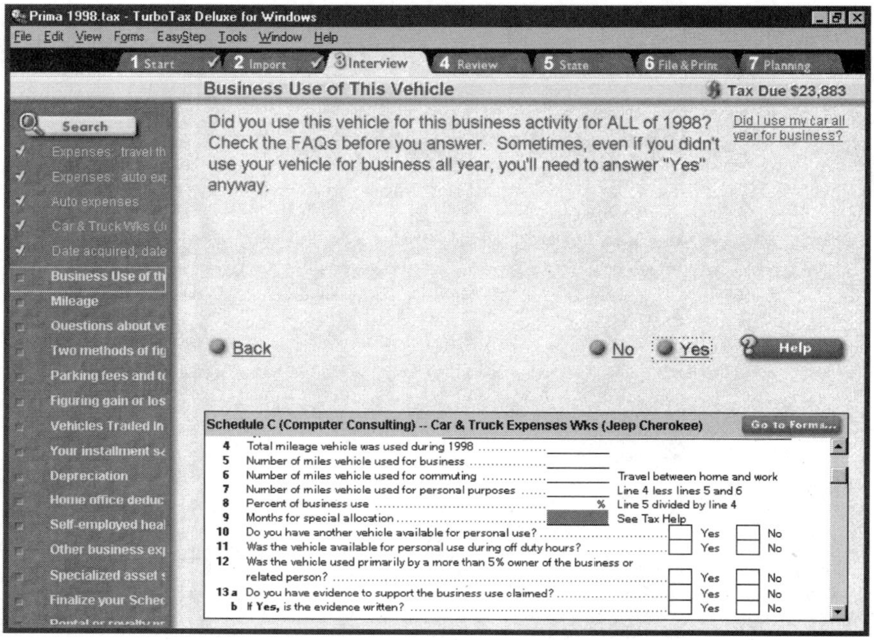

Figure 3.37

Read over the FAQs for some solid advice.

though this might not seem to be the appropriate response. For example, if you just bought the car in April of this year and have used it since then for business, you will answer Yes to this question.

After you respond Yes or No, the next screen asks you to enter the total miles you drove the car, the number of miles driven for business, and the number of miles driven commuting to work. (Home office miles to the refrigerator do not count!) Actually, miles driven to and from work (commuting) are not deductible. Be sure to keep your mileage log in with this year's tax documents. It is your only proof to the IRS as to how the car was used. You will need to buy a new log for 1999.

When you click on Continue, TurboTax will ask you to fill out a short questionnaire on how you use your auto in business. The responses will be transferred to Form 4562. Click on Continue when you are ready.

If you qualify for the standard mileage method (32.5 cents in 1998), Turbo-Tax lets you know and gives you the options of deducting your qualified business miles at the standard rate or entering the actual expenses.

TIP

In most cases the standard rate provides you with a higher (and quicker) auto expense. However, if you had unusually high maintenance costs this year or other high car expenses, you might want to use the actual expense method. You can always go back to this screen and select the mileage rate method and compare the two to be sure.

If you don't qualify for the standard mileage method, or you decide to use the actual expense method instead, TurboTax will list the categories for you and gather any lease expense information. Regardless of the method you choose, you can deduct your parking fees, taxi and bus fares, tolls, property taxes, and interest on car loans. When you are done entering expenses for that vehicle, TurboTax gives you the option of entering expenses for another.

Accounting for Business Assets

The rules surrounding the depreciation (expensing) of assets used in a business can be complex. TurboTax provides a video that covers the key issues and rules. Click on the Play button and review the video. Use the More Info button to read more about depreciation in the Help system. When you are ready to begin the interview, click on <u>Continue</u>.

If you have business assets to depreciate, TurboTax begins by asking you to enter a unique and descriptive name for the asset. Next (see Figure 3.38), you will need to enter the date you started using the asset (also known as the date placed in service) and the cost (including any costs of purchasing the asset). Then select an asset type from the drop-down list.

CAUTION

Enter your asset data wisely. If the cost that you report on this return is wrong, your deduction will be incorrect, and that could cause more problems down the road when you sell the asset. Take some time to read over the FAQs to learn more. You can also consult IRS Publications 946, 535, and 551 to get the big picture. When in doubt, contact your tax advisor with all your facts clearly listed out. Remember: the more organized you are and the more you understand the tax rules, the less expensive your tax advisor will be and the better advice your tax advisor will be able to give you.

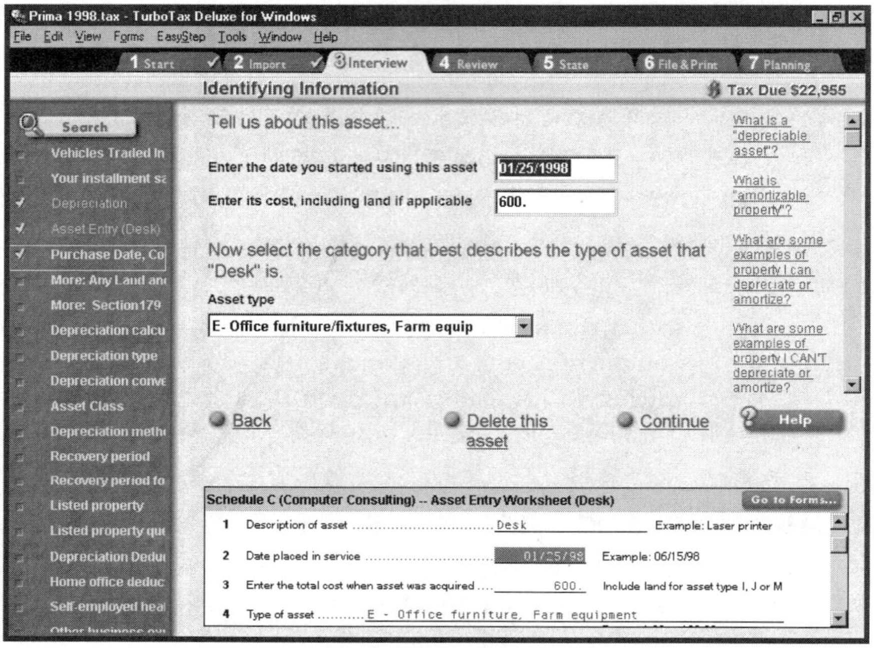

Figure 3.38

In order to compute tax depreciation, TurboTax needs to know more about the asset.

Click on <u>Continue</u>, and TurboTax will ask for the percentage of time that this asset was used for business. Enter the percentage and click on <u>Next</u>. Now comes the fun part. Figure 3.39 explains the Section 179 deduction that was covered earlier. Read over the <u>Eligibility Requirements</u> and the FAQs. Then consider if you need more tax deduction this year or if you'd rather push the expense out over the life of the asset (which does a better job of matching your business expense with your business income).

If this asset is not eligible for the Section 179 deduction, check the appropriate box. Otherwise, click on <u>Next</u> to continue. If the asset is eligible, the next Interview screen gives you the opportunity to decide how much of the asset's cost you want to deduct. TurboTax also provides <u>Recommendations</u> on whether to take a Section 179 deduction or not. Read over these recommendations and then enter the amount. Click on <u>Next</u> to continue.

At this point, TurboTax performs some calculations and saves your data for you. If you want to enter other assets, click on <u>Yes, Enter a New Asset</u>. Or you

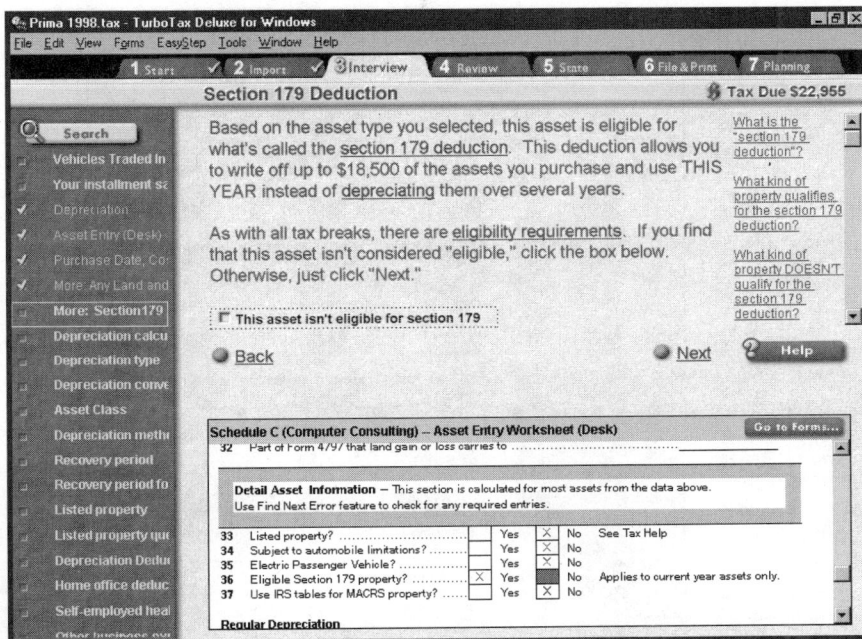

Figure 3.39

Not all assets are eligible for a Section 179 deduction.

can select <u>Yes, Update an Existing Asset</u>. Otherwise, click on <u>No, Done with Assets</u>.

Selling an Asset

In order to fill out the tax forms for an asset sale, you need to enter the asset into the system as described in the prior section. The first Interview question asks you to select which asset you sold. After you click on <u>Continue with This Asset Sale</u>, TurboTax displays the Interview screen shown in Figure 3.40.

Before answering these Interview questions, read over the FAQs and the Help screens on this topic. The tax treatment of asset disposals can be very tricky, so this would be a good time to read over IRS Publications 946, 535, and 551. When in doubt, present the facts to your tax advisor and ask for guidance.

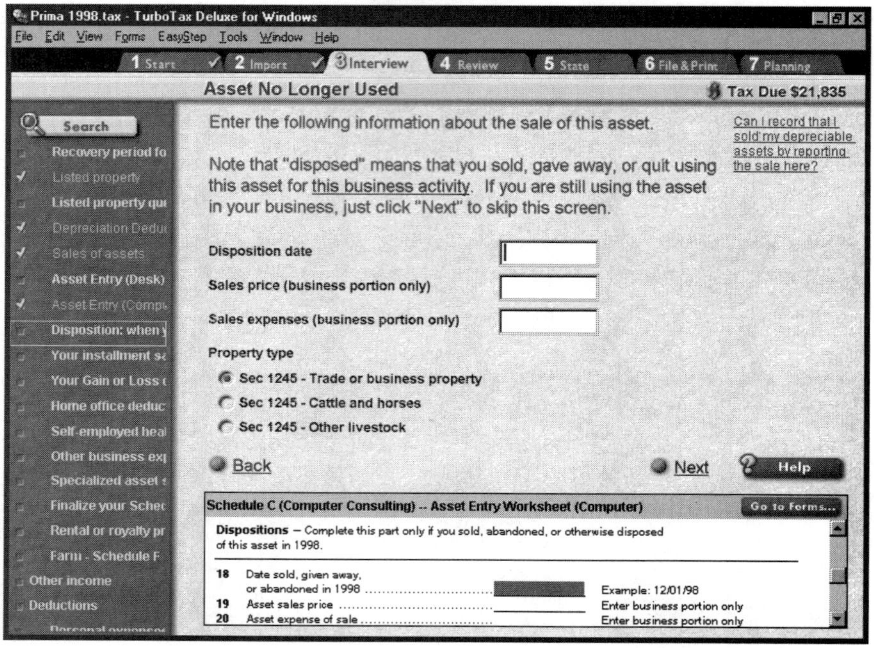

Figure 3.40

TurboTax walks you through the process of disposing of an asset as it relates to your taxes.

Enter the disposition date, sales price, and sale expenses and select a property type. Then click on <u>Next</u>. If you have any other asset sales, go ahead and enter them. Otherwise, TurboTax will take you to the next Interview topic.

Writing Off a Home Office

The Home Office Deduction Interview starts off with a very good video on tax opportunities and limitations. Take a moment to play the video before clicking on <u>Continue</u>.

As you can see in Figure 3.41, the first Interview question is about whether you want to take a home office deduction or not. The Help screen and hyperlinks provide you with a good background on what the IRS allows and what some of the long-term downsides are to taking a home office deduction. Use the Guide Me feature to have TurboTax walk you through the requirements and determine if your home office qualifies or not.

Once you have a good handle on your situation, click on <u>No</u> or <u>Yes</u> to continue. If you qualify, you will be prompted to edit your home office address

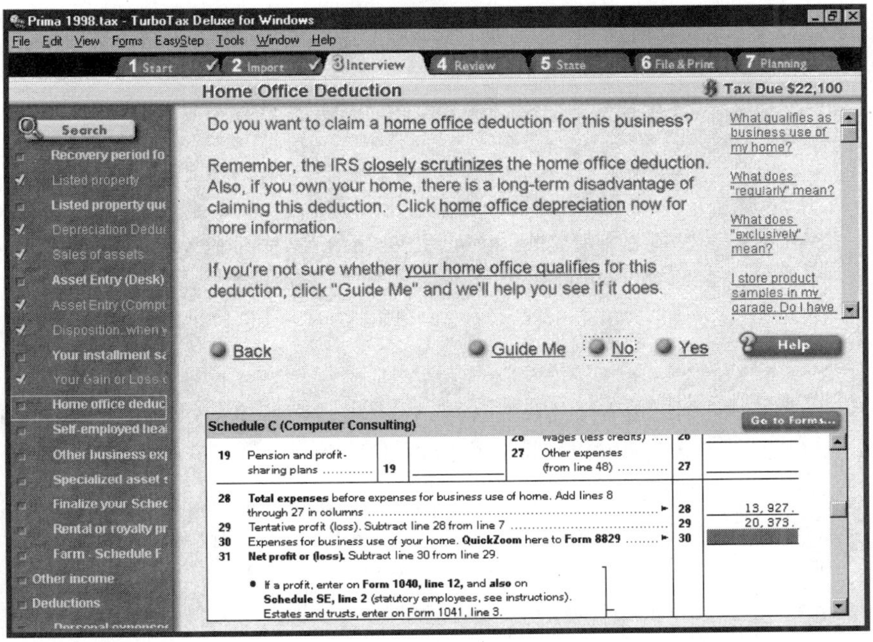

Figure 3.41

Not all home offices qualify as deductions.

as needed. This is the address listed on Form 8829 (Expenses for Business Use of Your Home). Next, TurboTax asks if you use the home office to provide day care. The IRS has special rules for day-care facilities, so if you do run a day-care facility from your home, review the FAQs to learn the nuances.

When you click on <u>Continue</u>, the Interview asks you to measure the area used for your home office and compare that to the total area of your home. The IRS allows you two methods of measuring a home:

- If the rooms are about the same size, you can measure based on the number of rooms (excluding bathrooms and closets)—for example, one room out of six rooms.

- The most precise method is based on square footage of the office and of the living space in the home (do not include the garage or unfinished basement).

IRS Publication 587 (Business Use of Your Home) provides many useful, practical examples of measuring a home and of which areas qualify (such as your garage if it's used for storing inventory). The ratio of business use to personal use is used to prorate the shared home expenses, such as mortgage, rent, heat, and electricity.

Enter the business area and the total home area, and then click on Continue.

NOTE If the home office area was used by more than one business, you need to enter a percentage to reflect this business. For example, suppose you and your spouse share a home office. If your business income was $20,000 and your spouse's business income was $40,000, then you would enter 33 percent (one-third of the total business income).

Read over the FAQs to see if any apply to your situation. Enter your income percentage (if less than 100 percent).

The next Interview question asks you to enter the gains from sales of assets that you used in your home business. In order to answer this question, you need to print out your Form 4797. If you didn't sell any assets, you do not need to do anything here.

To print Form 4797 and the supporting schedules, follow these steps:

1. Choose File, Print.
2. Choose Selected Forms.
3. Choose Form plus supporting details.
4. Click on Choose.
5. Select Form 4797 p1 Sale of Business Property.
6. Click on OK.
7. Click on Print.

Review the printout and determine if any of the assets sold at a gain (losses go on the next line) were used in the home office (this might include a copier, desk, or computer). Add up the gains from those assets only, and enter the amounts into the corresponding Interview field. Do the same for the losses from sales of home office assets.

When you are done, click on Continue. In the case of businesses with more than one home office, you need to allocate the total business expense between the two or more home offices. If this situation applies to you, enter the expenses allocated to this home office in the space provided. Otherwise, enter the total listed at the top of the Interview page (Schedule C, line 28). Click on <u>Continue</u> when you are ready.

When it comes to deducting the shared expenses (such as home mortgage interest and taxes), TurboTax does an excellent job of explaining the tax law to you through the use of videos, FAQs, and Help text (see Figure 3.42). Take a moment to view the video and review the FAQs in case any apply to you. As noted in the video, if you itemize your deductions, you only need to enter the mortgage interest and taxes once here, after which TurboTax takes care of allocating the appropriate amounts to your Schedule C and Schedule A (itemized deductions).

When you are ready, click on <u>Continue</u>. TurboTax prompts you to enter the direct and indirect expenses for your home (see Figure 3.43). Direct expenses are those that you incur only for the home office portion (such as repairing an office light fixture). Indirect expenses are expenses incurred for the entire home (such as heat, electricity, and water). Review the FAQs for more examples and information on deductibility.

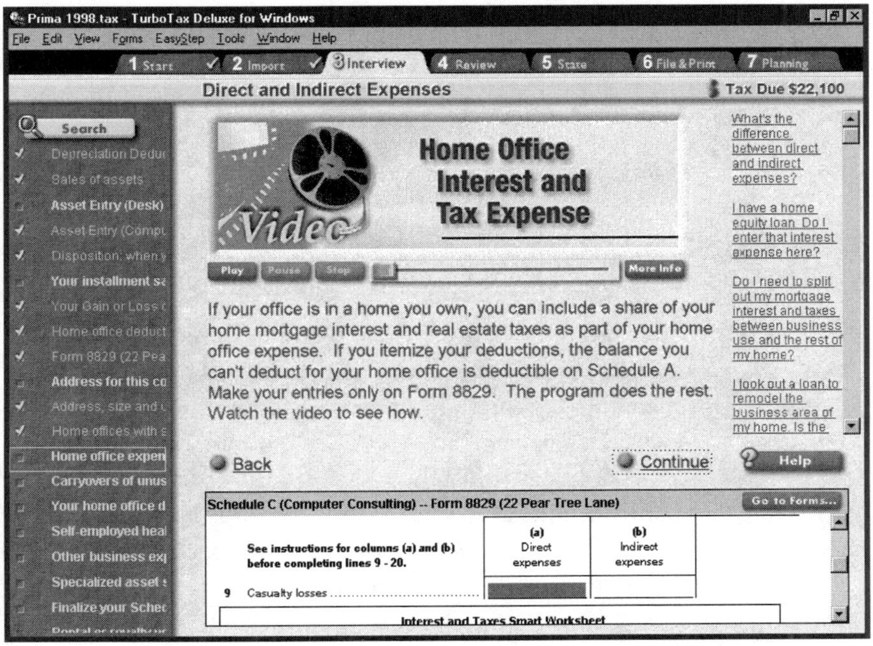

Figure 3.42

Your business may be able to deduct a share of the home interest and tax expense.

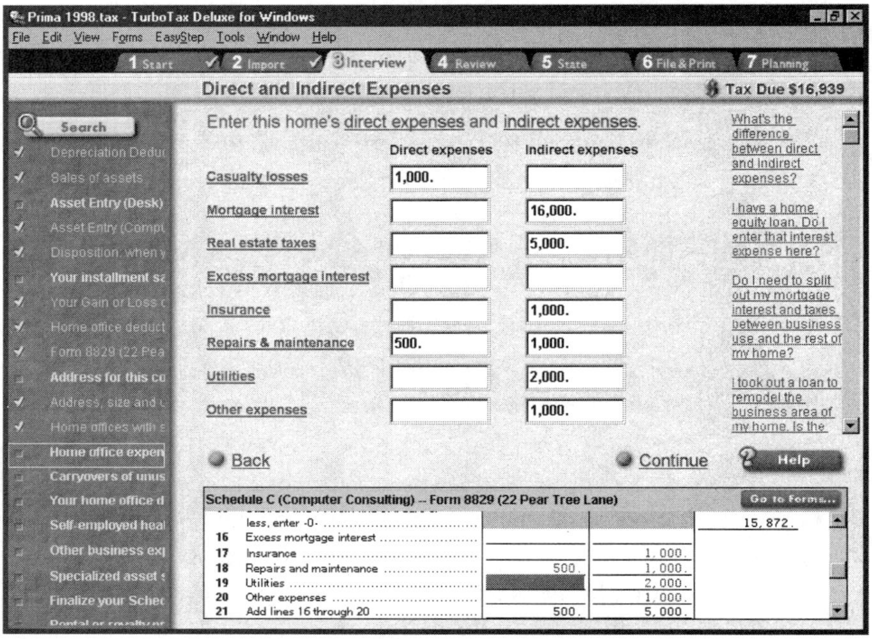

Figure 3.43

You can also deduct indirect expenses such as heat, electricity, and water.

Go ahead and enter your direct and indirect expenses. Click on Continue in order to move on to the next Interview question, which covers carryovers and excess casualty losses. To answer these questions, you need to have last year's return. Turn to Form 8829 (if you had one), and look for any carryovers. If you have any, enter the amounts in their respective fields. Click on Continue so that you can complete the home office data entry for this business. You can either edit an existing home office, create a new home office, or click on No, Done with Home Office.

The last question in the Schedule C net income area concerns whether you have any other business expenses. This is the last expense category on Schedule C. Click on Help or select Other Expenses to view a list of other typical expenses. Note that you should not expense to your business any charitable contributions. As a sole proprietor, you are to report charitable contributions as itemized deductions. You can, however, take as an advertising business deduction those costs involved in advertising in nonprofit newsletters, journals, or on team shirts.

Enter your other expenses (description and amount), then click on <u>Done</u> <u>with Other Expenses</u> to move ahead to the next Interview dealing with less-common situations. Here are the now-familiar at-risk and passive-activity questions. In addition to these is a query on whether you had any Section 179 carryover amounts (see last year's return) and whether you sold conservation property. Review the FAQs and IRS Publications listed on screen for a full description of these less-common situations. Check all that apply and click on <u>Next</u>.

The last screen provides you with an opportunity to edit an existing Schedule C, enter a new Schedule C, or click on <u>No, I'm Done with Schedule C</u>.

Reporting Rents, Royalties, and Supplemental Income

If you indicated back in Figure 3.28 that you had rental income, royalties or other supplemental income which is usually reported on Schedule E, Turbo-Tax now prompts you to name your Schedule E (see Figure 3.44).

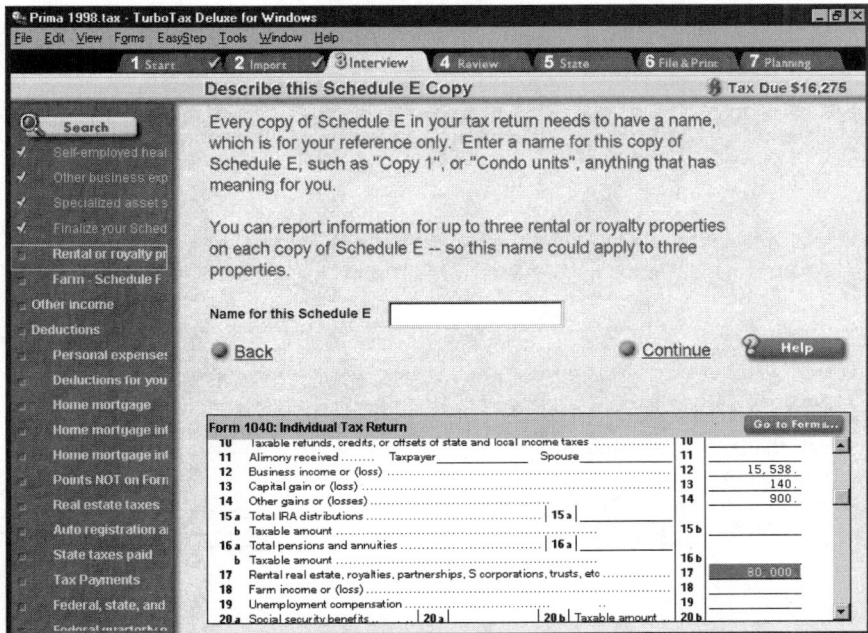

Figure 3.44

Each Schedule E can report up to three rental or royalty properties.

Enter a unique name for your first Schedule E and click on <u>Continue</u>. The next screen prompts you for more identifying information such as the owner, type of property (rental or royalty), and whether the property was disposed of or not during 1998. Answer <u>Yes</u> or <u>No</u> as applicable and click on <u>Continue</u>.

If you are not familiar with the tax rules pertaining to rental and royalty properties, take a moment to review the rules (see Figure 3.45). Click on <u>Yes, Review the Rules</u> and follow the Guide Me process. Pay particular attention to the video on Passive Activity Rules as this is the area most taxpayers do not fully understand.

After you have reviewed the rules, TurboTax prompts you for a description of the property, the type of property, and whether you materially participate in the property that generated income. Again, use the Guide Me feature if you are unsure of how the rules apply to your particular situation.

Figure 3.45

Review the tax rules with TurboTax before you start entering your data.

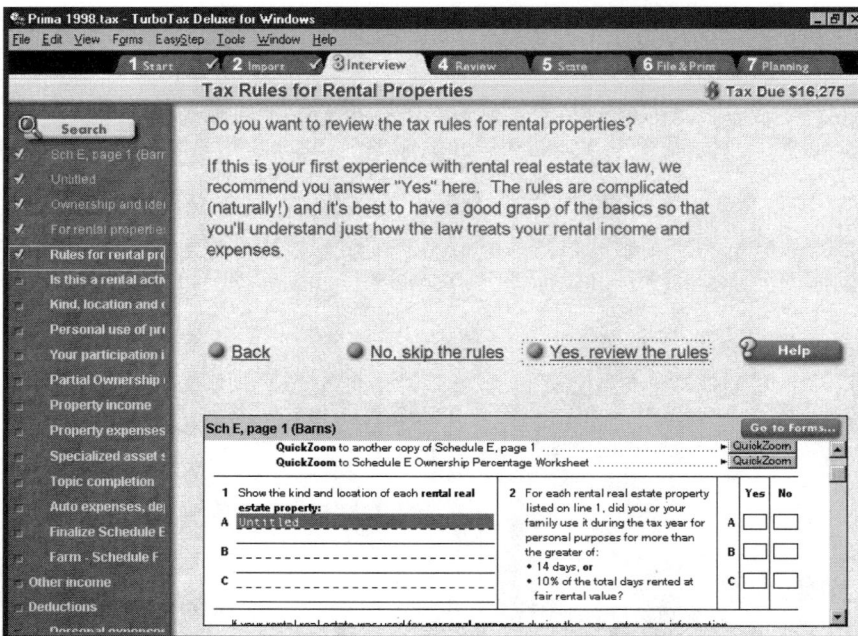

> Will Rogers once said that "income tax has made more liars out of the American people than golf has."

Follow the on-screen prompts to specify the ownership percentages and enter your income and expense data for this property. If you received a 1099-MISC for this property, TurboTax will give you an opportunity to enter those amounts. The expense data entry screen (see Figure 3.46) is very similar to the Schedule C expense area covered earlier in this chapter.

After you enter your expenses, TurboTax prompts you to specify the carry-overs, asset depreciation, asset sales and auto expenses related to the rental or royalty property. Again, the screens and procedures are the same as covered in the Schedule C section. When you have completed entering the data for this Schedule E, you can add up to two more properties on this Schedule E, create another Schedule E to enter more property data, or finish with Schedule E.

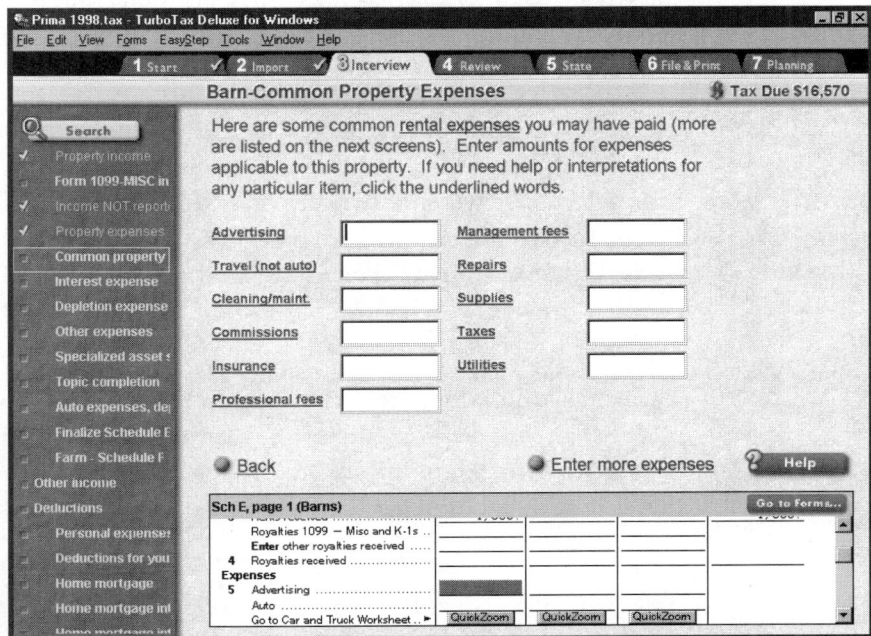

Figure 3.46

TurboTax uses the same data entry screens for Schedule E as were used for Schedule C.

Reporting Farm Income

If you are a farmer, you'll be happy to know that TurboTax can help you complete Schedule F (Profit or Loss from Farming) and the landowner's version, Form 4835 (Farm Rental Income and Expenses). The Interview process is similar for both operator-owners and landowner-renters. However, the rules and regulations surrounding farm tax law is complex and can be overwhelming for those new to it. Unless you've prepared your farm tax forms before, I strongly suggest that for this first time you do this with the help of your accountant or tax advisor (who is knowledgeable in farm tax law). The last thing you want to do is miss a tax credit or overpay your taxes!

The Interview for farming starts out very similarly to that just discussed for Schedule C sole proprietorships. First, you name your farm, and then you provide basic information, such as who owns the farm (such as you or your spouse), the principal farm product (such as milk), the principal agricultural activity code (options are provided), the EIN, and the method of accounting (cash or accrual). Next, TurboTax checks to make sure that you have materially participated (see earlier discussion in the section on partnership K-1s). Use the Guide Me feature and FAQs for help in answering these questions.

As you can see in Figure 3.47, TurboTax prompts you to list the income you received from common farming activities, including amounts from cooperative distributors. As you continue through the Interview, enter any agricultural program payments (usually reported to you on Form 1099-G), any commodity credit corporation loans (CCC loans), and crop insurance proceeds/disaster payments (Forms 1099-MISC or 1099-G). The last income question provides you with an opportunity to list any other income the farm might have received.

The expense questions are very similar to the Schedule C expense questions, except that the categories are farm-oriented. The FAQs try to provide you with answers to commonly asked questions; for a fuller discussion, read IRS Publication 225 (Farmer's Tax Guide).

The handling of vehicles and assets used in farming is identical to the Schedule C approach—except again, the tax law and terms are farm-oriented. The same is true also of the Interview process and questions concerning the sale of vehicles or assets used in the farming business. If necessary, review the earlier discussions on Schedule C and you'll be up to speed in no time.

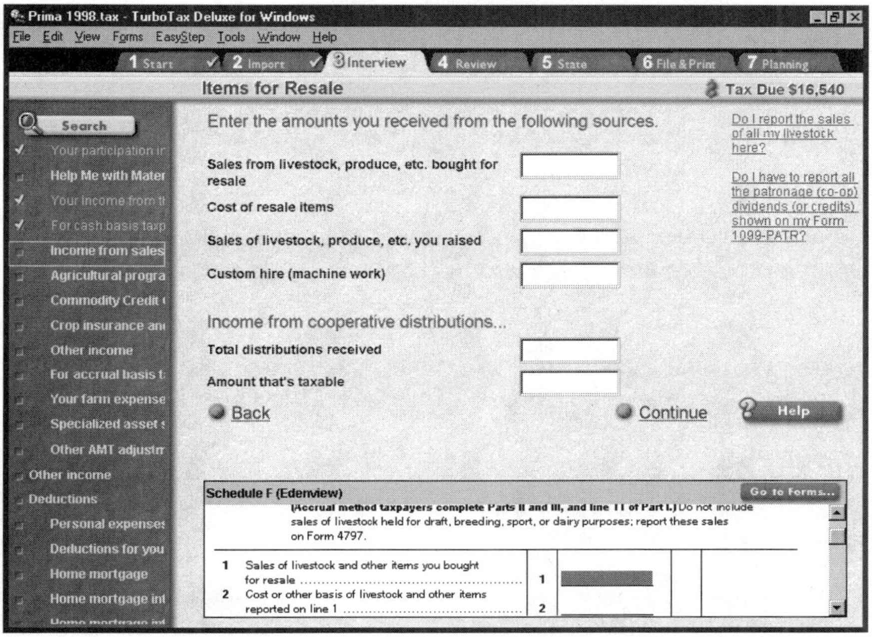

Figure 3.47

TurboTax can help you "milk" a few tax dollars back into your pocket.

If you had a profit from the farm business, you might be able to deduct health insurance coverage for yourself and your family. TurboTax walks you through the complicated rules and posts the appropriate deduction (if any) to your tax return.

The last expense question provides you with an opportunity to enter any other farming expenses (description and amount). The next Interview covers less-common situations. Here again are the now-familiar at-risk and passive-activity questions. In addition to these is a query on whether you had any Section 179 carryover amounts (see last year's return) and whether you sold conservation property. Review the FAQs and IRS Publications listed on screen for a full description of these less-common situations. Check all that apply and click on Next.

The last screen provides you with an opportunity to edit information on an existing farm, enter information for a new farm, or click on No, I'm Done with Farms.

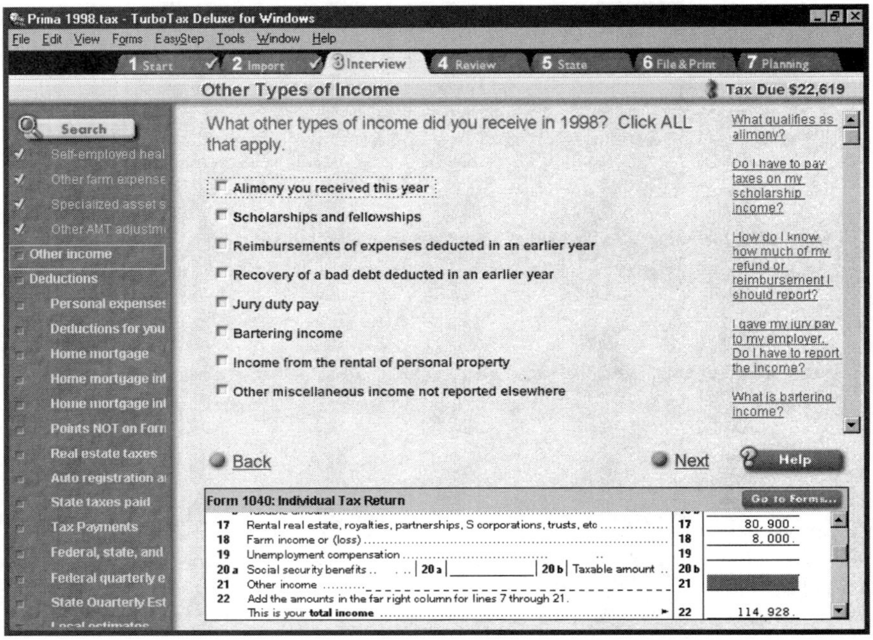

Figure 3.48

Be sure to list amounts for any other types of income you might have.

Entering Other Income

The last Interview question provides you with an opportunity to list any additional items of income (see Figure 3.48). Special rules apply to alimony, scholarships, and bartering income that you might have received. Click on the hyperlinks to learn more about how these rules affect your tax return.

What's Next?

Dinner! I'm starved. Hopefully your significant other and little tax deductions have your dinner all prepared and waiting for you. When you come back tomorrow morning, you'll explore the deductions and exemptions that you might be able to take, determine your tax credits and payments, and find out your total refund (or tax due).

Finishing Your Federal Tax Return

Good morning! If you are following the "In a Weekend" theme, it's Sunday morning and you're almost done with your federal tax return. Yesterday afternoon you entered your income amounts. This morning, you will enter the remaining adjustments to gross income, deductions, tax credits, and additional taxes due. As they say, there's no time like the present. So, dive right in.

Luckily, the IRS does not tax you based on your gross income. You are allowed several adjustments and deductions that reduce your taxable income. Even if you don't qualify for one of the "special rules," you can always count on the standard deduction (unless someone else claims you as a dependent—then they get the standard deduction). Your (hopefully) reduced taxable income is then multiplied by a tax rate based on your filing status (Married Filing Joint, Single, etc.), resulting in your initial tax liability. You can then reduce that tax liability with tax credits (if you qualify). However, the tax may increase if you owe other types of taxes, such as self-employment tax or alternative minimum tax. This session covers your deductions, your tax credits, and, most important, your prior tax payments. At the end of this session, you will know your tax due amount or the refund amount owed you by the IRS.

In this session, you will

- ✪ Learn about the adjustments to gross income
- ✪ Determine your standard tax deduction
- ✪ Enter your itemized deductions

- ✿ Enter your prior tax payments
- ✿ Review your tax liability
- ✿ Compute additional taxes due
- ✿ Explore the available tax credits

Adjusting Your Gross Income

Going to the chiropractor to get your back adjusted takes time and money. With TurboTax, your back doesn't get adjusted, but your gross income does—and you don't have to spend any more time or money. Throughout the Interview process, TurboTax has been collecting information from you on possible adjustments, deductions, credits, and payments that might apply to you. Many of the tax adjustments (such as IRA contributions and medical savings plans) have already been entered into the system and posted to the appropriate tax forms.

Take a moment to review your gross income (entered in the Saturday Afternoon session) and the current adjustments to gross income that TurboTax has already posted to your tax return.

NOTE If you are using Form 1040EZ, no adjustments or itemized deductions are allowed. You are allowed a standard deduction, the Earned Income Credit, and can enter tax payments from your W-2. However, that is all you can enter on a 1040EZ. So, as you are working through this chapter, if you see an itemized deduction, a tax credit, or a tax payment that you need to enter, your return type will automatically be changed by TurboTax to 1040A or 1040 when you enter that amount. If later you decide that the amount did not bring you any tax benefits, you can remove the amount and TurboTax will revert your return type back to 1040EZ.

If you are using Form 1040A, one adjustment to your gross income for IRA contributions is allowed as are a handful of tax credits, but you cannot itemize deductions. As noted above for 1040EZ tax returns, you can explore these other adjustments, credits, and payments (which will convert your 1040A to a 1040), and if you are not satisfied, you can remove the amounts and return to Form 1040A. Rest assured that, based on the data you enter, Turbo-Tax will print the appropriate forms.

Reviewing Your Work in Process

At any time during the Interview process, you can switch over to the tax forms to review your return or view tax forms not yet in your return. So far, you've been using the Go to Forms button (see Figure 4.1) to display the tax form for which the Interview question is collecting data. In some cases TurboTax collects data on a worksheet that later is posted to a tax form.

Use the menu to open a tax form by choosing Forms, Open a Form. Turbo-Tax displays the Open Form dialog box shown in Figure 4.2. Notice that at the top of the dialog box, you can set options:

- **Show My Return**. Lists all the forms in your tax return so far.
- **Open a Form**. Lists all the forms included with TurboTax, not just the ones you've used so far.

You can use the Open Form dialog box to see the first page of your tax return by following these steps:

1. Choose Forms, Open a Form.

Click here to see tax forms.

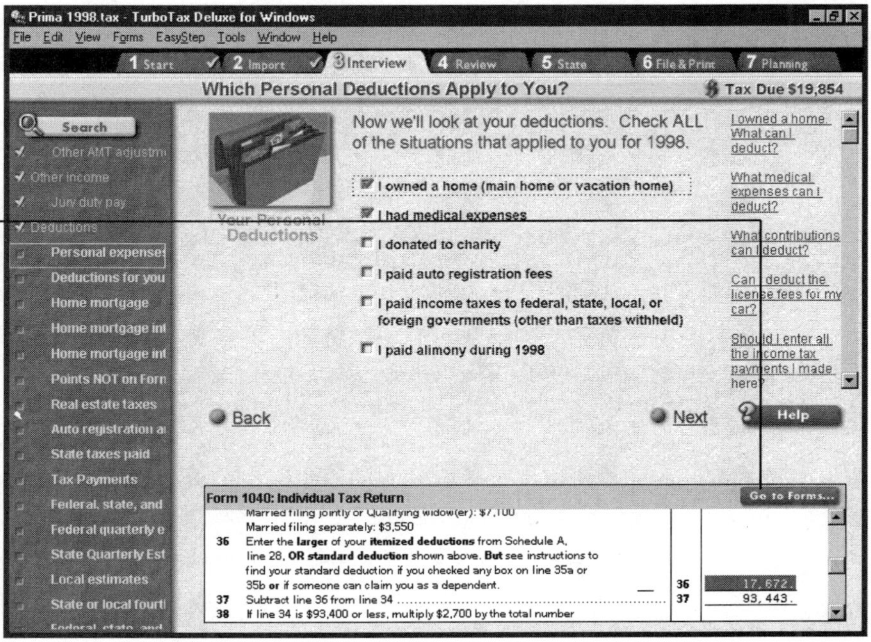

Figure 4.1

The current Interview topic shown here is your personal deductions.

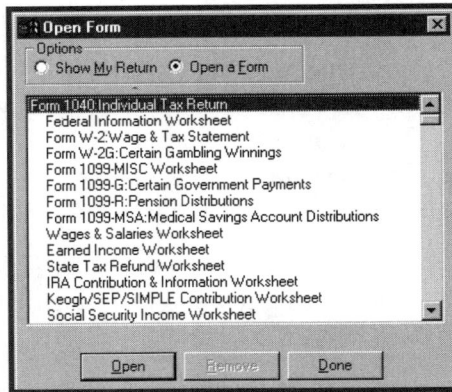

Figure 4.2

Use the Open Form dialog box to quickly jump to a specific tax form.

2. Select the option Show My Return.

3. Choose Form 1040, 1040A, or 1040EZ as applicable.

4. Click on the Open button. The form opens with the cursor in the current field.

5. Press Page Up as many times as needed to scroll up to the top of the form. Figure 4.3 shows the top portion of my fictitious family's Form 1040.

Read over your tax return. If you spot a mistake, such as an incorrect address or misspelled name, you can correct it right on the form (no need to return to the Interview). If you need more detail behind a number, click on the number. A magnifying glass appears to the left of the number (provided details exist for that number). When you click on the magnifying glass, TurboTax takes you to the supporting schedules and detail schedules (see Figure 4.4). This way you can drill down through your return and trace the numbers from the top down and back up again until you are comfortable with the amounts.

TIP Instead of using the magnifying glass, just double-click on a field, and TurboTax opens the underlying supporting schedule.

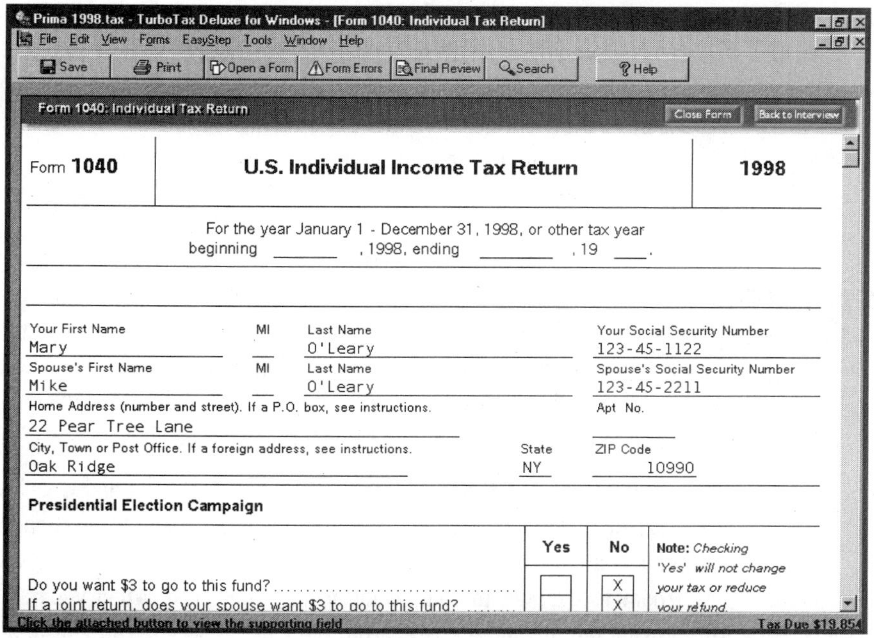

Figure 4.3

When you view the tax form, you can see where all your answers to the Interview questions went.

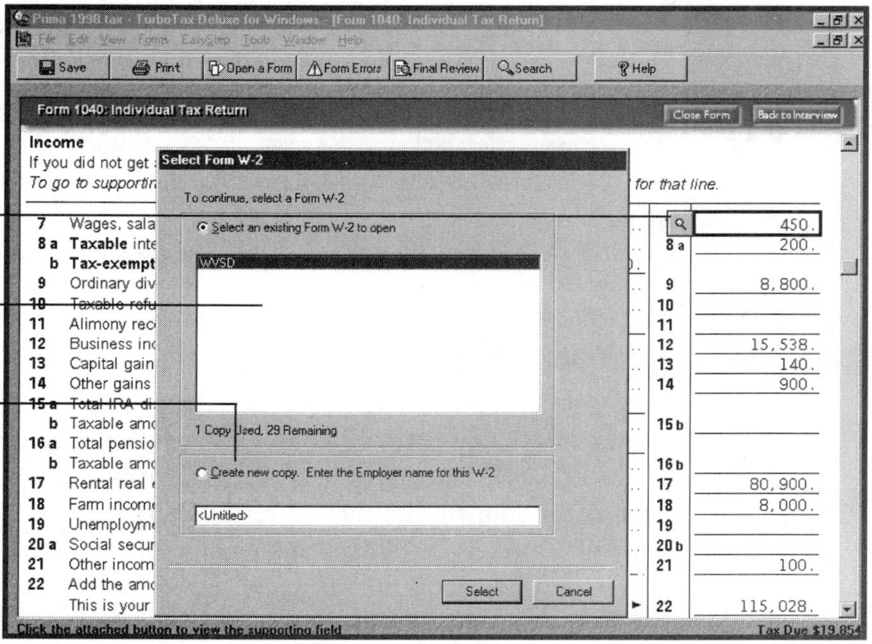

Click here ...

...to select a schedule here

... or create a new one here

Figure 4.4

Choose an existing schedule or create a new one.

NOTE   When changing amounts on a tax form, you always need to go to the bottommost level. For example, instead of changing your total wage amount on Form 1040, go to the W-2 that changed and edit the amount(s) there. TurboTax takes care of the math for you and posts the adjustments wherever necessary in your return.

CAUTION   If you try to edit Quicken imported data directly on the form, rather than using the TaxLink dialog box, TurboTax will display a warning message informing you that if you edit the data in TurboTax, the data will no longer be linked back to Quicken. To keep the live link between Quicken and TurboTax (and keep your financial and tax records in sync), always edit your imported data in Quicken and re-import it into TurboTax.

To edit imported Quicken data, choose File, TaxLink Import, Quicken TaxLink. When the TaxLink dialog box appears, locate the tax line amount to be changed, click on the Change Links button, and expand to select the detailed amount that you want to change. Click on Zoom to Quicken to change the value in Quicken. When you're done editing your data in Quicken, minimize Quicken (do not close Quicken) and edit data that is linked back to Quicken. TurboTax will automatically update the TaxLink dialog box to show your edited data. You can then click on Import to post the new data to the various tax forms.

NOTE   The Back to Interview button always takes you back to where you left off in the Interview, not to the Interview question for that tax form. To return to the Interview area for a tax topic, use the Interview Navigator.

Determining Your Gross Income

As you page down through your tax return, you will see the line for total income (line 22 on Form 1040), meaning your total gross income. The next section deals with the adjustments to gross income allowed by the IRS. Table 4.1 lists the adjustments allowed for Form 1040A and Form 1040 filers. If you had expected an adjustment amount that TurboTax is not showing, return to that topic in the Interview and review your responses. In the case of some self-employment adjustments, TurboTax has not yet completed the Interview on these topics. By the end of this session, your self-employment tax (if any) will be computed and the related adjustments will be determined and posted to this area.

TIP

You can always use the Interview Navigator's Search feature to search for a topic. Just click on the Search button in the Navigator to open the Navigation Search Dialog box (see Figure 4.5). Enter the word(s) you want to search for, and click on the Search button in the dialog box to view a list of Interview topics that deal with that issue. Select a topic and click on the Jump To button to go to that Interview topic. If the topic requires that you answer a prior set of Interview questions before advancing to that topic, you will be prompted to do so. For example, before TurboTax can determine the deductibility of alimony you paid, you first need to answer the questions in the Interview topic on other income. If the Navigator Search lists more than one topic, look for the topic that says, "Found under: interview."

Click here . . .

. . . to open this search dialog box

Figure 4.5

The Navigator Search feature can help you jump to the correct Interview topic.

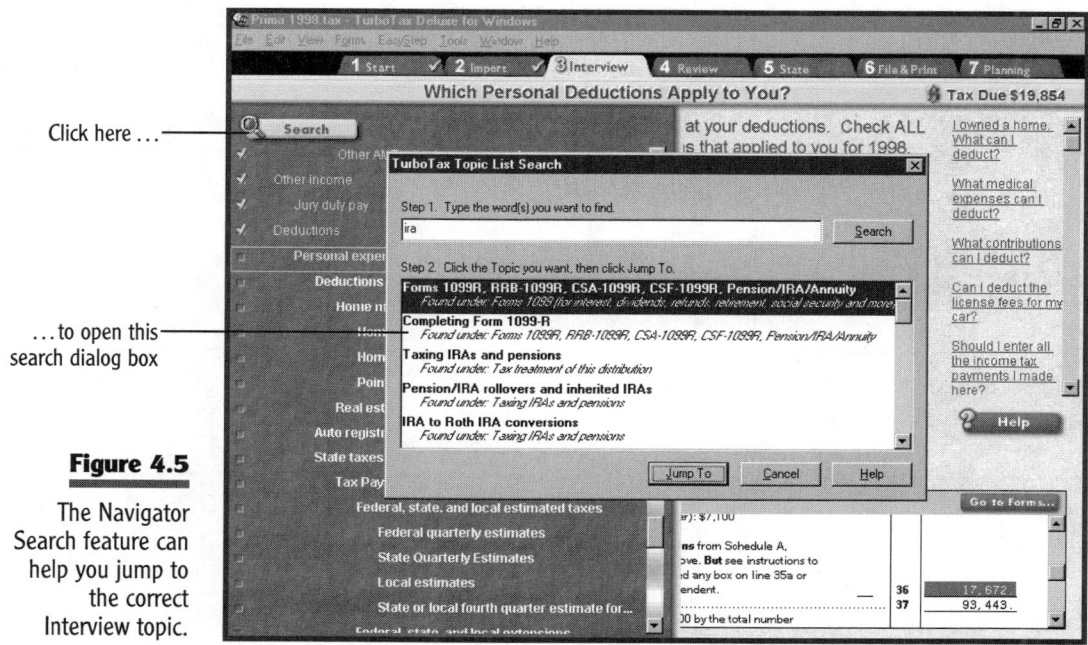

TABLE 4.1 ADJUSTMENTS TO GROSS INCOME

Adjustment	Description	See Interview Topic
IRA deduction	Deductions are allowed for contributions to qualified IRAs.	Contributions to retirement plans, IRAs, and MSAs; IRA custodial fees; and Form 1099R
Student loan interest	Deductions are allowed for interest on a qualified student loan.	Student loan interest
Medical savings account (MSA)	For self-employed taxpayers, or those employed by a qualified small business and who have high-deductible health coverage, deductions for contributions to an MSA may be allowed as an adjustment.	Form 1099-MSA; Contributions to retirement plans, IRAs, and MSAs
Moving expenses	Deductions are allowed for certain moves made because of job relocation.	Reimbursed moving expenses; Moving expenses
One-half of self-employment tax	For self-employed taxpayers, 50 percent of the additional self-employment tax you pay is deductible from your gross income.	Taxes on self-employment income
Self-employed health insurance	Forty-five percent of qualified health insurance premiums is deductible (subject to certain limitations) when payments are made by self-employed taxpayers and S-corp shareholders with greater than a 2 percent holding	Self-employed health insurance
Keogh, SEP, and SIMPLE plans	Contributions to retirement plans such as Keogh, SEP, and SIMPLE plans are deductible, subject to certain limitations.	Contributions to retirement plans, IRAs, and MSAs
Penalty on early withdrawal of savings	The interest penalty imposed by a financial institution for withdrawing savings before the maturity date is deductible (usually reported to you on Form 1099-INT, box 2).	Form 1099-INT; Other income

TABLE 4.1 ADJUSTMENTS TO GROSS INCOME (CONTINUED)		
Adjustment	**Description**	**See Interview Topic**
Alimony paid	Alimony payments you made during 1998 (as required in a divorce decree, separation agreement, or support decree), if taxable to the recipient, are allowed deductions for you.	Alimony you paid this year; Other income
Other adjustments	Certain other, less-common expenses are deductible, such as jury duty pay that you remitted to your employer, qualified performing artist expenses, and contributions to a 501(c)(18) pension plan.	Other income

Review the adjustments on your tax return. Use the Navigator to jump to the corresponding Interview topic to enter new data, or edit existing data through the Navigator. If you feel comfortable filling out the forms yourself, double-click on the field for the adjustment and enter your changes into the supporting schedule(s).

Determining Your Standard Deduction

In an effort to minimize record-keeping and auditing requirements, the IRS created the standard deduction. The standard deduction is an amount that is available to all taxpayers as an alternative to itemizing deductions. You should only settle for the standard deduction if it exceeds your allowable itemized deductions. TurboTax follows that sage tax advice and interviews you on all possible itemized deductions for your situation. TurboTax does not ask you for data about deductions that do not apply to you. For example, if you rent rather than own a home, TurboTax won't ask you to enter mortgage interest or property tax information.

Once you've entered all the information on itemized deductions, TurboTax compares the allowable deduction to the standard deduction and automatically selects the better of the two options for you. Table 4.2 lists the standard deduction amounts available to taxpayers based on filing status.

TABLE 4.2 STANDARD DEDUCTION AMOUNTS

Filing Status	Standard Deduction Amount
Single	$4,250
Head of Household	$6,250
Married Filing Joint	$7,100
Married Filing Separate	$3,550
Qualifying Widow(er)	$7,100

NOTE You can't itemize deductions and take the standard deduction too: each taxpayer must choose one or the other.

The amounts listed in Table 4.2 apply to most taxpayers. However, there are a few exceptions. The standard deduction amount is higher for taxpayers who are blind or who are 65 years old or older. TurboTax uses the higher amount, provided you checked the blind and/or 65 and over boxes in the initial Interview.

To double-check your initial Interview responses in TurboTax, choose Forms, Show My Return, and then open the Federal Information Worksheet. Figure 4.6 shows the Federal Information Worksheet for my fictitious family.

Dependents who can be claimed on another taxpayer's return have a lower standard deduction (for those under age 65 who are not blind, the amount is $700). The amount differs based on filing status, age, and blindness. Turbo-Tax uses the lower deduction, provided the Federal Information Worksheet contains the correct information (age, dependent filer, and blindness).

Married people who decide to file separately must use the same method. In other words, if you decide to use the itemized deduction method, your spouse must do the same. TurboTax cannot check this requirement across tax

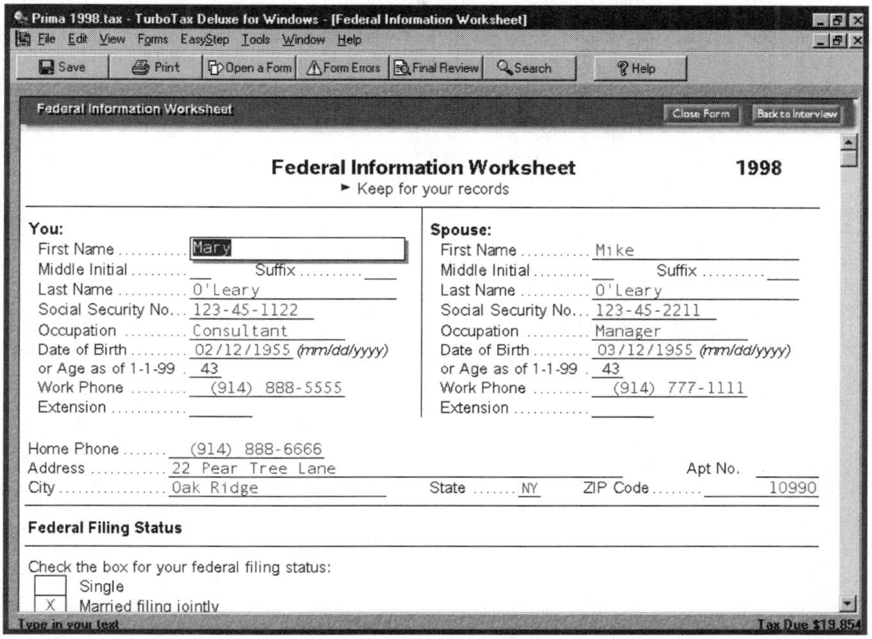

Figure 4.6

TurboTax uses the information on the Federal Information Worksheet to determine your standard deduction amount.

files. During the Review process, TurboTax will remind you of this need—but you must enforce this rule yourself.

◄◄◄

BUZZ WORD

Standard Deduction: The IRS allows you to reduce your adjusted gross income by a fixed amount, which is determined by filing status, age, and blindness.

Itemized Deduction: The IRS allows you to list specific expenses (such as medical bills, property taxes, and charitable contributions) instead of taking a standard deduction. The amount of these expenses is subject to certain limitations based on your adjusted gross income.

65 or Older: The IRS considers you 65 or older if your 65th birthday falls on or before January 1, 1999.

Blind: The IRS considers you blind if your doctor certifies in a letter that your vision, while you are wearing glasses or contact lenses, is no better than 20/200 in your best eye. Attach a copy of the letter to your tax return. If the letter states that your vision will never improve, future tax returns can just refer the IRS back to that first year's return.

◄◄◄

Itemizing Your Deductions

Even if you have always used the standard deduction in the past, you should familiarize yourself with the itemized deductions. The better you know the tax law, the better organized your tax and financial files will be. For example, if you didn't know that you could deduct the cost of TurboTax, you might throw the receipt away! (If you did throw the receipt away, ask the merchant for a copy soon.)

Understanding about itemized deductions can help you with tax planning too. Suppose you get a request in December for your annual March of Dimes contribution. If you are anticipating a large tax burden this year, you might want to pay it before the end of the year so that you get the deduction this year. On the other hand, if you think you won't be able to get an itemized deduction because of AGI limitations, you might want to postpone your contribution until January, hoping that next year's return will permit the deduction.

Some itemized deductions, such as medical and dental expenses, are limited to a percentage of AGI as a floor (.075 times your AGI is disallowed as a deduction). The result is that you are only able to deduct the amount over the floor. Other deductions are subject to a ceiling based on AGI. For example, some charitable donations are limited to 50 percent of your AGI. When all is said and done, the IRS then limits your total allowable deductions if your AGI exceeds a certain threshold ($124,500 MFJ, $62,250 MFS). The final limitation reduces your total itemized deductions by 3 percent of the excess of your AGI above the threshold amount. But only the itemized deductions subject to the 3 percent rule are reduced (medical, dental, investment interest, casualty losses, theft losses, and gambling losses are not subject to reduction).

This is the time you stand up and sing, "Hallelujah! TurboTax does all that math *and* keeps track of all the rules for me!" Feel free to do a little jig too.

> I tried hard to figure out my adjusted gross income. I adjusted it, and it's still gross.

Close any forms that you have opened, and then return to the Interview where you left off in Figure 4.1. TurboTax asks you to check all the situations that apply to you (such as whether you own a home or give to charity). Based on your responses, TurboTax customizes the Interview process to better match your situation. Go ahead and check the appropriate boxes, and then click on <u>Next</u> when you are ready.

Deducting Home Interest and Taxes

TurboTax begins by interviewing you (if you are a homeowner) on deductions for your home, such as home mortgage interest (see Figure 4.7). The video does a good job of explaining the deductibility of mortgage interest and points. Take a moment to read over the FAQs to see if any apply to you. When you are ready, click on <u>Continue</u> to start the Interview on mortgage interest and points.

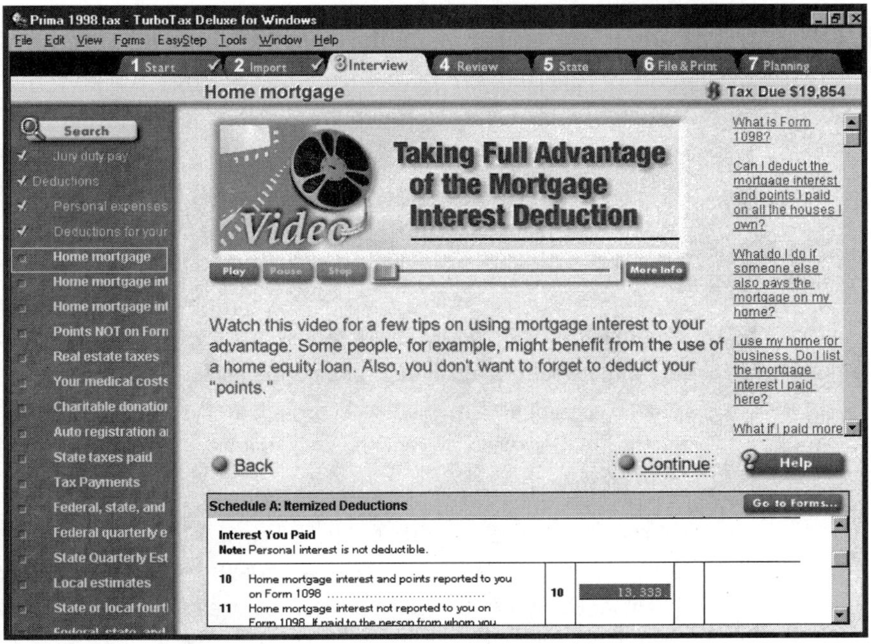

Figure 4.7

Points paid at closing may be deductible too.

Financial institutions are required to complete Form 1098 to report to the IRS the amounts you paid on mortgage interest and points paid at closing. Most lending institutions combine the Form 1098 reporting requirements with their own year-end statement, so if you can't find yours, look at the year-end statement (which may also list property taxes paid on your behalf, hazard insurance, and principal paid to date).

TurboTax asks if you received Form 1098 for your mortgage interest and points, or if you paid such amounts and didn't receive a Form 1098. Check the boxes as applicable, and then click on Continue. If you paid interest or points but received no Form 1098, TurboTax prompts you to enter the lender's name, address, and SSN or ID Number (if known).

Mortgage interest is only deductible if it relates to your primary home or to a second, vacation home. The rules regarding vacation homes are very strict, meant to deter those in the business of renting homes from taking the vacation home interest deduction. Refer to the Help system for more information on vacation home rules, or read over the sections on personal use of a vacation home in IRS Publications 17 and 527.

When prompted, enter the name of the lender and the mortgage interest plus points that you paid during 1998. Enter the amounts for each mortgage (Form 1098) on a separate line. Click on Continue, and then enter the real estate taxes that you paid on your home and/or vacation home (see Figure 4.8). Read over the FAQs to see if any of the issues presented apply to your situation. When you are done, click on Next.

TIP

You may have noticed by now that unless you check the appropriate box to let TurboTax know that you have data for a certain tax situation, TurboTax will not interview you on that topic. For example, in Figure 4.1 if you didn't check the box indicating that you had a home, TurboTax won't present you with Figure 4.8 asking you for the real estate taxes you paid on your home(s).

To correct the situation, just use the Navigator to move back to the "Which Apply To You?" screen, or use the Back button to move backward in the Interview process until you find the phantom check box. Check the box(es) you need and click on Next or Continue to register your answer and move ahead.

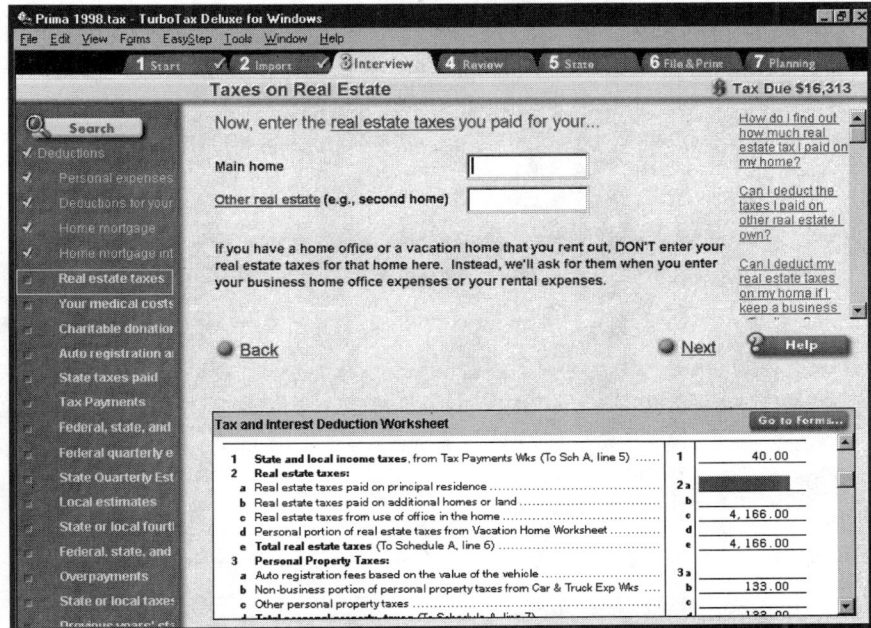

Figure 4.8

You can deduct the real estate taxes you paid on your home.

Deducting Medical and Dental Costs

After home mortgage interest, points, and taxes, the next Interview topic, "Common Medical Expenses," covers medical and dental expenses (see Figure 4.9). Although everyone has medical costs, Congress only allows a deduction for excessive medical costs. Medical expenses must exceed 7.5 percent of your AGI to be deductible. Once you do exceed the 7.5 percent AGI floor, then the amounts are deductible and not subject to any other floors (such as the 3 percent reduction for high AGI taxpayers).

If you have high medical costs, you are married, and both you and your spouse work, you might want to try filing separately so that one of you is able to deduct the medical costs. Doing so might lower your overall tax burden.

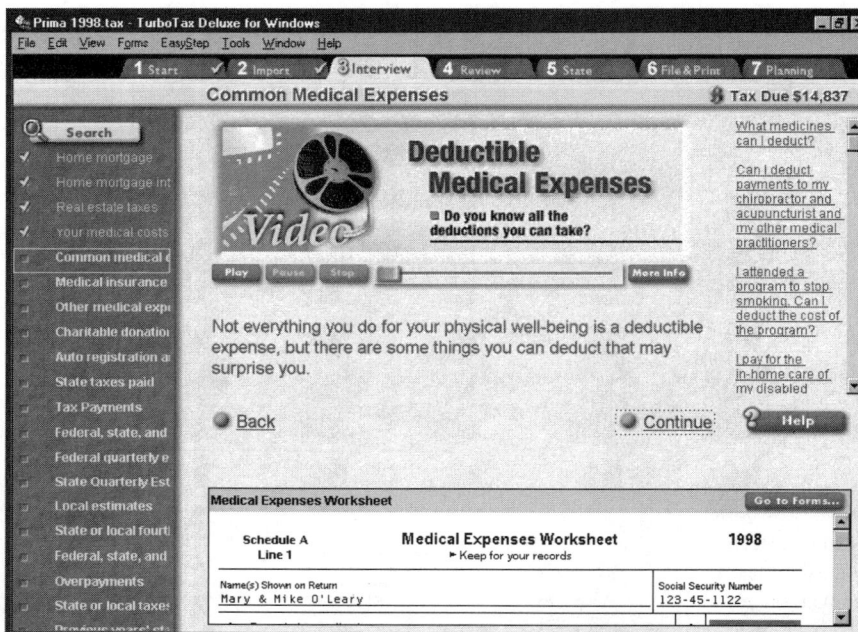

Figure 4.9

TurboTax provides a very good video on deducting medical expenses.

TIP

To save yourself some time here, check to see if you even have enough medical expenses to warrant entering this data. Choose Tools, Calculator to open the pop-up calculator. Point at the $ Tax Due button at the top of your screen to display the Tax Summary pop-up listing. If you can't see the Tax Summary because the calculator is in your way, move the calculator by dragging its title bar to a new location. The first item, Income and Adjustments, is your adjusted gross income (AGI). Enter this amount into the calculator and multiply it by .075. The result is the amount of disallowed medical expenses. If your medical and dental expenses do not even come close to the limitation, you might want to skip ahead to the next Interview topic (use the Navigator). For example, if your AGI is $50,000, you need to have more than $3,750 of medical expenses in order to have any medical deduction.

Medical expenses are one of the financial areas that you need to keep track of for tax purposes. If you use a program such as Quicken to electronically keep your checkbook, create a category called "medical" and record your payments to that category as they occur during the year. At year-end, print out a listing of the payments and check off those that are deductible. Of course you still need to keep your proof of the payments as being medical expenses (such as cancelled checks, bills from the doctor, and receipts for medicine).

But which medical and dental expenses are deductible? Play the video on deductible medical expenses for an overview. Then click on the More Info button to see a listing of IRS Publications. Publication 502 deals specifically with medical and dental expenses. In addition, read over the FAQs to see if any of the issues apply to your situation. The Tax Help area also provides you with specific examples of what is and is not deductible. Table 4.3 lists some examples of what you can and cannot deduct.

TABLE 4.3 EXAMPLES OF MEDICAL EXPENSES

Deductible Medical Expenses	Nondeductible Medical Expenses
Visits to doctors, dentists, chiropractors, acupuncturists, or other professionals who provide medical care.	Amounts paid out to a nurse to cook, clean, or do other housework.
Cosmetic surgery to correct a disfiguring disease, damage resulting from an accident, or a genetic disfigurement.	Cosmetic surgery done to enhance personal appearance.
Home remodeling to provide wheelchair access for a physically handicapped person.	New kitchen with counters too high for a wheelchair-bound person to use.
Artificial limbs, eyeglasses, contact lenses, hearing aids, prosthetic devices, Seeing Eye dog, or wheelchair.	Payment for otherwise qualified medical expenses of others (you can only deduct your paid expenses for yourself, your spouse, or your dependents). For the purpose of this rule, children and parents who would otherwise qualify as your dependent—except for the gross income test—can be treated as your dependent for medical expenses you pay.

TABLE 4.3 EXAMPLES OF MEDICAL EXPENSES (CONTINUED)

Deductible Medical Expenses	Nondeductible Medical Expenses
Air-cleaning system for allergy sufferer, pool for physical therapy when prescribed by a doctor, or a weight-reduction program prescribed by a doctor for treatment of a specific disease, hospital care, or lab fees.	Medical expenses of pets (too bad!) unless the animal qualifies as a medical need, such as a Seeing Eye dog.
Medicine, insulin, or telephone equipment for a hearing-impaired person.	Medicines or medical treatments deemed illegal in the state or location where you took the medicine or had the treatment.
Premiums paid for medical insurance, including most long-term care insurance contracts.	Expenses paid for things meant to improve your health, such as a vacation (darn!) and programs to help you quit smoking or lose weight.
Miles driven for medical purposes (10 cents per mile).	Health insurance reimbursements for medical expenses, which in themselves reduce otherwise deductible medical expenses.

CAUTION

Be sure to keep the proof of payment, doctor's letter, hospital bills, receipts, or any other items that support your deduction. When in doubt, consult your tax advisor.

When you are ready to proceed, click on <u>Continue</u>. TurboTax begins the Interview by asking you to fill in the amounts for various medical expenses (see Figure 4.10). Enter the medical costs that you believe to be qualified. For the total medical miles driven, you should have a mileage log that specifies where you drove to and from and the odometer reading at each location. To move to the next set of Interview questions, click on <u>Continue</u>.

The next set of Interview questions (see Figure 4.11) focuses on medical insurance premiums and medical savings accounts (MSAs). Medical insurance

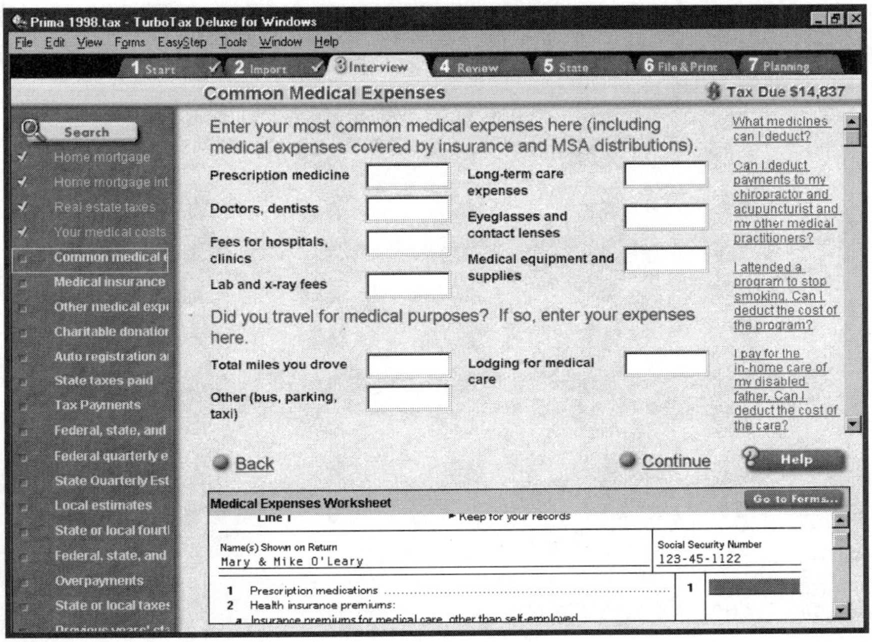

Figure 4.10

Eyeglasses and contact lenses are deductible medical expenses.

premiums that you pay—and on which you pay taxes—are deductible. For example, your employer may withhold medical insurance premiums from your paycheck—but if the amount isn't taxed, you can't deduct the premiums. The golden rule is that, if the amount is included in your gross income reported in box 1 of your W-2, then the medical premium you paid is deductible. Click on the Help button for more examples of nondeductible premiums.

If in this Interview you've already included a medical expense amount that was not net of the insurance company's reimbursement to you, enter the reimbursement amount in the Insurance Reimbursement box.

If you have an MSA and withdrew money during the year to pay medical expenses, enter the amount withdrawn in the MSA distribution received box. Do not enter your contributions to the MSA. TurboTax has already interviewed you on that item and posted the amount to Form 8853. If you missed this part of the Interview, use the Navigator's Search button to quickly move back and enter that information.

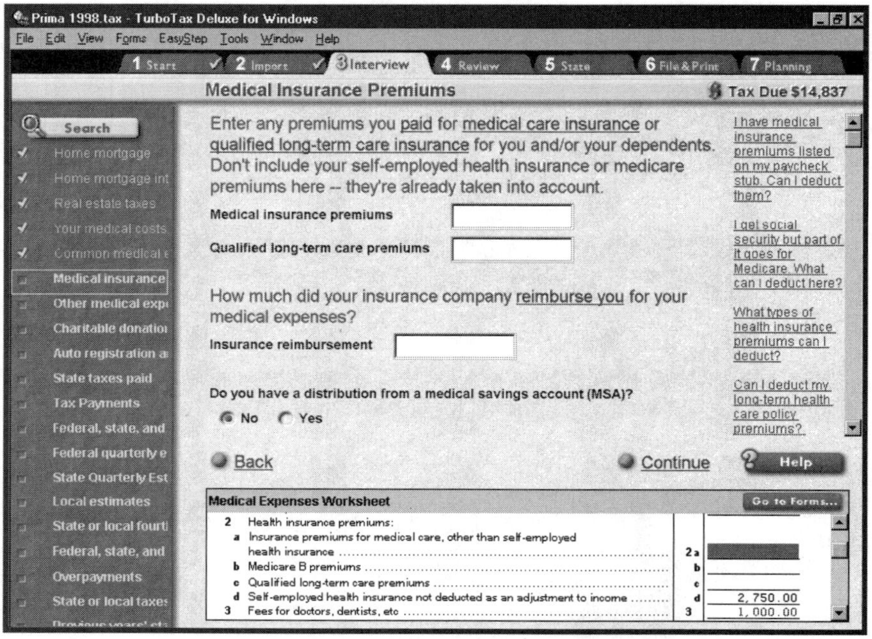

Figure 4.11

Medical insurance premiums might be deductible.

NOTE If you are self-employed and pay your own health insurance premiums, you should've already entered that amount as part of the Interview on your business (Schedule C, E, or F). TurboTax lists the amount on the Medical Expenses Worksheet's line 2(d) at the bottom of your screen. If you don't see an amount there, or if you need to check on the source of the amount there, right-click on the amount on line 2(d), and then choose Data Source from the pop-up menu. When the Data Source dialog box appears (see Figure 4.12), scroll down to review the source amounts. Then click on any amount to view the source form, schedule, or worksheet.

The last Interview question on medical expenses asks you to list any additional medical expenses that the Interview hasn't covered yet. At the top of the screen (see Figure 4.13), there is a link to the IRS Publication on medical expenses. The FAQs also provide some additional examples of deductible

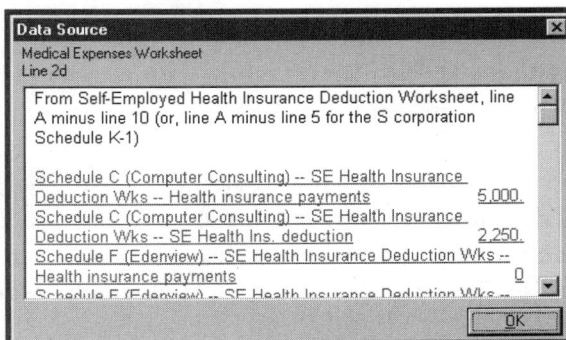

Figure 4.12

The Data Source dialog box lists all forms that support the selected amount.

and nondeductible medical expenses. When you are ready, enter a description of the medical expense and the amount for each deductible expense that you have. When you are finished, click on <u>Done with Medical Expenses</u> to go to the next Interview topic.

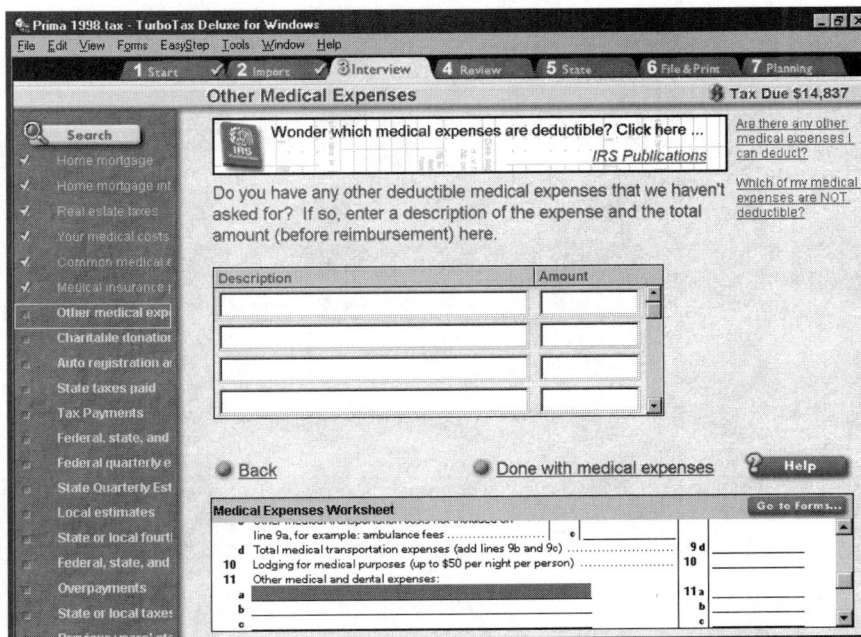

Figure 4.13

Enter your other medical expenses in the table provided.

Deducting Charitable Donations

It is always better to give than to receive, but it's okay to get a deduction for it too! So says Congress and the IRS. Keep in mind, however, that there are limitations and stringent record-keeping requirements based on the type of charity and donation. Furthermore, not all nonprofit organizations qualify as deductible donation charities. To start off, play the TurboTax video on deductible charitable donations (see Figure 4.14). Then review the FAQs, which provide many practical examples of charitable deductions.

When you click on <u>Charitable Donations</u>, the Tax Help window appears and provides you with the various rules and regulations. Table 4.4 helps you sort through these rules and summarizes the record-keeping and compliance requirements of each.

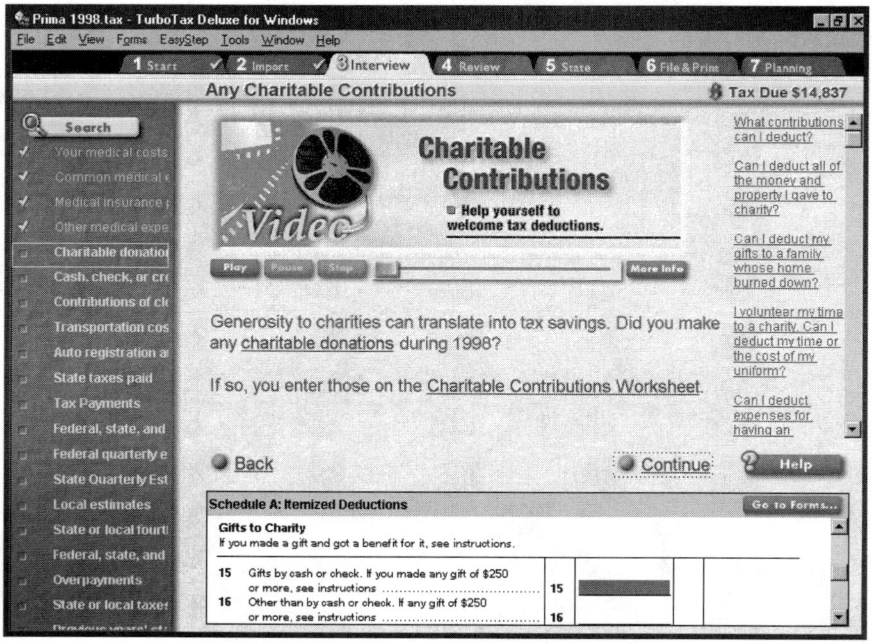

Figure 4.14

Not all charitable donations are deductible.

TABLE 4.4 CHARITABLE CONTRIBUTION RULES

Type of Donation	Record-Keeping and Compliance Rules
A single cash contribution less than $250 to a qualified charity	Keep the cancelled check or receipt as proof of donation.
A single cash contribution of $250 or more to a qualified charity	Keep the cancelled check and a letter or document from the charity acknowledging your donation, the amount, when received, and the purpose of the donation. If you received any goods or services in return (such as a dinner), the letter must indicate the fair market value of the goods or services received (this becomes the nondeductible portion).
A single noncash contribution less than $250 to a qualified charity	Keep a record of the name of the charitable organization, the location of where the contribution was made and the date, a reasonable description of the property donated, and if practical, a written acknowledgement from the organization containing this information. In addition, keep any records that pertain to the original cost basis of the item and its current fair market value. If you donated the property based on any condition, you will need to explain the conditions too.
A single noncash contribution of over $250 but less than $500	The same requirements apply as for noncash contributions less than $250, but you must have something in writing from the organization, which must state if you received any goods or services in return for the donated property (including the fair market value of those goods or services).
Noncash contributions of over $500 but less than $5,000	Form 8283 must be filed (which requires more details on the method used to determine the fair market value and other facts).
Single noncash contributions over $5,000	Form 8283 must be completed and in Part IV, the charitable organization must acknowledge the receipt of property.

NOTE   Timing can be everything!

- Contributions made by check that are mailed and dated on the last day of 1998 are deductible in 1998.

- Checks postdated to 1999 but mailed in 1998 are not deductible until 1999.

- Donations made by credit card are deductible when the charge is made.

- Donations made by online banking are not deductible until the payment date shown on the statement.

You can also deduct your out-of-pocket expenses having to do with the charitable organizations to which you donate your time and efforts. In 1998 you can deduct 14 cents per mile (up from the previous year's 12 cents) for the use of your car in giving service to charities. As with other mileage deductions, you need to keep an accurate mileage log. Parking fees, tolls, bus fare, and other transportation costs incurred on behalf of a charity are also deductible, as long as the charitable organization doesn't reimburse you for these costs. However, you cannot deduct the value of your donated time or services.

Contributions are subject to the 3 percent AGI floor. This means that your total allowable contributions will be reduced by 3 percent of your AGI if your AGI exceeds the limitation ($124,500 MFJ, $62,250 MFS).

In addition to this overall limitation, the IRS has spun quite a messy web with minilimitations by type of charity. Luckily, TurboTax keeps track of the threshold amounts for you and does all the tricky math. But if these limitations apply to you, you might be interested in the rules so that you can understand what TurboTax did.

If your total contributions are 20 percent of your AGI or less, you can skip this section because the limitations do not apply to you (consider yourself lucky!). For the rest of us Good Samaritans, here's the scoop. First, you need to ask someone at your charitable organization if it is a "50 percent limit" charity. Most of the time you should get the answer right off the bat. Some examples of 50 percent organizations include religious or educational

FIND IT ON ▶
THE WEB

WHICH ORGANIZATIONS ARE CHARITABLE?

How do you know that an organization qualifies as being a charitable organization? Well, for starters you can consult IRS Publication 526 (Cumulative List of Organizations), which lists qualified charitable organizations that have filed with the IRS. (This publication is not included in TurboTax, so call 800-TAX-FORM for a copy or refer to the online version at www.irs.ustreas.gov) You can also ask someone at the organization whether or not it qualifies— you should be able to get this information from most organizations.

In general, nonprofit organizations created in or under the laws of the United States and organized for charitable, religious, scientific, literary, or educational purposes or for the prevention of cruelty to children or animals qualify. Therefore, contributions to war veterans organizations, churches, synagogues, public parks, volunteer fire companies, the Red Cross, and the Boy Scouts are all qualified donations.

If you get something in return for your donation, the fair market value of the service or product that you receive is not deductible. For example, your dues to a religious organization are fully deductible. However, the tuition and book fees paid for your child to attend a religious school are not deductible. If you pay $50 for a Muscular Dystrophy Association fund-raising dinner, which has a fair market value of $35, you can only donate the remainder of $15.

Payments to homeowner associations, lobbying groups, chambers of commerce, social clubs, and sports clubs are not qualified donations. Even the value of the blood you donate to the local blood bank is not deductible (although it is an honorable donation). By the way, did you hear the one about the bloodsucking IRS agent?

organizations, hospitals, and publicly supported charities. Armed with this knowledge, you can then figure out the limitations:

- Contributions to a 50 percent limit charity are limited to 50 percent of your AGI.

- Contributions of capital gain property to a 50 percent limit charity are limited to 30 percent of your AGI.

- Contributions of capital gain property to a non-50 percent limit charity are limited to 20 percent of your AGI.

Of course, there are many loopholes and exceptions. If money is at stake, it's best to consult your tax advisor for guidance.

When you are ready, click on <u>Continue</u> so that you can customize the Interview to better meet your needs (see Figure 4.15). Based on your responses, TurboTax interviews you about your cash contributions, noncash contributions, transportation donations, and contribution carryovers.

Click on <u>Continue</u> to start entering your contribution amounts. For each cash contribution, TurboTax asks you to list the charitable organization's

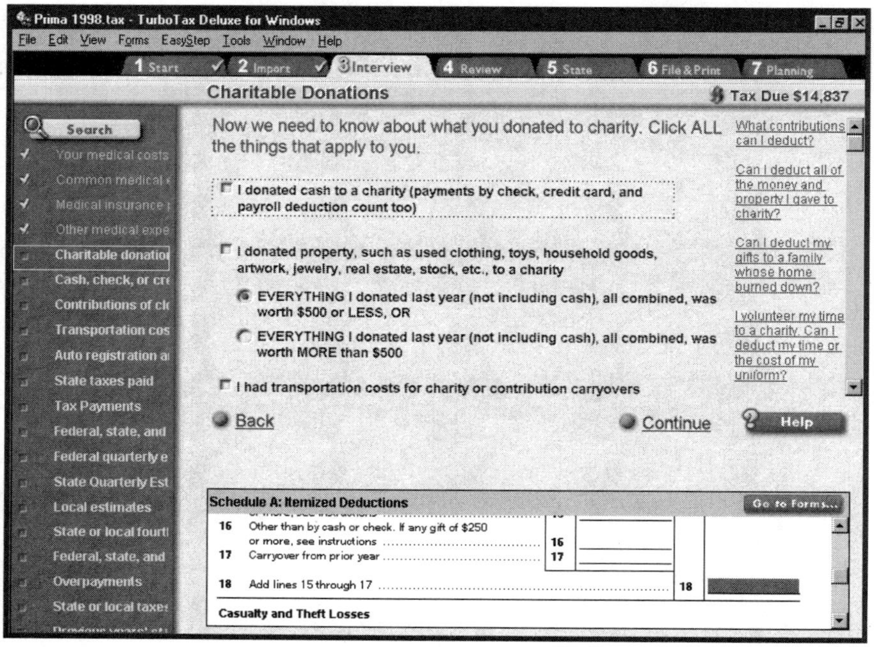

Figure 4.15

Review the FAQs for advice that may pertain to your situation.

name and the amount donated. If you made cash donations to a 30 percent charity, be sure to click on the Yes radio button at the bottom. Click on <u>Continue</u> to move ahead. If the donations were made to 30 percent charities, you must specify the organization type for each contribution and click on <u>Continue</u> again.

The next screen asks you about your noncash charitable contributions. Check the boxes which best describe your property donations and then click on <u>Continue</u>. For each property donation, TurboTax asks you to list the charitable organization's name, address, and describe the donated property. You will need to provide the donation date and value (including how you determined the value). Check the appropriate radio button to indicate the organization type as 50 percent, 30 percent, or a capital gain donation to a 50 percent or 30 percent organization. When you are finished, click on <u>Continue</u> to move ahead.

If you drove your vehicle while donating time to a charitable organization or had other transportation costs, enter those figures (see Figure 4.16). At the bottom of this screen, you can also let TurboTax know if you have any

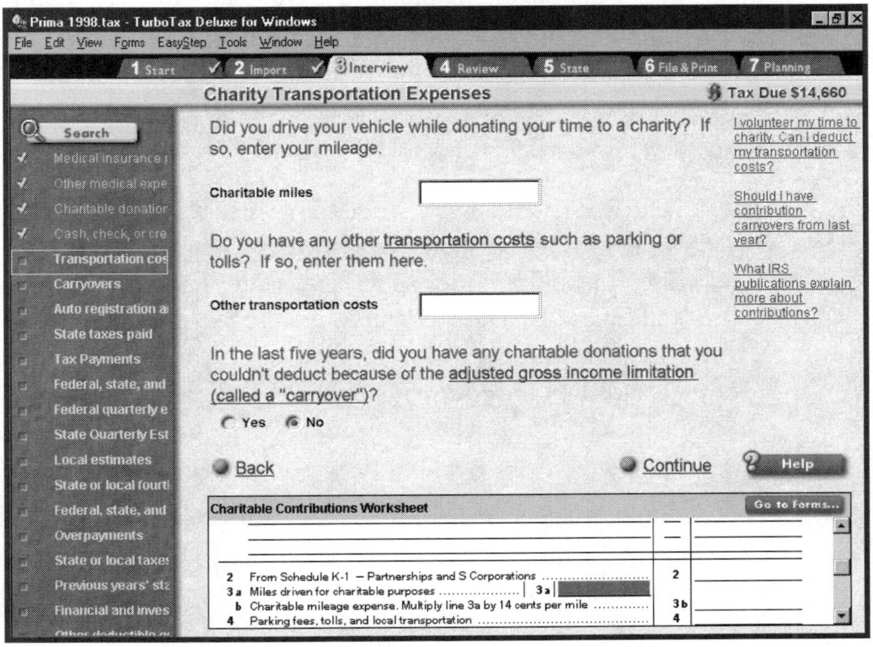

Figure 4.16

You can deduct the transportation costs you incurred for charity.

charitable contribution carryovers from previous years' returns (the past five years). If you rolled over your amounts from last year's TurboTax file, these amounts will be automatically carried over for you. Otherwise, review your returns for the past five years and note the contribution carryover amount, if any (see Form 8283 for the previous years' returns).

Take a Break

This would be a good place for you to take a break and stretch your legs a bit. So, go get some coffee, make some popcorn, or just walk around a little. When you come back, you'll continue entering your remaining deductions and any adjustments to gross income that you haven't been interviewed on yet.

Taking the Tax out of Taxing

The IRS realizes that to tax you on your tax payments would be, well, double taxation. You can take as a deduction taxes that you paid to state and local governments. TurboTax uses this opportunity to also ask you about any other tax payments that you have made for federal and state purposes that relate to this tax year, such as estimated tax payments and overpayments from previous years applied to this year.

Deducting Vehicle Taxes

The first Interview question on taxes pertains to a little-known deduction for your auto registration fees. If you use a car for business as well as for personal use, TurboTax not only reminds you of this nifty little deduction but also automatically takes into account the personal portion of your auto registration fee (see Figure 4.17). You can also deduct personal property tax or license fees for your car or other vehicles (including boats and recreational vehicles). Read over the FAQs to learn more about the deductibility of car license fees and personal property taxes.

Enter the personal property tax amounts for your vehicles, and click on Next.

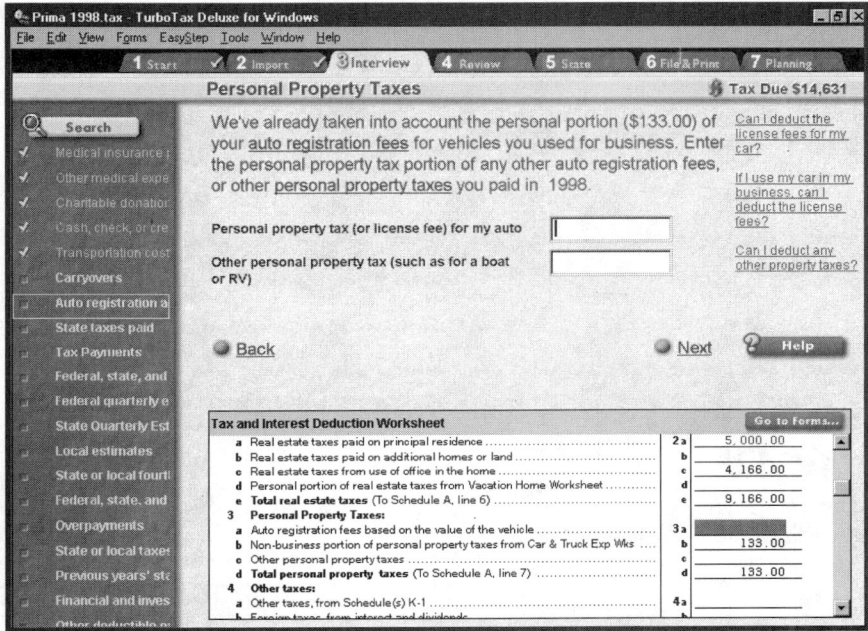

Figure 4.17

You can deduct the personal property taxes on your boat, airplane, or trailer

Entering Tax Payments

The next set of Interview questions provides you with an opportunity to customize the Interview process to meet your needs. Notice in Figure 4.18 that TurboTax asks you about all the taxes you paid to the IRS or states, not just the deductible portion. Some of the information that you enter here (such as state income taxes paid during the year) is used on Schedule A as a deduction. Some of the other information goes on Form 1040 or your state tax return in the section on taxes that you already paid for this year. Amounts from your W-2 for federal and state taxes withheld have already been posted to the correct form by TurboTax.

TIP

Unless you used TurboTax last year and rolled over your previous year's data into this year, you will need to pull out last year's federal and state returns and look at your tax payments. If you paid taxes, locate the cancelled check as proof that the IRS or the state received your payment. This will also serve as proof for any tax deduction you may take. If your bank doesn't provide you with cancelled checks, use your bank statement.

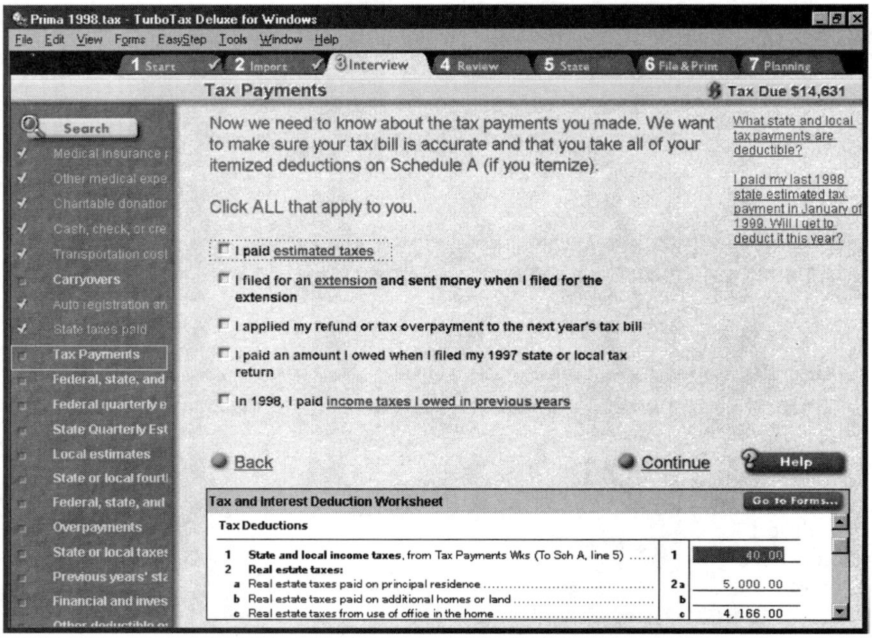

Figure 4.18

Don't forget to get credit for the taxes you have already paid!

◄◄◄◄◄◄◄◄◄◄◄◄◄◄◄◄◄◄◄◄◄◄◄◄◄◄◄◄◄◄◄◄◄◄◄◄◄◄◄

BUZZ WORD

Estimated Taxes: Taxes paid to federal and/or state taxing jurisdictions in addition to the taxes withheld from a paycheck. Estimated tax payments are usually made quarterly based on an estimate of the tax you expect to pay for that year. Sole proprietors and taxpayers with high nonwage income usually must pay estimated taxes to avoid underpayment penalties. TurboTax advises you of this need if it applies to your situation.

Extension: If you require additional time to gather and report the details of your tax return, you can send IRS Form 4868. Form 4868 grants you an automatic four month extension of time to file your completed tax return. On the extension form, you estimate your tax liability to the best of your abilities. You must pay any tax due with your extension. Most states follow the federal method. Note though that interest and penalties on late payment of any taxes not paid will still be imposed, regardless of the extension.

◄◄◄◄◄◄◄◄◄◄◄◄◄◄◄◄◄◄◄◄◄◄◄◄◄◄◄◄◄◄◄◄◄◄◄◄◄◄◄

TIP

If you use financial software such as Quicken, run a report for tax payments to get a quick listing of all taxes you've paid during 1998!

Start by looking at last year's federal and state returns. Then follow this handy checklist:

✔ Determine if you paid taxes during 1998 for your 1997 taxes. If so, pull out the cancelled checks and keep as proof for this tax return filing.

> ✔ If you paid state taxes with your 1997 tax return when you filed it in 1998, you can deduct the state tax payment on your 1998 federal tax return.

✔ Then look to see if you had an overpayment on your federal or state tax returns. Did you ask to have the overpayment sent to you (you would then see a deposit of the funds in your bank account) or applied to next year's (1998) taxes?

> ✔ If you received a refund of state taxes paid, then you need to list that money as income on your 1998 tax returns. Federal tax refunds do not constitute taxable income.

> ✔ If you applied the overpayment to your 1998 taxes, then you get credit for the additional payment and get to deduct any state taxes applied to 1998 taxes.

✔ Then look through your cancelled checks or financial software to see if you paid any additional taxes as a result of an audit, amended return, or estimated tax return.

> ✔ Additional state taxes paid resulting from an audit or amended return are deductible for federal purposes in the year paid.

> ✔ Estimated tax payments reduce your tax liability upon filing your 1998 return. The state portion is deductible for federal purposes in the year paid.

> ✔ Look for estimated state tax payments paid in 1998 for 1997 tax estimates. These are deductible in 1998.

> ✔ Local income tax payments are deductible too.

CAUTION The January 15 estimated state tax payment paid in 1999 is not deductible until you file your 1999 tax return. Similarly, the January 15 estimated state tax payment paid in 1998 is deductible on your 1998 tax return even though it applies to your 1997 estimated taxes!

Of course, TurboTax takes care of applying all these rules and making sure that you don't accidentally deduct a federal tax payment or miss a state tax deduction for 1998. All you need to do is gather the data and check the boxes that apply to you. Then, click on Continue to move on with the Interview.

The Interview provides you with a video on federal, state, and local estimated taxes and asks you to check boxes to indicate who you paid estimated taxes to: federal, state, or local. After you do this, click on Continue and begin entering the date paid and amount per quarter (see Figure 4.19).

Review the FAQs to learn about the importance of providing the exact date paid, the state and local codes, and dealing with overpayments. Enter your quarterly payment dates and amounts. If you have overpayments or other federal payments, click on I Have More Federal Estimated Tax Payments,

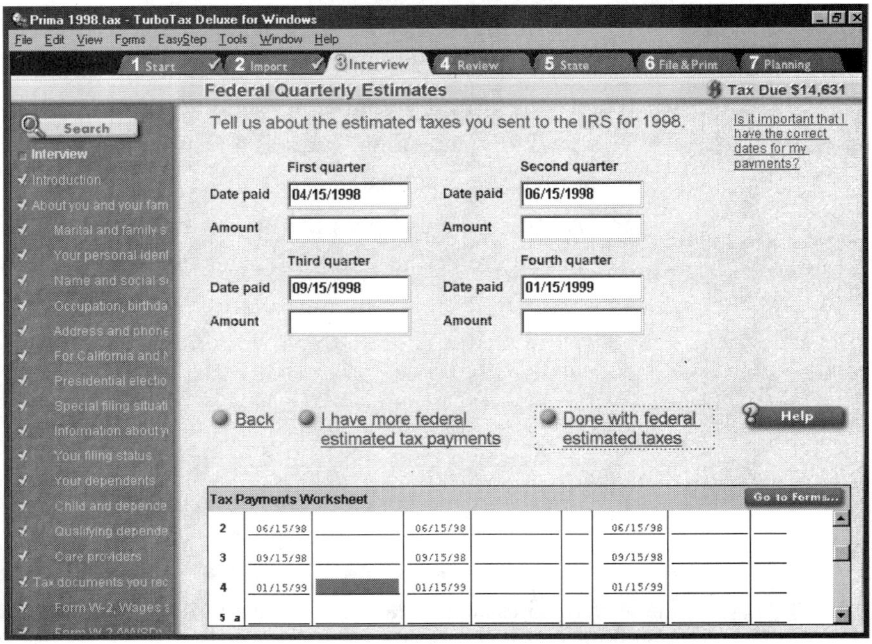

Figure 4.19

Be sure to enter the exact date paid so TurboTax can check for underpayment penalties and apply these to the correct tax year.

and enter those dates and amounts on the next screen. When you are finished, click on <u>Done with Federal Estimated Taxes</u>.

Next, do the same for state quarterly estimated payments (see Figure 4.20). When you are finished, click on <u>Done with State Estimated Taxes</u>. And then do the same for any local tax estimates that you paid.

If you paid a fourth quarter state or local estimated tax for 1997 in 1998, enter the amounts when prompted.

If you filed an extension, TurboTax asks you to enter the amounts paid. Next, the Interview asks you to enter any overpayments from 1997 that were applied to 1998. If you paid state or local taxes with your 1997 tax returns, TurboTax prompts you for those amounts and then asks if you had any other taxes paid during 1998 (such as from an audit or amended return).

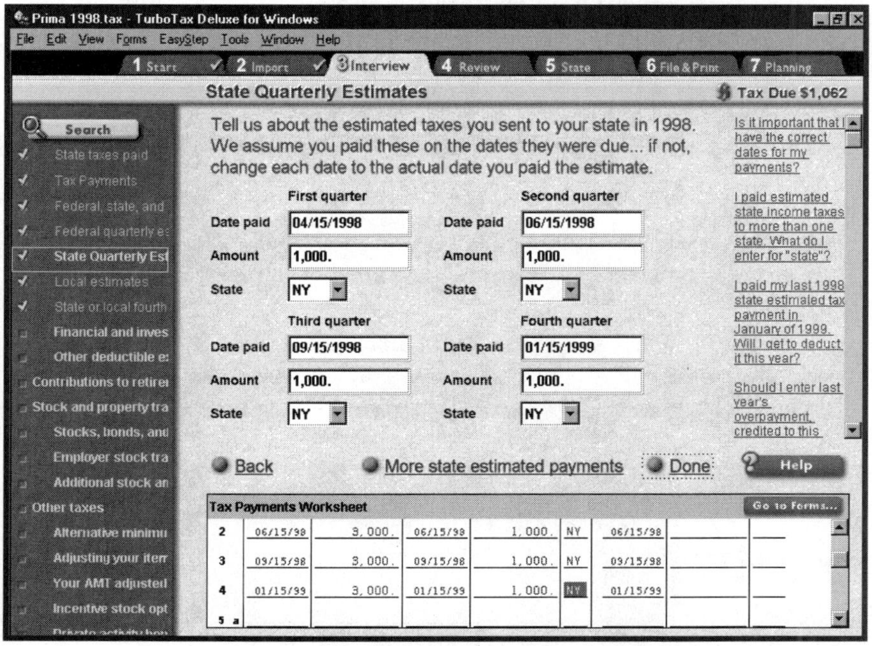

Figure 4.20

Enter your State Quarterly Estimates and other state tax payments here.

The last Interview question on taxes paid provides you with an opportunity to list any other deductible taxes, such as foreign taxes or certain inheritance taxes. Read over the FAQs to learn more about which taxes are deductible and which are not. When you are finished, click on <u>Done with Deductible Taxes</u>. This concludes the Interview on income taxes paid.

Deducting Financial Expenses

As you can see in Figure 4.21, there are many financial-related expenses that you might be able to deduct. You can, for example, deduct the fees paid to a tax preparer, a tax advisor, or an investment advisor; IRA custodial fees; and the cost of TurboTax as well as even the cost of this book! As with all deductions, make sure you have a receipt and proof of payment. In the case of tax software and books, it is a good idea to keep both with your tax records in case of an audit. You can only deduct amounts paid for in 1998. So, if you bought your tax software and tax book in 1999, file the receipt away in your 1999 tax deduction file for use on your 1999 tax return.

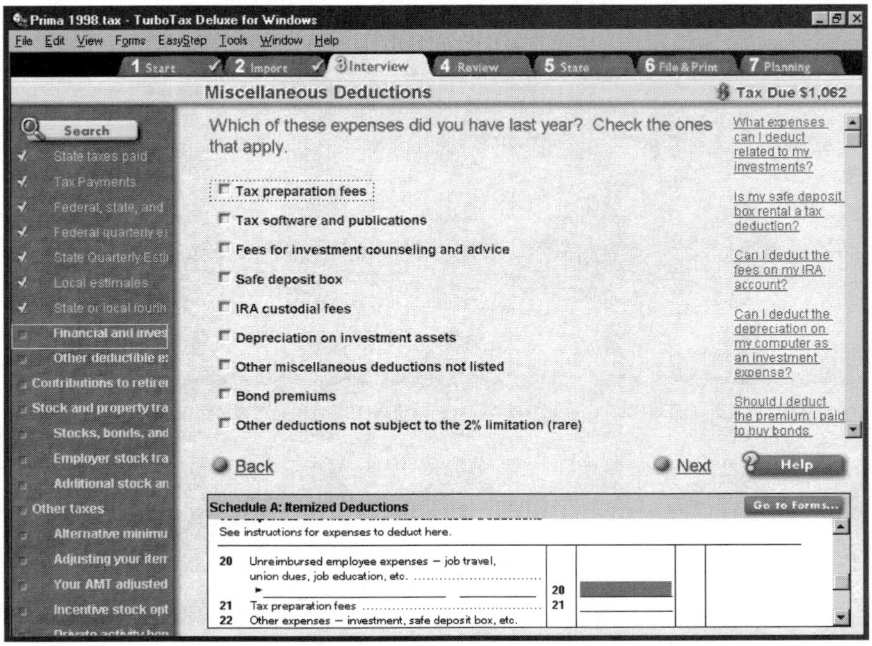

Figure 4.21

You can deduct the cost of a safe deposit box used to store your investment assets or records.

TIP

TurboTax comes with a money-back satisfaction and a tax law accuracy guarantee that most tax preparers don't provide. The 100 percent accuracy guarantee says: "If you pay an IRS or state penalty because of a calculation error in TurboTax, Intuit will pay you the penalty plus interest." Should you need to take Intuit up on this offer, you will need the software and receipt to prove Intuit's error and your reliance. So, be sure to store your tax software, data, and books with your tax files in a computer-friendly area (no dampness or excessive heat, which could damage the CD or your data disk).

Check the deductions that apply to you, and then click on <u>Next</u>. TurboTax prompts you to enter the amounts for each item, one at a time. Be sure to read over the FAQs and follow any relevant Help hyperlinks on each Interview screen to learn more about payments that are and aren't deductible.

> Why do politicians always promise no new taxes, but never say anything about making the old ones lower?

The last Interview question on miscellaneous deductions provides you with an opportunity to list other expenses subject to the two percent AGI limitation (which is most miscellaneous deductions). Other deductions not subject to the two percent AGI limit (such as federal estate tax, gambling losses up to gambling winnings reported as income, and certain repayment of social security benefits) will be requested in the next Interview screen. You can learn more about these miscellaneous deductions in Tax Help. When you are done, click on <u>Continue</u> to enter any other miscellaneous deductions not subject to the two percent AGI limitation. When you are finished, click on <u>Done with Miscellaneous Deductions</u>.

Deducting Other Expenses

As the Interview process on deductions winds to a close, TurboTax asks if any of the situations in Figure 4.22 apply to you. Many of these items include hyperlinks that take you to further explanations about the possible deduction and rules. Carefully review the Tax Help associated with any items that

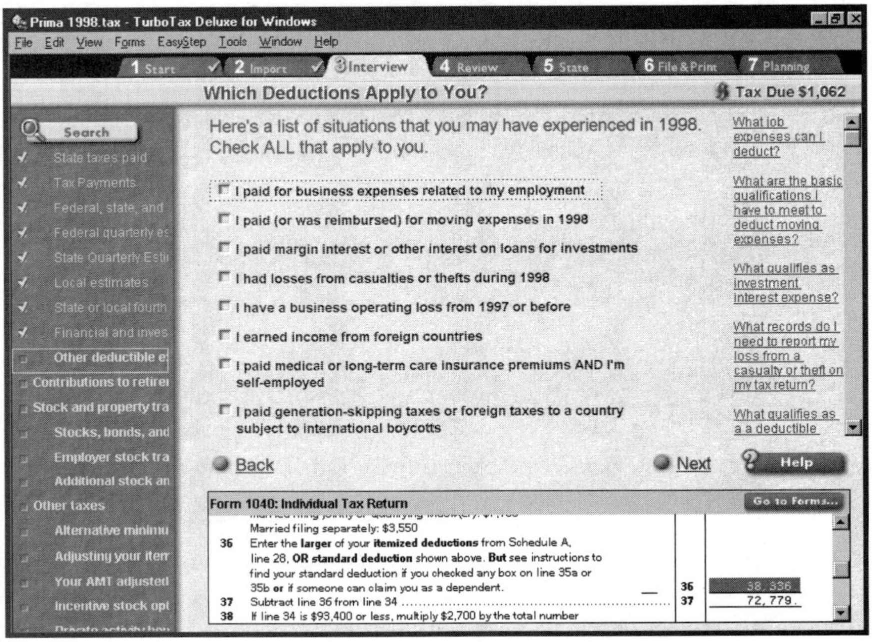

Figure 4.22

Don't overlook a possible deduction related to work or a move.

you feel may apply to you. Check the boxes that you wish to be interviewed on, and then click on <u>Next</u>.

Deducting Employee Business Expenses

Employee business expenses for which your employer reimbursed you in total do not need to be listed on your tax return at all. But, if your employer didn't reimburse you 100 percent for expenses that you incurred for work, you may be able to deduct them (see Figure 4.23). To learn more about deductible employee business expenses, review the FAQs.

Some expenses (such as union dues, subscriptions to trade publications, and uniforms) are not reimbursed by your employer but are necessary for you to maintain or improve your job skills. Here is a brief list of some deductible job-related expenses for which your employer may not be reimbursing you:

✿   Uniforms that cannot be used as regular clothing (regardless of whether or not they were purchased in a uniform shop)

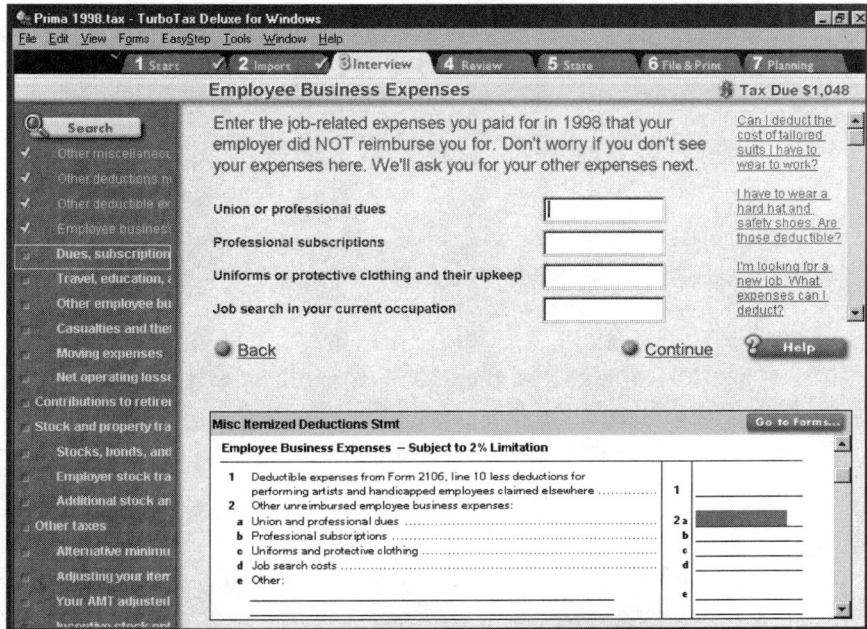

Figure 4.23

Certain job-related
expenses
are deductible on
your tax return.

- Tools that you don't expect to last more than one year
- Long-distance phone calls made for work from home (that aren't reimbursed)
- Costs involved in seeking a new job including cost of resumes, employment agencies, and phone calls (but not the travel expenses related to that job search, which go on Form 2106)
- Dues to unions (if required in order to work), dues to professional organizations (such as the American Institute of Certified Public Accountants), and subscriptions to publications directly related to your job
- Cost of education to maintain or improve your job skills, but not those that qualify you for a new job
- Medical examinations required by your employer (but not reimbursed)

As with all deductions, be sure to keep the receipt and cancelled check to prove the expense and the payment. Enter the amounts that apply to you, and click on <u>Continue</u> when you are ready to move ahead.

The next Interview screen explains that Form 2106 (Employee Business Expenses) must be completed if you or your spouse have travel, entertainment, educational, or home office expenses related to an employer. If so, click on Yes. If not, click on No.

Completing Form 2106

If you or your spouse did need to complete Form 2106, the Interview will ask you to provide an occupation name for each 2106. You will need to complete a separate 2106 for each job. The next Interview question (see Figure 4.24) asks who the 2106 is for and allows you to enter unreimbursed expense amounts for business gifts, education, and trade publications. Enter any applicable amounts, and then click on Continue to move forward.

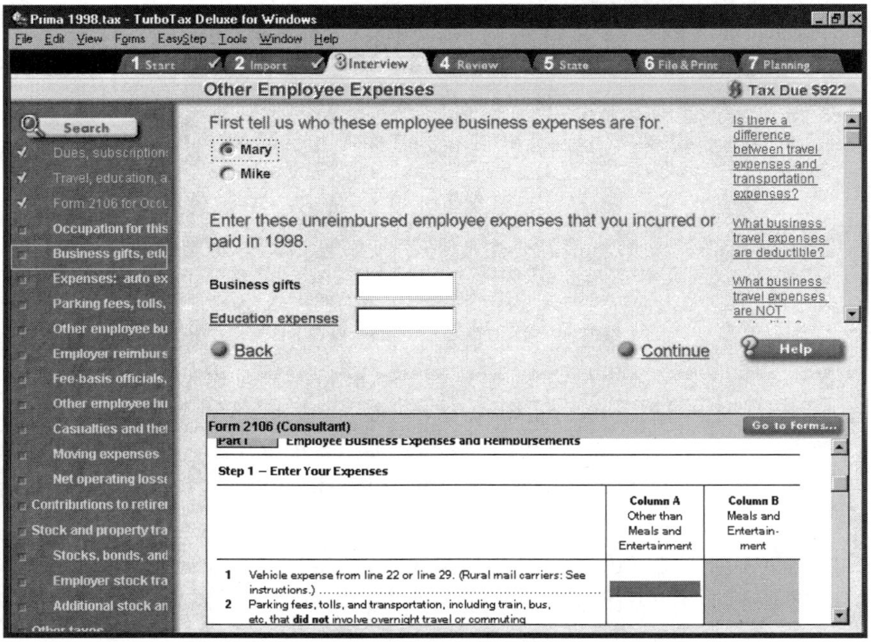

Figure 4.24

Some job-related expenses must be reported on Form 2106.

TIP

> You can deduct educational expenses if they were required by your employer or if they maintain or improve your job skills. You cannot deduct educational expenses that would lead to a new trade or business or if the education merely helps you meet the minimum requirements of your existing job. IRS Publication 508 (not included in TurboTax) provides you with more information on educational expenses.

Next, the Interview asks if you've incurred any auto expenses, purchased assets, disposed of assets, or had home office expenses related to your job. Check all that apply. TurboTax then walks you through the various rules and helps you enter your amounts. The Interview process for auto expenses, asset purchases, asset disposals, and home office expenses is identical to the Interview process for Schedule C (Profit or Loss from Business), which was covered earlier. Please refer back to Saturday Afternoon's session for guidance on answering these Interview questions.

The next Interview question (see Figure 4.25) prompts you to enter any transportation, travel, or meal expenses related to your job but for which your employer did not reimburse you. Review the FAQs for more information on what expenses are deductible. At the very least, you need to be aware of the following issues:

○ **Transportation.** Transportation to and from your regular place of business is not deductible. However, if your employer requests that you drive to a client's site or take a bus to a warehouse for work purposes, the transportation costs that you incur—but for which you are not reimbursed—are deductible.

○ **Travel.** Overnight trips for work are considered to be travel and should be reported separately on the travel line. Expenses not reimbursed by your employer for transportation, hotel, cabs, tips, laundry, and other incidentals are deductible. Expenses for your own personal pleasure (such as movies or sightseeing and travel expenses of family members accompanying you) are not deductible.

✪ **Meals and Entertainment.** Only meals and entertainment directly associated with your business are deductible. The IRS is very strict in this area, and the rules can be complicated. Always write on the back of your meal or event receipt the names of the businesspeople with you, notes on the business purpose, and if possible, the name of the project or task discussed. For a full discussion of nondeductible meals and entertainment expenses, see IRS Publication 463 (not included with TurboTax). And when in doubt, consult your tax advisor for specific regulations or case support if necessary.

Enter your transportation, travel, and meal expenses as applicable, and then click on <u>Continue</u> to move ahead. The next Interview question provides you with an opportunity to list any other employee business expenses that you haven't been asked to enter yet. Click on the FAQ for a listing of other business expenses that you might be able to deduct. Enter your amounts, and then click on <u>Continue</u>.

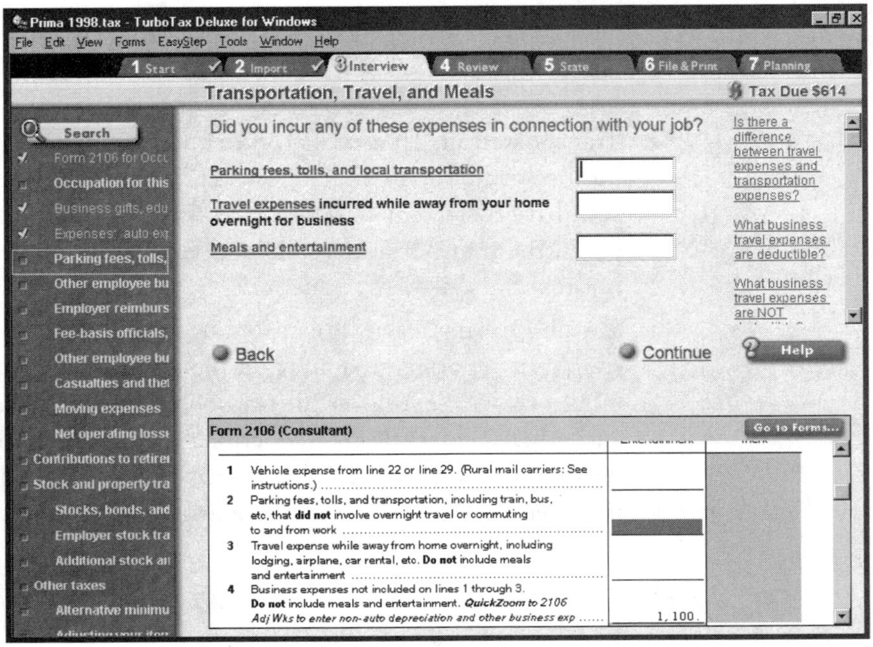

Figure 4.25

You may be able to deduct travel and meal expenses for which your employer didn't reimburse you.

Lastly, the Interview asks if your employer reimbursed you for any job-related expenses that weren't reported on your W-2. Choose the appropriate response, and enter any applicable amounts when prompted.

Deducting Casualty and Theft Losses

The next screen provides you with a video on disaster tax relief (see Figure 4.26). Play the video and click on Continue to move ahead. TurboTax explains where to report a casualty or theft gain (not loss). Read over the explanation and click on Continue to begin the Interview process for Casualty and Theft Losses.

If you suffered damage as the result of some unforeseen event, or if you lost something as the result of a theft, you might be able to qualify for a

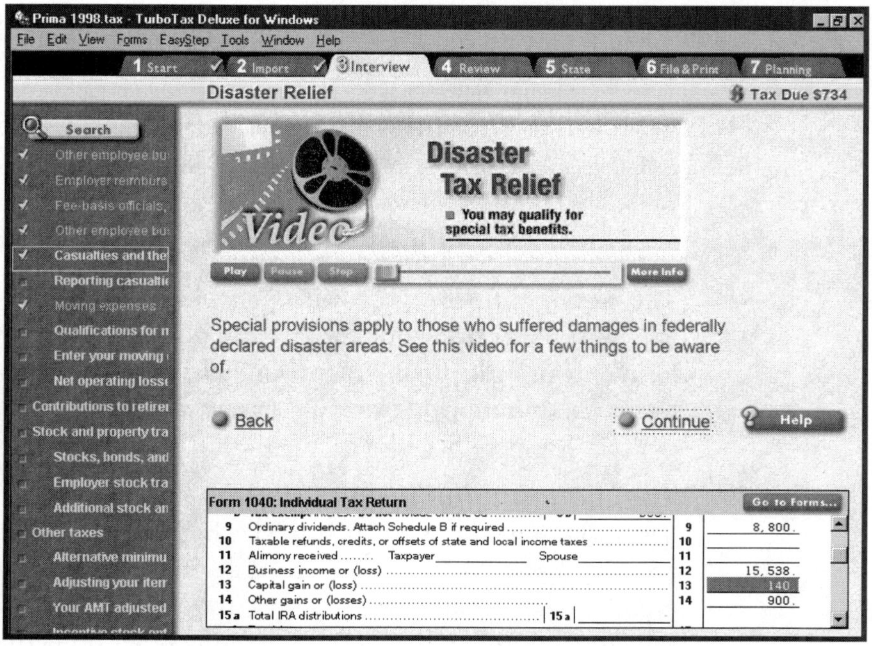

Figure 4.26

If you sustained a loss due to a federally declared disaster, TurboTax helps you determine the proper tax treatment.

deduction. A casualty loss is defined by the IRS as a sudden event, an unexpected event, or an unusual event. Disasters such as tornadoes, fires, earthquakes, storms, hurricanes, and floods are examples of IRS-approved casualty loss events. Other casualty losses that take longer to occur (such as termite infestations) do not qualify for a deduction. Government-ordered condemnation and demolitions do qualify, even if they continue over a long time span, just because the taxpayer has no say in such matters.

To deduct a theft loss, you will need to prove:

- That your property was taken (keep on file a police report or an insurance adjuster's report).
- That you owned the property (keep your purchase receipt, videotapes, or an insurance rider separately listing the property).
- The specifics of the crime (where stolen, when you discovered the theft, etc.).

TIP If your insurance paid for the entire casualty loss or theft, you do not need to report the event on your tax return. However, if the insurance only paid for part of the loss, or if it didn't pay for any, you can file Form 4684 to claim a deduction. Casualty losses are reduced by 10 percent of your AGI. So, if the loss is valued at less than 10 percent of your AGI, you can skip this section.

The TurboTax Interview provides you with a tip on how Form 4684 works. You must file a Form 4684 for each casualty or theft event. Furthermore, the form only provides four lines for you in which to list the properties lost. TurboTax uses additional Form 4684s as needed. When you are ready to begin, click on Ready to Start Form 4684.

The Interview begins by asking you if the casualty or theft pertains to business or personal property. If you have both, start by entering your personal property losses. Next, provide a brief description of the event, the date of the event, a description of the property, the date acquired, and other property value/use information. Continue entering other properties and other events as needed (see Figure 4.27).

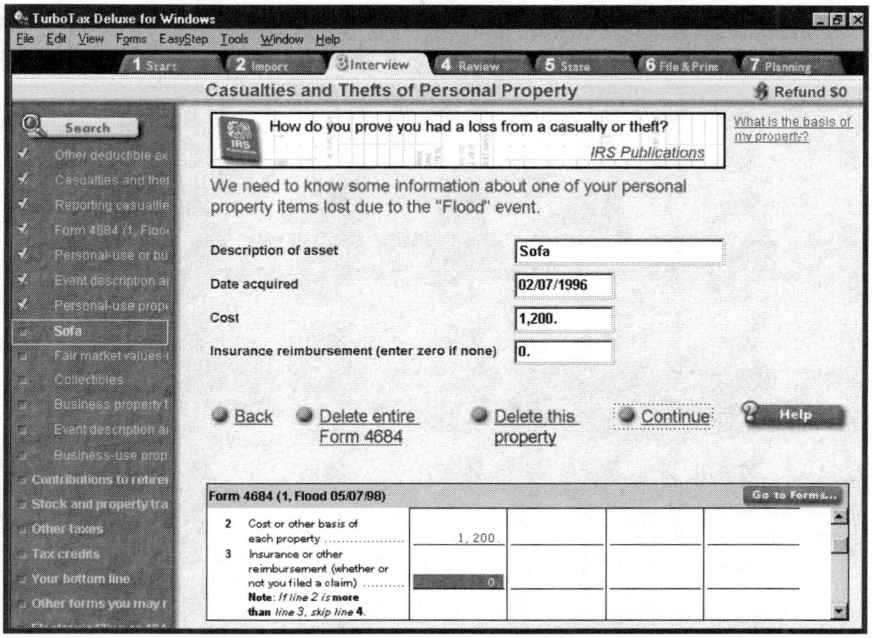

Figure 4.27

You must itemize the properties lost or damaged in a casualty or theft event.

Deducting Moving Expenses

Moving expenses used to be itemized deductions that you could take on your Schedule A. But in recent years the rules have become stricter. You now report the allowable moving expense (if any) on page one of your return, as an adjustment to gross income. TurboTax opens the Interview on this topic with an offer for you to review the rules and a video (see Figure 4.28). Take TurboTax up on the offer, and you are bound to sleep better tonight!

Here's a brief overview of what qualifies these days for moving expenses:

○ Your move must be job-related (such as a new job or a transfer).

○ Your new job must be at least 50 miles further away from your old house than the old job was. For example, if you drove 8 miles to your old job from your old house, your new job must be at least 58 miles away from your old house.

○ You must work at the new job (or for someone else in that geographic region) for at least 39 weeks during the first 12 months at your new

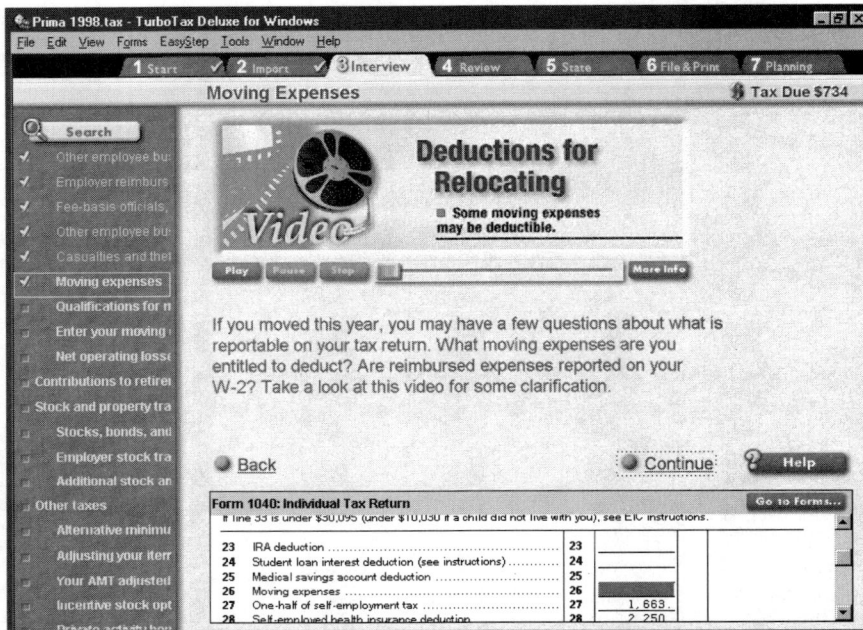

Figure 4.28

Some moving expenses related to your employment can reduce your gross income.

home. If you are self-employed, you have the burden of continuing for 78 weeks in the first 24 months at the new location.

If you meet these requirements, then you get to deduct from your gross income the costs of:

○ Transportation and storage of household goods and personal effects (see Tax Help in TurboTax for more details).

○ Travel and lodging while moving your family to the new home, but not meals—so it's McDonald's for all!

Click on Continue. TurboTax lists the conditions under which you do not need to complete Form 3903 to deduct your storage fees on Schedule A. Read over the rules and click on Continue to move forward. Enter the name of your new place of work and click on Continue. TurboTax lists the qualifications you must meet in order to deduct moving expenses (see Figure 4.29). Check the boxes which pertain to your situation. Click on Continue and start entering your data. Next, enter your expenses for transportation and storage and for travel and lodging. The last item asks you to enter any

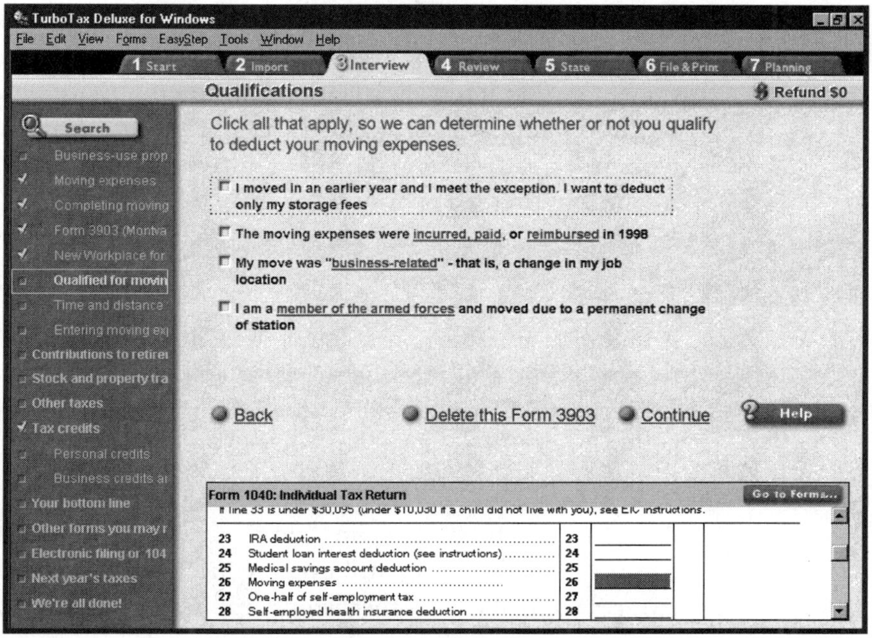

Figure 4.29

Click on the hypertext to learn more about the tax ramifications of each item.

employer reimbursement that you received. If you entered all the amounts on your W-2, TurboTax will have already posted the amount from box 13 with a code of "P" here. If your employer gave you a lump sum, it would be reported in your gross salary income (box 1). Enter that exact reimbursement amount here.

The last Interview screen for moving expenses reports to you the results of your moving expense entries. Income will occur in situations where your expenses are less than the amount your employer reimbursed to you. Otherwise, you will have an adjustment to gross income, which will lower your AGI—always a good thing for your itemized deductions and those other AGI-based limitations.

Contributions to Retirement Plans

If you contribute money to a retirement plan such as an IRA, a SEP, or a Keogh, you may be able to deduct some part of your contribution from your gross income. If necessary, use the Navigator to go to the topic Contributions to Retirement Plans. Go ahead and play the video on this topic to get a good overview on the issues you face. When you are ready, click on <u>Continue</u>. The first Interview question asks you to specify which type(s) of retirement accounts you contributed to for 1998. Keep in mind that for many types (such as an IRA and SEP) you have up until April 15, 1999, to make a contribution for 1998.

Contributing to an IRA

An individual retirement account (IRA) is an investment account set up for the sole purpose of meeting the tax rules Congress creates for IRAs. Back in the early 80s, Congress wanted to encourage taxpayers to save for retirement, and realized that tax breaks are the fastest way to shape consumer spending, so they created the IRA.

An IRA is a retirement savings account in which you can contribute up to $2,000 annually. The contribution reduces your gross income, which in turn reduces your AGI. In other words, you invest tax-free dollars and earn tax-free interest in an IRA now while you are in a high tax bracket. Later, when you retire and are in a much lower tax bracket, you will pay the income tax only on the amount that you withdraw each year.

Of course, as with all tax benefits, Congress has specified limitations, rules, and regulations that must be followed or you will incur tax, penalties, and interest:

- ✿ IRAs must be set up at a bank or stock brokerage firm that will act as the IRS's watchdog, making sure that the account meets the IRA rules.

- ✿ Each taxpayer (you and your spouse) is entitled to an IRA contribution up to the lesser of $2,000 or 100 percent of earned income (alimony counts as earned income for this purpose).

- ✿ The IRA contribution amount is limited by your participation in a qualified retirement plan provided by your employer, such as a 401(k). Starting in 1998, a spouse who is not an active participant in an employer plan will not be treated as an active participant merely because his or her spouse is a participant.

- ✿ The AGI reduction amount is limited by your modified AGI (basically AGI without regard to IRAs and certain social security benefits) on a sliding scale. In 1998 the regular IRA contribution has been reduced to zero for single taxpayers with an AGI of $40,000, or $60,000 for joint filers. These amounts will continue to expand over the years until 2007, when the contribution amount goes to zero for single taxpayers with an AGI of $60,000, or $100,000 for joint returns.

⚙ IRA distributions received before age 59½ are generally subject to a penalty. Furthermore, if you don't begin taking minimum distributions by age 70½, other penalties will be assessed.

TurboTax applies all these rules based on the information that you provide about your IRA. But you need to know what type of IRA you have. The original IRA described above is now called a *traditional deductible IRA*. You can also have a *nondeductible IRA* in which you can make contributions of taxed money. The earnings accumulate tax-free until withdrawn.

TIP If your traditional IRA contribution is limited by AGI phaseout, consider opening a nondeductible IRA or a nondeductible Roth IRA (see the Roth IRA discussion in the next section).

CAUTION If you contribute more than the allowable amount to a traditional IRA, whether deductible or not, the excess contribution may be subject to a cumulative penalty of six percent. Cumulative means that if you don't catch your error until a few years later, the tax is on the resulting excess for each year.

Contributing to a Roth IRA

Named after Bill Roth, the U.S. senator who thought it all up, the Roth IRA has sparked a lot of interest and confusion over the past year. In case you haven't heard, the Roth IRA allows you to boost your retirement income while helping with your estate planning. First, unlike regular IRAs, you don't have to withdraw money from your Roth IRA when you reach 70½ years of age. Upon your death, the Roth IRA passes to your beneficiaries, largely tax-free, and continues to grow tax-free under rules similar to those governing regular IRAs. Any money withdrawn by your beneficiaries is tax-free, whereas money drawn from a regular IRA would be taxable to the beneficiary. Furthermore, as long as you and/or your spouse have taxable income, you can continue to make contributions to a Roth IRA (in regular IRAs this is not permitted after age 70½).

Another key advantage of a Roth IRA is that you can withdraw any part of your annual contribution to the IRA (but not the income earned in the IRA) at any time for anything without incurring a penalty or tax. If you are older than 59½, you can also withdraw the earnings tax- and penalty-free (provided your Roth IRA is at least five years old). Regular IRAs do not permit any premature withdrawals without inflicting stiff penalties and taxes unless you meet specific exceptions (for example, if you are a first-time home buyer, you have qualified education expenses, or you have disabilities or certain medical expenses).

The annual nondeductible Roth IRA contribution amount is limited to $2,000, provided you have taxable income of at least that amount. Furthermore, the allowable contribution is reduced to zero based on a sliding scale, reaching zero for single taxpayers with a modified AGI of $110,000, or $160,000 for joint returns.

If you want, you can convert a regular IRA to a Roth IRA (but only if your modified AGI is less than $100,000). The part of the amount which is rolled over that was deducted from your gross income in previous years is taxable. If the rollover is completed by January 1, 1999, you can spread the tax out over four years. Otherwise, the entire tax must be paid to avoid the penalties for early withdrawal. If you roll over a regular IRA to a Roth IRA and then change your mind, you can revert back to the regular IRA provided you complete the transfer back to a regular IRA by the due date of your return (April 15, 1999, for 1998 returns).

NOTE If you cannot or do not make contributions to a deductible IRA or Roth IRA, you can make contributions to a nondeductible IRA. However, in total, your contributions to all IRAs in a taxable year cannot exceed $2,000 plus a similar amount for your spouse.

Entering Your IRA Information

If you made contributions to a traditional IRA for 1998, or you will do so by April 15, 1999, check the Traditional IRAs box in Figure 4.30 and answer Yes when asked the question again. The Interview then prompts you to enter the contribution amounts and basis in the IRA, for you and your spouse (see Figure 4.31). Review the FAQs to see if any of the issues noted apply to your situation. You can also click on the Tax Help hyperlinks to learn more about the terms used here.

Refer back to your 1997 year-end IRA statements for the basis amount. Note that in the contribution area, you only enter the contribution amount for the traditional IRA. However, in the basis area, TurboTax needs to know your entire IRA basis for years 1997 and earlier. The basis includes any SIMPLE and IRA-SEP accounts that you have. When you are ready, click on <u>Continue</u> to move on to the next question.

TurboTax can tell from certain data you entered earlier (such as your W-2 and 1099s) if you or your spouse participate in a retirement plan at work.

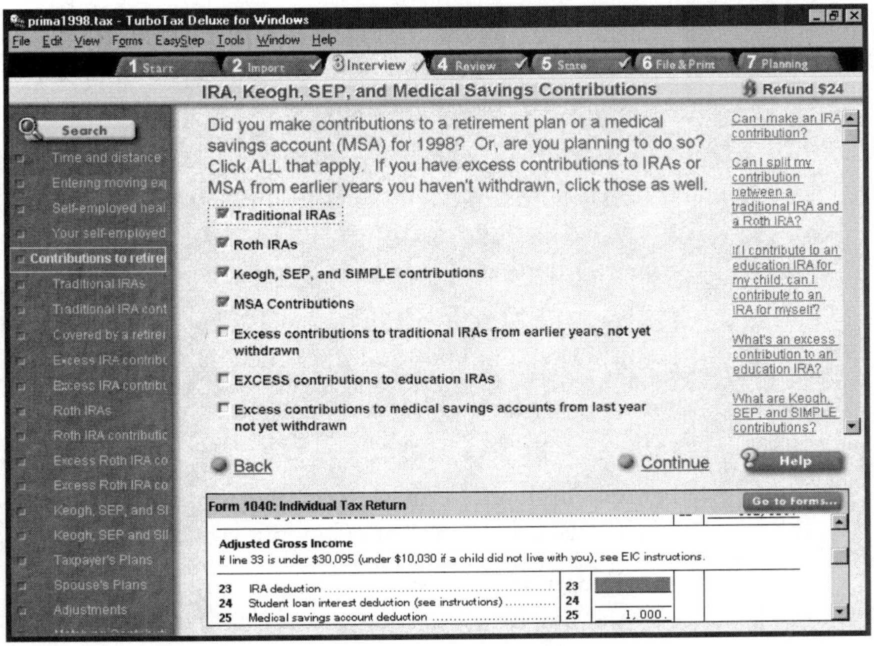

Figure 4.30

Contributions to a retirement plan can lower your AGI.

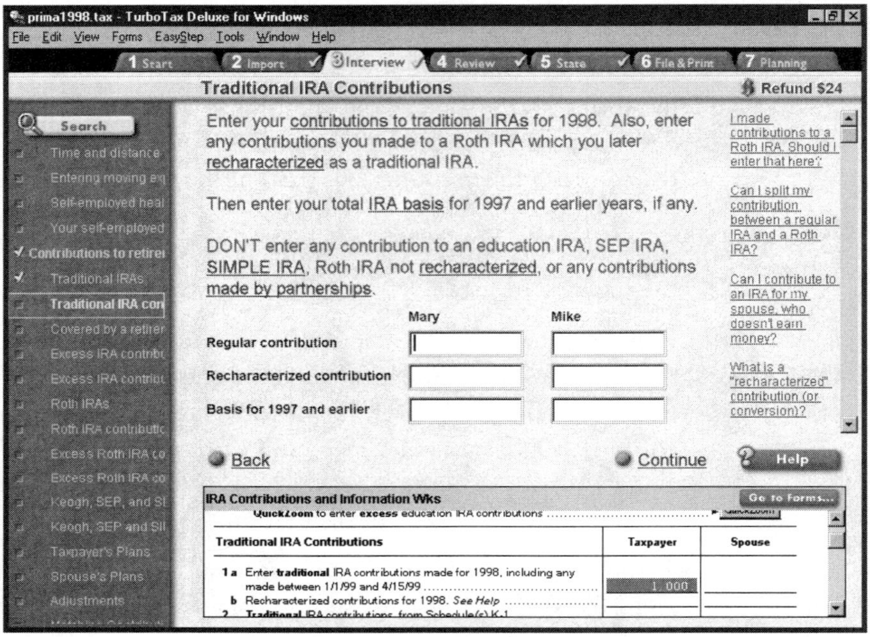

Figure 4.31

Enter any contributions to traditional IRAs here.

This next part of the Interview reports that information and may ask you to confirm that one of you does not participate in a retirement plan at work. Answer <u>Yes</u> or <u>No</u> as appropriate.

The next set of Interview questions asks if you contributed to a Roth IRA. If so, click on <u>Yes</u>. Figure 4.32 prompts you to enter the contributions to a Roth IRA without regard to any conversion amounts. TurboTax will interview you on that conversion separately.

Review the FAQs, hyperlinks, and Tax Help. When you are ready, enter your contribution amounts, and then click on <u>Continue</u>.

Contributing to a Keogh, SEP, or SIMPLE Plan

For self-employed businesses and small businesses that cannot bear the burden of a 401(k) retirement plan, Congress created several simpler retirement plans:

○ **Keogh**. A Keogh (also known as an HR10 plan) can be set up by a self-employed business as a *defined contribution plan* or a *defined*

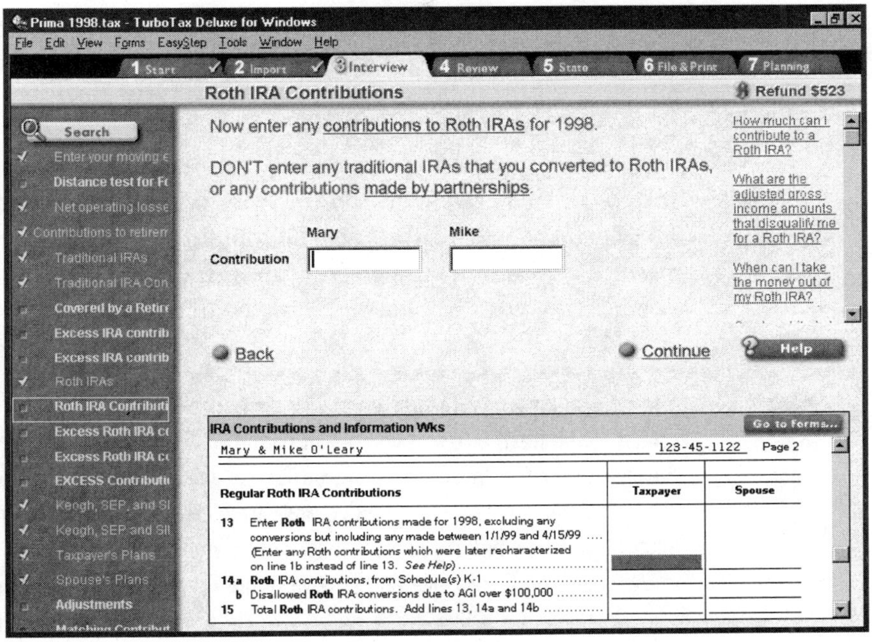

Figure 4.32

Enter contributions to your Roth IRA here.

benefit plan. Your contributions (and therefore your deduction from gross income) are limited by your earned income from the business. You must establish the plan by the end of the tax year and the plan must be in writing. Specific rules govern which employees must be covered and when they are vested.

○ **IRA-SEP.** A Simplified Employee Pension (SEP) plan can be established at any time up to the due date of the self-employed business owner's tax return (including extensions). The plan must be in writing and allows self-employed business owners without employees to set up a more flexible IRA. Contributions are limited to 15 percent of compensation up to $24,000. A SEP must cover all employees aged 21 and older who earn more than $400 during the year.

○ **SIMPLE.** The newest kid on the block, SIMPLE plans are for employers with 100 or fewer employees who each earn $5,000 or more. Employers contribute dollar for dollar (limited to $6,000 annually) up to 3 percent of compensation what the employees contribute.

The TurboTax Interview asks if you or your spouse contributed to a Keogh, SEP, or SIMPLE plan. Check the appropriate box, and then click on <u>Continue</u>. As you can see in Figure 4.33, TurboTax lists the various types of plans and allows you to enter the amounts for each. A really nifty tool that TurboTax provides for Keogh and SEP plans is the Maximize check box. Instead of having to guess the amount that you can contribute, you can click on Maximize and TurboTax will compute the maximum contribution for you! Once you know the maximum, you can then decide how much money you actually want to contribute by the due date of your return.

NOTE

● ●

The calculations in TurboTax happen automatically when you move from one Interview screen to the next, or when you are in Forms view and move from one form to the next. In the case of the Maximize feature, TurboTax has one more question to ask you before advancing to the next screen. Once you've answered it, TurboTax will report to you the maximum amount. At that point, if you want to lock in an amount (as opposed to leaving it set to "maximize"), click on <u>Back</u> twice and enter a figure up to that maximum amount.

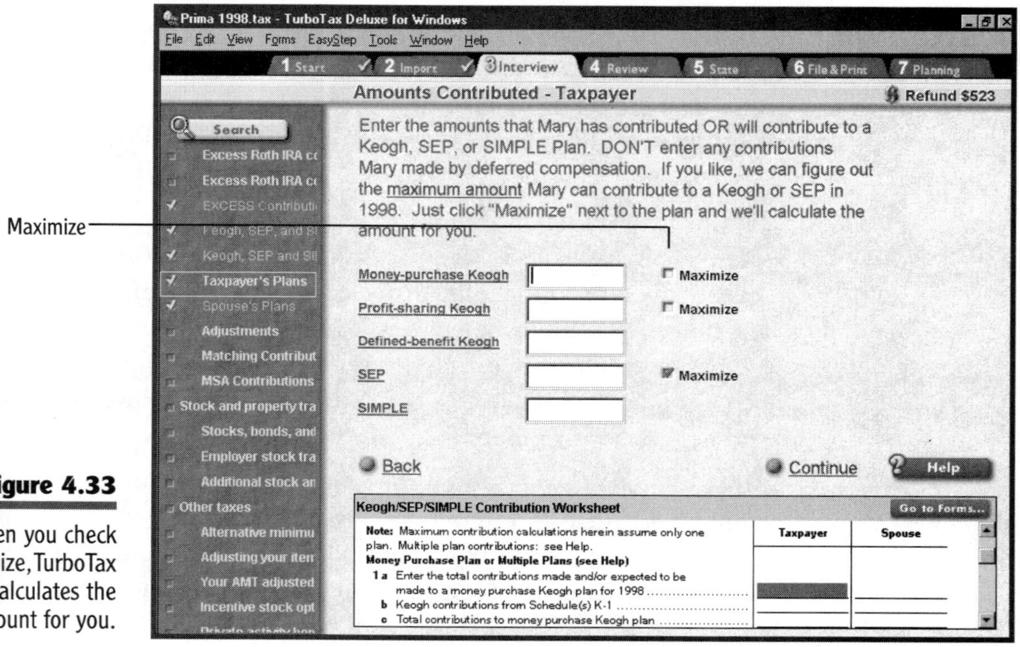

● ●

Maximize

Figure 4.33

When you check Maximize, TurboTax calculates the amount for you.

Review the FAQs, hyperlinks, and Tax Help. When you are ready, enter your amounts or use the Maximize feature to determine the maximum allowable contribution. Click on Continue to move ahead to the next Interview topic.

If you are self-employed, TurboTax gives you an opportunity to adjust the self-employment income. The adjustment to self-employment income usually only occurs when the taxpayer has more than one business, when the taxpayer suffers a business loss, or in certain partnership situations. When in doubt, consult your tax advisor for help in determining the reduction amount, if any.

Enter the adjustment amount, and then click on Done with Adjustment. If you checked the Maximize check box, TurboTax will display the maximum deduction amount allowed.

Contributing to an MSA

The last adjustment to your gross income that TurboTax asks you about concerns contributions to a medical savings account (MSA). An MSA is a tax-free account that works very similarly to an IRA, except that you withdraw the funds to pay "qualified" medical expenses that aren't covered by your health insurance. Self-employed individuals and employees of small businesses (of 50 or fewer employees) can set up MSAs. As with IRAs, various rules, limitations, and penalties apply:

- Establish the MSA with a qualified MSA custodian (usually offered by health insurance companies) by contributing cash to the account. The amount you contribute is up to you, but it should be close to the amount you expect to need. Contributions are also limited as noted below.

- Contributions to MSAs are limited to 65 percent (for individuals) or 75 percent (for families) of the health insurance deductible. For example, if a family of four has an annual deductible amount of $1,500, the most the family could contribute to an MSA in a year would be $1,125. Of course, the contribution could be less.

✿   If at any time you become covered by another health plan, the entire amount in the MSA becomes taxable income in that year and is subject to a penalty of 15 percent.

The good news is that so long as you continue to qualify, the MSA balance accumulates tax-free. When you turn 65, you can withdraw the funds for any purpose, subject to income tax but with no penalties. Until then, you can withdraw funds (or have your MSA make payments) to pay for qualified medical expenses not covered by the health insurance plan. The qualified medical expenses do include the deductible amount and health insurance premiums, which makes this a great tax-planning tool.

CAUTION

◆ ◆

To avoid the 15 percent penalty and additional taxable income, keep your contributions down to a reasonable amount, which you feel certain you can use up in each year. If you marry someone with coverage or get a new job, stop making contributions and use up the remainder in the account before the new plan takes effect.

◆ ◆

The TurboTax Interview on contributions to MSAs begins by asking if you or your spouse contributed to an MSA. Click on <u>Yes</u> or <u>No</u>, as applicable.

After a few questions about your health insurance coverage and your spouses health plan(s), TurboTax will prompt you to enter the amounts (see Figure 4.34). Notice that you shouldn't include any employer contributions, excess contributions, or amounts rolled over from another MSA. Click on <u>Continue</u> when you are ready to move ahead.

As you can see in Figure 4.34, the Interview questions help you determine the MSA contribution limit based on your health plan deductible, wage earnings, and type of coverage. To learn more about the tax rules surrounding MSA, click on the FAQ <u>What Is a High-Deductible Health Plan?</u> Follow the hyperlinks to learn more about each of the items requested. Enter your information, and then click on <u>Continue</u> to move ahead. TurboTax calculates your return and asks if you have another MSA for which to enter data, if you want to edit an MSA that you already entered, or if you are done entering MSAs. Select the appropriate option.

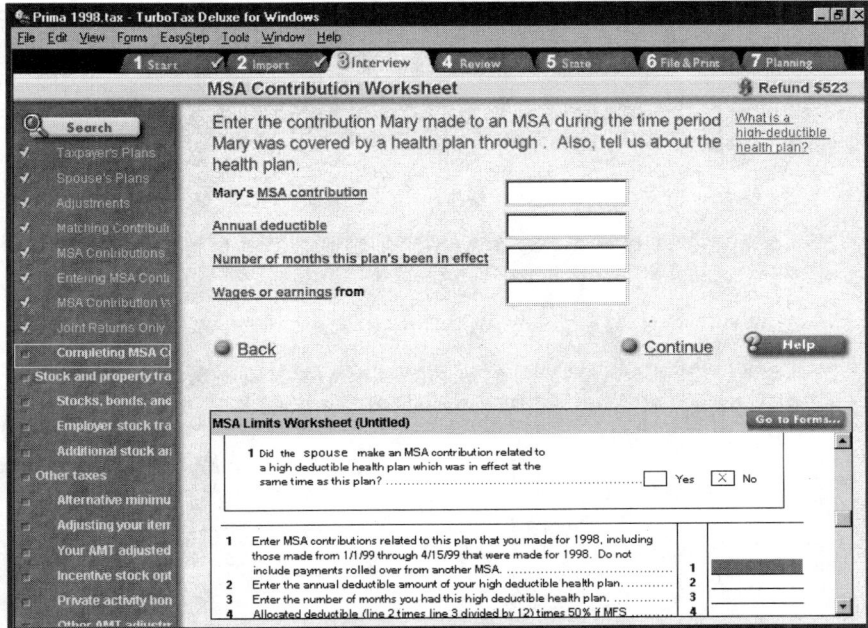

Figure 4.34

First, you need to enter the MSA contribution amounts.

Sales of Property

In the Saturday Afternoon session on entering gross income, you had an opportunity to enter gains or losses from the exchange of property for a self-employed business (Schedule C), a partnership (Schedule K-1), from rental and other activities (Schedule E), and from a farming business (Schedule F). TurboTax prompts you once more to enter any information on gains and losses from sales of property (see Figure 4.35).

Check any boxes that apply to you, and then enter the required information. Refer back to the Saturday Morning session as needed. As always, review the FAQs, follow the hyperlinks for further explanation, and when in doubt, consult your tax advisor for guidance.

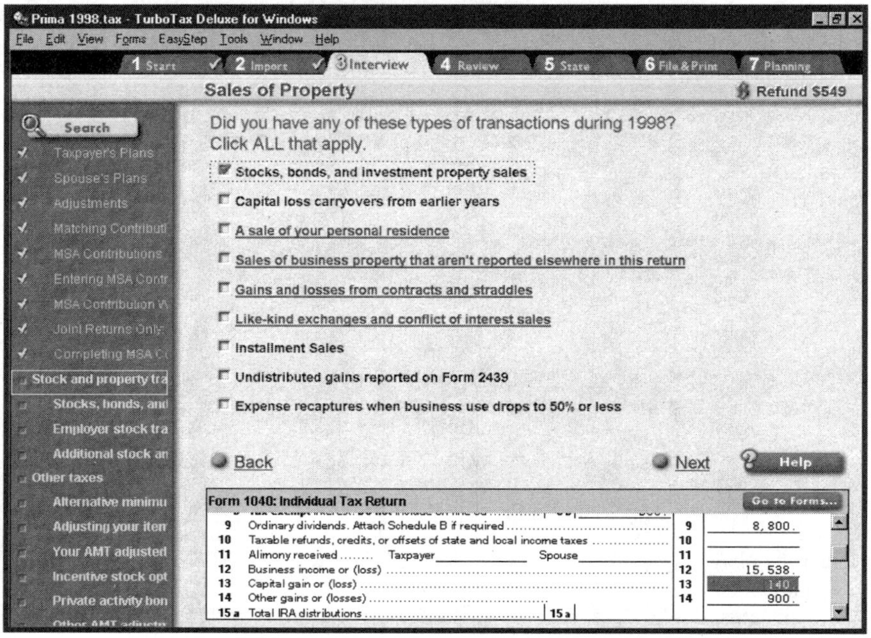

Figure 4.35

The IRS wants to know about any property sales you had during the year.

Reviewing Your Tax Liability

Now would be a good time to review the changes to your tax return from this morning's work. Follow these steps to review your adjustments to income and your itemized deductions, and then to see the preliminary tax calculation. The last three topics for this morning will cover what other taxes you may owe, tax credits you may be able to take, and other tax forms you may need to complete.

1. From the menu bar, choose Forms, Show My Return.

2. Choose Form 1040: Individual Tax Return.

3. Click on Open.

4. Page up to line 22, your total income. Slowly scroll down so that you can see the Adjusted Gross Income section, as shown in Figure 4.36.

5. To see the detail behind any number, double-click on the amount.

6. All the supporting forms that you open will stay open until you click on Close Form. When you are done reviewing the AGI area, close the supporting forms and return to Form 1040.

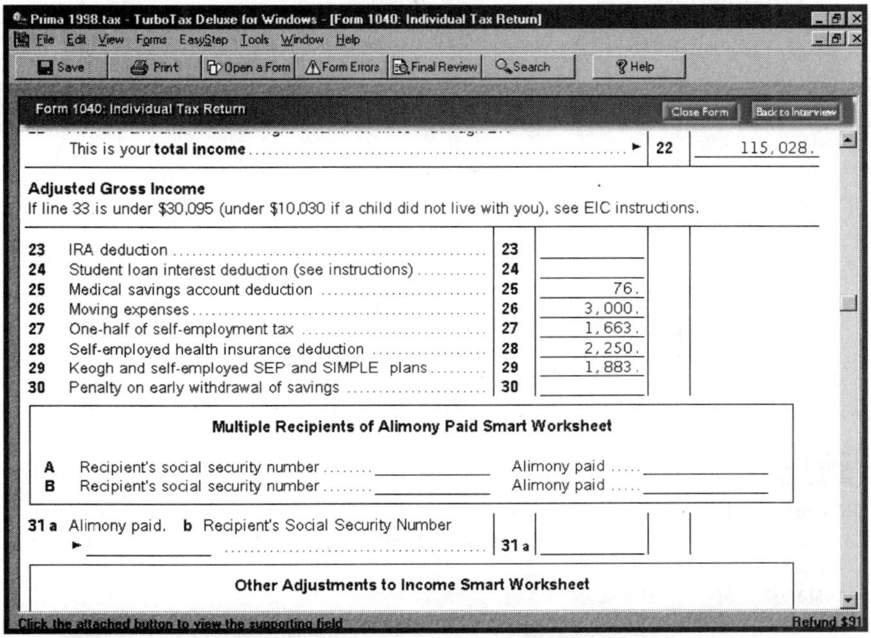

Figure 4.36

All the adjustments to gross income that you can take are listed here.

7. Continue to scroll down until lines 34 through 37 display. You should be able to see your AGI amount on line 34 and the itemized or standard deduction amount on line 36 (see Figure 4.37).

8. Double-click on the amount for line 36. If you itemized deductions, Schedule A appears. Scroll down and review the amounts and limitations. Drill down to the supporting forms, schedules, and worksheets as needed. For standard deduction taxpayers, a worksheet showing the calculation appears.

9. Close any open supporting forms, schedules, or worksheets and return to Form 1040.

10. Scroll down and note the exemption amount that TurboTax computed for line 38. If your AGI exceeds $93,400, double-click on this amount to see how TurboTax applied the limitation and computed line 38 for you. Close the supporting worksheet when you are done.

11. Scroll down so that you can see the taxable income listed on line 39 and the tax calculation (see Figure 4.38).

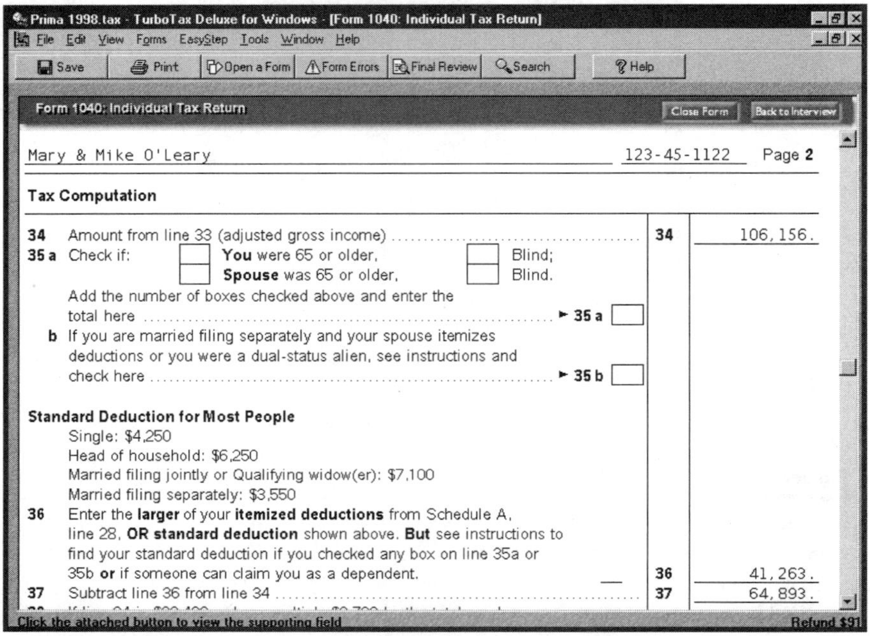

Figure 4.37

TurboTax selects whichever is better for you—the standard or itemized deduction.

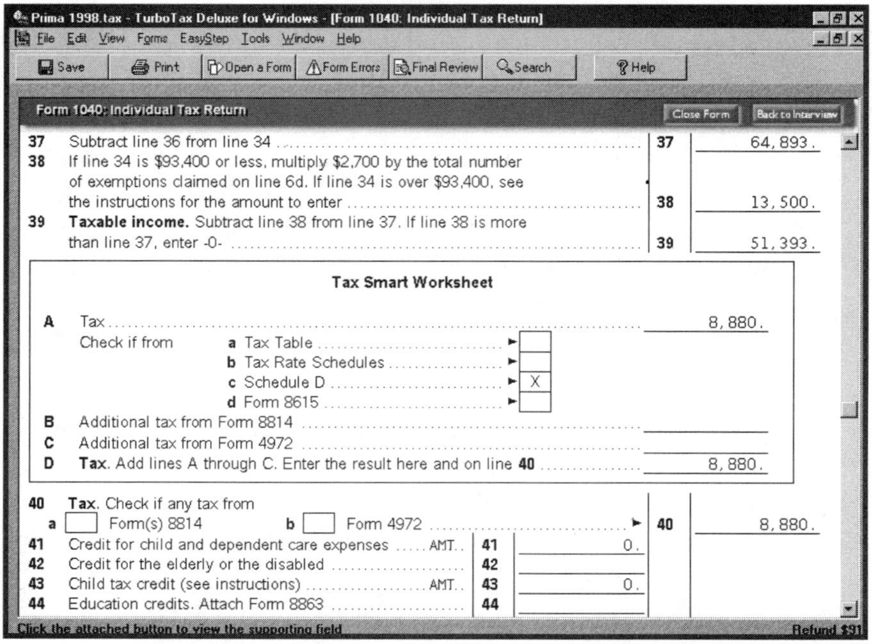

Figure 4.38

TurboTax calculates your tax for you.

12. If you'd like to, scroll down slowly through the remainder of the form and note the remaining sections to be completed, on tax credits, other taxes, payments (for which you've already entered the data), and the all-important refund due/amount owed.

13. Return to the Interview.

Computing Additional Taxes Due

As if income taxes weren't enough of a burden, you may have to pay additional taxes with your return. Taxes such as self-employment tax, the social security and Medicare taxes on household employees, and taxes on tips not reported to your employer, just to name a few, must all be reported on your tax return. As you can see in Figure 4.39, TurboTax reviews all the information you have entered thus far and takes the liberty of noting the additional taxes that you must pay.

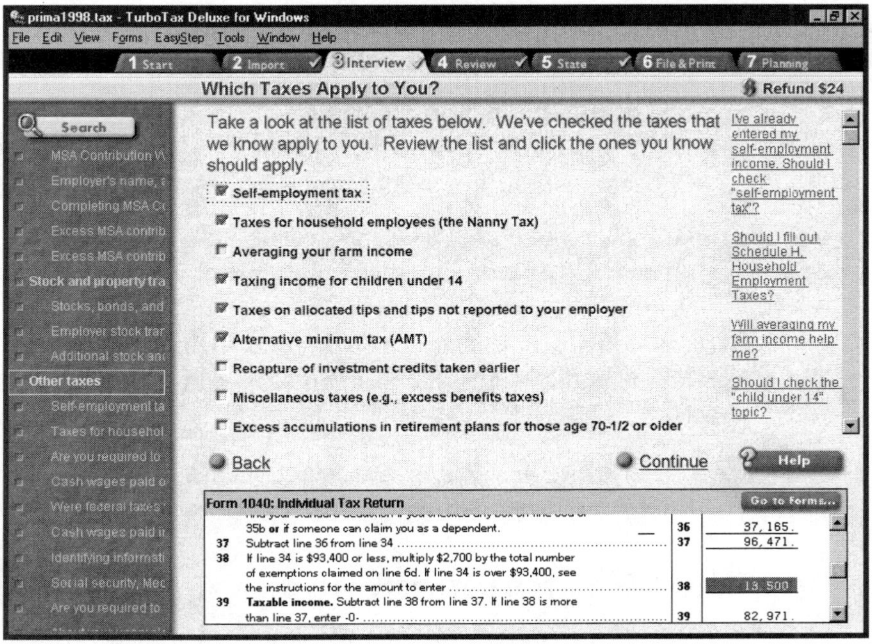

Figure 4.39

Income tax isn't the only tax paid for on your federal tax return.

Take a moment to click on the hyperlinked items and read over the Tax Help screens to make sure that you understand what each tax is for and whether or not it applies to you. Check all that apply, and then click on <u>Next</u>.

Paying the Nanny Tax

If you pay cash wages of $1,100 or more to household employees or in-home care providers for your dependents, you must pay the Nanny Tax on Schedule H. The Nanny Tax is the social security tax and Medicare tax required to be paid by employers. For purposes of this tax, your spouse, your children, and students under age 18 are not subject to the Nanny Tax.

TurboTax opens the Interview with several questions geared toward making sure you actually owe a Nanny Tax for someone. Read over the FAQs, hyperlinked explanations, and Tax Help. Next, enter your employer identification number (EIN). Note that this is *not* your social security number. If you don't have an EIN yet, enter "applied for" and call 800-TAX-FORM to get Form SS-4 (Application for Employer Identification Number) or visit the IRS Web site at **www.irs.ustreas.gov/prod/forms_pubs/forms.html**. Either you or your spouse will become the "employer."

FIND IT ON ▶
THE WEB

Next, TurboTax prompts you to enter the wage and tax withheld information (see Figure 4.40). Click on the FAQs to see if any of the issues raised pertain to you. Enter your amounts, and then click on <u>Continue</u> to move ahead.

The Interview continues with questions about the unemployment tax (FUTA) and state unemployment taxes that you may owe. Enter any applicable amounts. Consult the FAQs and Tax Help as needed. At the end, TurboTax displays the Nanny Tax that you owe and lists it on your tax return.

> I believe we should all pay our tax bill with a smile. I tried, but they wanted cash.

Paying Self-Employment Tax

To the extent that you owe self-employment tax, TurboTax has already interviewed you on that topic as part of your Schedule C self-employed business, Schedule F farm business, or Schedule K-1 partnership business. At this

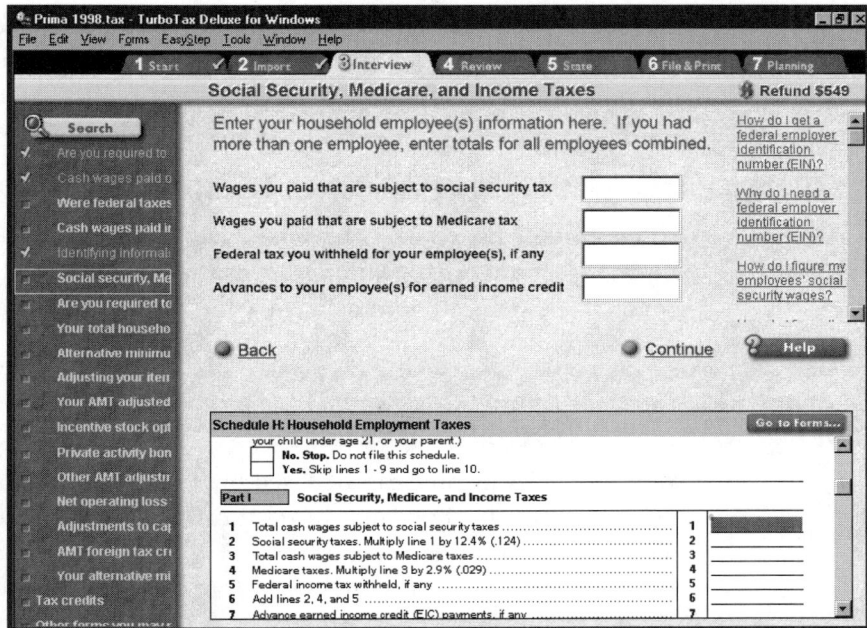

Figure 4.40

Household employment taxes should be paid with your return.

point, you can review or edit your self-employed income data entry or review the Self-Employed Tax Worksheet and form SE.

TIP

To view the details behind any number on your 1040, just double-click on the amount. Drill down to the supporting schedules and worksheets. Click on the Print button anytime to print copies as you go along. For example, to learn more about the self-employment tax on line 50, double-click on the line 50 amount. TurboTax displays the Schedule SE Adjustments Worksheet. To view the actual Schedule SE, click on the QuickZoom button for the short or long form. To get more details about any amount, double-click on the amount to drill down further.

Paying Tax on Tips

Tips that you received but did not report to your employer should be reported on Form 4137 (one per taxpayer). If this applies to you, check the box for unreported tips for you or your spouse and follow the Interview process. You will be asked for the amount, any tips paid out of a tip-sharing pool, and the employers that weren't notified of the tip amount.

Determining the Alternative Minimum Tax

Based on the answers you've given so far, TurboTax has already determined if you owe an alternative minimum tax (AMT) or not. If you do, click on Yes so you can review your data entry for Form 6251 (Alternative Minimum Tax—Individuals). If not, click on No to continue.

Paying Tax on Kiddie Income

Your children's income can be taxed on your return or you can opt to file a separate return for the child. In most cases, reporting the child's income on their own return results in a tax savings. The option to report a child's income on your return is provided mainly as a convenience for you.

You may elect to report a child's income on your return if the child has investment income of less than $6,500 consisting only of interest, dividends, capital gains, and nontaxable distributions. The election is made on Form 8814. The first $650 of a child's taxable income is exempt from tax, and the next $650 is taxed at 15 percent. Any amount in excess of $1,300 is taxed at the parent's tax rate. Both the parent and the child must meet certain requirements to gain this tax benefit (the lower tax rate on the first $1,300).

In the Interview, select whether you want to file a separate return for the child or if you want to add the child's income to your return. If you choose the latter, TurboTax will walk you through the process of filling out Form 8814. If you decide to file the child's return separately, you will need to save your tax file and create a new one for each child.

TIP Review the FAQs, Tax Help hyperlinked information, and Guide Me features to help you decide if the advantages of including the child's income on your return outweigh the tax consequences.

Paying Other Taxes

Other, less-common taxes that you may owe include excess benefit taxes and certain recapture taxes. If these apply to you, read over the FAQs, follow the Tax Help hyperlinks, and use the Guide Me features to help you enter the correct information. When in doubt, consult your tax advisor.

Exploring Tax Credits

Tax credits are great, if you can get them—so get them while you can. Unlike adjustments to gross income and itemized deductions that simply reduce your taxable income, tax credits give you your money back dollar for dollar. Suppose your tax liability is $5,000. If you qualify for a tax credit of $500, you will only need to pay $4,500.

Figure 4.41 shows you the initial tax credit Interview screen. If TurboTax can determine (from the data you've entered thus far) any credits that you might

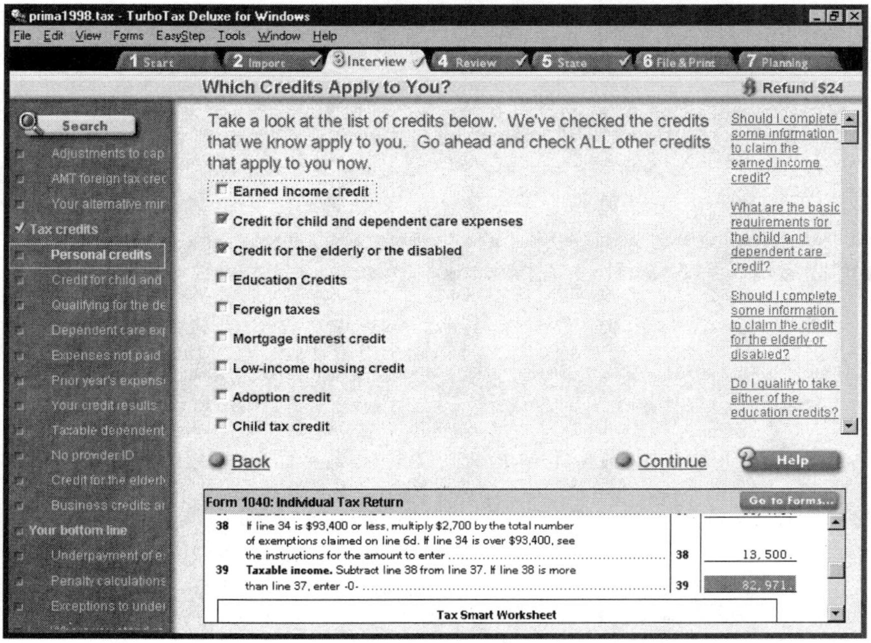

Figure 4.41

Tax credits reduce your taxes dollar for dollar.

be able to take, the box is checked for you. Check any others that might apply, and then click on Next.

NOTE Note that some tax credits result in a refund, whereas others are limited to your tax liability. TurboTax knows the difference and will limit your tax credit refund as needed.

Child Tax Credit

The Child Tax Credit is $400 for each qualifying dependent child under age 17. To claim the credit you must complete a complicated IRS worksheet which may result in you filing Form 6251, Alternative Minimum Tax (AMT), to determine if your credit is limited by AMT. The good news is that TurboTax does all of this for you and reports to you the credit amount you qualify for or explains why you are not eligible for the child care credit. When you are ready to move ahead to the next topic, click on Next.

TIP To view the details of the child care credit calculation, double-click on the amount (even if its zero) on line 43. TurboTax will display the tax credit form and allow you to drill down to the supporting schedules and worksheets.

Earned Income Credit

The Earned Income Credit (EIC) is provided to low income taxpayers who support children, and a limited credit is permitted to certain taxpayers without qualifying children. In 1998, the EIC can be up to $2,271 for one qualifying child, $3,756 for more than one child, or $341 for no qualifying children. Unlike the Child Tax Credit, the EIC is a refundable credit (the credit amount is not limited to your tax liability).

After a few questions on other types of earned income, TurboTax computes the EIC. If you do not qualify for the EIC, TurboTax explains why. To review the EIC calculations, click on the Go to Forms button.

Dependent Care Credit

The Dependent Care Credit is for working taxpayers who pay care costs which allow them to work (such as day-care for a child or elderly dependent). The credit amount is 20 percent to 30 percent of up to $2,400 of care expenses for one dependent or up to $4,800 of expenses for more than one dependent. The credit is reduced for AGI over $28,000.

TurboTax provides a Guide Me mini-interview to walk you through the qualifying dependent rules. Take a moment now to click on Guide Me and determine if your dependent(s) qualify. Or if you know for sure that your dependent(s) do qualify, click on Yes, I Qualify.

The next Interview screen explains that the Dependent Care Credit is also available for a spouse who is disabled or a full-time student during 1998. Click on the item which best matches your situation and click on Continue. TurboTax calculates your Dependent Care Credit and completes Form 2441, Child and Dependent Care Expenses, for you.

Educational Credit

The Educational Credit Interview begins with a video on how the two new education credits can help you reduce the costs of higher education. The Hope Education Credit provides you with at most a $1,500 credit per year, but only for the first two years. The video explains the specific limitations and rules. The second credit is the Life-Time Learning Credit, available for any number of years and provides at the most $1,000 per year. The two credits are mutually exclusive. That is, you can not use both for the same student in the same year. The video provides you with a good overview of the specific limitations and rules. You can also click on the More Info button to learn more about the credits. When you are ready to begin the interview, click on Continue.

TIP If you do not qualify for a credit, based on the information already entered into TurboTax (such as AGI over the limitation amount), TurboTax won't take you through the Interview screens. Instead, TurboTax explains why you do not qualify for the tax credit. If you need to change a previous answer or amount, use the Go to Forms button or Back to find and correct your data entry.

They say that death and taxes are inevitable. At least death doesn't get worse every year!

Other Credits

The other tax credits which you may be eligible for include:

- Foreign Tax Credit
- Disabled Tax Credit
- Mortgage Interest Credit
- Low-Income Housing Credit

In the Which Credits Apply to You? screen (refer to Figure 4.41) you should have checked off the boxes for the credits you think you might be able to take. TurboTax will walk you through entering any additional data and let you know if you do or do not qualify for the tax credit.

What's Next?

Lunch already? Today is probably going much faster for you, and that's good. You worked hard yesterday, entering all your taxable income information. Now you will be able to reap the benefits of that hard work and let the computer do the work for you. After lunch you'll review your draft tax return and correct any omissions or errors. You will determine if you owe any underpayment penalty and prepare your final return for submission to the IRS. Then you will install your state TurboTax tax program(s). After that, you'll be all set to file your tax returns and store this year's tax documents away.

Reviewing and Filing Your Returns

- ✿ Filing for an Extension
- ✿ Using TurboTax Review
- ✿ Finding Deductions
- ✿ Setting Up Your State Return
- ✿ Filing Your Returns Electronically

Good afternoon! If you are following the "In a Weekend" theme, it's Sunday afternoon and you're almost done with your federal tax return. This morning you entered your remaining adjustments to gross income, deductions, tax credits, and additional taxes due. This afternoon you will review your federal tax return, fill out any remaining tax forms, correct any errors or omissions, work with your state tax return, and determine whether you'll file your return electronically or go the old-fashioned route and file via the U.S. Postal Service. As important as it is to maintain good tax records and enter your data properly, it is even more important to review your tax return thoroughly. You'd be surprised how even the smallest error can convert a tax refund to a tax liability. Once your federal return is finalized, you can then move on to preparing your state tax return and filing your returns.

In this session, you will

- Determine any additional tax forms to be filed
- Select a filing method and review your payment options
- Run automatic Reviews
- Delete unnecessary forms and schedules
- Review Audit Alerts and tax-planning tips
- Complete your state tax return
- File your tax return
- Organize and store your 1998 records

Filing Additional Tax Forms

You left off this morning at the Interview topic "Other Forms You May Need to File." As you can see in Figure 5.1, TurboTax lists popular forms that many taxpayers need to file with their returns. Any forms that TurboTax has determined that you must file are already checked off.

Table 5.1 provides a brief description of each tax form listed. Form 2210, Form 4868, and Form 8822, the key forms that most taxpayers need to file at one time or another, are covered in more detail later this afternoon. If you need to use one of the other tax forms, just apply the skills you learned this morning: read over the FAQs, click on the hyperlinks, and read over the Tax Help screens. When in doubt, consult your tax advisor.

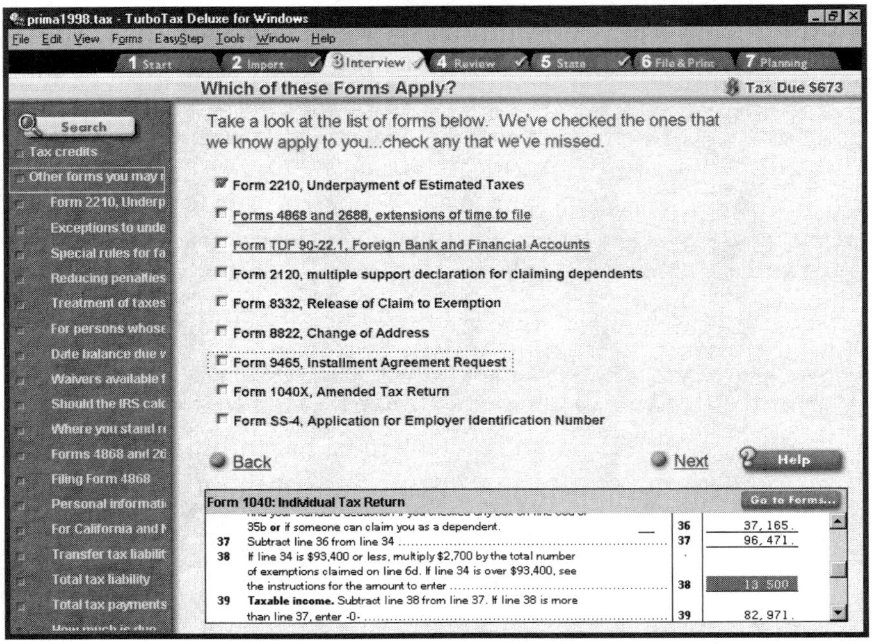

Figure 5.1

You may need to file one of these additional tax forms.

TABLE 5.1   ADDITIONAL TAX FORMS

Tax Form	Name	Description
2210	Underpayment of Estimated Tax by Individuals, Estates, and Trusts	If you have self-employment income or investment income, you must pay estimated taxes during the year to cover enough of the tax liability. If you don't pay enough, you may need to file Form 2210 to prove you did pay enough or to compute the penalty and interest if you didn't pay enough tax during the year.
4868 and 2688	Application for Automatic Extension of Time to File and Application for Additional Extension of Time to File	If you don't have enough time to gather your tax data by April 15, the IRS allows you to pay the tax and automatically get an extension for filing the detailed tax return until August 15 (use Form 4868). If by August 15 you still can't file the details, use Form 2688 to ask for an additional extension to October 15.
TDF 90-22.1	Foreign Bank and Financial Accounts	If you have banking or other financial accounts in foreign countries with a combined balance of more than $10,000, you must file this form. TurboTax will walk you through the process of filling out the form. Note that you do not file this form with your tax return. Instead, mail the form to U.S. Dept. of the Treasury, P.O. Box 32621, Detroit, MI 48232-0621. TurboTax's Help screens provide you with this address and more information on preparing and signing the form.
2120	Multiple Support Declaration	As discussed in yesterday morning's section "Claiming Dependents," you must file Form 2120 if you and others together provide more than 50 percent of someone's support. You all must decide who will get the exemption. The person who gets the exemption must attach to their return Form 2120 signed by each person who contributes more than 10 percent.

TABLE 5.1 ADDITIONAL TAX FORMS (CONTINUED)

Tax Form	Name	Description
8332	Release Claim to Exemption	Use this if you are a custodial parent wishing to release a claim to a child's exemption amount on your return. The noncustodial parent must include a signed copy of this form with his or her tax return. TurboTax's Interview does an excellent job of walking you through the rather complex rules surrounding the dependency and support requirements. IRS Publications 501 and 504 also provide you with a good discussion of the issues, along with practical examples on using this form.
8822	Change of Address	If you moved to a new address since the last tax return filing, you must file Form 8822. Just like your Ma, the IRS likes to keep tabs on you!

Underpaying Estimated Taxes

Income taxes are collected throughout the year by way of withholding on your wages (W-2) and certain transactions subject to backup withholding (some 1099s). If you have other income from self-employment or investments, you may already be in the habit of paying your income taxes throughout the year via quarterly estimates paid to IRS and state tax authorities.

If you don't pay enough of your tax liability on time during the year, the IRS assesses you a penalty and charges interest on the late payment. Most states impose their own late payment penalty and interest charges too. As you can imagine, this could result in a huge unexpected tax liability when you file your return. In tonight's session on tax planning, you will learn how to stay on top of this issue so that you pay in enough taxes to avoid the underpayment penalty.

CAUTION

◆◆

Don't assume that just because you have withholding taken from your paycheck that you can't have an underpayment penalty. Always check your estimated tax liability. Withholding may not cover your tax liability if you have other income such as interest, dividends, or a state tax refund. Note that the tax estimate includes additional taxes such as the Alternative Minimum Tax (AMT) and Self-Employment Tax (SET or FICA).

◆◆

You do not have to pay a penalty or file Form 2210 if either of the following is true:

✪ Your 1998 tax liability net of the withholding tax is less than $1,000

✪ Your 1997 tax liability was zero or you received a refund

Furthermore, you will not owe a penalty if you paid taxes in during 1998 that equal or exceed one of the following:

✪ 90 percent of this year's tax liability

✪ 100 percent of last year's tax liability; or if your AGI is more than $150,000 ($75,000 MFS), 110 percent of last year's tax liability

NOTE

● ●

The IRS may waive the underpayment penalty if you can show you failed to pay the estimated tax in on time due to a casualty, disaster, or other unusual, unforeseen event. Even changes to the tax law sometimes qualify as "unforeseen" events that prevent taxpayers from properly estimating their tax liabilities.

To apply for the waiver, attach an explanation to Form 2210 and any documentation (such as a flood insurance claim) that supports your request. In most cases, the IRS is understanding of these hardships.

● ●

The TurboTax Interview opens by letting you know whether or not you need to file Form 2210. If your screen looks like Figure 5.2, then you need to file Form 2210. You should click on Yes to see if you can reduce or eliminate the penalty.

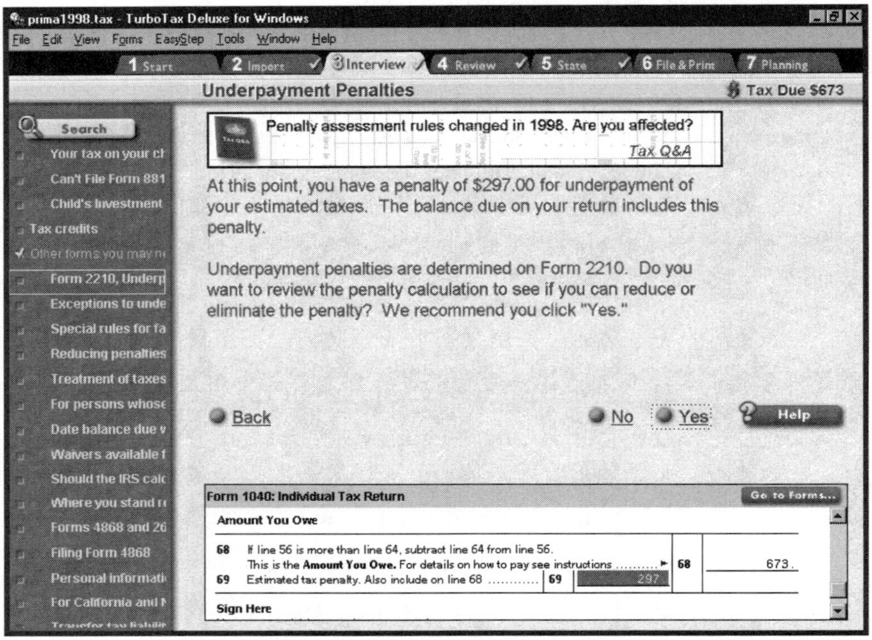

Figure 5.2

Even if TurboTax shows a penalty, you may be able to reduce the amount owed.

In order to determine whether you qualify for one of the exceptions, Turbo-Tax needs to ask you a few questions about your prior year's tax return. If you used TurboTax last year and rolled your prior year's data into this year's return, TurboTax will show you last year's data (giving you an opportunity to change any amounts as needed to match the tax return you filed). You will need to provide the following 1997 information:

- Filing status
- AGI (Form 1040, line 32)
- Tax liability (Form 2210, line 8; or Form 1040, line 53)

If you didn't have a tax liability in 1997, or if you didn't file a tax return last year, leave the 1997 Tax Liability for Form 2210 field blank. Click on Next.

If you qualify for one of the exceptions, TurboTax will explain that no underpayment penalty applies to your return. If you change your tax return data later on, you should revisit this area to make sure that no underpayment penalty applies because of this change.

TIP

■ ■

If you plan to file your tax return early and you owe an underpayment penalty, be sure to change the date that TurboTax uses to determine the penalty. By default, TurboTax uses April 15, 1999, as the filing date. To change this date for purposes of the penalty calculation, use the Interview Navigator to search for the topic "Date Balance Due Will Be Paid," and then enter the date you plan to file your tax return.

■ ■

If you left the Tax Liability field blank, TurboTax will display a list of questions that determine if you meet a specific exception (see Figure 5.3). You must answer Yes to all the questions in order to qualify. Click on Yes or No as applicable. If you qualify, TurboTax will explain that no 2210 penalty applies to your return.

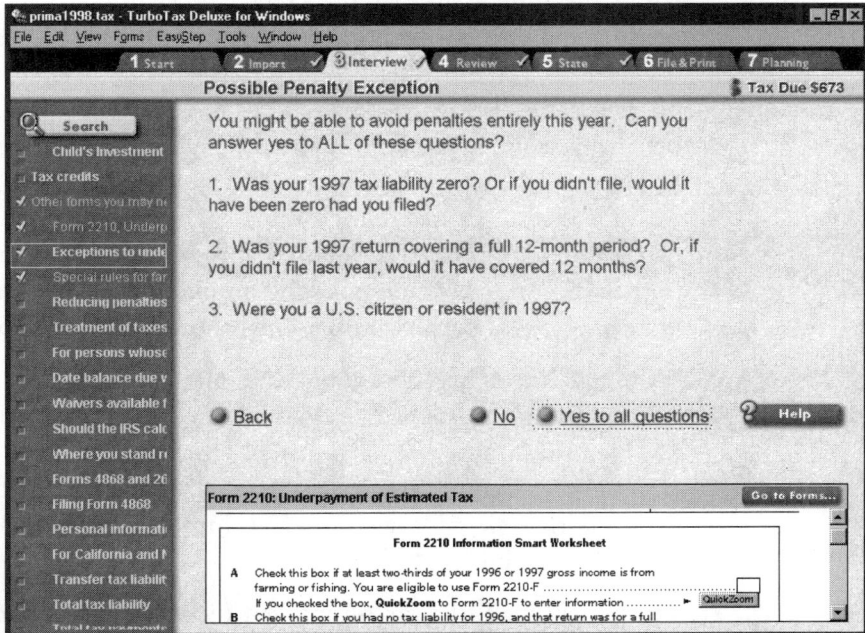

Figure 5.3

If you meet an exception, you may not owe a penalty.

NOTE

Farmers and fisherman who derive at least two-thirds of their gross income from farming or fishing are eligible to file Form 2210-F (Underpayment of Estimated Tax by Farmers and Fishermen). Form 2210-F allows farmers and fisherman to pay only one estimated tax payment by January 15 of the following year. Therefore, the payment for 1998 must be made by January 15, 1999. Alternatively, farmers and fisherman can elect to file their 1998 tax return, by March 1, 1999, instead of making an estimated tax payment by January 15, 1999.

Unfortunately, TurboTax does not provide an Interview process for Form 2210-F. In order to complete Form 2210-F, you must switch to the Forms method, and open Form 2210. Check box A at the top of Form 2210 (Form 2210 Information Smart Worksheet), and click on the QuickZoom button to enter data into Form 2210-F. The Tax Help screens are still available, and you should be sure to check the FAQs too. See IRS Publication 225 (Farmer's Tax Guide) for more information.

If you still owe a penalty, the last special rule that TurboTax will explore for you is the annualized method. Generally, taxes that you pay through withholding and estimated payments are applied ratably to the four quarters in a tax year. If you or your spouse received your taxable income seasonally or irregularly during 1998, you may be able to lower your underpayment penalty by annualizing your income. The annualization method was created to help taxpayers in seasonal businesses to better match their tax liabilities with the income earned. For example, if you own a Schedule C business that makes holiday gift baskets, you probably earn most of your money at the end of the year. Annualization takes the timing of your income into account and doesn't impose a penalty until you have earned enough to owe taxes.

Although TurboTax does not have an Interview for the annualization method, filling out Schedule AI using the Forms method is easy enough to do. Here is an overview of the steps to follow in completing Schedule AI (Annualized Income Installment Method). If you need to select this topic from the Interview Navigator, search for "Reducing Penalties By Annualizing Your Income."

1. When the TurboTax Annualized Income Method Interview screen asks you if you want to annualize your income, click on Yes.
2. Select Go to Forms.

3. Click on the QuickZoom button on line F to access Form 2210, Schedule AI.

4. Enter your income amounts on line 1 by quarter, as received during the year.

5. When you are done, click on the Back to Interview button. Follow the screen prompts to move through the remaining estimated tax screens. The last Interview screen will recompute your penalty and let you know if one is still owed.

TIP

By default, withholding taxes are applied ratably as four equal quarterly payments. You can elect to treat the tax withheld as paid when it was actually withheld. In some cases where you changed jobs during the year or received a big raise, this may help lower your penalty. To make this election, use the Interview Navigator to go to the topic "Treatment of Taxes Withheld."

The last few Interview questions verify the date you will be filing your return, ask if you meet a penalty waiver exception, and inform you of any penalty owed.

Filing for an Extension

Sometimes no matter how hard you try, April 15 comes around and you still don't have all of your tax papers in order. Employers, financial institutions, and partnerships are all required to send you the tax forms you need (such as W-2s and 1099s) by February. But occasionally you don't get the forms you need in time to file your return. Realizing that you may need extra time to file your return, the IRS makes life easy for you by providing you with an "automatic" extension (Form 4868). When you send in Form 4868, you get an additional four months to file your return (instead of being due April 15, your return is due by August 15).

The good news is that the extension is automatic—no explanation is needed. The bad news is that you still must pay your tax liability by April 15. TurboTax helps you estimate the tax due and complete Form 4868. If you have already filed Form 4868 and need an additional extension to

October 15, 1999, TurboTax will transfer the appropriate information and help you complete Form 2688.

NOTE If you need to file Form 2688 to get an additional two month extension, note that you must provide the IRS with an adequate explanation. If you file Form 2688 without filing Form 4868, the IRS will only grant you an extension if you are late because of an undue hardship.

TurboTax begins the Form 4868 Interview by offering to explain how to file for an extension. Choose <u>Yes, Tell Me How to File for an Extension</u> to have TurboTax guide you through the process (similar to the Guide Me feature). Or, choose <u>No, Start Entering Extension Information</u> to begin the Interview process.

After verifying your personal information (name, address, and social security number), TurboTax asks if you want to transfer the data you've entered thus far on Form 4868 (see Figure 5.4). Alternatively, you can choose not to transfer the total tax liability and tax payment amounts and instead enter

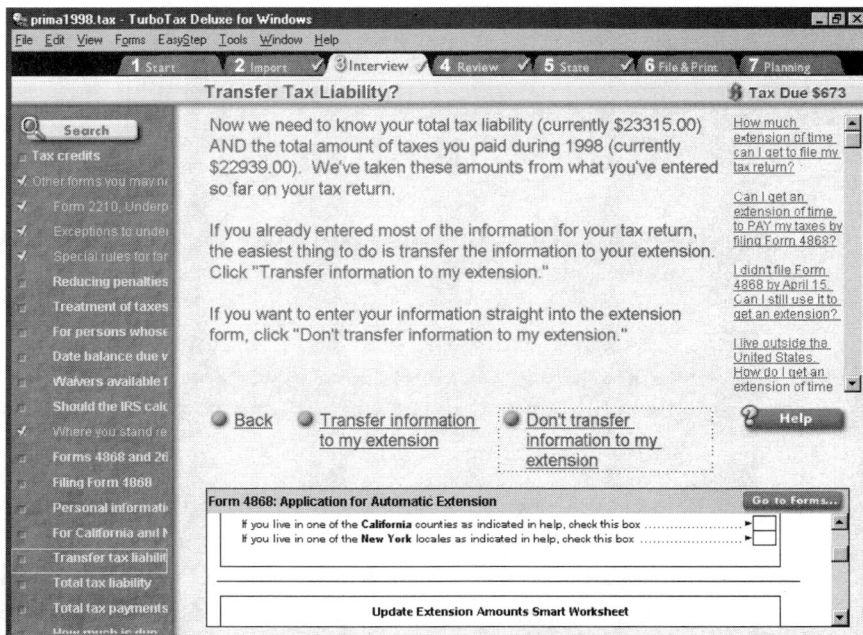

Figure 5.4

TurboTax fills in the tax liability and tax payment amounts for you if you want.

OH NO! TODAY IS APRIL 15TH!!!

If you're just joining us at this point in the book, I'll guess that it's pretty close to April 15 and you need to file an extension today. No problem. Just choose <u>Don't Transfer Information to My Extension</u>, and then enter your expected tax liability and the total tax payments that you've made for the 1998 tax year (including withholding on W-2s and 1099s as well as any estimated tax payments). It's always better to overestimate your tax due and get a refund later than to underestimate and owe interest and incur a penalty.

If you haven't created a tax file in TurboTax yet or if you need to use Turbo-Tax to estimate your tax liability for 1998, follow these steps:

1. If you haven't installed TurboTax, do so now.

2. If you haven't created a new tax file, choose File, New Tax Return.

3. Click on the Interview tab (tab 3).

4. Click on <u>Let's Start My Return</u>, and then enter your personal information. For help on determining your filing status and dependents, see the Saturday Morning section "Entering Personal Information."

5. Proceed to the next Interview topic, Tax Documents You Received.

6. Check the appropriate boxes if you have the time to enter your gross income amounts. Refer to the Saturday Afternoon session, "Starting Your Federal Tax Return," for help on entering your data.

7. If you are short on time, instead of entering the details, click on the Go to Forms button (bottom right corner of your Interview screen). Scroll down to line 21 (other income), and enter the total amount of your gross income from all sources. To itemize the amounts and let TurboTax add up the numbers for you, double-click on the amount to create a supporting details schedule. When you are done, click on the Back to Interview button.

NOTE

By entering your gross income without any adjustments or itemizing deductions, you will probably be paying more tax than you need to. If you are certain of an adjustment or deduction that reduces your gross income, subtract it from your gross income amount or list it on the schedule for other income as a negative number.

8. Your tax liability will be displayed in the top right corner of the Interview, just below the Planning folder tab.

9. Click on the Search button in the left portion of the screen (the Interview Navigator).

10. Type the number 4868, press Enter, and click on the Jump To button. This takes you to the beginning of the Interview for filing an extension (the topic of this section).

11. After you complete the Interview on filing an extension and you print and mail in your extension with your check (be sure to sign the extension!), you can relax and start back at the beginning of the book. If you entered amounts in other income that do not belong there, remember to delete them.

those figures yourself. Those two numbers are the only amounts entered on Form 4868, other than any gift tax that you may owe.

April 15th, the day taxes are due, is the same day the Titanic went down.

CAUTION The IRS will consider your automatic extension void if you don't estimate a reasonable tax liability. The IRS's concept of reasonable is based on the gross income reported by your employers (W-2s) along with other income sources (1099s, K-1s, etc.). As a general rule of thumb, it is better to overestimate your taxable income than to owe interest and penalties for late filing, not to mention the addition of a nonfiling penalty, which is imposed when an extension is denied.

If you chose to transfer your data to the extension form, TurboTax displays the amounts for you and gives you the option of changing the amounts as needed. Otherwise, TurboTax prompts you to enter your tax liability and tax payments.

If you also need to file an extension for gift tax or a generation skipping transfer (GST), TurboTax will prompt you for that information and post the appropriate amounts to your Form 4868. Consult the FAQs and Tax Help screens for more information on these additional taxes. After advising you to update your extension for any changes to your tax data prior to filing Form 4868, TurboTax lets you know where to send the form.

> **TIP** To quickly print your Form 4868, click on the Go to Forms button. When the form opens, click on the Print button in the toolbar (just below the menu bar) and the Print button in the dialog box. Sign it and add your check, and you're ready to mail it!

Changing Your Address

Another form you will probably need at one time or another is Form 8822 (Change of Address). This form lets the IRS know where to mail your tax forms package and where to send you notices. Most taxpayer problems with the IRS stem from miscommunication. Keeping the IRS informed of your proper address is one step you can take to avoid problems. You can access this form from within the Interview by checking Form 8822, Change of Address (refer to Figure 5.1).

Figure 5.5 shows the first TurboTax Interview screen for Form 8822. Check the appropriate boxes to let TurboTax know how to handle the tax data you've already entered and how this address change affects your return.

Click on <u>Continue</u> and TurboTax will interview you on the address, old spouses (not that all spouses are old), and the other returns (if any) that are affected by this change of address.

Selecting a Filing Method

Next, you need to decide how you want to file your return (see Figure 5.6). TurboTax allows you to file electronically, via a computer-scannable return

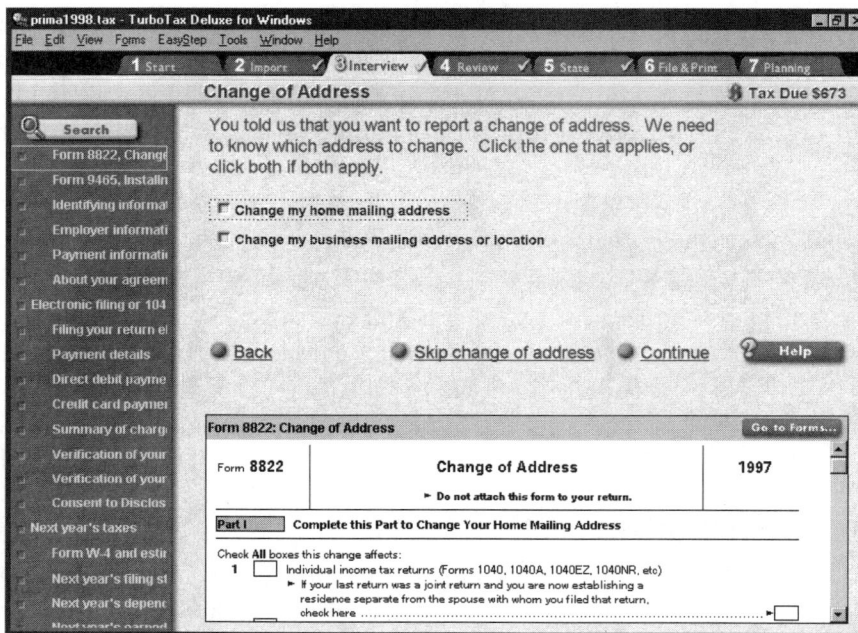

Figure 5.5

TurboTax needs to know if the address you entered earlier is the new or old address.

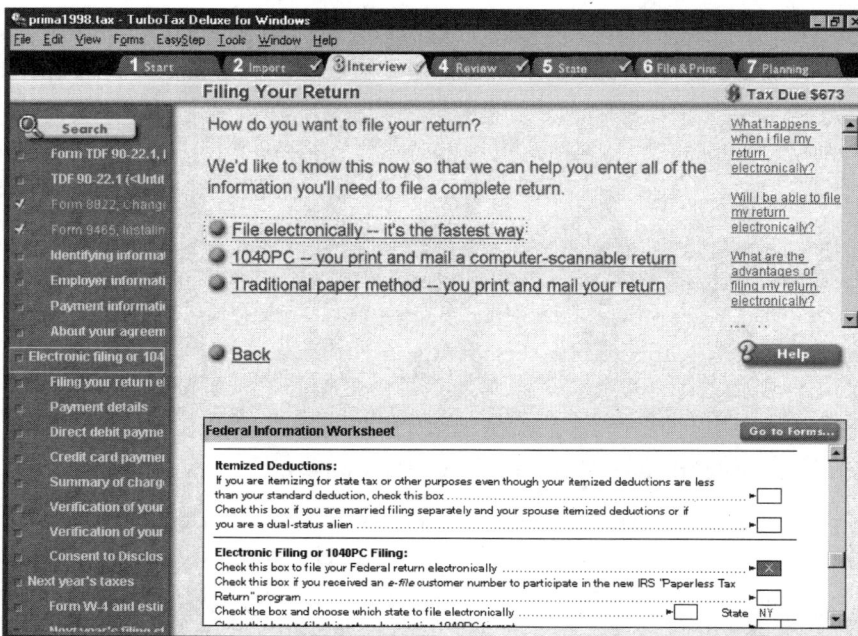

Figure 5.6

TurboTax helps you determine which filing method is best for you.

that you mail in, or using the old-fashioned paper-based method. The IRS allows you to file electronically as long as you meet certain requirements.

Why File Electronically?

It is natural to be skeptical of new processes, but the advantages to filing electronically far outweigh the cons. Some advantages to filing electronically are as follows:

- ✿ Your return is delivered to the IRS more quickly.
- ✿ Free electronic filing (for one return) is included with TurboTax Deluxe.
- ✿ TurboTax can confirm the delivery for you (at no extra charge).
- ✿ There is greater accuracy at the IRS because your data doesn't need to be rekeyed.
- ✿ You'll get your refund sooner because of faster delivery and processing time at the IRS.
- ✿ You can file prior to April 10, 1999, but you don't have to pay the taxes due until April 15, 1999. (Wow!)

On the con side, I can only find one disadvantage to filing electronically: you don't get the opportunity to have your filing certified as having been delivered by the U.S. Postal Service. The certification and return receipt services of the U.S. Postal Service provide you, the taxpayer, with court-approved proof that you did file your return on time. Even in these days of the IRS accepting tax filings by express mail services such as Federal Express and Airborne Express, I still drive down to the post office and pay extra fees to have the delivery certified and get a return receipt. Old habits are hard to break. But more importantly, I like that warm, fuzzy feeling of knowing that, should the IRS claim I didn't file my return on time, I can produce proof that holds up in court. I'm sure that as we all become more automated, the IRS and the courts will begin to recognize e-mail certifications.

NOTE

As I wrote this book, the U.S. Postal Service was getting ready to launch an electronic Internet stamp. E-Stamp Corporation's SmartStamp software allows you to download postage from the Internet and then print the stamp with an ordinary ink-jet or laser printer. E-Stamp (list price of about $169) for Windows 95, 98, and NT is scheduled for release in early 1999. Basically you will weigh your package and then enter the data (weight and address). The software links to the E-Stamp Web site (**www.estamp.com**), verifies the address, computes the postage due, prints the stamp (on label peel-off paper or directly on the envelope), and then deducts the postage cost (plus a small yet-to-be determined fee) from your account.

FIND IT ON ▶
THE WEB

Looks like electronic certifications of delivery may not be so far away in the future.

Why File Using the 1040PC Format?

The 1040PC format produces a printout of your return (only the lines with amounts) in a scannable format. After receiving a 1040PC in the mail, the IRS scans it into a computer. Although not as convenient for you as electronic filing, the 1040PC format provides several benefits over filing a paper-based return.

- ✿ Uses less paper and less ink
- ✿ Reduces processing time at the IRS (your data doesn't need to be rekeyed)
- ✿ Increases accuracy at the IRS (again because your data doesn't need to be rekeyed)

TIP

If you decide to file electronically or use the 1040PC method and need to attach a copy of your federal tax return to your state tax return, you can attach a printout of the electronic file (as if you had mailed the return) or a 1040PC printout. Note that over half of the states now accept electronic filing of their own state tax returns.

Choosing Your State Filing Method

Review the FAQs on the various filing methods and select your preferred method from the list (click on the method's hypertext). You can always decide to change to another method after you review your return. Regardless of the method you select, the next Interview question asks how you would like to file your state tax return. As you can see in Figure 5.7, many states now support electronic filing (click on the down arrow next to These States Support Electronic Filing to see the states listed).

To file your state return electronically, select your state from the drop-down list, and then click the option button for Yes. If not, select the appropriate No response. When you are ready, click on <u>Continue</u> to move on to the next Interview question.

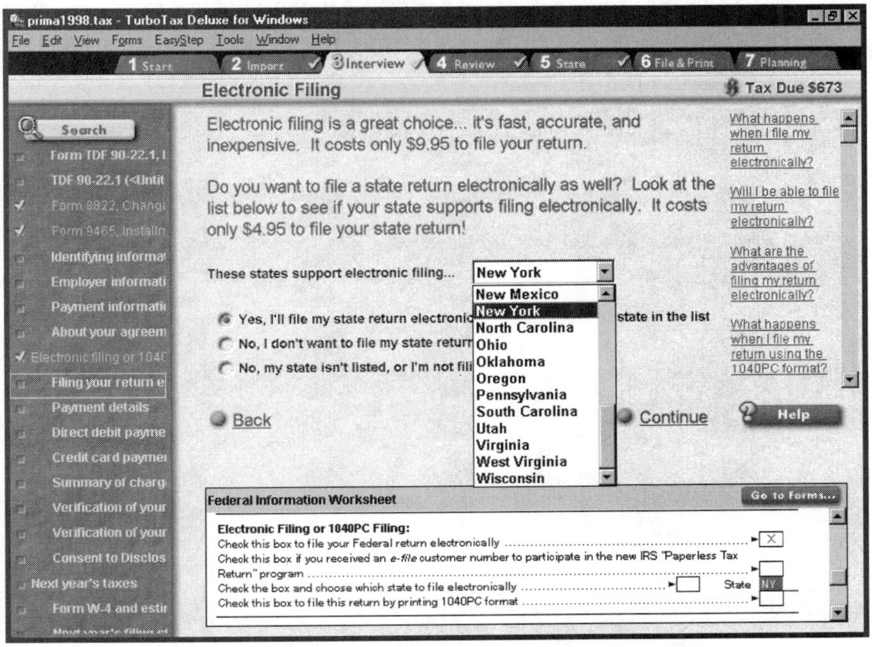

Figure 5.7

You might be able to file your state tax return electronically too!

Paying Your Taxes

If you owe taxes, you need to determine how you will pay your tax liability (see Figure 5.8). You can provide the IRS with your bank account number, and the IRS will automatically withdraw the taxes from your account. Or you could provide a credit card number, and the IRS will charge your credit card for the amount due plus the credit card company fee. Of course the IRS will be happy to do it the old-fashioned way and cash the check that you mail in. So many ways to pay taxes! Select your preferred method, and then click on Continue.

NOTE At the time I wrote this book, the IRS was still finalizing arrangements with several credit card companies (MasterCard, Discover/Novus, American Express, and possibly, Visa). All agreements provide that the taxpayer (not the IRS) pays the usual merchant fee. When you use your credit card at a store, the merchant at that store pays about a three percent fee to the credit card company. There's no word yet on what the fee will be for taxpayers.

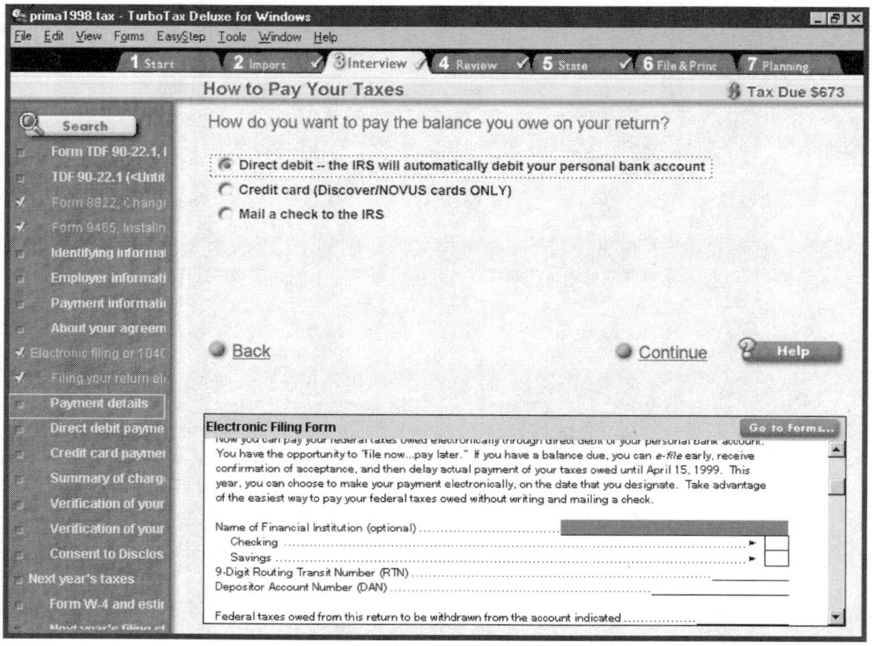

Figure 5.8

Nowadays you can pay your taxes with a credit card.

After you select a payment method and provide bank account or credit card numbers as needed, click on Continue. TurboTax advances to the Interview topic "Next Year's Taxes."

Moving On to Review

Your screen should now look like Figure 5.9. But instead of planning for next year's tax return just yet (this will be covered more fully tonight in the discussion on tax planning), you should review what you've entered thus far for this year's tax return. Choose No to move ahead to the Review tab.

Updating TurboTax

Before you start to review your tax return, TurboTax wants to make sure that you are working with the most up-to-date program, tax forms, and tax rules. If you have Internet access, click on Update TurboTax (see Figure 5.10) to connect to the TurboTax Web site, where you can update your system.

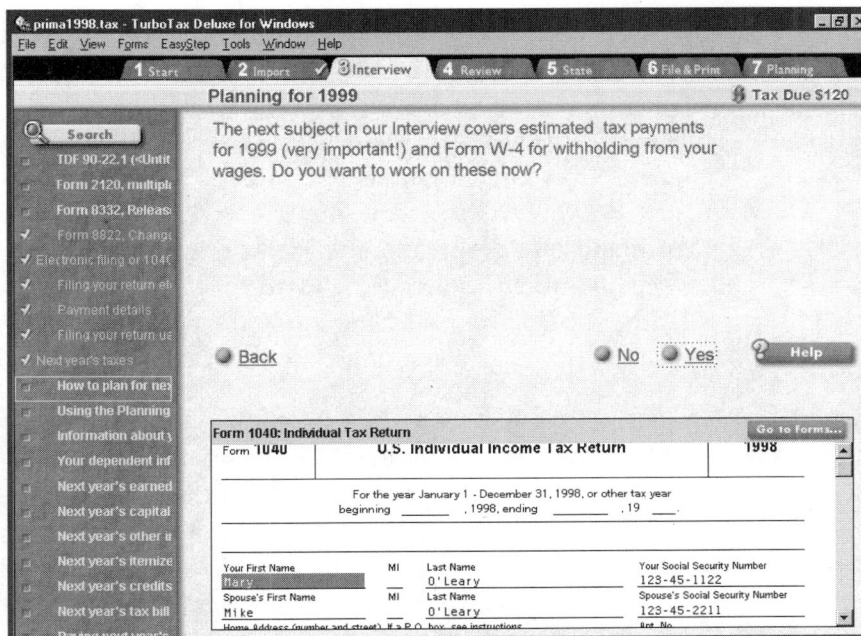

Figure 5.9

Instead of preparing your estimated 1999 taxes, click on No to start the 1998 tax Review process.

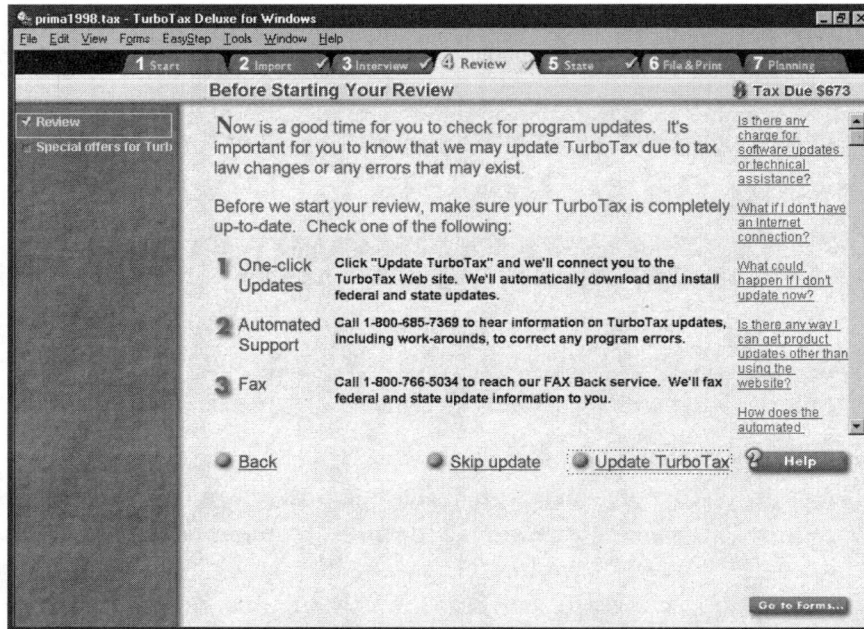

Figure 5.10

Before starting your review, be sure to update TurboTax.

If you don't have access to the Internet, choose <u>Skip Update</u>. Then call Intuit at 800-264-5943 and ask for an update disk to be mailed to you (takes about a week to receive it). You can also use the Automated Support phone number (800-685-7369) to hear information on TurboTax updates, program errors, and solutions to common problems. The FAX Back service provides you with this same information, but in a more detailed, printed format (and a quick turnaround). To reach the FAX Back service, call 800-766-5034 and press 2 to request a faxed catalog of all FAX Back documents for TurboTax Deluxe. Once you know the document you want, call the FAX Back number again and press 1 to enter the document number(s).

◆ ◆

CAUTION   I highly recommend that you do not file a tax return using TurboTax until you have a chance to update your program. The original TurboTax Deluxe 1998 CDs were manufactured in late November 1998. Although most of the tax law is set by then, many of the tax forms are not. Furthermore, as with any software product, bugs exist. Program errors can cause your tax return calculations to be off, your forms to print incorrectly, or worse yet, your electronically filed tax return to be filed in Bangladesh. Not that I've ever had any program error in TurboTax cause my return to be wrong. But then again, I always do the update. Plus I wait until April 1 to work on my return, knowing full well that the bugs will have been worked out by then for sure.

◆ ◆

Running Automatic Reviews

After you have updated your copy of TurboTax (or ordered the update disk), TurboTax prompts you to select the automatic Review processes that you would like to run (see Figure 5.11). The Review process checks for

- Missing items
- Incomplete items
- Missed deductions
- Items that would trigger the IRS audit flag
- How your return compares with the average return
- Ideas on how to reduce your tax burden next year

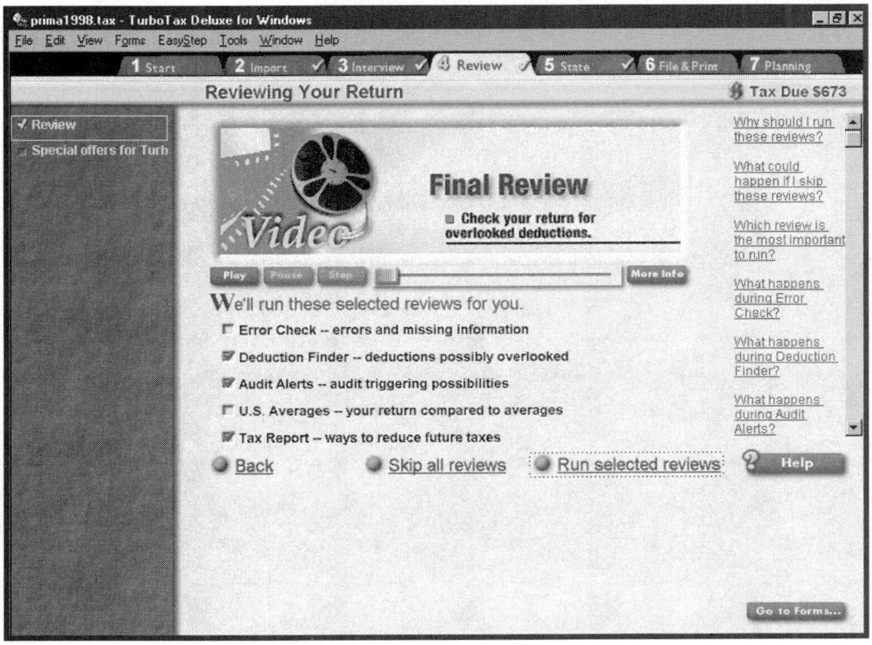

Figure 5.11

TurboTax can check your tax return for errors, missed deductions, and audit issues.

Table 5.2 lists and describes the various Review routines that TurboTax provides. By default, TurboTax takes the liberty of selecting all Reviews to be run. The process is so quick that I highly recommend you let TurboTax do all the Reviews.

TIP

If you change amounts or Interview answers on your return after you run the Reviews, be sure to run them again. TurboTax will wipe the slate clean and re-review your return from the bottom up with lightning speed. An ounce of prevention is sure to save you tax dollars in the long run!

TABLE 5.2 TURBOTAX AUTOMATIC REVIEWS

Tax Review	Description
Error Check	Checks all tax forms, schedules, and supporting details looking for incorrect and incomplete items. It also cross-checks your return for incompatible data, amounts too high/too low, and estimated data. This is the most important Review and should be run again if you change anything in the Interview or on any forms.
Deduction Finder	Looks for deductions for which you qualify but didn't take. It also looks for planning opportunities for next year.
Audit Alerts	Scans your return for areas that tax experts would question, such as inconsistencies or unusual deductions. It also looks for items that the IRS has focused on in the past. If you get an Audit Alert, this does not indicate that your return will be audited but simply alerts you to common audit issues.
U.S. Averages	Compares your return to the national averages for returns filed in the previous year (1997). It helps you see how your return compares to others in your tax bracket.
Tax Report	Summarizes your return and suggests ways in which you might be able to reduce taxes in the future.

TIP

To get an overview of the Review process, play the video.

When you are ready, click on <u>Run Selected Reviews</u>. TurboTax displays the One Moment dialog box while it runs the various Review processes. When completed, you will see the results, one Review topic at a time. Figure 5.12 shows you the topic "How Error Check Works." Notice that the Interview Navigator appears at the left, listing the errors found. (Wow, those poor O'Learys have so many errors!)

TIP

Are you curious about how Error Check works? Click on the hyperlink <u>Here</u> on the screen "How Error Check Works" to view a complete description from Program Help in the Help system.

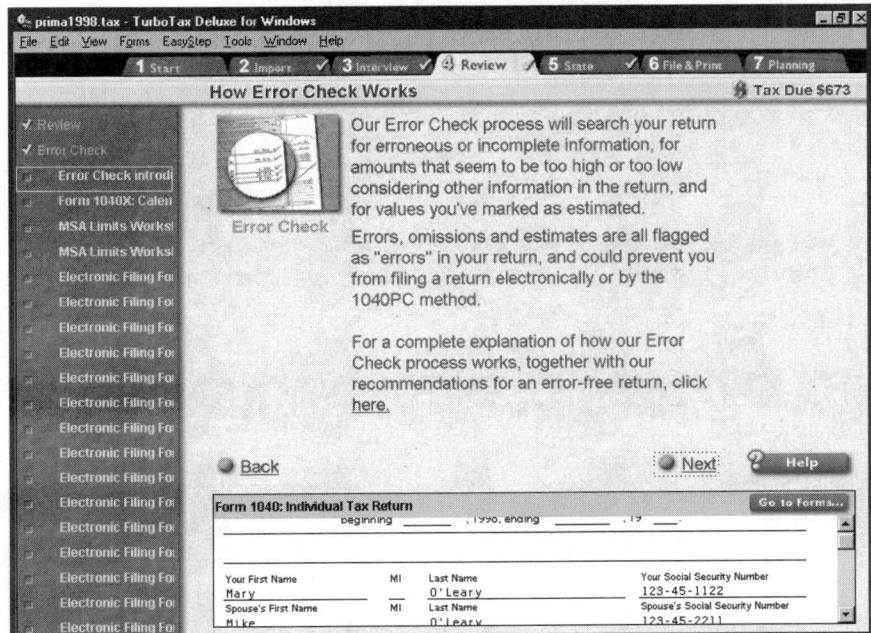

Figure 5.12

You can review your tax return using the familiar Interview process.

When you are ready to continue, click on <u>Next</u>. Figure 5.13 shows you a sample error found in the tax return of my fictitious family. TurboTax explains to you what is missing. In this case, on Schedule B, a 1099-DIV for IBM (a dividend received from IBM) lacks some information. The Turbo-Tax Reviewer knows that box 2a on that 1099-DIV should be greater than or equal to the sum of boxes 2b, 2c, and 2d. A FAQ provides help on what kind of information is needed. At the bottom of the screen, the supporting form or schedule appears with a Go to Forms button.

TIP   TurboTax provides you with a Print button. If you can't resolve the error or omission at this time, print the page and follow up on the issue later.

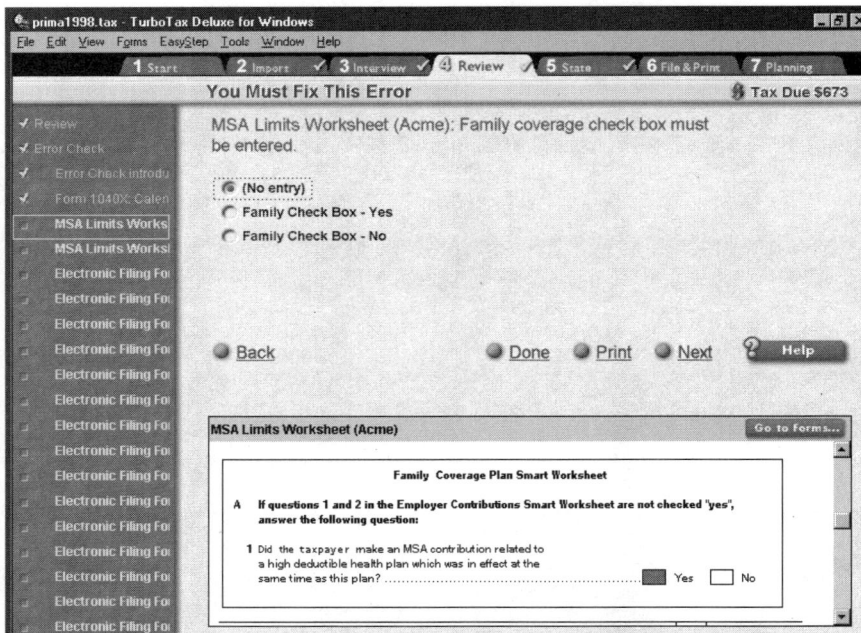

Figure 5.13

TurboTax explains the error or omission and provides you with an opportunity to correct the situation.

So, what should you do when the TurboTax Reviewer finds an error or omission such as this? First, find your source document and compare the information there with the data you entered in TurboTax. After that you have several options:

○ If indeed the amount is missing or incorrect and you know how to correct the error, enter the correct information in the space(s) provided.

○ If your source document appears to be in error, contact the issuer and request a correct document to be provided to you *and* the IRS.

○ If TurboTax is out in left field (usually not the case), print the error page and on it write out an explanation (for yourself) why you believe the amount/data entry is correct as is. Keep this filed with your return. Four or five years from now if you are audited, at least your memory will be refreshed.

○ If you don't understand the issue or error, print the page and discuss it with your tax advisor.

Click on <u>Next</u> to continue to the next error.

Deleting Forms and Supporting Detail Lists

In some cases you will notice a long list of missing items from a form that you started to use, but then realized didn't apply to you. When this happens you should delete the form from your tax return. To delete a form, schedule, or supporting detail list from your return, follow these steps:

1. If you are in the midst of reviewing your return, use the Go to Forms button.

2. From the menu bar choose Forms, Show My Return.

3. Click on the form, schedule, or supporting detail list that you need to delete from your return.

4. Click on the Remove button.

5. Repeat steps 3 and 4 as needed.

CAUTION

◆◆◆◆◆◆◆◆◆◆◆◆◆◆◆◆◆◆◆◆◆◆◆◆◆◆◆◆◆◆◆◆◆◆◆

You will be unable to delete a form or schedule if it is required or requested by the data you have entered. For example, on Form 2210 if you check the box indicating that you want to use the annualized method, TurboTax won't let you delete Schedule AI, which contains that information. So first you should clear the check box or other information that requires the form or schedule. Click on the Remove button to delete the unneeded form or schedule.

◆◆◆◆◆◆◆◆◆◆◆◆◆◆◆◆◆◆◆◆◆◆◆◆◆◆◆◆◆◆◆◆◆◆◆

6. Click on the Back to Interview button to continue clearing errors.

NOTE

•••

If you delete a form that has supporting detail schedules associated with it, the supporting detail schedules will automatically be removed.

If a form includes amounts from other forms, the Remove These Forms dialog box appears with a list of the other forms (see Figure 5.14), allowing you to Remove Listed Forms or Cancel.

Note also that you cannot delete the Federal Information Worksheet or the State Assistant Worksheet.

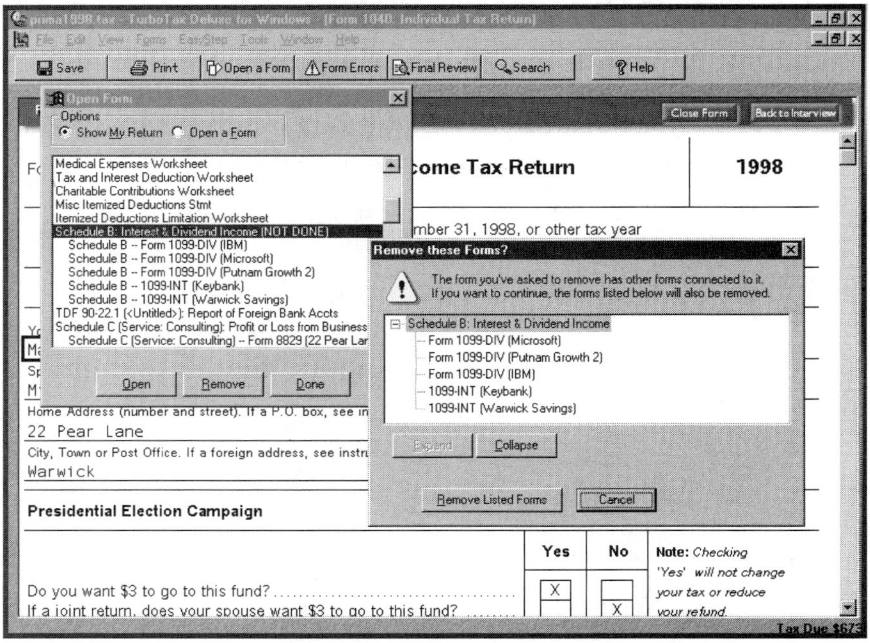

•••

Figure 5.14

When you delete a form that contains amounts from other forms, TurboTax displays this dialog box.

Continue through the errors, correcting what you can, deleting unnecessary forms, and printing the errors that you need to research further. When you reach the end, Error Check Conclusion, read over the message and click on <u>Next</u> to continue.

Checking Overrides

An *override* occurs when the amount you have entered into a field replaces TurboTax data that has been computed or posted from another form or schedule in your return. For example, the total income amount on line 22 is a calculated field (TurboTax adds up all your gross income and enters the total on line 22). It is a sign of a flexible program when you are allowed to override calculated or automatic fields. This feature recognizes that you, the user, are in control. But just like driving a car, you need to proceed with caution and know what you are doing.

Why would you want to override a calculated or automatic amount? Well, here are some possible reasons:

✪ Under the direction of your trusted tax advisor, you decide to take an aggressive tax position on a tax issue that goes against the current tax law. For example, you decide you have enough facts and are willing to go to Tax Court to fight for your right to claim a deduction that the IRS currently disallows.

✪ You are unable to download the latest version of TurboTax via the Internet, but their FAX Back service alerts you that a calculated field is incorrect. You use your calculator and enter the proper amount using the Override feature.

✪ The IRS or a state taxing authority informs the public of an error on a form or in the tax logic of that authority, but for which TurboTax hasn't provided an update yet. You get the taxing authority's notice in writing from a reliable source and use the Override feature in Turbo-Tax to correct your return accordingly.

CAUTION

◆◆◆◆◆◆◆◆◆◆◆◆◆◆◆◆◆◆◆◆◆◆◆◆◆◆◆◆◆◆◆◆◆◆◆◆◆

Do not use the Override feature to modify TurboTax's calculated results unless you have a very good reason to do so. If you do not understand where a number came from, use the Data Source feature to drill down and find the source data. Always change the underlying source data rather than override a top level summarized or carried forward amount.

For example, if the amount in box 1b of your 1099-DIV is wrong, don't use the Override feature to change the total taxable dividends on page one of your 1040. Instead, drill down to the 1099-DIV and fix the amount you entered for that dividend in box 1b.

◆◆◆◆◆◆◆◆◆◆◆◆◆◆◆◆◆◆◆◆◆◆◆◆◆◆◆◆◆◆◆◆◆◆◆◆◆

Note that overrides are not necessarily errors, but if an override occurs and you don't know why, you should investigate and correct the situation if necessary.

To override a calculated field on a form, follow these steps:

1. Right-click on the amount in the form or schedule.
2. Choose Override.
3. Type in the new amount and press Enter. Overrides appear in red on your screen.

Here are some reasons not to use the Override feature:

- TurboTax does not update amounts that have been overridden. For example, if you override the total dividend income amount on your 1040 and later add in a new 1099-DIV, TurboTax will be unable to update your total dividend income to include that new amount. Once you override a field, that field will always require manual computation.
- Overriding tax law rules that TurboTax follows violates your warranty with regard to that override and its effects.
- Overrides may lead to questions from the IRS, delay your refund, or invalidate your electronic filing.

To cancel an override, follow these steps:

1. Right-click on the overridden amount (in red).
2. Choose Cancel Override. TurboTax recalculates the return and displays the calculated amount.

Go ahead and click on <u>Next</u> to have TurboTax find any overridden amounts in your return. Cancel any overrides that you do not want on your return.

When you are done, click on <u>Next</u> to move on to the next Review, the Deduction Finder.

Finding Deductions

Throughout the Interview process, TurboTax tries to make you aware of tax-reduction opportunities through additional deductions, exceptions, or other avenues that you might qualify for. The Deduction Finder in the Review section goes through your return and identifies which suggestions you haven't acted on yet. The result is the list you see in the Navigator section of Figure 5.15. Many of these items look familiar because you've been asked about them during the Interview process or you've seen them discussed in the FAQs.

Click on <u>Next</u> to start reviewing the deductions and other suggestions TurboTax has for you. Read over each suggestion and determine if it might apply to you. Print the suggestions that are of interest but for which you need to gather more information. When you're ready to take advantage of a suggestion, click on the Go to Forms button and enter your data.

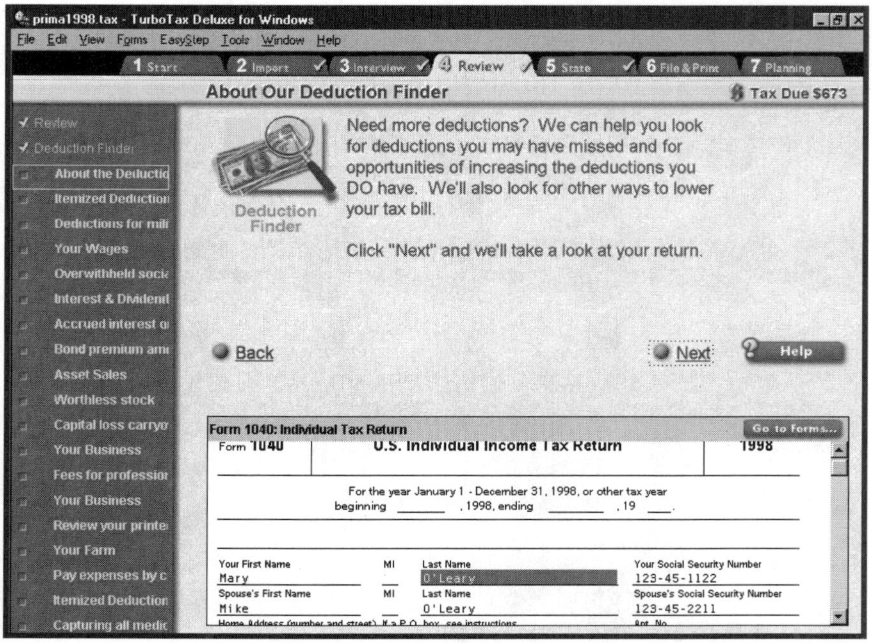

Figure 5.15

The Deduction Finder gives you one last chance to reduce your tax burden.

You know it's a bad day when your income tax refund check bounces.

TIP　At any time while reviewing the suggestions of the Deduction Finder, you can click on the Done button to skip the remaining suggestions and go directly to the next Review topic.

Reviewing Audit Alerts

The Audit Alerts feature (see Figure 5.16) looks through your return and brings to your attention any odd items. Just because TurboTax brings an item to your attention as an Audit Alert doesn't mean that your return will be audited. The Audit Alerts feature is meant to add an expert's eye to the process of reviewing your tax return. Sometimes when you've been working so long with so many details, you can't see the forest for the trees. The Audit Alerts feature looks at the forest.

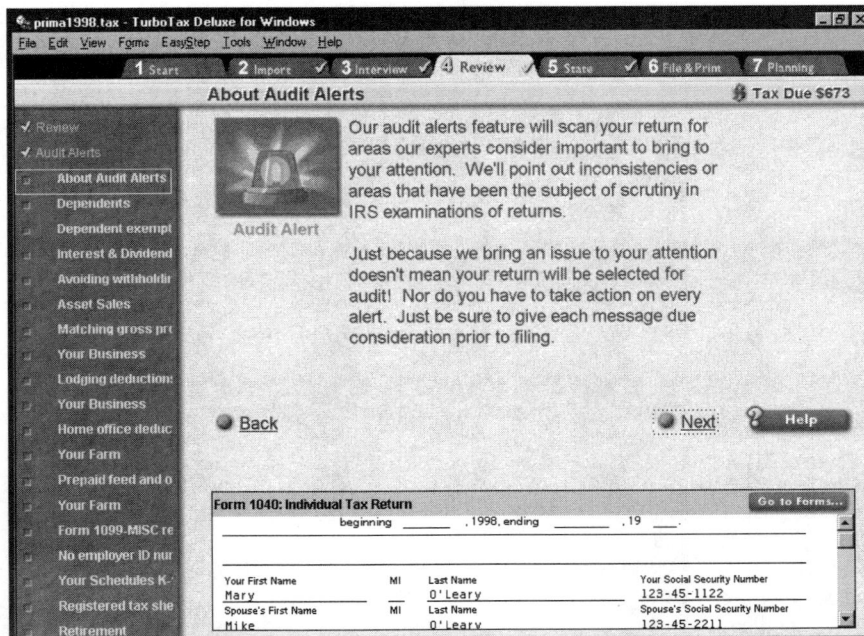

Figure 5.16

The Audit Alerts feature looks for inconsistencies in your return.

Click on <u>Next</u> to begin reviewing the Audit Alerts. Some of the alerts are standard questions such as "Can anyone else claim one of your dependents on their return?" In other cases the Audit Alert points out a withholding tax on a 1099 that you may be able to prevent for next year by providing your SSN. Or the Audit Alert may advise you of your own filing responsibilities as a business owner (Forms 1099 and W-2) and the penalties for noncompliance. In any event, the Audit Alerts will provide you with valuable information.

TIP When you see an Audit Alert that affects next year's return, or that could be used in your tax planning, click on the Print button and file the idea away in your 1999 tax file.

Comparing Averages

Paying taxes is one experience that we all have in common with one another. Well, that and McDonald's. The TurboTax U.S. Averages Review feature (see Figure 5.17) compares the amounts on your return to the spring 1998 version

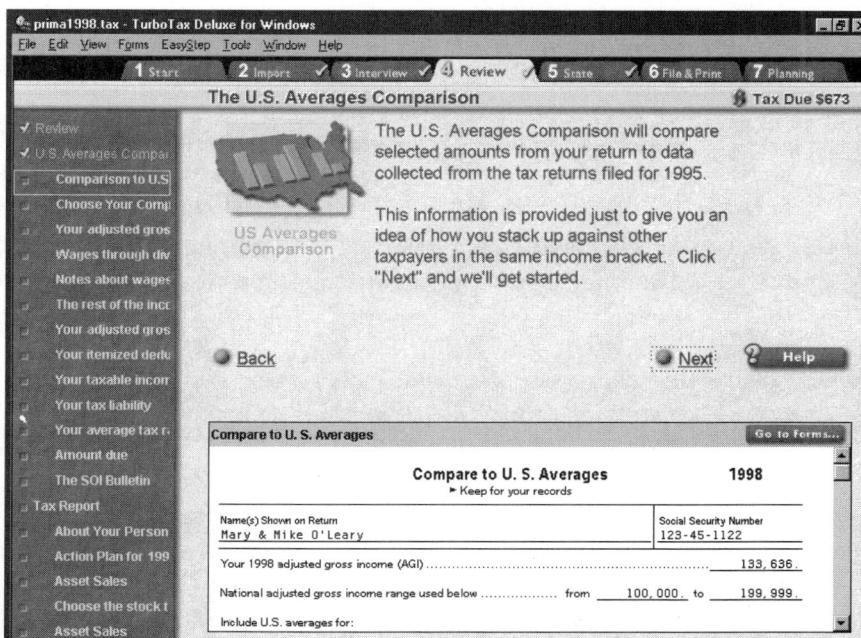

Figure 5.17

TurboTax compares your return to the national averages.

of the Statistics of Income (SOI) bulletin, a report compiled by the IRS every three months. This bulletin contains analysis of income, deduction, tax, and credit information, including the number of returns filed and the total amounts reported for each item.

TIP

Visit the SOI Web site (**www.irs.ustreas.gov/prod/tax_stats**) for the latest averages and more fun statistics.

By comparing your return to the national averages, you can gain a better perspective on how your return looks to the IRS, from a statistical standpoint. Furthermore, you will know how your return compares to returns of other taxpayers in your tax bracket. If you seem to be paying more taxes than other taxpayers at your income level, you may need to change your tax-planning strategies. On the other hand, if you pay less than most folks earning a similar income, then you can give yourself a pat on the back.

Click on Next to start the U.S. Averages Review. First, TurboTax asks if you want to see the averages for all tax lines or just the lines on your return for which you have amounts. Choose all return lines if you want to see the averages even for those lines you left blank. Otherwise, leave the default choice of just your lines with amounts. Then click on Next.

After informing you of how your AGI stacks up against the nation, Turbo-Tax will start to take you through your return, line by line. As you can see in Figure 5.18, the Compare to U.S. Averages form at the bottom of your screen shows you your actual tax return amounts, the national average, and the difference. Continue to click on Next and notice how the text above explains the national statistics, while the form displayed at the bottom of the screen shows how your amounts compare to the national average.

When you reach the deduction area, note how close or far off your deduction amounts are as compared to the national average. These differences may signify the need for better record keeping or tax planning. Toward the end of this Review, TurboTax reports your average tax rate and compares it to the national average. This is a very good gauge of where your tax return falls in the scheme of things. The comparison of tax due, however, is relatively meaningless since everybody has different withholdings and estimated payments.

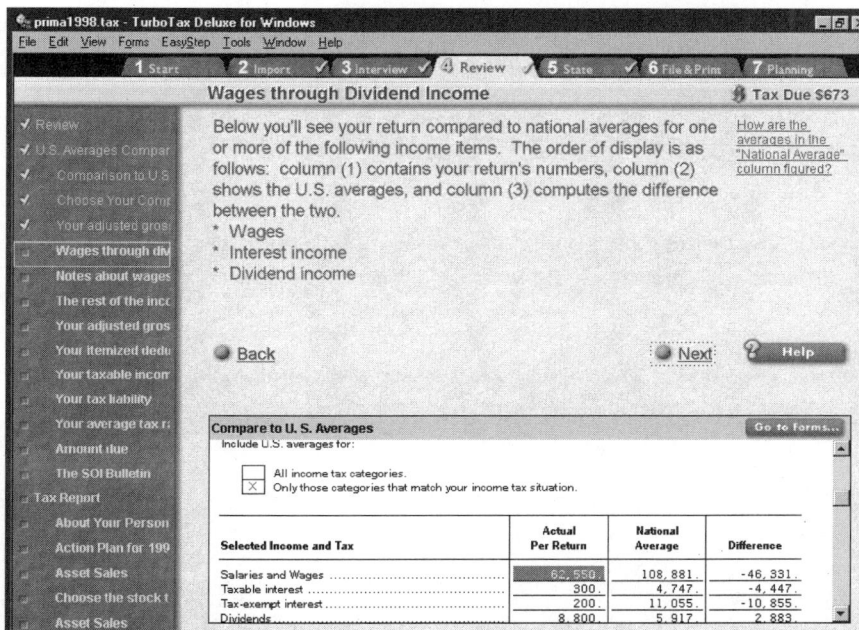

Figure 5.18

You can see in the Compare to U.S. Averages form how your amounts stack up to the national average.

Getting Your Tax Report Card

The Tax Report Reviewer (see Figure 5.19) provides you with an action plan for 1999 tax planning. The plan summarizes your 1998 tax return highlights and then provides specific tax-planning tips in the areas where you have income or need deductions. You can use Next to view the plan one screen at a time, or you can print the entire Tax Report right away.

NOTE If you prefer to review the Tax Report onscreen, continue to click on Next to move through the tax-planning tips. You can always print a single tip by clicking on Print and selecting Print This Tip.

To print your Tax Report, follow these steps:

1. Click on Print. The Print Review dialog box appears.
2. Select the Print Tax Report option.

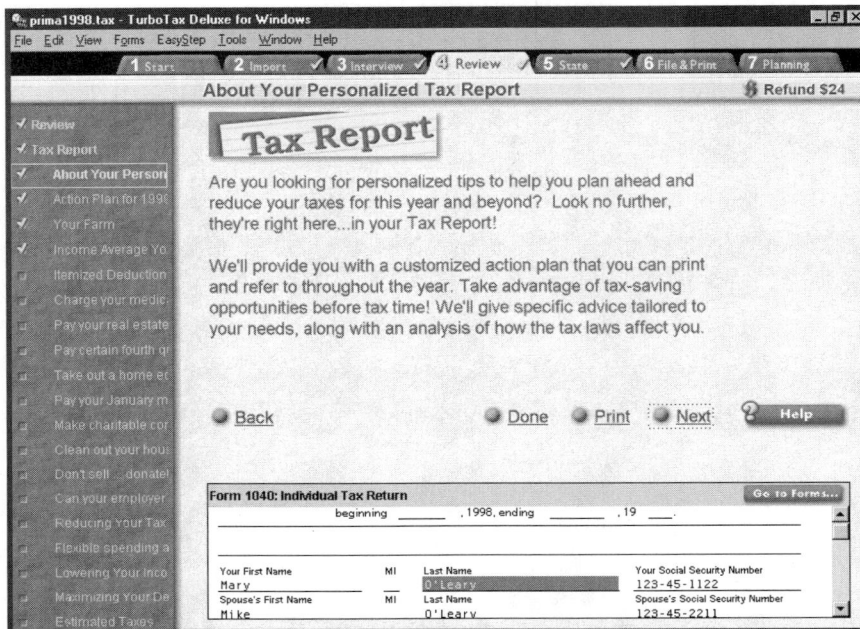

Figure 5.19

The Tax Report
provides you with
a personalized
tax plan.

3. If necessary, click on the Setup button to set up or change your printer.

4. Click on Print. Figure 5.20 illustrates the first page of the 10-page Tax Report for my fictitious family, the O'Learys.

TIP To quickly end your on-screen review of the Tax Report, click on Done.

Finishing Your Review

When you finish with your last Review item, TurboTax gives you the option of running the Review again. To finish the Review process, click on Skip Review. TurboTax asks if you want to connect to the Internet and explore the special offers on products and services that may be of interest to you. Click on Special Offers to see what is available, or click on Skip Special Offers to end the Review process (you'll find yourself on the State tab).

```
                        Tax Report for Mary O'Leary
                               Tax Year 1999

          1998 Tax Summary

          Income and Adjustments:    $134,336
          Deductions:                 $37,584
          Taxable Income:             $83,252
          Total Tax:                  $23,367
          Total Payments:             $22,939
          Refund / Tax Due:            $-729


          About Your Personalized Tax Report

          Are you looking for personalized tips to help you plan ahead and reduce your taxes for this
          year and beyond?  Look no further, they're right here...in your Tax Report!

          We'll provide you with a customized action plan that you can print and refer to throughout
          the year. Take advantage of tax-savings opportunities before tax time! We'll give specific
          advice tailored to your needs, along with an analysis of how the tax laws affect you.

          You can review your Tax Report on-screen and we'll show you valuable tips as you go. Just
          click the highlighted words for more detailed explanations. You can also print the entire
          Tax Report now. Just click "Print", then click "Print Tax Report."

          Action Plan for 1999

          1.  Asset Sales

              •  Choose the stock to trade

                 Are you planning to sell stock that you've bought at various times throughout the
                 years?  Choose the "lot" of stock you sell carefully:  it can make a big difference
                 in the amount of gain or loss you report.

                 Say you have 100 shares of XYZ Company stock which is currently selling for $100
                 share.  You bought 25 shares at $43 per share and 75 at $75 per share.  You know
                 you'd like to sell only 20 shares of this stock ... which actual shares should you
                 sell?

                 The answer depends on what's going on in the rest of your return.  For example, if
                 you have capital losses this year, sell the $43 shares:  your gain of $1,140 will
                 absorb the losses.  You may want to instruct your broker in writing exactly which
                 shares you want to sell.

          2.  Asset Sales

              •  Income Average Your Farm Profits!

                 Income Average Your Farm Profits

                 Can you lower your tax by averaging your farm income? It may be worthwhile to check
                 this out...

                 If your tax liability was lower in the last three years, you could benefit from this
                 1997 law change. Click "Tell Me More" and we'll see if it's a benefit to you.


                                          1                        10/29/1998
```

Figure 5.20

The Tax Report printout provides you with solid tax-planning advice for 1999.

Take a Break

Now would be a good time to take a break, before you prepare your state tax returns and file your returns. Refill your coffee cup, go let the dog out (or in), and see if any donuts are left in the cupboard. When you return, you'll work on your state tax return(s), file your tax returns, and organize your tax records for storage.

Setting Up TurboTax State

All states except for Alaska, Wyoming, South Dakota, Nevada, Texas, and Washington impose some type of income taxation. Most states follow the federal model, while others such as Florida, New Hampshire, and Tennessee impose a flat tax on investment income such as your portfolio, interest, or dividend income. Some states take a large chunk of your money (New York, Oregon, Maryland, Massachusetts, Wisconsin, Rhode Island, Maine, Minnesota, and Utah are at the top of the list, as is Washington, D.C.), whereas others take less for income taxes (Louisiana, North Dakota, Delaware, Missouri, Mississippi, New Mexico, and Alabama are at the bottom of the list).

So, unless you live in a state that has no income tax, you must also file a state income tax return by April 15, 1999. If you earned income in other states that is subject to tax in those states, you may need to file more than one state tax return. Or if you moved from one state to another during the year, you probably need to file partial-year returns with your previous home state and your new home state.

Luckily, TurboTax can help you automate the process of completing state returns using the same skills and methods that you just learned in preparing your federal return. TurboTax transfers all of your financial and tax data from the federal return to the state tax return. At this point in most cases, 80 percent of your state tax return is already complete. All you need to do is address the unique state tax rules and adjust for state tax deductions, after which your state tax return will be done.

Unfortunately, TurboTax Deluxe does not come with any state software. You need to purchase your state software (for each state) separately. Think of each state's software package as a completely different set of logic, using different forms and being just as complicated as the federal area. When you purchase the state tax software, you are really only paying for the cost to research the state tax laws, as well as to create and maintain the state tax software. TurboTax state programs are cheaper than the federal program, at $27.95 per state versus the $44.95 for federal. But if you have several states to prepare, this can certainly add up. At the very least, you might consider purchasing your home state program. You might be able to use some of the backup schedules from the home state program to help you make short work of those other state returns. Although the tax logic for many states is complex, TurboTax State makes preparing your state tax return a breeze.

NOTE Whereas the federal version of TurboTax Deluxe ships in December, the state versions of TurboTax do not ship until mid-January to mid-February (varies by state). The main reason for this delay is that most states do not release their tax forms until they've had a chance to see what has changed on the federal tax forms. Also, state legislators wait to finalize their tax laws until after the federal government closes its tax law books.

Ordering TurboTax State

You can order your state program on disk by contacting Intuit

- By phone (800-4-INTUIT)
- By mail, using the order form that came with your TurboTax Deluxe CD

FIND IT ON ▶
THE WEB
- On the Internet at **www.intuit.com/quicken_store**

TIP If you are a registered TurboTax user, you are sent a Customer Savings Form so you can order your TurboTax federal and state programs in advance. Prices are generally cheaper, and occasionally Intuit throws in a free software gift to sweeten the deal (in the fall of 1998, Intuit gave away free copies of Rand McNally's TripMaker to early orderers). Also by ordering early, in the fall of the tax compliance year, you get to deduct the expense in that year!

But the easiest way to order your state module is by using the built-in Buy and Download State feature (see Figure 5.21) in late February or early March. The download only takes 10–15 minutes, and TurboTax automatically installs the state application for you. If you go with the disk method instead, you will need to install the file yourself.

CAUTION Don't forget to update your TurboTax State modules. To do so, choose Tools, Update. If you don't have an Internet connection, use the FAX Back service to determine if any updates to your State module exist. If so, then call Intuit at 800-4-INTUIT to order an update disk to be sent to you.

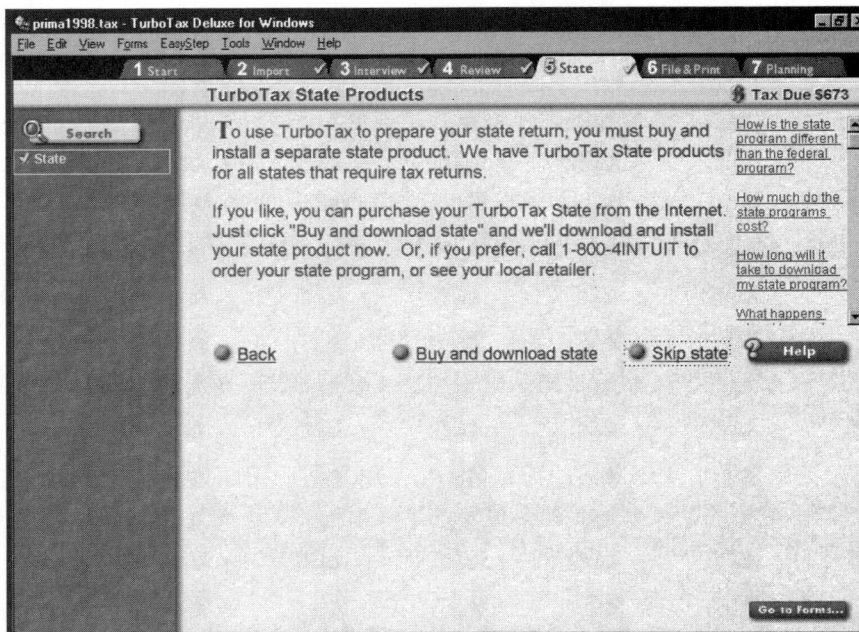

prima1998.tax - TurboTax Deluxe for Windows

File Edit View Forms EasyStep Tools Window Help

1 Start   2 Import   ✓ 3 Interview   ✓ 4 Review   ✓ 5 State   ✓ 6 File & Print   7 Planning

TurboTax State Products   💲 Tax Due $673

Search
✓ State

To use TurboTax to prepare your state return, you must buy and install a separate state product. We have TurboTax State products for all states that require tax returns.

If you like, you can purchase your TurboTax State from the Internet. Just click "Buy and download state" and we'll download and install your state product now. Or, if you prefer, call 1-800-4INTUIT to order your state program, or see your local retailer.

How is the state program different than the federal program?

How much do the state programs cost?

How long will it take to download my state program?

What happens

● Back   ● Buy and download state   ● Skip state   ❓ Help

Go to Forms...

Figure 5.21

The TurboTax State folder offers information on how you can order your state program.

Completing the State Interview

At the time this book was published, the various TurboTax State 1998 modules have not been released. Please refer to PRIMA TECH's Web site for an up-to-date section on completing a State tax Interview and reviewing and filing your state tax returns. The address is **www.prima-tech.com/turbotaxstate**.

FIND IT ON ▶
THE WEB

Filing and Printing Your Return(s)

You've now reached the sixth folder tab, File & Print (see Figure 5.22). When you went through the Review process, TurboTax asked you how you wanted to file your return. As part of the Review diagnostics, TurboTax verified that you could file using that method. The three methods of filing are

✿ Electronic filing

✿ 1040PC filing

✿ Paper-based filing

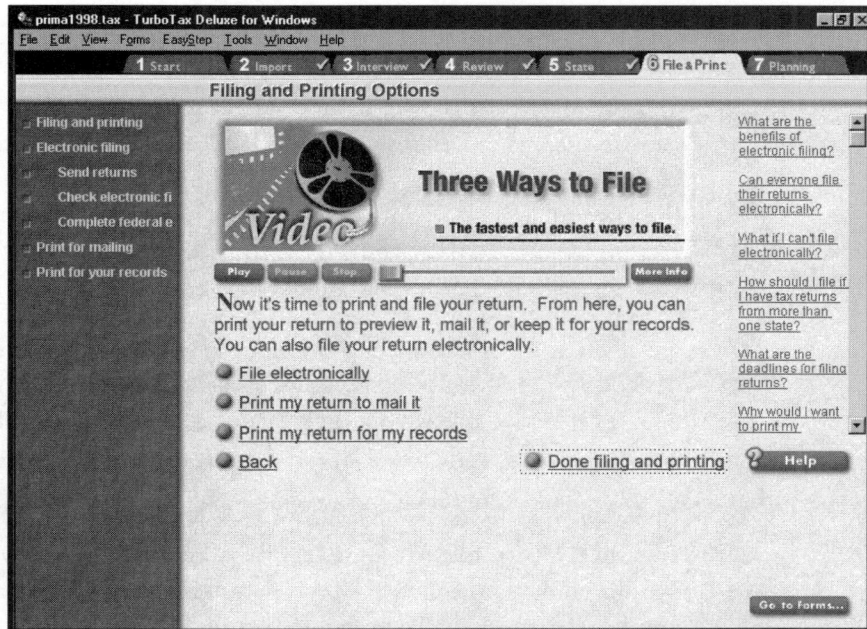

Figure 5.22

Play the video to get an overview of your filing and printing options.

In addition, many states permit you to file electronically through a phone setup (such as in New Jersey) or using an abridged (1040PC type) scannable return. If you are not allowed to use one of these modern methods, Turbo-Tax will let you know that you must file a conventional paper-based return.

TIP Read over the FAQs to learn more about electronic filing, multiple state tax filings, deadlines, and tax return print options.

Filing Electronically

If you decided to file your return electronically, click on File Electronically. Filing electronically means that your return will be transmitted via your modem through an Internet connection to Intuit's secure Web server. The security protocols are the same protocols as used by banks, ATMs, and credit card companies, so you don't need to worry about your private information being read by computer hackers. When Intuit's Electronic Filing Center receives your tax data file, Intuit's computer converts your file into a standardized IRS-approved format and then transfers your data to the IRS.

You can check on the status of your return in TurboTax. Just use the Navigator to search for the topic "Check Electronic Filing Status." Once there, click on <u>Connect Now to Get Status</u>. TurboTax dials up and then displays the current status of your return. Usually within 24–48 hours the process is complete, and the IRS sends back to you, through Intuit's Electronic Filing Center, a confirmation and an electronic receipt.

TIP Out of town and curious about the status of your recently filed electronic return? Call 520-901-3271 or surf out to **www.turbotax.com/efstatus** for basic status information.

If you filed your tax return electronically last year, the IRS assigned you a Personal Electronic Filing Customer Service Number (PEF-CSN). You should enter that number when prompted, before you transmit your file. If you file your return electronically with a PEF-CSN, you do not need to fill out and mail in a signature form (Form 8453-OL). Most states have their own version of Form 8453-OL. TurboTax will remind you to print, sign, and mail these forms too.

NOTE Unless you have a PEF-CSN, don't forget to fill out, sign, and mail in Form 8453-OL! Electronic signatures on tax returns (scanned signatures) are not yet accepted by the IRS. Instead, for the first year that you file electronically, you must fill out, sign, and mail in Form 8453-OL. If applicable, your spouse must sign too. The IRS and the state taxing authorities use this form as proof that you personally consented to electronically transmit that data file to the IRS. If you don't have a PEF-CSN and don't submit a Form 8453-OL, your return will be considered by IRS as "unsigned." Historically, an unsigned return is an "unfiled" return, subject to late fees, nonfiling fees, and interest on the taxes due.

Your Deluxe version of TurboTax provides you with one free electronic federal tax return filing. If you have more than one federal return to file, you will need to pay $9.95 per federal transmission. Federal regulations prohibit you from electronically filing more than three federal tax returns. State electronic filings cost $4.95 per state. Filing fees must be paid at the time of filing by using a credit card or having the amount deducted from your bank account. Some states do charge sales tax on this service (which is deductible as part of the cost of preparing your tax return for federal purposes).

TIP

FIND IT ON ▶
THE WEB

Tax professionals can register with the IRS and use Intuit's ProSeries to electronically file an unlimited number of returns. To learn more about ProSeries, visit the ProSeries Web site (**http://www.proseries.com**). There you will find directions on how to file Form 8633 (Application to Participate in the IRS *e-file* Program). To order ProSeries, call 800-934-1040.

Figure 5.23 shows a list of the four basic steps you must complete to file electronically. This provides you with a good overview of the process. The following is a more detailed list that takes you step by step through the screens.

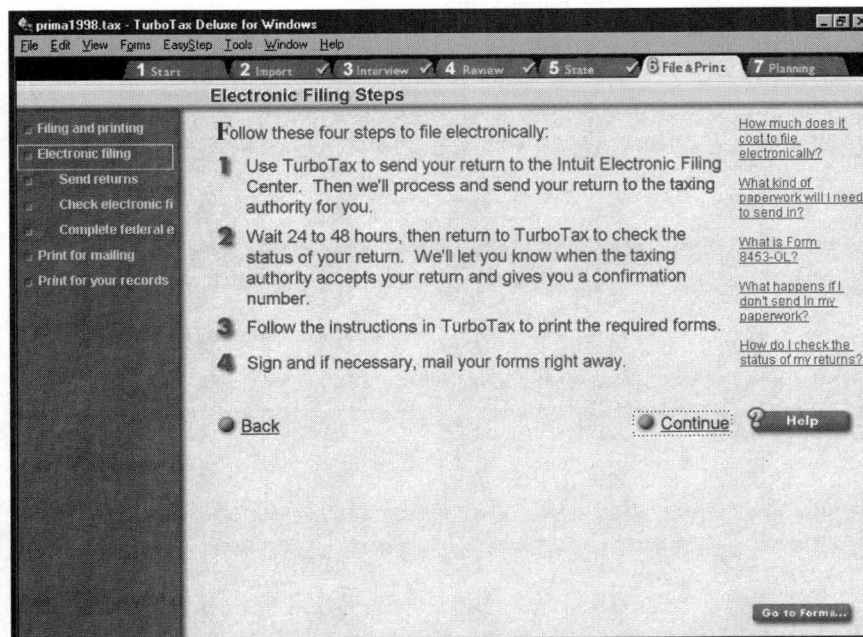

Figure 5.23

Filing electronically
is as easy as 1, 2,
3, and 4!

◆ ◆

CAUTION You will not be able to electronically transmit your return until you have completed and cleared all Review items. Your tax return must pass the Final Review before TurboTax will permit you to transmit the data.

Furthermore, your modem must be able to transmit the data at a speed of at least 9600 baud. Most computers and modems sold in the past two years are at the much faster speed of 28.8 or 56 kilobits per second. You can check the speed by right-clicking on the My Computer icon (located on your desktop), choosing Properties, and selecting the Device Manager tab. Next, double-click on Modem to see the name of your modem. Select your modem name and click on Properties. The Modem tab should list the maximum baud rate. Close the System dialog boxes and return to TurboTax.

◆ ◆

1. Click on <u>Next</u> to select the returns that you want to file electronically (see Figure 5.24). Make sure your modem is plugged in and turned on.

2. Select the returns that you want to transmit. You can select all (federal and states), just a few, or only one.

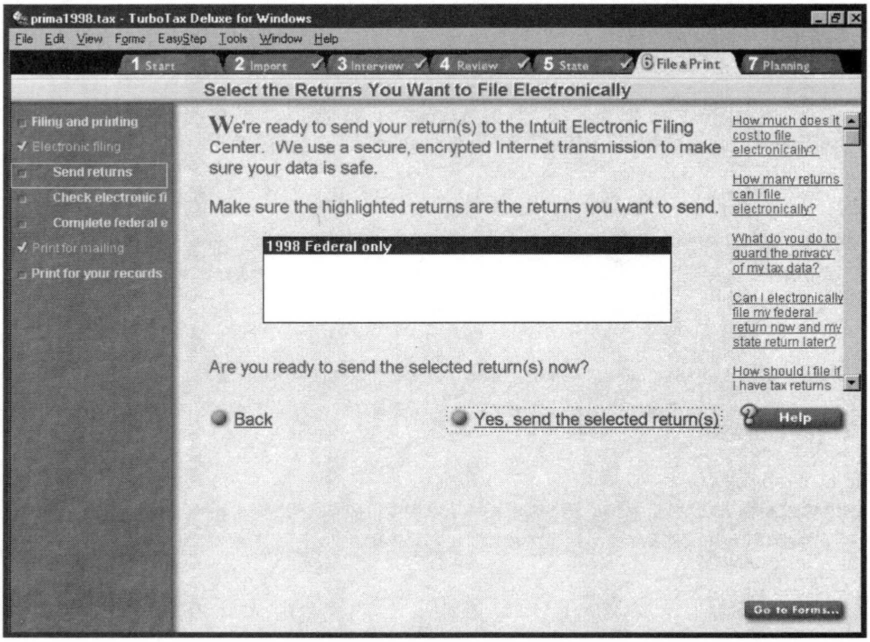

Figure 5.24

You can send just your federal return now and send your state returns later.

3. Click on <u>Yes, Send the Selected Return(s)</u> to transmit your tax data to the taxing authority.

4. After transmitting, TurboTax will prompt you to print Form 8453-OL and/or the state versions of this form, if needed. Sign and mail in these forms by the tax return deadline.

5. If you owe taxes, TurboTax will prompt you to print Form 1040-V (Payment Voucher) to accompany your check. (If you elected to pay taxes online with a credit card or bank account debit, you will not need Form 1040-V.) The state versions of this payment voucher will also print. Be sure to mail your payment in by the deadline.

◆ ◆

CAUTION Do not mail Forms 8453-OL and 1040-V in the same envelope! Each form goes to a different address. TurboTax will print the mailing instructions for you, including the address. To save yourself time, print two copies so you can cut out address labels and paste them right onto the envelopes. Also, see the certified mail/registered receipt tip in the " Proving You Filed on Time " section later this afternoon.

◆ ◆

6. Refer to the section "Organizing Your 1998 Tax Records" later this afternoon for instructions on how to print a copy of your returns for yourself.

WHAT IF MY ELECTRONIC RETURN IS PENDING OR REJECTED?

Here's what to do if your tax return is pending or rejected:

Pending: Wait another day or two, and then recheck your return's status. Chances are that processing at the IRS is just backlogged. If your return is still pending after four days, call 520-295-3351 for assistance.

Rejected: In most cases the rejection is due to a data entry error, such as an incorrect social security number, or to a taxpayer name change. The SSN and names of taxpayer, spouse, and dependents *must* match IRS records, otherwise the electronic file will be rejected. Directions on how to fix the error appear in the Current Status screen. If the problem is not fixable, you will need to file a conventional paper-based return.

7. After 24–48 hours, start TurboTax and choose EasyStep, Filing. The Electronic Filing Status screen opens.

8. Click on the Get Current Status button to view the status of your electronically filed returns.

Practicing origami using your tax return means:

A) Your electronic tax filing went through okay.

B) You're not receptive to paying taxes this year.

C) You've decided to open a new business—an origami shop.

Filing a 1040PC Return

Referring back to Figure 5.22, click on <u>Print My Return to Mail It</u>. This displays the Print for Mailing screen shown in Figure 5.25. Be sure that the 1040PC box is checked. When you click on Print, TurboTax will print the 1040PC abridged, scannable version of your tax return, complete with

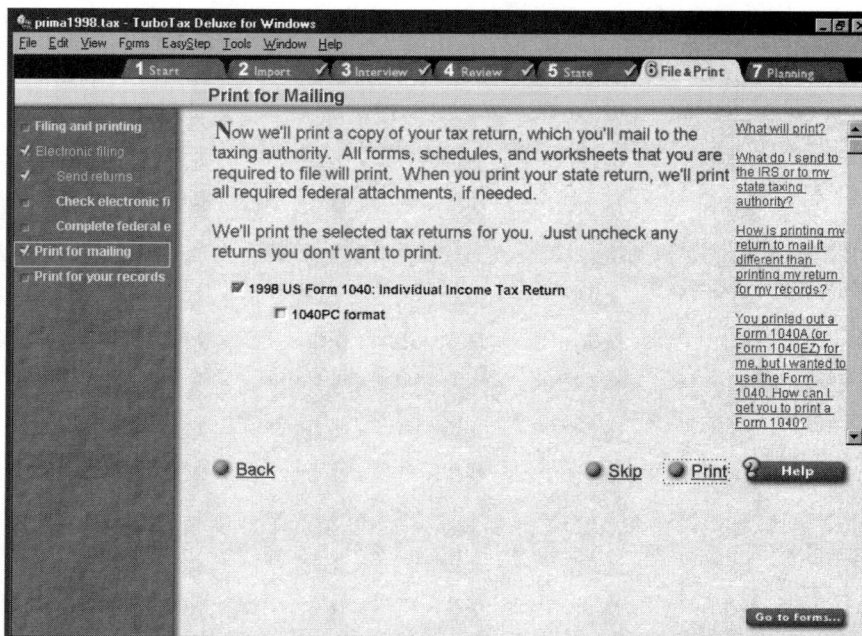

Figure 5.25

TurboTax prints your 1040PC and state returns for you.

instructions. When the IRS receives your 1040PC, they will scan it into their computers.

CAUTION

You should not print a tax return that contains errors. Make sure that you have completed the Review process and cleared all errors in the Error Check Review before printing a final return.

If you must print a tax return that contains errors (TurboTax will warn you that the return still contains errors), immediately mark each and every page with a highlighter or crayon. You don't want to accidentally mix up your draft return pages with the final return. I usually change names on page one of Form 1040 to "Draft xx/xx/xx," where xx/xx/xx is the date. That way each and every page is date stamped and gets labeled as "draft."

To file your 1040PC federal tax return, follow these steps:

1. Sign and date the 1040PC where indicated. If applicable, your spouse must sign also. Be on the lookout for additional forms that also require you to sign (such as Form 8283) or forms that require you to get the signatures of others (such as Schedules H and R). Refer to the TurboTax filing instruction page for a complete list.

2. Use a paper clip (do not staple, and no spindling either!) to attach your W-2s and any other required documents to the back, upper left corner of your 1040PC.

3. If you owe taxes, attach your payment check by paper clip as well.

4. Neatly fold your 1040PC and documents, and insert them into an envelope.

5. Address the envelope to the filing center listed by TurboTax on the instruction page.

TIP

Print two copies of the instructions. Keep one for your files, and use the other to cut out a mailing label to paste onto your envelope.

Also, see the certified mail/registered receipt tip in the " Proving You Filed on Time " section. And refer to "Organizing Your 1998 Tax Records" for instructions on how to print a copy of your returns for yourself.

Filing Paper-Based Returns

Referring back to Figure 5.22, click on <u>Print My Return to Mail It</u>. This displays the Print for Mailing screen. Be sure that your federal and/or state tax return boxes are checked. When you click on <u>Print</u>, TurboTax will print the tax returns selected, complete with instructions.

The IRS accepts tax returns on white or cream-colored paper only. The paper must be 8½ by 11 inches and have a weight of at least 18 lb. (most copier paper is 20 lb.). Most states follow the federal lead, although they seem to prefer 20 lb. white paper.

TIP If TurboTax prints a Form 1040EZ or 1040A and you later decide you'd prefer to file a regular Form 1040, you can force TurboTax to print a Form 1040. To do so, open your Federal Information Worksheet and check the box for Calculate Form 1040 Regardless. Save your tax return, run the Review process, and then go back to the File & Print tab.

To file your paper-based returns, follow these steps:

1. Sign and date the returns where indicated. If applicable, your spouse must sign also. Be on the lookout for additional forms that also require you to sign (such as Form 8283) or forms that require you to get the signatures of others (such as Schedules H and R). Refer to the TurboTax filing instruction page for a complete list.

2. Staple your W-2s and any other required documents to the front of your return, where indicated.

3. If you owe taxes, attach your payment check too.

4. TurboTax prints your tax return in the correct order for filing.

TIP If you have shuffled the papers around a bit in the process, here's a little-known tip. The first page or two should be your Form 1040, 1040A, or 1040EZ. Thereafter, refer to the "Attachment Sequence No." in the top right corner of each form (just below the 1998) to determine the proper order. Notice that the sequence order does not follow the actual form number order. That would be too logical!

5. Find an envelope large enough to hold your tax return. If it is more than five pages, you probably should use a 12-by-9-inch envelope instead of a regular letter-size envelope.

6. Address the envelope to the filing center listed by TurboTax on the instruction page. To save time, print two copies of the instruction sheet. Save one copy for your files, and use the other to cut out an address label to paste onto your envelope.

7. Be sure to apply the proper postage for the odd weight, and mail by the deadline!

Proving You Filed on Time

All too often, IRS or state taxing authorities send notices to taxpayers charging penalties and interest for late filing or nonfiling, when in actuality the taxpayer filed on time. Unless you have proof that you filed your return on time, the taxing authority will win in court and you will have to pay the penalty.

Save yourself the grief and aggravation of a questionable filing by paying the U.S. Postal Service a couple bucks to provide you with proof of mailing date and date received by the IRS. The two forms that you should get and fill out in advance are

❖ A receipt for certified mail (about $1.35)

❖ A return receipt (about $1.10)

You can go to the post office and pick up these two forms (or a supply, if you file quarterly returns) and fill them out ahead of time. When you go to mail your return, you can pay for both services and your postage all at once. The certification proves that your return was postmarked on that day. The return receipt is a postcard that accompanies your return, is signed by the IRS as received, and is then mailed back to you. Keep both with your return (or with your estimates) as proof of timely filing.

Bumper sticker: Save Our Trees. Stop Printing Tax Forms!

TIP   Unfortunately, TurboTax doesn't print these U.S. postal forms for you. But you can purchase Certified Mailer Software and computer-printable forms from Southern Business Forms (504-733-2374). I use these products throughout the year and appreciate the time savings. One less item to worry about as I rush to the post office!

Making the Deadline

For the 1998 calendar year, you must file your tax returns by April 15, 1999. This means that the postmark on your envelope must be no later than midnight on April 15, 1999. Traditionally, the IRS has only accepted the postmark from the U.S. Postal Service as being valid. Beginning in 1998, the IRS now accepts the "postmark" of certain private companies such as Federal Express, Airborne Express, DHL Worldwide Express, and USA Overnight. The cost of overnight service is usually higher than a U.S. Postal Service mailing on April 15. A certified, return receipt service, is still my preferred method of filing.

If you file estimated payments, the first quarterly estimated payment for 1999 is also due on April 15. Unfortunately, your estimates go to a different address, so you can't put the two in the same envelope. I strongly recommend you spend the extra bucks to get your estimated payment filings certified and to get a return receipt. You'll learn more about estimates in tonight's session on tax planning.

TIP   Make a copy of each tax payment check before you send it in. File the copy with your copy of the tax return for easy reference next year.

The Buck Stops Here

In the end, regardless of whether you hired a tax accountant to prepare your return, paid a tax expert to review your self-prepared return, or just used TurboTax to complete your return, *you* are filing your tax return. Mistakes can happen to tax preparers, tax experts, and yes, even computer systems.

If you can, wait a few days, maybe even a week, so that your mind is fresh. Then find someplace quiet, far away from the computer, where you can spread out your source documents and printed tax returns. Begin with the federal tax return. Read every line, line by line—even your address and social security number. When you get to a number that is the total of many numbers on another schedule or form, trace the number back. Pull out a calculator (never trust a computer—I'm a programmer myself, so please take this advice) and add up the numbers. You should understand where each number comes from and how it was computed. If the IRS audits you, you won't be able to say, "But I relied on the computer." A computer is just a tool, like a calculator or a car. You are always the driver.

This process will only take you an hour or two (depending on how many state tax returns you have). But in the end, you will have more confidence in your returns and in TurboTax. (After eight years of using TurboTax, I have yet to find a mathematical mistake that the program has made, though I have found many of my own!) You will also be astonished to realize how much you've learned this weekend. This exercise will tie it all together for you and help you organize your tax records even better for 1999.

Organizing Your 1998 Tax Records

The first step is to print a copy of your tax returns for your records. Referring back to Figure 5.22, click on Print My Return for My Records. This will display the Print for Your Records screen shown in Figure 5.26. Be sure that the box is checked for each federal and state return that you want to print. When you click on Print, TurboTax will print the tax returns with all supporting details and schedules (including the worksheets with your raw data, which weren't filed with the taxing authority). Because of the details being printed, this print job will take longer than the returns took to print.

TIP

Periodically, I've been asked by financial institutions and investment advisors for copies of my prior year's tax returns. Instead of running out to make copies at a copy center, I've gotten into the habit of printing two extra copies of each federal and state tax return (as filed). This is in addition to the copy with full detail for my file. Then when someone asks for a copy of a prior year's return, I can just pull it out of the tax file. Then I can spend my time doing something other than tax work.

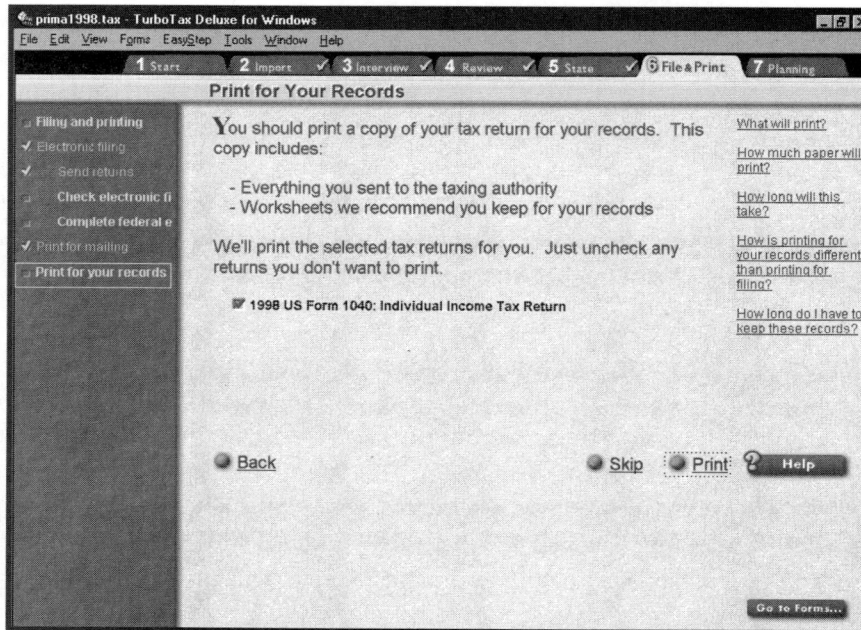

Figure 5.26

Printing a copy for
your records is
very important.

Backing Up Your Data

Backing up your computer files is an important task most computer users become accustomed to. However, when it comes to your financial data and tax data, you need to do double-duty. Do not just rely on your current back-up system to save this year's tax data. In addition to your normal computer backup routines, follow the steps below to save a copy of your 1998 tax data onto a disk. Then keep this disk with your TurboTax Deluxe CD, any state software disks, and your other 1998 tax documents.

1. Choose File, Save to save your current tax file to your hard disk, as usual.

2. Place a blank formatted disk in the floppy disk drive (usually drive A).

3. Choose File, Save As. The Save Tax Return dialog box appears with the Save In folder set to your current hard disk location, the File name set to the name you gave this return, and the Save As type set to Tax Files (*.tax).

4. Click on the down arrow in the Save In box, and select your floppy disk drive (which is where you just inserted the blank disk).

5. Click on the Save button. TurboTax saves the currently open tax file to the floppy disk.

6. To reopen the copy on your hard disk (if you need to work on it some more), Choose File. Recently opened files are listed at the bottom of the File menu. The first file name is the tax return copy on the floppy disk, the second file name is the copy on your hard disk.

7. Repeat the process if you change any tax data.

Storing 1998 Tax Files

Before you head out to Casa Maria's to celebrate, you should organize your tax records for 1998 while everything is fresh in your mind. The human body has amazing healing powers, and in a few days all of this will just be a blur. If you need to substantiate any dollar amount on your return two or three years from now, the blur will give you a huge headache. So, take the time now to put your 1998 tax records in order.

A box with a lid, such as a file box or a copier paper box from work, will do the trick. Label the outside of the box in big clear letters "1998 Tax Records." Inside, arrange the information in folders or envelopes clearly labeled as follows. The order places the most frequently needed information up front, with the less likely needed information in the back.

- **1998 TurboTax Materials.** Use this folder for your 1998 TurboTax Deluxe CD, manuals, state disks, and data file disk.

- **1998 Correspondence with Taxing Authorities.** If voluminous, your correspondence may need to be kept in several folders.

- **1998 Tax Estimates.** File here your computation basis for estimated taxes due, copies of checks, Estimated Tax returns, and proof of filing.

- **1998 Federal Tax Return.** Keep a recommended two copies of your return as filed with the IRS.

- **1998 State Tax Returns.** Keep a recommended two copies of your return as filed with the state.

- **1998 Federal—My Copy.** File here all detail schedules as printed and any handwritten schedules not entered into TurboTax, in addition to a copy of your federal return.

- **1998 State—My Copy.** File here all detail schedules as printed and any handwritten schedules not entered into TurboTax, in addition to a copy of your state return.

- **Source Documents.** Use this folder to store your W-2s, 1099s, etc., including any correspondence with issuers in which you request to have corrections made.

- **Paystubs.** Though some folks toss these, I keep mine with the current tax year.

- **Account Statements.** Include your account statements and cancelled checks here.

- **Adjustments for AGI.** In this folder, file your proof of adjustment taken, if it's not being kept in the Account Statements folder.

- **Itemized Deductions.** File here your proof of deduction taken, including receipts, letters from charities, mileage logs, etc. You may need to use several folders (one for each deduction type) if your documentation is voluminous.

- **Tax Payments.** In this folder, file your proof of tax payments, if it's not being kept in Account Statements or Source Documents folders.

- **Tax Credits.** In this folder, file your proof of tax credit basis, if it's not being kept in Account Statements or Source Document folders.

- **Business Records.** Keep documentation to prove all amounts on Schedules C, E, or F as applicable. Depending on volume, you might need several boxes per business.

- **WIP.** For work in progress, this is where I keep printouts of the draft tax returns as I work on them, along with my notes on what changed and why, clearly marked as being a draft with a line drawn through each page.

Other records such as birth certificates, deeds, and alimony arrangements should be copied—keep a copy with your tax files, but be sure to place the originals in a safe deposit box. Because your 1998 Tax Records box contains a CD and disks, be sure to store it in a computer-friendly environment (not in direct sunlight, not in a basement that floods, etc.).

Setting Up 1999 Tax Files

Take a good look at your 1998 tax files before you store the box away in that spare bedroom. Consider if your situation in 1999 will change to include a Schedule C business or a move across the country. Set up files or envelopes now to capture that information. In your business files, create files to hold receipts and other forms of proof that support deductions and deposits. With the files set up in advance, all you need to do is move the documents from your mail, purse, or briefcase into the proper file. Next year when you need to prepare your tax return, you'll be able to pull out this set of files and enter data right into TurboTax. No more sifting through the shoebox for a receipt! And, more importantly, no more missing tax deductions!

TIP Having the 1999 tax files set up early in 1999 helps you plan for your tax liability better too. You'll learn more about this in tonight's session.

What's Next?

Dinner! A golden rule among tax professionals is that we never do tax planning on an empty stomach! You should be proud of all you have accomplished this weekend. In tonight's bonus session you will learn how to use TurboTax to develop and maintain a tax plan that is tailored to your needs.

Tax Estimates and Planning

- ✿ Preparing Tax Estimates
- ✿ Forecasting Your Taxes
- ✿ Creating a Tax Plan
- ✿ Managing a Tax Audit
- ✿ Knowing Your Rights

After spending a weekend organizing your taxes and preparing your federal and state tax returns, you're probably full of great ideas on how you will save tax dollars in 1999. Well, tonight you will put those ideas into motion. First, you will prepare your estimated tax returns for 1999. Then, you will review the tax plan that you printed out during the Review process. You'll be able to test out your tax-planning ideas with the built-in Tax Planner that comes with TurboTax. You will create what-if scenarios to see the tax effects of various tax-planning ideas. At the end of this chapter, you will also learn how to file an amended return, manage a tax audit, and gauge your tax costs throughout the year.

In this session, you will

- ✪ Prepare tax estimates
- ✪ Review tax-planning ideas
- ✪ Forecast taxes with Tax Planner
- ✪ Create what-if scenarios
- ✪ Learn how to amend your return
- ✪ Find out how to manage a tax audit

Preparing Tax Estimates

As you learned this morning, income taxes are collected throughout the year by way of withholding on your wages (W-2) and certain transactions subject to backup withholding (some 1099s). If you have other income from self-employment or investment income, you may already be in the habit of paying your income taxes throughout the year via quarterly estimates paid to IRS and state tax authorities.

If you don't pay enough of your tax liability in on time during the year, the IRS assesses you a penalty and charges interest on the late payment. Most states impose their own late payment penalty and interest charges too. As you can imagine, this could result in a huge unexpected tax liability when you file your return. In this session, you will learn how to stay on top of this issue so that you pay in enough taxes to avoid the underpayment penalty, without paying too much of your money to the taxing authorities too early.

You do not have to pay a penalty or file Form 2210 if either of the following is true:

- Your 1998 tax liability net of the withholding tax is less than $1,000
- Your 1997 tax liability was zero or you received a refund

Furthermore, you will not owe a penalty if you paid taxes in during 1998 that equal or exceed one of the following:

- 90 percent of this year's tax liability
- 100 percent of last year's tax liability; or if your AGI is more than $150,000 ($75,000 MFS), 110 percent of last year's tax liability

Are you withholding enough taxes on your W-2 and 1099s to cover your tax liability? If not, can you avoid paying an underpayment penalty? Or are you withholding too much tax, forfeiting the interest that you could have earned if that overpayment had been invested or kept in a savings account? These are tough but important questions that TurboTax can help you answer. Managing your tax payments is the first tax-planning strategy that you will learn to implement tonight.

> **Q.**   What's the difference between a tax advisor and an angry bull?
>
> **A.**   The tax advisor charges more.

Returning to the Interview

In order to review your tax withholding and prepare your tax estimates, you will need to return to the Interview tab. TurboTax will pick up the Interview where this afternoon's session left off, on the topic Planning for 1999 (see Figure 6.1). Click on <u>Continue</u> to begin the Interview on estimated tax payments and withholding taxes.

Determining Your Correct Withholding Level

The first Interview topic is Form W-4, Employee's Withholding Allowance Certificate. When you start a job, your employer is required to get a Form W-4 from you. The W-4 tells the employer how to withhold tax from your paycheck. The basic information on a W-4 tells the employer

○ Whether to withhold at the single or lower married rate

○ How many withholding allowances you claim (each allowance reduces the withholding amount)

○ Whether you want any additional amount withheld

Figure 6.1

The Interview process will walk you through the issues and help you prepare tax estimates.

TIP

If you work only part of the year, your withholding may be too high. Ask your employer to use the part-year method instead to better match your withholding with your income. See IRS Publication 505 for more information.

Whenever your situation changes (a marriage, a divorce, new dependents), you should complete a new W-4 to update your employer on your new withholding level. If you claim an exemption from withholding, your employer will not withhold any taxes from your paycheck. You can claim an exemption from withholding for 1999 only if the following are both true:

- In 1998 you had a right to a refund of all federal income tax withheld because you had no tax liability.
- In 1999 you expect the same to occur.

TIP

Review your W-4 information annually to ensure adequate withholding.

Click on <u>Continue</u> to move through the next set of screens. You will be asked for or about the following information:

- Your filing status (be sure to change if different in 1999)
- Increased standard deduction (be sure to check the box if you must itemize in 1999, as opposed to estimating your tax liability using just a standard deduction)
- Your personal exemptions (enter the total number of dependents you expect to have in 1999)
- Your earned income from employment and self-employment for you and your spouse (see Figure 6.2)
- Your 1999 capital gains and losses (see Figure 6.3)
- Other income you expect to earn in 1999 and any adjustments to your income (such as from IRA contributions, moving for work, or an MSA contribution)
- Your 1999 itemized deductions (be conservative here—only enter amounts you know for sure that you will incur in 1999)

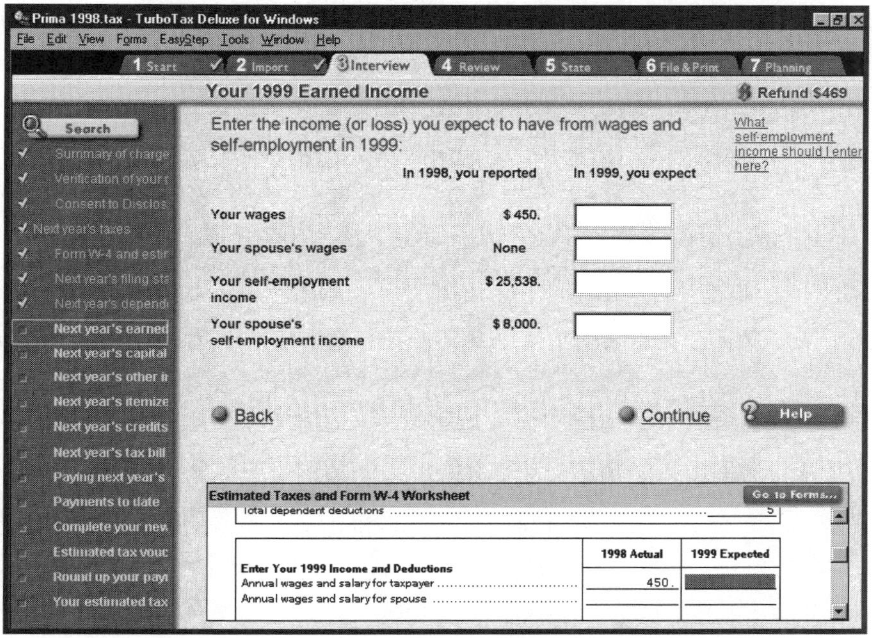

Figure 6.2

Enter your expected 1999 earned income in the 1999 column.

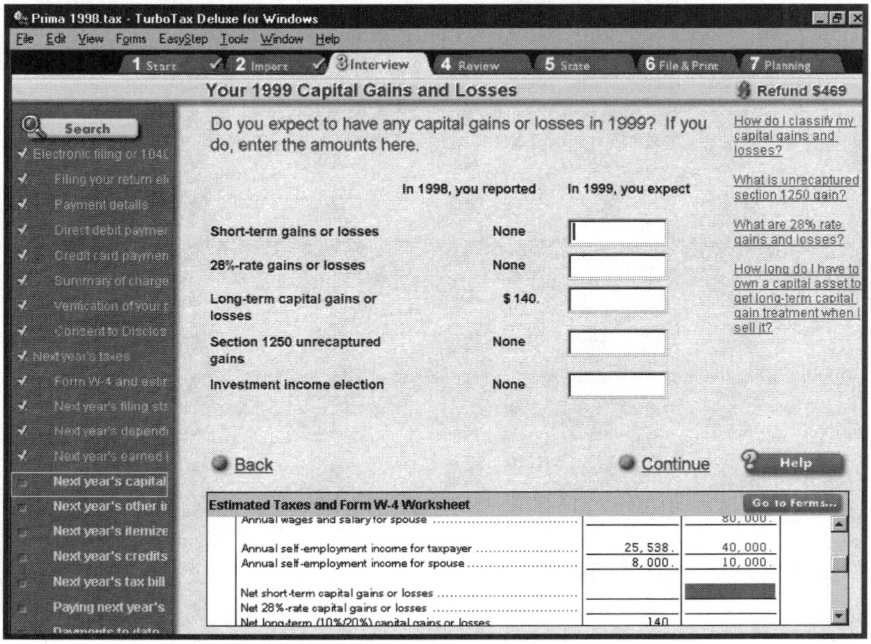

Figure 6.3

The Interview shows you the amounts you reported for 1998 and fills in whatever it knows of 1999 for you.

○ Your 1999 tax credits and other taxes (except for self-employment tax, which TurboTax computes for you and enters on the line below)

After you have entered your estimated tax data for 1999, TurboTax computes the tax due and displays your estimated tax bill (see Figure 6.4). If you need to change any of your estimates, click on Back to move back one Interview screen at a time, or use the Navigator to jump to a specific topic. To see the full Estimated Taxes and Form W-4 Worksheet, click on Go to Forms.

After reviewing your estimated tax bill, click on Continue to move past the data-gathering stage. The Interview now asks if you would like to prepare a W-4, prepare estimated tax returns (called vouchers), or prepare both. I strongly suggest you prepare both. If after the process you decide you don't need to submit one or the other, at least you know that your existing withholding will cover your 1999 tax bill. If your situation changes, you can just return to this portion of the Interview and update your data before printing new forms. Choose the option you decide to prepare (see Figure 6.5).

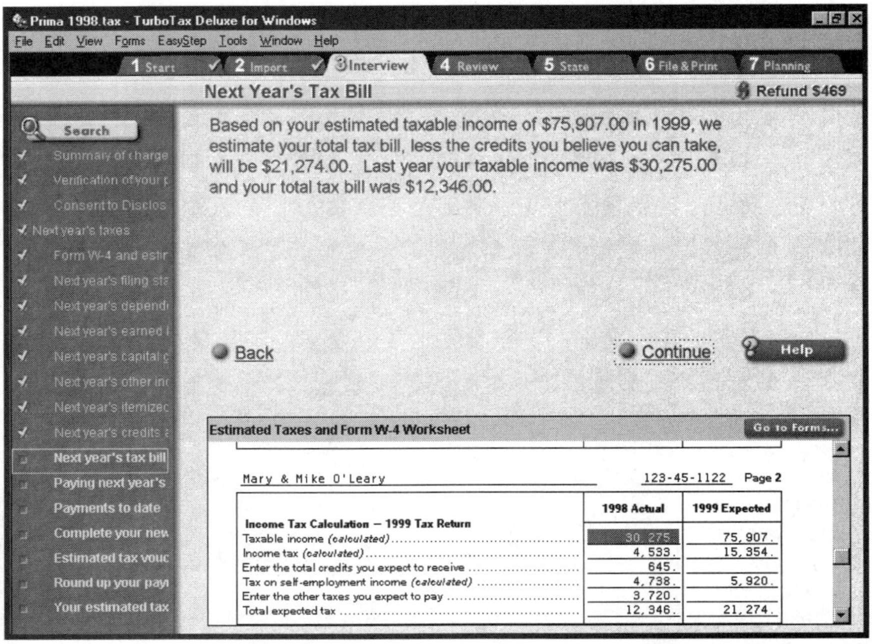

Figure 6.4

The highlights of your 1999 projected tax data appear at the bottom of your screen, side by side with your 1998 actual amounts.

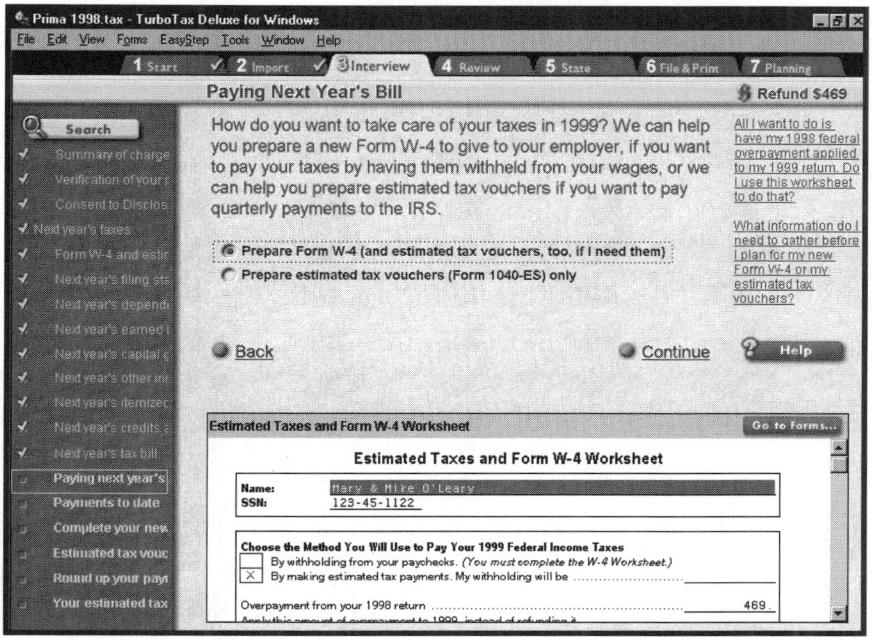

Figure 6.5

You can prepare a W-4 and/or 1040-ES for 1999.

Preparing Your W-4

First, TurboTax asks if you have already paid any estimated tax payments or had any withholding from your paychecks for 1999. If so, enter the amounts for you and your spouse. Consult the FAQs to learn more about how withholding and estimated tax payments effect your W-4 withholding. When ready, click on Continue to move ahead.

The next few screens prompt you to enter

○ Your expected salary

○ Salary that you've received so far this year

○ Frequency of pay periods (weekly, monthly, etc.)

○ Paydays you have left in this year

Enter the requested information, using Continue to move through the interview process. At the end, TurboTax Displays your W-4 results and lets you review the Additional Information for Form W-4 (use Go to Forms button to view). Click on Continue to move ahead to the next interview topic.

Preparing Your 1040-ES

For calendar-year taxpayers, estimated taxes are paid on a quarterly basis, with due dates as follows:

- First quarter due April 15
- Second quarter due June 15
- Third quarter due September 15
- Fourth quarter due January 15

Note that if the due date falls on a national holiday or a weekend, then the due date is moved to the next business day. For purposes of the 1999 estimated tax payment deadlines, this only affects the payment due January 15, 2000. Because this is a Saturday, your fourth quarter estimate is not due until Monday (January 17).

As with your tax returns, you should mail your payment using the U.S. Postal Service's certified, return receipt service. This way you will have proof that you filed on time in case a 2210 penalty is levied on you. And remember what you learned this afternoon: the estimated payments go to a different address than your annual income tax returns.

NOTE States generally follow the federal government's lead when it comes to estimated tax payments, paycheck withholdings, and deadlines. Consult your state income tax instruction booklet or the TurboTax State tax module for more information. TurboTax State tax modules help you complete state tax estimates and print the forms for you.

If you decided just to prepare estimated tax vouchers, TurboTax begins the interview by asking you how conservative you want to be. As shown in Figure 6.6, the safest method is to base your estimated taxes for 1999 on 105% of your 1998 Federal Tax liability. By doing so, you will pay in more than you need to legally pay (in order to avoid an underpayment liability). I highly recommend using this conservative 105% method, if you can afford to make the resulting tax payments. If cash is short, and you do not anticipate owing as much tax as you did this year, choose the legally required 90% (or if a higher income bracket, 100%) method. Farmers and fishermen can take advantage of an even lower requirement (66⅔%), if you qualify (see FAQs for details).

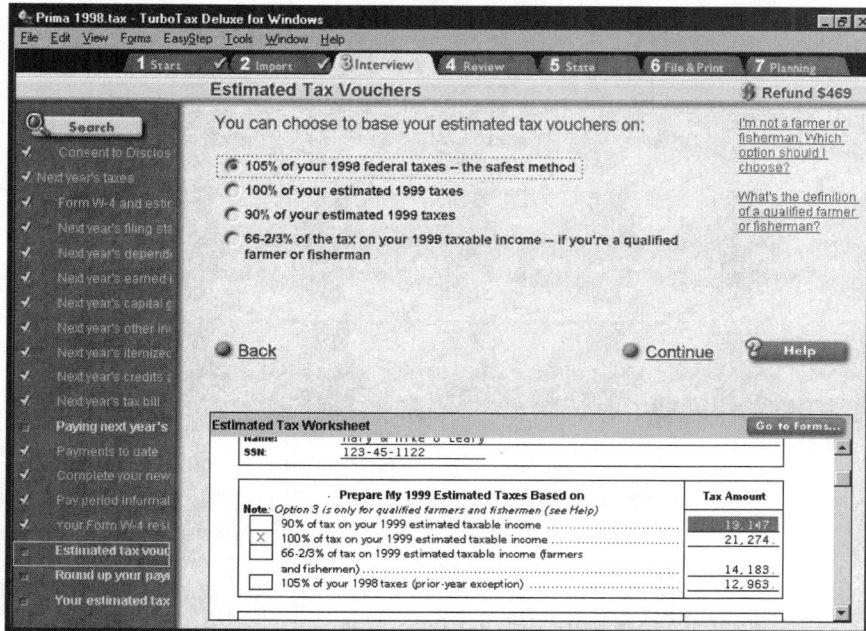

Figure 6.6

Paying 105% of your previous year's tax bill is the safest method.

CAUTION

Keep in mind however, that regardless of the method you use, in the end you will have to pay all of your 1999 tax liability come April 15, 2000. If you pay estimates which total less than your actual 1999 tax liability, you will need to save for the ultimate 1999 tax bill.

TIP

Note that the IRS doesn't pay you interest if you overpay taxes. By paying in too much in estimated tax payments, you are essentially giving the IRS an interest-free loan. If you have good financial self-control, then you might be better off only paying the IRS the minimum due (generally 90%), and depositing the remaining expected tax due in a high-yield, safe investment account or fund. Each time you pay the IRS, deposit the remaining "expected" tax due into your tax savings account. Do not borrow or pay bills from your tax savings account. Come April 15, 2000, you'll have all the money you need to pay the IRS and some interest income to boot!

This Tip and the previous Caution apply to your state tax estimates too.

When ready, select a method to base your estimated tax vouchers on and click on <u>Continue</u>. The next screen asks if you want to round up your payments (such as from $1,356 to $1,400). Adjust the quarterly payments as needed and click on <u>Continue</u>. TurboTax displays your estimated tax vouchers.

> What is the difference between tax avoidance and tax evasion?
>
> The jail walls.

Reviewing 1998 Tax Data

One of the easiest ways to learn how to lower your tax liability in the future is to take a good look at your prior year's tax situation. The Review tab that you used in this afternoon's session provided you with several tools you can use to create a tax plan for 1999:

- Deduction Finder
- Audit Alerts
- Tax Report

If you skipped these Reviews earlier, take a moment now to return to this afternoon's session and reread "Moving On to Review" for specific instructions on how to conduct these Reviews. If you did go through this process, bring out your notes and printouts from this morning.

TIP Use a three-ring binder as your tax-planning ideas book. Create tabbed sections for Dependents, Wages, Self-Employment Income (Schedule C, E, and F information), Other Income, AGI, Itemized Deductions, Tax Credits, and Tax Payments/Estimates. As you read over the Reviews for deductions, Audit Alerts, and Tax Report, write up your ideas and questions, and then file them into the appropriate section. As you surf the Internet, talk with friends, and meet with your financial planner, put everything in this binder. You will find this binder helpful year-round and across tax years as you try to decipher the opportunities and risks of each idea.

Forecasting Your Taxes

TurboTax comes with a built-in Tax Planner, which helps you implement your tax-planning ideas. The TurboTax Tax Planner allows you to create two hypothetical tax scenarios (case studies) so that you can compare and contrast tax strategies. When you look at the scenarios side by side, you see how each idea affects your bottom line. For example, suppose you were considering investing in an IRA. You could use the Tax Planner to see the tax savings from the IRA contribution.

Click on the last folder tab, Planning (see Figure 6.7). Play the video to get an overview of the Tax Planner and how it works. When you are ready, click on <u>Run Planners</u>. The next screen tells you about the new tax rules for 1999 and beyond. Click on <u>Planning for Next Year</u> to view Tax Help, which lists the key tax law changes. When you are ready to close Tax Help, click on the tax planner that you want to use (Tax or IRA planner).

Figure 6.7

Use the Tax Planner to create what-if scenarios and see the tax effects of your planning ideas.

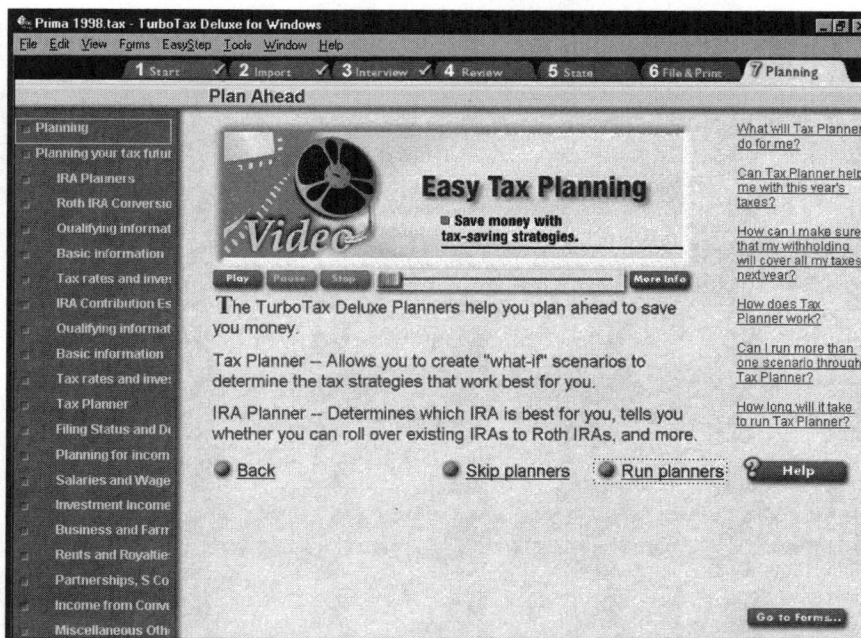

Creating a Tax Plan

The first step is to select the tax year (1998 or 1999) for each plan. If you want to see the multiyear effect of a tax-planning idea, you may want to make Plan 1 the year 1998 and Plan 2 the year 1999. On the other hand, if you want to compare and contrast several planning options in the same year, set both plans to 1998 or 1999. Click on <u>Continue</u> so you can start the tax-planning process.

Notice in Figure 6.8 that, as with the Tax Estimate and W-4 Planner, the Tax Planner has extrapolated your 1998 tax data and automatically posted the data to your two plan years. This saves you from having to re-enter your data and provides you with your base year amounts. Now all you need to do is adjust the data to reflect your anticipated income and tax situation for those years.

Click on <u>Continue</u> as needed to move through the screens. For tax areas with supporting schedules and detail worksheets, the Tax Planner allows you to work with the details. For every key tax election or area, the Tax Planner will give you a chance to change your tax data.

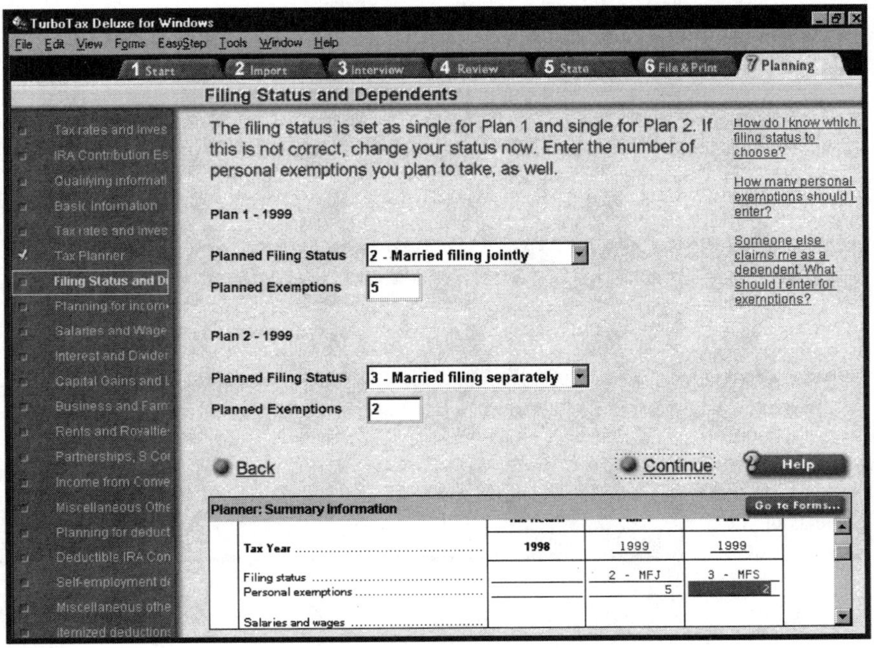

Figure 6.8

You can make adjustments to your data for each tax plan if you expect your situation to change in the future.

The specific areas that the Tax Planner will quiz you about include

✿ Salaries, wages, and withholding

✿ Investment income

✿ Business income

✿ Rents, royalties, partnerships, etc.

✿ Income from converting to a Roth IRA

✿ Other income or loss

✿ Adjustments to income

✿ Standard deduction and itemized deductions

✿ Personal exemptions

✿ Income tax, credits, other taxes and payments

TIP Tired of being interviewed? At any point, you can click on Go to Forms and work directly with the Tax Planner Summary Information Worksheet.

The Tax Planner Summary Information Worksheet at the bottom of your screen has eight supporting worksheets. If you decide to work directly with the worksheets, be sure to drill down to the appropriate supporting worksheet and enter data there, instead of at the top summary level.

Although the Tax Planner does most of the calculations, there are a few that you must do offline to create an accurate tax plan. You must calculate the following items:

✿ Allowable amounts for AGI deductions such as IRA deduction, self-employment retirement plan deduction, self-employed health insurance plan deduction

✿ Deductible amount of passive-activity losses

✿ Deductible amount of interest expense deduction and casualty losses

✿ Deductible amount of 20 percent and 30 percent limit charitable contributions

- Amount of other taxes due, such as AMT and early withdrawal penalties

- Amount of credits such as the elderly or disabled credit

If you have these amounts in a tax plan year, refer back to the Interview topic using the Navigator and use the Help screens or Forms to determine the correct amount to use in your plan.

NOTE You can only run two scenarios at a time. To compare more than two scenarios, run the Tax Planner as many times as needed and print out the plan in detail at the end. You can then lay the plans out and compare side by side more than two scenarios.

At the end, TurboTax will offer to review your tax plan, giving you suggestions and advice (see Figure 6.9). It is certainly worth getting the free advice, so go ahead and click on <u>Review My Plan</u>. Read through the tax advice screens, using the <u>Continue</u> button as needed to page through them.

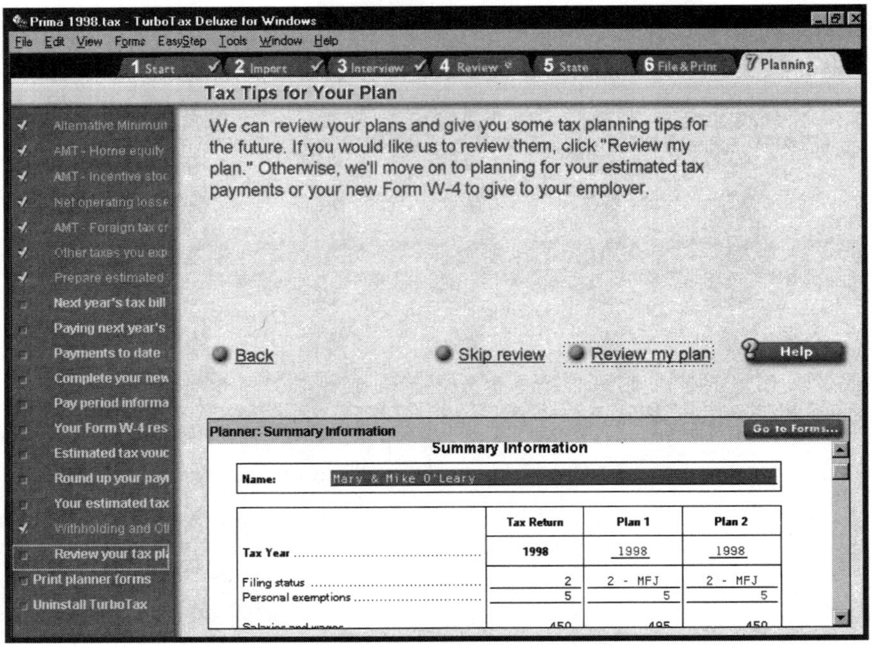

Figure 6.9

TurboTax can use the Reviewer on your tax plan to give you feedback and more tax-planning ideas.

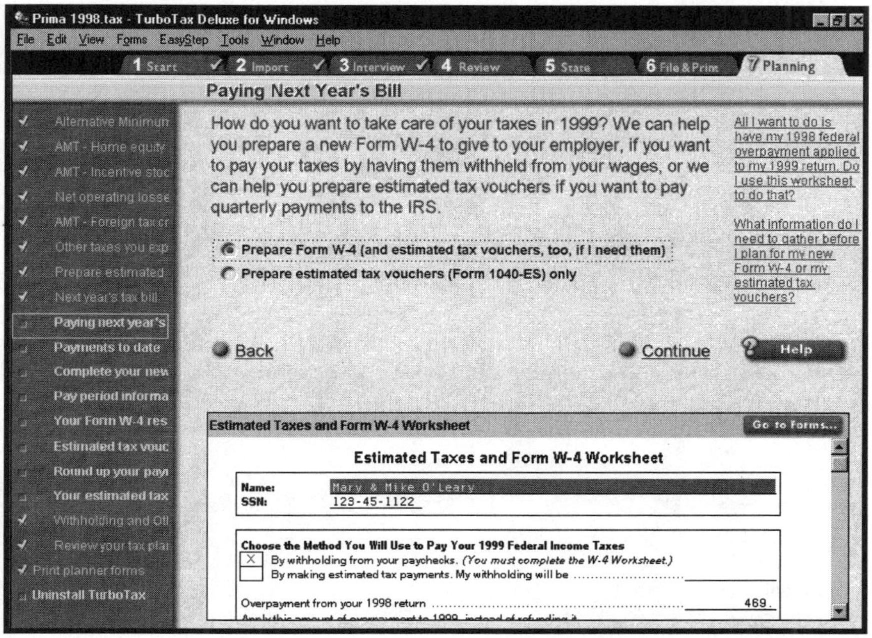

Figure 6.10

You can prepare a W-4 or 1040-ES based on a tax plan.

Planning for Estimated Taxes

Based on your tax plans (Plan 1 or 2), TurboTax can help you prepare your W-4 or Form 1040-ES estimated tax payment vouchers. To do this, select a plan (see Figure 6.10). Then choose either Estimated Tax Payments or W-4 Worksheet. The last tax planner screen allows you to print your tax plan, your W-4, or 1040ES.

Planning for Your IRAs

If you're not sure you should open an IRA, or if you have an IRA that you're considering converting to a Roth IRA, TurboTax's Tax Planner can help you evaluate the costs and benefits (see Figure 6.11). Take a moment to view the video on making IRA contributions (see Figure 6.12). To learn more about IRAs, click on the More Info button and read IRS Publication 590.

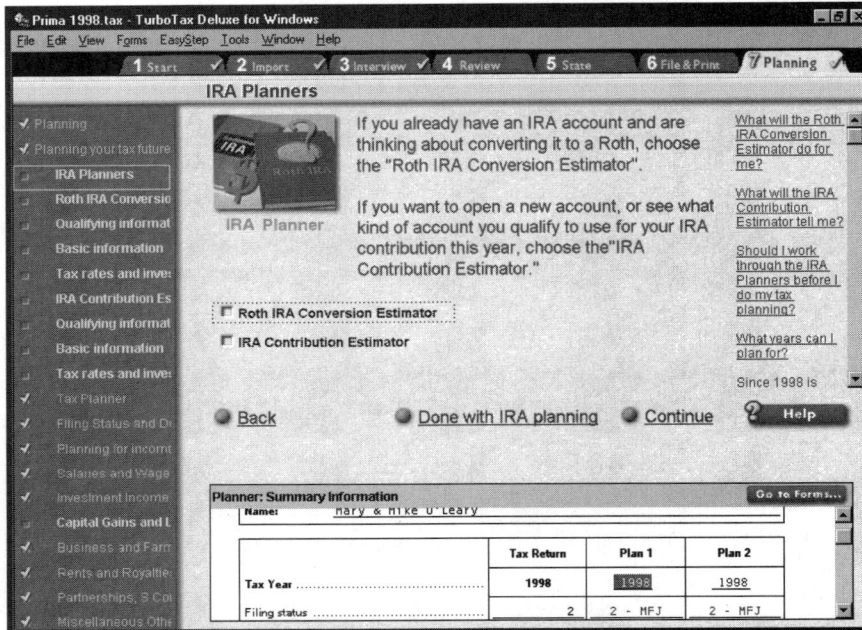

Figure 6.11

TurboTax can help you determine if an IRA will save you taxes.

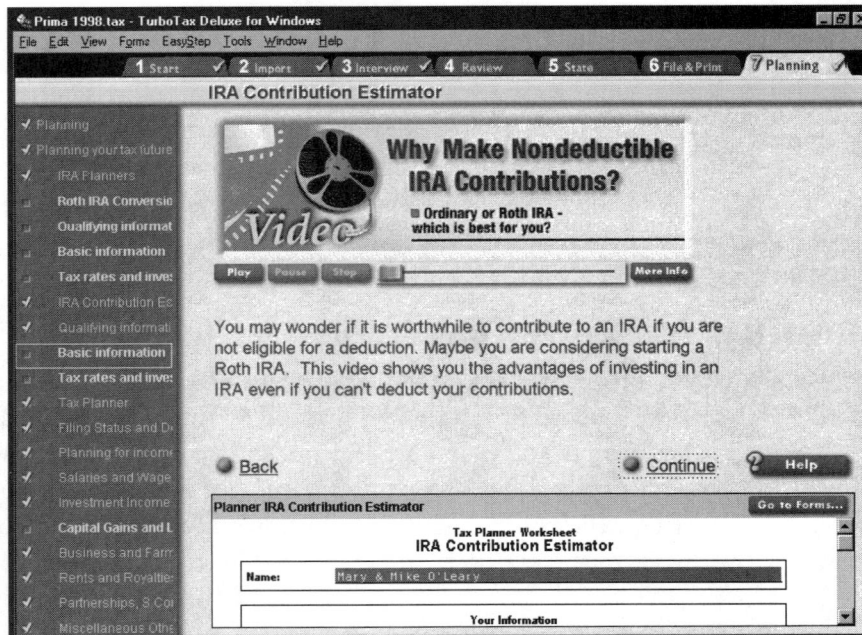

Figure 6.12

The IRA Contribution Estimator asks you for some basic information.

The IRA Planning session is split into two topics:

- Roth IRA Conversion Estimator
- IRA Contribution Estimator

Choose the first topic if you already have a traditional IRA and you want to know whether it would be worthwhile to convert it to a Roth account. Choose the second option if you don't know which kind of IRA to open. Once you've chosen an option, click on <u>Continue</u>.

If you choose the second option, TurboTax will prompt you to select a tax year (1999 or 2000), a filing status, and to enter your estimated AGI for that year (refer to your tax plan for this amount—it doesn't post automatically).

Click on <u>Continue</u> to advance to the next set of questions. You will need to enter

- The age at which you'll start and stop making contributions
- Whether or not you or your spouse have a retirement plan at work

Click on <u>Continue</u>. TurboTax will then explain the contribution limitation rule. Next, you are asked to estimate your annual contribution, enter the age at which you will begin withdrawing from the IRA, and indicate how long you will continue withdrawing from the IRA. Continue to the next question, which prompts you to enter your expected tax rates and rate of return on your investment (such as interest). Based on this information, TurboTax computes your traditional and Roth IRA tax savings (see Figure 6.13). When you are done, click on <u>Done with IRA Contribution Estimator</u>.

If you choose to estimate a Roth IRA conversion, you will be asked when you plan to convert your IRAs, your filing status, and your AGI range (see Figure 6.14). The AGI range selections are more than $100,000 or $100,000 and less. If your AGI is more than $100,000, you cannot convert your existing traditional IRAs to the Roth IRA. For further information on the AGI limits, consult the FAQs and Friday night's discussion of IRAs.

Click on <u>Continue</u>, and as long as your expected AGI is $100,000 or less, you will be prompted for information regarding your existing traditional IRAs (see Figure 6.15). Be sure to read over the FAQs for important information that may pertain to your situation. Then you will be asked for the

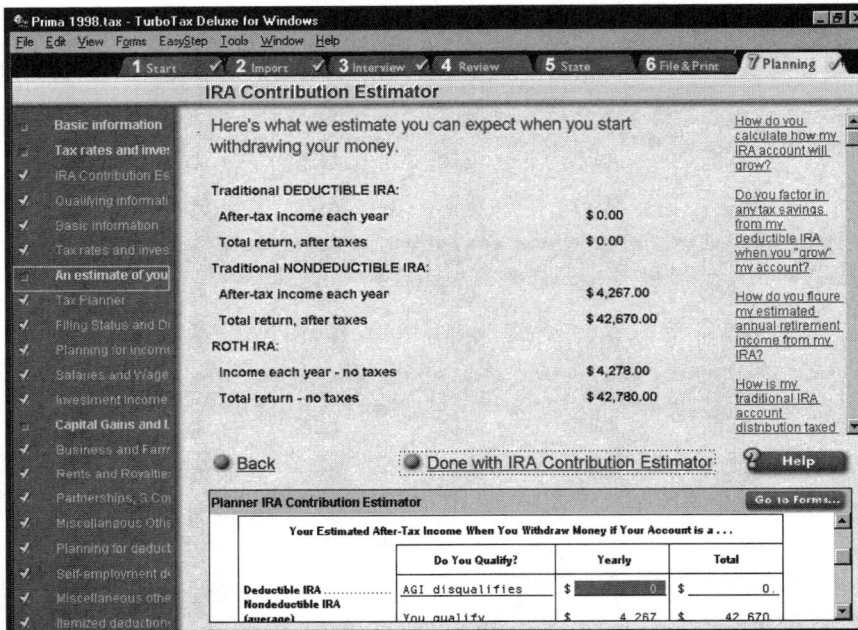

Figure 6.13

At a glance, you can see the benefits of the IRA that is right for you.

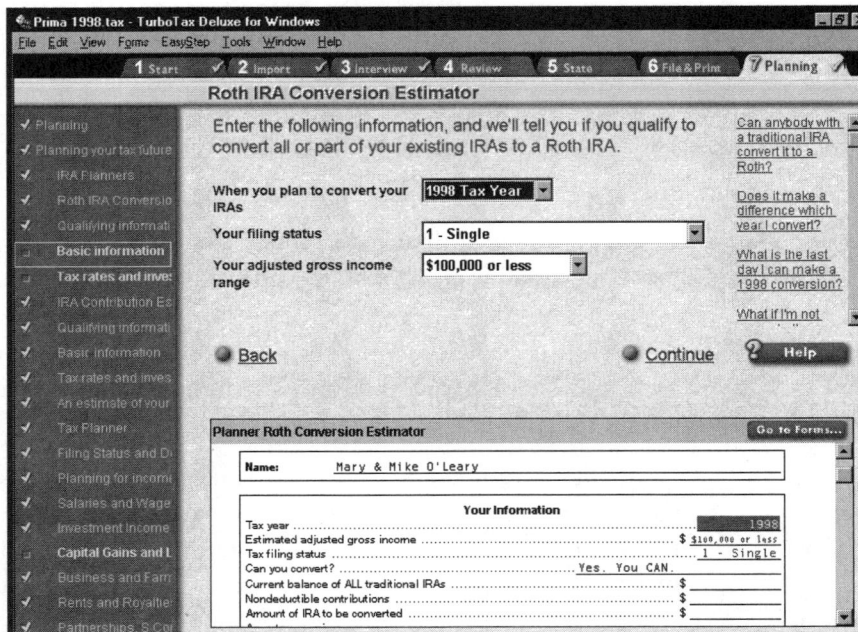

Figure 6.14

TurboTax can determine the tax cost/benefit of converting to a Roth IRA.

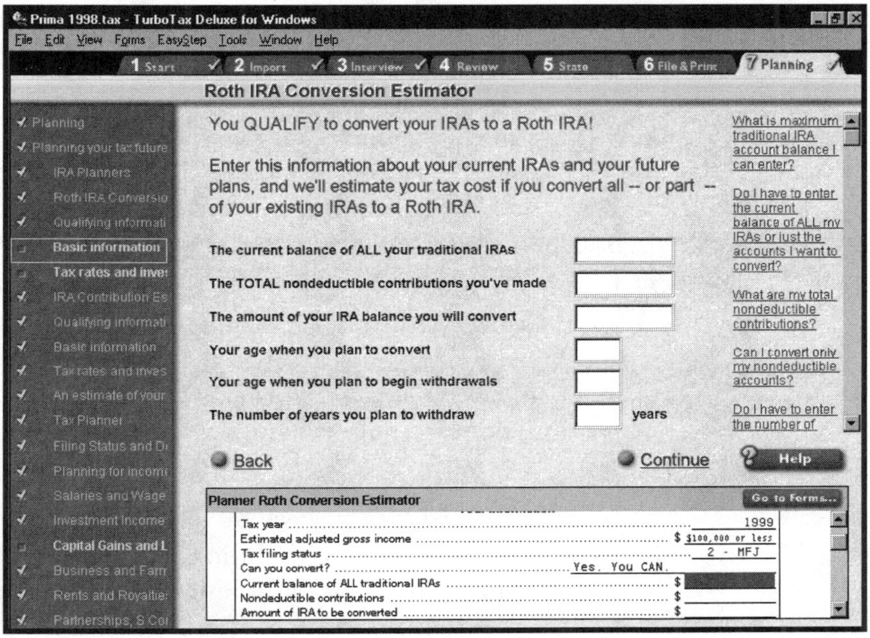

Figure 6.15

Make sure you enter the background information on your existing IRAs.

same tax rate and interest rate (rate of return) information. When you click on <u>Continue</u>, you will see the same type of report as shown in Figure 6.13.

How do you know you've met a good tax advisor?

There's a loophole with the same name.

Implementing Your Tax Plan

You've done good work this weekend, but without implementing your ideas, you won't save a dime in taxes. Here are some tips to help you put your ideas into practice.

○ Automate your checkbook with a product like Quicken. Financial software does more than just print checks and maintain your checkbook register. With it you can set up reminders for your tax estimates and alerts for taxable transactions, as well as keep an eye on your tax deductions throughout the year. Financial software such as Quicken also provides you with detailed reports, which are a great help at tax time.

○ Set up a three-ring binder for tax planning and keep it where you pay your bills or file receipts away. In the front of the binder, tape down a 1999 and 2000 monthly at-a-glance calendar (the kind you find at the back of pocket day-timers). Highlight all due dates.

○ During the year, when your tax situation changes (new job, marital status change, house move, opening an IRA, etc.), open up TurboTax and adjust your tax plan accordingly. Recheck your W-4 and tax estimates to make sure you pay enough taxes, but not too much. Print the updated plan and file it away in your tax-planning binder.

○ When you adjust your tax plan for an increase or decrease in your income, consider how the change might affect your deductions too.

○ As taxable transactions occur during the year, organize your tax records immediately (don't wait until you file your return to get your records in order). For example, if you sell an asset at a gain, gather up your records from the purchase (to prove your basis) and from the sale (to prove the selling price plus any costs to sell), and then staple them together. File it all in your tax folder for 1999; or if it's a large transaction, move the entire folder to your 1999 tax records file drawer.

○ Capture the flag! No, I mean the receipts. Either set up folders for each tax deduction area or designate a large file or box that will serve that purpose. When you get a receipt for a taxable or deductible transaction, write a brief description on the back or staple it to a clean piece of paper and document the transaction there. Write yourself a note such as "Charitable deduction—old clothes given to Salvation Army." Then put the receipt and documentation in the appropriate folder or box—not in your sock drawer. At the end of the year, you will have everything you need in one place, all prelabeled.

○ Before investing in any "tax shelter," consult with a reputable CPA or tax advisor. Unfortunately, many scam operations exist today that take your hard-earned dollars on the promise of high earnings and no taxes. If the deal sounds too good to be true, it probably is. It's always best to get a second opinion from an independent, reliable CPA or tax advisor.

✿ Tax laws have a tendency to change during the year, and sometimes the changes even affect prior years (retroactive tax law changes). If you have access to the Internet, you can keep up to date on tax law changes via TurboTax's Web site and the Intuit Web sites. Personal income tax newsletters such as the J.K. Lasser Monthly Tax Letter provide you with clear, concise coverage of tax law changes (815-734-1104, $24 for a one year subscription) in hard copy. Your CPA or tax advisor may also be able to provide you with a monthly or quarterly update bulletin. Just remember, you file and plan in the spring, but if the tax law changes in the summer, you'll need to revise your tax plan accordingly.

Take a Break

Now would be a good time for you to get up and stretch. Walk around a bit and clear your mind. Grab a drink and a healthy snack (popcorn is a vegetable, right?). When you come back, you'll learn how to file an amended return and what to do if you are audited.

Amending Your Return

It's never too late when it comes to taxes; although if you owe money, you will have to pay interest and maybe penalties too. If you discover an error on a return that you already filed, the best thing to do is file an amended return (Form 1040X) as soon as you can. The same goes for state tax returns. (States have their own version of an amended return.)

You can amend a federal tax return within three years after you originally filed your return, or within two years after you paid the tax that was due for that tax year. The most current version of Form 1040X is used, regardless of the year being amended.

TIP IRS Publication 17 (Your Federal Income Tax) provides you with a detailed discussion of amending your return and how to file Form 1040X.

Although the Interview process doesn't cover amended returns, TurboTax does include a Form 1040X in the Forms library. Just choose Forms, Open a Form and scroll down to the bottom of the list. Then page up twice. Sandwiched in between Form 1040-V (Payment Voucher) and the W-2 is Form 1040X (Amended U.S. Individual Income Tax Return). Select 1040X and click on the Open button. Form 1040X opens on your screen in Forms method (see Figure 6.16).

If you need to amend your 1998 tax return, enter "98" in the box after "This return is for calendar year 19__." After you press Enter, TurboTax will copy the corrected amounts from the TurboTax data file (to column C) and compute the difference (column B). You only need to enter the amounts originally reported (column A).

If you are amending a return prior to 1998 (such as for 1997 or 1996), you will need to enter the amounts as originally reported (or amended per an audit or a prior 1040X), as well as the change or correct amount. TurboTax will fill in the net change or correct amount column as needed (if you fill in

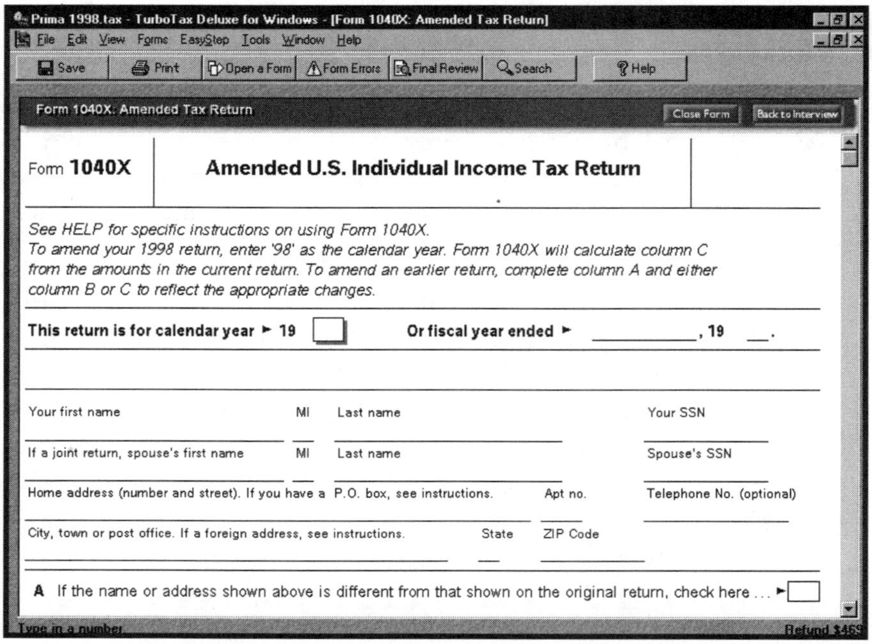

Figure 6.16

If you need to file a corrected tax return, use Form 1040X.

column B, TurboTax will compute column C and vice versa). It's up to you which column you'd rather enter your data into, B or C. TurboTax will squeeze out the difference and fill in whichever column you do not complete.

TIP If you moved or changed your name since you filed the original return, be sure to check the box on line A.

Work your way through the form, filling out the lines as needed with your original tax return amounts, along with the change or correct amount. When it comes to supporting your change, you should keep the following issues in mind:

- If you are amending a year other than 1998, you will need to get copies of the prior year's IRS forms and schedules. For example, if you change an itemized deduction, you will need to show how it affects Schedule A. Some taxpayers just make a copy of their prior year's "as filed" tax form, "white-out" the old totals, and write in the new totals. Others prefer to get a blank form and rewrite the entire schedule.

- Be sure to use the proper standard deduction, personal exemptions, and tax rates for the year you are amending.

- In general, be sure to give the IRS a complete description and support for the amendment you make to your return.

CAUTION Although you can file a 1040X to change your filing status, you can't change from Married Filing Joint to Married Filing Separately for tax return years prior to 1996.

It takes longer to process 1040X forms than regular tax returns. It may take up to three months to get your refund, but of course any tax due must be paid with your amended return.

TIP Any time you amend your federal return, chances are that the state tax return will need to be amended too. Call your state or visit the state's Web site for the proper amended tax form.

Being Unable to Pay Taxes

If you can't pay the tax that is due with your amended tax return, or any tax return for that matter, you can work out a payment plan with the IRS. Form 9465 (Installment Agreement Request; see Figure 6.17), which is included in TurboTax, must be filed in a timely manner. Both the taxpayer and the spouse must sign the agreement.

In most cases the IRS will work with you and agree to the installment payment plan. Note, however, that you will be charged interest (currently 8 to 10 percent) and penalties (about .05 percent per month) on the late amount. You will also be charged a one-time processing fee of $43. Before you sign up with the IRS, shop around and see if you can get a better interest rate on a loan from a bank.

NOTE

You can only have one installment plan with the IRS at a time. When you sign the installment loan agreement, you agree to pay your future taxes on time by making estimated payments or through withholding on your paycheck.

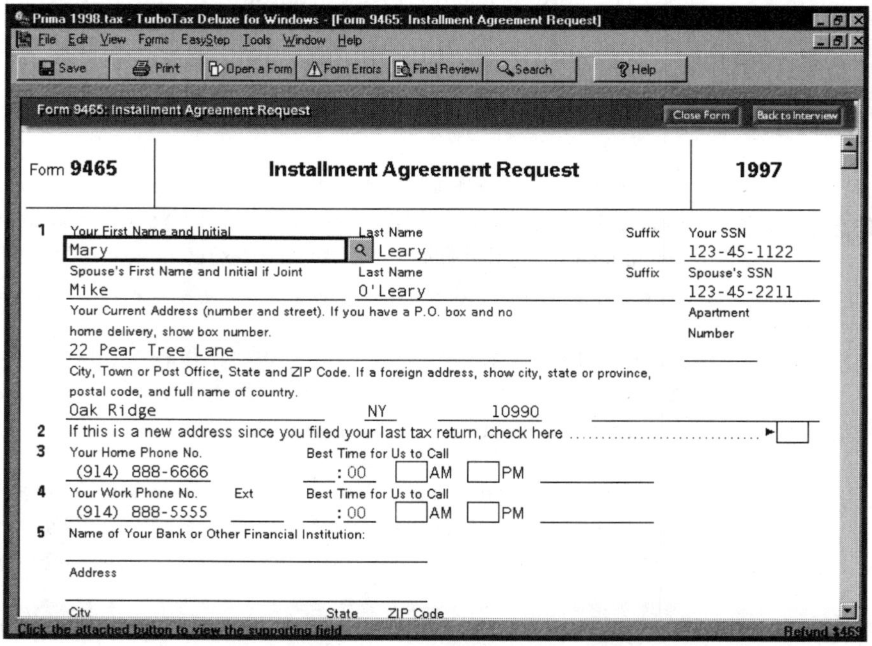

Figure 6.17

If you can't pay your taxes, file Form 9465 and ask to arrange a payment plan.

Managing a Tax Audit

Nothing instills fear in the hearts of Americans like a letter from the IRS. Well, almost nothing, except a letter from the IRS announcing that an auditor would like to meet with you.

Tax audits, examinations, and desk reviews of your tax returns (federal and state) have got to rank up there with root canals. And the root canal might be preferable for many of us.

Well, don't panic. First and foremost, take comfort in knowing that you have taken the time to organize your taxes. Whenever you ventured into an unknown tax area, you researched the topic and consulted a tax advisor if necessary. Often the taxing authority is just missing a 1099 or has the incorrect SSN. Any mismatch in the computer will send up a flag and issue you a notice. Occasionally, the IRS conducts audits or reviews of a specific sector of the public, such as lawyers or pizza parlor owners. Audits provide the IRS with valuable insights into what is "normal" in that business or profession. Information from these audits is used to establish standards and guidelines for reviewing similar returns.

> "The trick is to stop thinking of it as your money."
>
> —A Tax Auditor (who wants to remain anonymous, for obvious reasons)

Types of Audits

Regardless of the reason for the tax audit, you should know that there are many different types of audits. Some are quick and easy, while others could go on for a while.

✪ **Statement of Changes to Your Account**. The IRS is bypassing you and just changing your return. You have the right to question the adjustment and contest the changes. Usually a call to the IRS (at the 800 number given on the form) clarifies the reason for the change. If the IRS is in error, gather together your proof, explain in a cover letter the mistake, and respectfully ask for the correction to be made. Send your response in writing to the IRS using the post office's certified, return receipt service. Wait two weeks and if you don't hear back, call again.

- **Request for Additional Information**. The IRS sends you a letter asking for additional information to support a number on your tax return or a tax law position (which differs from the IRS's interpretation of the tax law). Almost one-third of audits are conducted via mail. Do not ignore these letters. Respond with a clear, concise cover letter, and include a copy of the IRS's letter to you as well as the additional information requested. Send the documents to the address provided, using the post office's certified, return receipt service.

- **Office Examination**. The IRS sends a letter notifying you of the date, time, and location of your audit. You should bring along a copy of your tax return as filed and any substantiation materials that the IRS requests. For example, if the subject of the audit is a large charitable contribution deduction, bring the letter from the charity that supports that deduction. About 50 percent of all IRS audits are office exams. Do not stand up the IRS—they don't take it well. Always call in advance if you need to reschedule or if you run into problems meeting at the appointed time.

- **Field Audit**. The IRS sends a letter notifying you of the date and time of the audit to be held at your place of business or home. This method is used about one-third of the time and is usually chosen because of the complexity of the issue—or to examine the business assets or the building or home office. Whereas an office exam usually centers on a list of specific issues, field audits often create more lists of issues than just the initial audit topic.

Audit Triggers

The IRS uses statistical analysis to rate returns against the norm. Weights are assigned to various items on a return, and then the returns are ranked to determine which ones have the greatest potential for error. The statistical model that the IRS uses is based on the results of taxpayer audits over the years. The IRS doesn't publish the exact benchmarks, but you can get an idea from TurboTax as to where you fall compared to other taxpayers. The TurboTax Review provides you with a report that compares various parts of your return to the national average. If you haven't had a chance to run that report yet, click on the Review tab and select Review U.S. Averages. While you are there, you might want to run another helpful Review: Audit Alerts. The Audit Alerts feature looks through your return and lets you know if anything looks odd or out of sync. It's about the same as having a tax advisor review your return.

Here is a list of issues that might raise the old IRS audit flag:

- Someone (usually not a friend) informs the IRS that you are omitting income from your return. The good news is that the IRS audits the informer too!
- You deduct losses from a tax shelter.
- You report gains or losses from a complex transaction without clearly explaining the situation.
- Your itemized deductions exceed IRS guidelines (see Table 7.1).
- You receive cash income that the IRS believes is easy not to report properly.
- Your contributions to charity are higher than the IRS believes someone at your income level can afford.
- You or your spouse conducts a home business that may actually be a hobby or tax shelter scheme.
- You are a shareholder in a closely held corporation that is being audited.
- A prior year's audit resulted in taxes being due.
- You claim excessive medical and dental deductions year after year that exceed the IRS guidelines.

> **Q.** What is black and tan and looks good on an overzealous tax auditor?
>
> **A.** A Doberman

Table 7.1 lists the average amount of deductions by AGI range based on tax returns filed in 1996. TurboTax checks for this when you run the U.S. Averages Review, but you might find this table handy for tax-planning purposes.

TABLE 7.1 AVERAGE ITEMIZED DEDUCTIONS IN 1996

AGI	Medical and Dental	Taxes	Interest	Charitable Contributions
<15,000	5,637	1,884	5,088	1,224
<30,000	4,498	2,189	5,427	1,389
<50,000	4,323	3,083	5,903	1,511
<75,000	4,903	4,410	6,756	1,816
<100,000	6,706	6,108	8,176	2,330
<200,000	11,682	9,514	11,141	3,478
>200,000	36,912	36,657	24,987	19,204

Preparing for an Audit

Remember that your auditor is your friend, as long as you have nothing to hide. Tax auditors have families and hobbies—and they must file the same tax forms that you do. So, take a deep breath and pull out your tax records from that tax year. Review the return to refresh your memory on what happened in that year. The better you kept your tax records, the easier this process will be. Find the tax form, schedule, and line item that the IRS is questioning. Look in your bank statements, cancelled checks, and other tax documents until you find the proof you need to substantiate the amount on your return. If you can't find the proof, try to contact the vendor, payer, employer, or other party to the transaction—they may have a copy of the receipt or be able to vouch for you.

Go back to your return and look for other problems. Use TurboTax, for that tax year (if you have it) or for the current year, to help you find problems. If you are starting from scratch, use the current year's version of TurboTax and create a new tax file with a name like "My 1996 Tax Audit." Enter all of the

data from your return as filed. Since you don't have the TurboTax version for that tax year, the tax computations and tax rates will be wrong. You'll need to use overrides and compute these items yourself. Run the Reviews for Audit Alerts and National Averages. Gather any additional substantiation materials you may need for these other possible audit issues. By anticipating these other items, you will be calmer and better able to respond as an organized and prepared taxpayer (always impressive to auditors).

TIP Don't take all of your records to the exam. Only bring with you the exact documents that the agent requested. Don't volunteer information. Answer the questions truthfully, but don't bring up topics other than the issue at hand.

If it appears certain that you will owe taxes, consider what amount feels reasonable before the audit begins. Many audits end with the IRS auditor and the taxpayer negotiating a reasonable sum to settle on. This saves you and the IRS the time and expense of a long, drawn-out court battle.

You may appoint a CPA, an enrolled agent, or an attorney to represent you before the IRS. To do so, fill out Form 2848 (order it from the IRS or get it online at the IRS Web site). And certainly consult with a tax expert if you feel that your situation is gray (your interpretation of the tax law differs from the IRS's and you believe you are correct) or you need specific tax law advice. If you think the IRS will charge you with fraud, consult a tax attorney before you enter the exam. The attorney will explain the exact rules and inform you of your rights as a taxpayer and as a citizen.

TIP Don't let the IRS agent hurry you into an audit or exam meeting. The Taxpayer Bill of Rights stipulates that you must be given adequate time to get ready. If an agent shows up at your door without notice, be firm on your right to reschedule. If the auditor takes offense, call the local IRS office and ask for a different auditor.

Use your common sense and best manners when dealing with an agent on an audit. Avoid personal and emotional responses. Be firm, but polite. If the agent acts unprofessionally, you do have the right to ask that another agent handle your case. Note that you also have the right to tape the interview (audio only), provided you notify the agent in writing at least 10 days in advance of the meeting. If the IRS tapes the interview, you can request a transcript within 30 days.

Stick to the list on the notice you received, and make sure that the auditor does the same. You only have to answer the questions that pertain to the items on that list. For example, if the letter lists Schedule A charitable contributions, you do not have to answer questions about your dividend income on Schedule B. Politely respond, "I'm sorry, but I didn't come prepared to answer that question. It wasn't on the list you gave me." If you satisfy the auditor on the listed issues, the case will be closed. If not, the auditor may issue you more lists called Information Document Requests (IDRs). At a future meeting, you will then need to answer questions about those other issues.

Handling Audit Changes

Rarely does an audit result in you getting money back. However, if this happens to you, celebrate and pat yourself on the back for all the time you spent organizing your taxes and learning TurboTax.

But if the audit ends with the auditor suggesting changes to your return that result in a tax to be paid, you will be asked to sign Form 870 (Waiver of Restrictions on Assessment and Collection of Deficiency in Tax and Acceptance of Overassessment). By signing Form 870, you give up your right of appeal to both the IRS Office of Appeals and the Tax Court. However, you can still file a claim in Federal District Court or the Court of Federal Claims, unless you have agreed not to do so on Form 870.

Once you sign Form 870, the IRS has the right to assess you for the tax deficiency with any applicable interest and penalties. In the case of a refund, Form 870 is used to claim that refund.

If you disagree with the auditor on the changes, you have several options:

✪ Discuss the issue with the auditor over the phone or in person. Try to discern if there was any miscommunication. Ask if you can provide

further proof to substantiate your claim. Believe it or not, it's actually in the auditor's best interest to resolve issues in order to avoid the expense involved in handling disputes.

✿ If the auditor won't budge, ask to have a personal meeting (not on the phone) with the office manager. The manager has the power to reverse an auditor's findings. Managers will always want to back their people, but when faced with the facts, they must judge fairly (see "Knowing Your Rights" below).

✿ If all else fails, and you're sure that you are correct and that the IRS is wrong, file an appeal with the IRS. You can appeal on your own or hire a tax professional to help or to represent you. I strongly recommend that you hire a tax professional to assist you through the process. For more information, see IRS Publication 5 (Appeal Rights and Preparation of Protests for Unagreed Cases).

Knowing Your Rights

In 1998, Congress passed a new set of laws designed to protect taxpayers from abuses committed by IRS personnel. You can get a copy of these laws from the IRS or any taxpayer advocacy group. One of the many rights you have is that the IRS must inform you of the effect of the tax action being taken, what you can do, and what your rights are. Exercise your rights. When you meet with a revenue agent, ask for a complete explanation of the issues and procedures. You have other rights too, such as the right to a hearing before the IRS can enforce a tax lien or seize property. Your tax advisor can help you with knowing and exercising your rights.

What's the difference between a taxidermist and a tax collector?

The taxidermist only takes the skin.

Printing Forms from the IRS Web Site

Here are step-by-step instructions on how to print forms from the IRS Web site:

1. Open your Web browser and connect to the Internet.
2. Type in the Web site URL **http://www.irs.ustreas.gov/prod/forms_pubs/forms.html** and press Enter.
3. Once the Web page loads, your screen will look like Figure A.1.

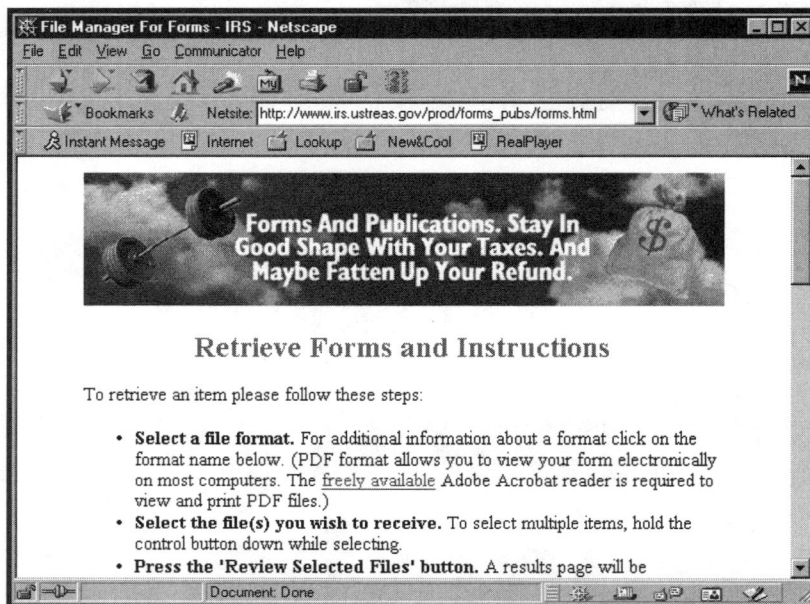

Figure A.1

Printing forms and instructions from the IRS Web site is fast and easy.

4. Scroll down until you can see the file format selection area (see Figure A.2).

5. Select a file format (either PDF, PCL, PostScript, or SGML Text, the last of which merely gives you the instructions in a text-only format).

TIP

FIND IT ON ▶ THE WEB

If your PC cannot read any of the file formats listed, do not despair. Point your Web browser to **www.adobe.com/prodindex/acrobat/readstep.html** and download the free Adobe Acrobat Reader. The Acrobat PDF (portable document format) is fast becoming the standard in distributing documents on the Internet, so you'll be able to use this free plug-in not only at the IRS site but at other Web sites as well. The download and installation processes take about 15 minutes. When you are done, be sure to exit your Web browser and restart your computer before attempting to use your new PDF reader.

6. Scroll down a bit farther, until you can see the Review Selected Files and Clear Selections buttons (see Figure A.3).

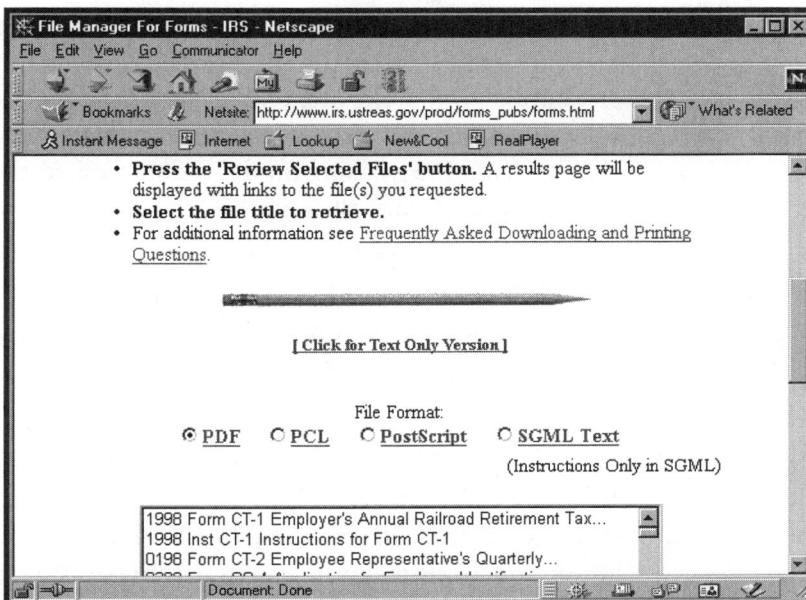

Figure A.2

You can choose whichever file format you prefer.

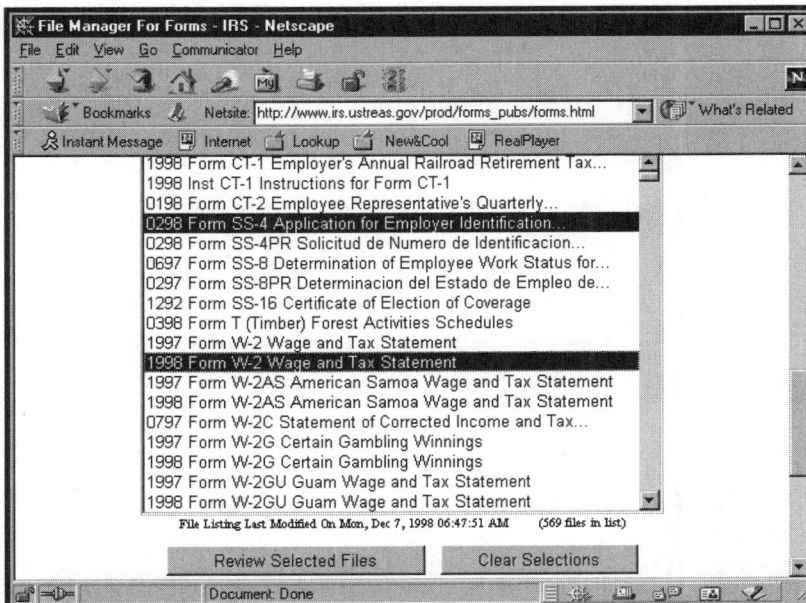

Figure A.3

You can select several tax forms at once.

7. Scroll through the tax form list until you locate the tax form(s) you want to view and print. To select several contiguous forms, hold down the Shift key while clicking on the first and last items in the list of tax forms you want. To select several noncontiguous forms, hold down the Ctrl key while clicking on the various desired tax forms. To deselect all tax forms, click on the Clear Selections button.

8. Once you've made your selections, click on the Review Selected Files button.

9. The IRS displays a listing of the tax forms you requested (see Figure A.4). The file format and size is noted for each, along with each form's name.

10. Click on a form name to download and view the form. Once the form appears, you can print it.

11. If you requested more than one form, use your Web browser's Back button to return to your form request list. Click on another form and print as needed.

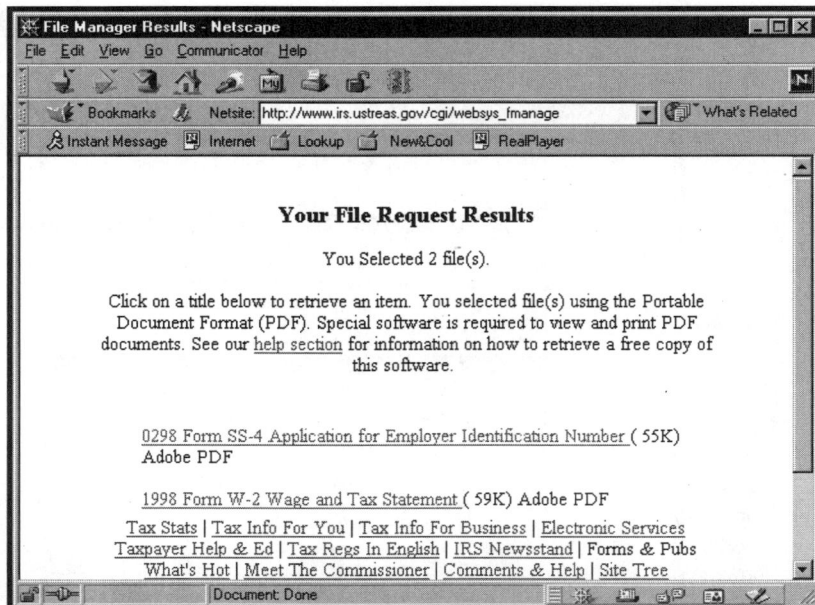

Figure A.4

The IRS lists your requested tax forms.

APPENDIX B

Helpful Lists

This appendix contains a collection of lists that you might find helpful in completing your federal and state tax returns. You will find

- ✪ A tax record checklist
- ✪ Tax-planning tips
- ✪ A list of top 10 errors to avoid
- ✪ Hot tax audit alerts
- ✪ Employee vs. independent contractor guidelines
- ✪ Web site addresses for state tax agencies
- ✪ Addresses for where to file your federal and state tax returns

Tax Record Checklist

Use the following as a basic checklist of tax records that you should keep.

Your income records should cover

- ❏ All W-2s and 1099s
- ❏ Other employee compensation
- ❏ Interest and dividends
- ❏ Rents and royalties
- ❏ Sales of stock, personal residence, and other property
- ❏ Alimony
- ❏ Pensions and annuities
- ❏ Unemployment compensation

- ❑ Social security and railroad retirement benefits
- ❑ Business and farm income
- ❑ Partnership and trust income
- ❑ State and local income tax refunds
- ❑ Gambling and lottery winnings
- ❑ Scholarships and fellowships
- ❑ Other miscellaneous income

Your deduction and credit records should cover

- ❑ Tax return preparation fees
- ❑ Medical expenses
- ❑ Home mortgage interest
- ❑ Investment interest and expenses
- ❑ Charitable contributions, both cash and property
- ❑ Out-of-pocket expenses for volunteer services
- ❑ Union and professional dues
- ❑ Child and disabled-dependent care expenses
- ❑ Job search expenses
- ❑ Retirement plan contributions
- ❑ Expenses for business use of car (including mileage log)
- ❑ Business travel and entertainment expenses
- ❑ Alimony paid
- ❑ Moving expenses
- ❑ Real and personal property taxes
- ❑ Casualty and theft losses
- ❑ Qualified educational expenses
- ❑ Vocational and job-related expenses
- ❑ Forfeited interest
- ❑ State and local income tax payments
- ❑ Business credits
- ❑ Home office and/or sole proprietor business expenditures

Tax-Planning Tips

Here are some more tax-planning tips:

- ✿ To avoid paying long-term capital gains tax on stock that you sell, consider donating the stock to a qualified charitable organization (the contribution would be valued at fair market value).

- ✿ Unload investments that have done poorly before the end of the tax year. In addition to offsetting this year's capital gains, you can use the losses to reduce your ordinary income by as much as $3,000.

- ✿ Replace personal debt (such as car loans and credit card bills) with mortgage debt. Interest expense on mortgage loans is deductible whereas consumer interest is not.

- ✿ Consider the after-tax yield of an investment when comparing the returns on different investments.

- ✿ Consider giving gifts to your children. You may be able to shift income to them since children are usually in lower tax brackets and pay less in taxes. Even if your children are subject to the "kiddie tax," you may still save money due to the child's lower tax bracket base.

- ✿ Make your IRA and Keogh contributions early in the year. Your money will grow faster than if you wait until the last minute (something I'm guilty of!).

- ✿ Contribute the maximum to your 401(k) plan early in the year.

- ✿ If you roll over a pension distribution to an IRA account, be sure you do it in a timely fashion. Otherwise you might be taxed on the full amount. Also note that in some cases there is a 20 percent withholding tax on lump-sum distributions.

✿ Revisit your tax plan quarterly. Use a financial software package such as Quicken to help you track and manage taxable transactions.

Top Ten Errors to Avoid

1. Entering an override amount in TurboTax that wasn't updated for a later change. *Solution:* Use the Review tab to find and review overrides before printing the return. After printing, use a calculator to check the override amount and do the math for all the lines or forms using that amount.

2. Missing deadlines. *Solution:* Know when your estimated payments, tax returns, and special tax elections must be made. For example, the last day to make an IRA contribution for the 1998 tax year is April 15, 1999, whereas the last day to set up a Keogh is December 31, 1998.

3. Incorrectly taking a personal exemption. *Solution:* If you, your spouse, or your child can be claimed as a dependent on someone else's return, do not take a personal exemption for that person on your return. TurboTax prompts you for this information. If you are not sure, contact the other taxpayer and clear up the issue before filing your return.

4. Missing signatures. Be sure to sign your tax return on all forms that require a signature. Also, be sure to sign your tax payment check before sealing the envelope! It's a good idea to write your social security number on the check too.

5. Providing an incorrect spelling of a taxpayer name or an incorrect social security number.

6. Forgetting to attach Copy B of W-2s.

7. For Schedule C taxpayers with a home office deduction, entering mortgage interest and property taxes on Schedule A and on Schedule C. *Solution:* In TurboTax, only enter the mortgage interest and property taxes during the Home Office Deduction Interview. TurboTax will automatically prorate the allowable deductions as needed between Schedule A and Schedule C.

8. Not reporting income for which the IRS has received a 1099.

9. Reporting a deduction for an expense without having the proper proof of payment and purpose.

10. Putting the state tax label on the envelope for the federal tax return and vice versa.

Hot Tax Audit Alerts

Categories of taxpayers or tax-related items that have reportedly piqued the interest of many an auditor include

✿ Workers in a business in which substantial cash payments are often made (most often happens with doctors, lawyers, store owners, and waiters).

✿ Self-employed taxpayers who report gross receipts of $100,000 or more on Schedule C.

✿ Operators of one of the following "high audit risk" companies: bed-and-breakfasts, art dealers, entertainment concerns, gas stations, liquor stores, mortuaries, pawnshops, restaurants and bars, taxi services, and used-car dealers.

✿ Deductions or business expenses that seem out of proportion with the reported income.

✿ Returns signed by an accountant or a tax preparer who is on the IRS list of "problem preparers" who have repeatedly violated the law.

- Discrepancies between your tax return and the information reported to the IRS on Forms W-2 and 1099.

- Married taxpayers who file separate returns. In general, the IRS has found inconsistencies between the two returns.

- Schedule F (farm) losses, particularly when the taxpayer has a sizable salary income.

- Returns that claim the Earned Income Credit. The IRS has found abuse in this area and tends to scrutinize such claims.

Employee or Independent Contractor?

(From IRS Publication 15A, Section 2)

An employer must generally withhold income taxes, withhold and pay social security and Medicare taxes, and pay unemployment taxes on wages paid to an employee. An employer does not generally have to withhold or pay any taxes on payments to independent contractors.

Common-law rules. To determine whether an individual is an employee or an independent contractor under the common law, the relationship of the worker and the business must be examined. All evidence of control and independence must be considered. In any employee-independent contractor determination, all information that provides evidence of the degree of control and the degree of independence must be considered.

Facts that provide evidence of the degree of control and independence fall into three categories: behavioral control, financial control, and the type of relationship of the parties as shown below.

Behavioral control: Facts that show whether the business has a right to direct and control how the

worker does the task for which the worker is hired include the type and degree of

- Instructions the business gives the worker. An employee is generally subject to the business's instructions about when, where, and how to work. Even if no instructions are given, sufficient behavioral control may exist if the employer has the right to control how the work results are achieved.

- Training the business gives the worker. An employee may be trained to perform services in a particular manner. Independent contractors ordinarily use their own methods.

Financial control: Facts that show whether the business has a right to control the business aspects of the worker's job include

- The extent to which the worker has unreimbursed business expenses. Independent contractors are more likely to have unreimbursed expenses than employees. Fixed ongoing costs that are incurred regardless of whether work is currently being performed are especially important. However, employees may also incur unreimbursed expenses in connection with the services they perform for their business.

- The extent of the worker's investment. An independent contractor often has a significant investment in the facilities he or she uses in performing services for someone else. However, a significant investment is not required.

- The extent to which the worker makes services available to the relevant market.

- How the business pays the worker. An employee is generally paid by the hour, week, or month. An independent contractor is

usually paid by the job. However, it is common in some professions, such as law, to pay independent contractors hourly.

✿ The extent to which the worker can realize a profit or incur a loss. An independent contractor can make a profit or loss.

Type of relationship: Facts that show the parties' type of relationship include

✿ Written contracts describing the relationship the parties intended to create.

✿ Whether the business provides the worker with employee-type benefits, such as insurance, a pension plan, vacation pay, or sick pay.

✿ The permanency of the relationship. If you engage a worker with the expectation that the relationship will continue indefinitely, rather than for a specific project or period, this is generally considered evidence that your intent was to create an employer-employee relationship.

✿ The extent to which services performed by the worker are a key aspect of the regular business of the company. If a worker provides services that are a key aspect of your regular business activity, it is more likely that you will have the right to direct and control his or her activities. For example, if a law firm hires an attorney, it is likely that it will present the attorney's work as its own and would have the right to control or direct that work. This would indicate an employer-employee relationship.

IRS help. If you want the IRS to determine whether a worker is an employee, file Form SS-8, Determination of Employee Work Status for Purposes of Federal Employment Taxes and Income Tax Withholding, with the IRS.

State Tax Agencies: Web Sites

Here is a handy listing of the state tax Web sites:

Alabama Department of Revenue
http://www.ador.state.al.us/

Alaska Department of Revenue
http://www.revenue.state.ak.us/

Arizona Department of Revenue
http://www.revenue.state.az.us/

Arkansas Revenue Division
http://www.state.ar.us/revenue/rev1.html

California Franchise Tax Board
http://www.ftb.ca.gov

Colorado Department of Revenue
http://www.state.co.us/gov_dir/revenue_dir/home_rev.html

Connecticut Department of Revenue Services
http://www.state.ct.us/drs/

Delaware Division of Revenue
http://www.state.de.us/govern/agencies/revenue/frame_m.htm

District of Columbia Office of the Chief Financial Officer
http://www.dccfo.com/

Florida Department of Revenue
http://sun6.dms.state.fl.us/dor

Georgia Department of Revenue
http://www2.state.ga.US/Departments/DOR/

Hawaii Department of Taxation
http://www.state.hi.us/tax/tax.html

Idaho State Tax Commission
http://www.state.id.us/tax/home.html

Illinois Department of Revenue
http://www.revenue.state.il.us

Indiana Department of Revenue
http://www.ai.org/dor/index.html

Iowa Department of Revenue and Finance
http://www.state.ia.us/government/drf/index.html

Kansas Department of Revenue
http://www.ink.org/public/kdor

Kentucky Revenue Cabinet
http://www.state.ky.us/agencies/revenue/revhome.htm

Louisiana Department of Revenue
http://www.rev.state.la.us/

Maine Revenue Services
http://janus.state.me.us/revenue

Maryland Comptroller of the Treasury
http://www.comp.state.md.us/

Massachusetts Department of Revenue
http://www.magnet.state.ma.us/dor/dorpg.htm

Michigan Department of Treasury
http://www.treas.state.mi.us

Minnesota Department of Revenue
http://www.taxes.state.mn.us

Mississippi State Tax Commission
http://www.mstc.state.ms.us/

Missouri Department of Revenue
http://dor.state.mo.us

Montana Department of Revenue
http://www.mt.gov/revenue/rev.htm

Nebraska Department of Revenue
http://www.nol.org/home/NDR/

Nevada Department of Taxation
http://www.state.nv.us/taxation/

New Hampshire Department of Revenue
Administration
http://www.state.nh.us/revenue/revenue.htm

New Jersey Division of Taxation
http://www.state.nj.us/treasury/taxation/

New Mexico Taxation & Revenue Department
http://www.state.nm.us/tax/

New York Department of Taxation and Finance
http://www.tax.state.ny.us/

North Carolina Department of Revenue
http://www.dor.state.nc.us/DOR/

North Dakota State Tax Department
http://www.state.nd.us/taxdpt/

Ohio Department of Taxation
http://www.state.oh.us/tax/

Oklahoma Tax Commission
http://www.oktax.state.ok.us/

Oregon Department of Revenue
http://www.dor.state.or.us/default.html

Pennsylvania Department of Revenue
http://www.revenue.state.pa.us/

Rhode Island Division of Taxation
http://www.doa.state.ri.us/tax/

South Carolina Department of Revenue
http://www.dor.state.sc.us/

South Dakota Department of Revenue
http://www.state.sd.us/state/executive/revenue/revenue.html

Tennessee Department of Revenue
http://www.state.tn.us/revenue/

Texas Comptroller of Public Accounts
http://www.cpa.state.tx.us/

Utah State Tax Commission
http://www.tax.ex.state.ut.us

Vermont Department of Taxes
http://www.state.vt.us/tax/index.htm

Virginia Department of Taxation
http://www.state.va.us/tax/tax.html

Washington State Department of Revenue
http://www.wa.gov/DOR/wador.htm

West Virginia Department of Tax & Revenue
http://www.state.wv.us/taxrev/

Wisconsin Department of Revenue
http://www.dor.state.wi.us

Wyoming Department of Revenue
http://revenue.state.wy.us/

A very nice, up-to-date state links page can be found at the Federation of Tax Administrators (FTA) Web site at **www.taxadmin.org/fta/link/link.html**. This Web site also has links to many other tax resources.

Where to File

This table is a listing of addresses for filing federal and state income tax returns:

State	Federal Returns	State Returns
Alabama	IRS Memphis, TN 37501-0002	If a refund or no tax is due: Alabama Income Tax Refund P.O. Box 154 Montgomery, AL 36135-0001 If tax is owed: Alabama Income Tax Division P.O. Box 2401 Montgomery, AL 36140-0001
Alaska	IRS Ogden, UT 84201-0002	No personal income tax.
Arizona	IRS Ogden, UT 84201-0002	Arizona Department of Revenue P.O. Box 29002 Phoenix, AZ 85038-9002

State	Federal Returns	State Returns
Arkansas	IRS Memphis, TN 37501-0002	If a refund or no tax is due: Department of Finance & Administration State Income Tax P.O. Box 1000 Little Rock, AR 72203-1000 If tax is owed: Department of Finance & Administration State Income Tax P.O. Box 2144 Little Rock, AR 72203-2144
California (for the counties of Alpine, Amador, Butte, Calaveras, Colusa, Contra Costa, Del Norte, El Dorado, Glenn, Humboldt, Lake, Lassen, Marin, Mendocino, Modoc, Napa, Nevada, Placer, Plumas, Sacramento, San Joaquin, Shasta, Sierra, Siskiyou, Solano, Sonoma, Sutter, Tehama, Trinity, Yolo, and Yuba)	IRS Ogden, UT 84201-0002	If a refund or no tax is due: Franchise Tax Board P.O. Box 942840 Sacramento, CA 94240-0000 If tax is owed: Franchise Tax Board P.O. Box 942867 Sacramento, CA 94267-0001
(for all other counties)	IRS Fresno, CA 93888-0002	If a refund or no tax is due: Franchise Tax Board P.O. Box 942840 Sacramento, CA 94240-0000 If tax is owed: Franchise Tax Board P.O. Box 942867 Sacramento, CA 94267-0001
Colorado	IRS Ogden, UT 84201-0002	Colorado Department of Revenue 1375 Sherman Street Denver, CO 80261

State	Federal Returns	State Returns
Connecticut	IRS Andover, MA 05501-0002	If a refund or no tax is due: Department of Revenue Services P.O. Box 150420 Hartford, CT 06104-0420 If tax is owed: Department of Revenue Services P.O. Box 150440 Hartford, CT 06104-0440
Delaware	IRS Philadelphia, PA 19255-0002	If a refund or no tax is due: Delaware Division of Revenue P.O. Box 8765 Wilmington, DE 19899-8765 If tax is owed: Delaware Division of Revenue P.O. Box 508 Wilmington, DE 19899-0508
District of Columbia	IRS Philadelphia, PA 19255-0002	Not applicable.
Florida	IRS Atlanta, GA 39901-0002	No personal income tax.
Georgia	IRS Atlanta, GA 39901-0002	Georgia Income Tax Division P.O. Box 740380 Atlanta, GA 30374-0380
Hawaii	IRS Fresno, CA 93888-0002	Hawaii is divided into four tax districts. Taxpayers should file their returns and pay their tax with the taxation district office in which they reside or have their principal place of business. The four taxation district offices are: Oahu District Office P.O. Box 3559 Honolulu, HI 96811-3559

State	Federal Returns	State Returns
Hawaii (continued)		Maui District Office P.O. Box 913 Wailuku, HI 96793-0913
		Hawaii District Office P.O. Box 1377 Hilo, HI 96721-1377
		Kauai District Office P.O. Box 1688 Lihue, HI 96766-5688
		Taxpayers who don't reside in or have a principal place of business within Hawaii should file with:
		Oahu District Office P.O. Box 3559 Honolulu, HI 96811-3559
Idaho	IRS Ogden, UT 84201-0002	Idaho State Tax Commission P.O. Box 56 Boise, ID 83756-0201
Illinois	IRS Kansas City, MO 64999-0002	Illinois Department of Revenue Springfield, IL 62719-0001
Indiana	IRS Cincinnati, OH 45999-0002	Indiana Department of Revenue P.O. Box 40 Indianapolis, IN 46206-0040
Iowa	IRS Kansas City, MO 64999-0002	Iowa Income Tax Processing Department of Revenue and Finance Hoover State Office Building Des Moines, IA 50319-0120
Kansas	IRS Austin, TX 73301-0002	Kansas Income Tax Kansas Department of Revenue Topeka, KS 66699-1000

State	Federal Returns	State Returns
Kentucky	IRS Cincinnati, OH 45999-0002	If a refund is due: Kentucky Revenue Cabinet Frankfort, KY 40618-0006 If tax is owed: Kentucky Revenue Cabinet Frankfort, KY 40619-0008
Louisiana	IRS Memphis, TN 37501-0002	Department of Revenue P.O. Box 3440 Baton Rouge, LA 70823-3440 (Taxpayers may also deliver tax forms and payment to any of the department's regional offices.)
Maine	IRS Andover, MA 05501-0002	Maine Revenue Services Income/Estate Tax Division 24 State House Station Augusta, ME 04333-0024
Maryland	IRS Philadelphia, PA19255-0002	Comptroller of the Treasury Revenue Administration Division Annapolis, MD 21411-0001
Massachusetts	IRS Andover, MA 05501-0002	Massachusetts Department of Revenue P.O. Box 7003 Boston, MA 02204 For refunds, send to: Massachusetts Department of Revenue P.O. Box 7000 Boston, MA 02204
Michigan	IRS Cincinnati, OH 45999-0002	If a refund, a credit, or no tax is due: Michigan Department of Treasury Lansing, MI 48956 If tax is owed: Michigan Department of Treasury Lansing, MI 48929

State	Federal Returns	State Returns
Minnesota	IRS Kansas City, MO 64999-0002	Minnesota Individual Income Tax St. Paul, MN 55145-0010
Mississippi	IRS Memphis, TN 37501-0002	Bureau of Revenue P.O. Box 23050 Jackson, MS 39225-3050
Missouri	IRS Kansas City, MO 64999-0002	If a refund or no tax is due: Department of Revenue P.O. Box 500 Jefferson City, MO 65106-0500 If tax is owed: Department of Revenue P.O. Box 329 Jefferson City, MO 65107-0329
Montana	IRS Ogden, UT 84201-0002	Income Tax Division Department of Revenue P.O. Box 6308 Helena, MT 59604-6308
Nebraska	IRS Ogden, UT 84201-0002	Nebraska Department of Revenue P.O. Box 94818 Lincoln, NE 68509-4818
Nevada	IRS Ogden, UT 84201-0002	No personal income tax.
New Hampshire	IRS Andover, MA 05501-0002	No personal income tax. New Hampshire has a flat tax (5 percent) on some interest and dividend instrument income.
New Jersey	IRS Holtsville, NY 00501-0002	If a refund or no tax is due with or without the Homestead Rebate Application: State of New Jersey Division of Taxation CN 555 Trenton, NJ 08647-0555

State	Federal Returns	State Returns
New Jersey (continued)		If tax is owed: State of New Jersey Division of Taxation CN 111 Trenton, NJ 08645-0111 Homestead Rebate Applications mailed without income tax returns: State of New Jersey Division of Taxation CN 197 Trenton, NJ 08646-0197
New Mexico	IRS Austin, TX 73301-0002	New Mexico Taxation and Revenue Dept. P.O. Box 25122 Santa Fe, NM 87504-5122
New York (for New York City and New York counties of Nassau, Rockland, Suffolk, and Westchester)	IRS Holtsville, NY 00501-0002	State Processing Center P.O. Box 61000 Albany, NY 12261-0001
(for all other counties)	IRS Andover, MA 05501-0002	State Processing Center P.O. Box 61000 Albany, NY 12261-0001
North Carolina	IRS Memphis, TN 37501-0002	North Carolina Department of Revenue P.O. Box R Raleigh, NC 27634-0001
North Dakota	IRS Ogden, UT 84201-0002	State Tax Commissioner State Capitol 600 E. Boulevard Avenue Bismarck, ND 58505-0550

State	Federal Returns	State Returns
Ohio	IRS Cincinnati, OH 45999-0002	If a refund, a credit, or no tax is due: Ohio Department of Taxation P.O. Box 2679 Columbus, OH 43270-2679 If tax is owed: Ohio Department of Taxation P.O. Box 2057 Columbus, OH 43270-2057
Oklahoma	IRS Austin, TX 73301-0002	Oklahoma Tax Commission P.O. Box 26800 Oklahoma City, OK 73126-0800
Oregon	IRS Ogden, UT 84201-0002	If a refund or no tax is due: REFUND P.O. Box 14700 Salem, OR 97309-0930 If tax is owed: Oregon Department of Revenue P.O. Box 14555 Salem, OR 97309-0940
Pennsylvania	IRS Philadelphia, PA 19255-0002	Pennsylvania Dept. of Revenue 4 Revenue Place Harrisburg, PA 17129-0004
Rhode Island	IRS Andover, MA 05501-0002	State of Rhode Island Division of Taxation One Capitol Hill Providence, RI 02908-5801
South Carolina	IRS Atlanta, GA 39901-0002	SC1040 or SC1040NR- Refunds or No Tax Due: Long Form Processing Center P.O. Box 101100 Columbia, SC 29211-0100 SC1040A- Refunds: Short Form Processing Center P.O. Box 101104 Columbia, SC 29211-0104

State	Federal Returns	State Returns
South Carolina (continued)		All Balance Dues: Taxable Processing Center P.O. Box 101105 Columbia, SC 29211-0105
South Dakota	IRS Ogden, UT 84201-0002	No personal income tax.
Tennessee	IRS Memphis, TN 37501-0002	Tennessee does not impose a tax on wages and salaries. There is an income tax (6 percent annually) on certain dividend and interest income. For all returns: Tennessee Department of Revenue Andrew Jackson Building 500 Deaderick Street Nashville, TN 37242
Texas	IRS Austin, TX 73301-0002	No personal income tax.
Utah	IRS Ogden, UT 84201-0002	Utah State Tax Commission 210 N 1950 W Salt Lake City, UT 84134
Vermont	IRS Andover, MA 05501-0002	Vermont Department of Taxes 109 State Street Montpelier, VT 05609-1401
Virginia	IRS Philadelphia, PA 19255-0002	File tax returns at the address specified by the Commissioner of Revenue, Director of Finance, or Director, Department of Tax Administration, for the city or county of residence.

State	Federal Returns	State Returns
Washington	IRS Ogden, UT 84201-0002	No personal income tax.
West Virginia	IRS Cincinnati, OH 45999-0002	Department of Tax and Revenue P.O. Box 1071 Charleston, WV 25324-1071
Wisconsin	IRS Kansas City, MO 64999-0002	If a refund or no tax is due: Wisconsin Department of Revenue P.O. Box 59 Madison, WI 53785-0001 If tax is owed: Wisconsin Department of Revenue P.O. Box 268 Madison, WI 53790-0001
Wyoming	IRS Ogden, UT 84201-0002	No personal income tax.

Glossary

A

Accelerated Cost Recovery System (ACRS). A method of depreciating an asset (such as a car), allowing you to deduct the cost over a period of time, faster than a straight-line method (cost divided by life of asset). Used for most assets placed in service from 1981 to 1986. For assets placed in service after January 1, 1987, see *Modified Accelerated Cost Recovery System (MACRS)*.

Accrual basis. A method of record keeping in which you report income when earned and expenses when incurred, even though you may not receive or pay out the cash until later. Most companies are on an accrual basis. Most individuals are on a *cash basis*.

Adjusted basis. A term used to describe the value of an investment (such as a stock or a bond) after adjusting for costs to improve, depreciation, or other amounts that either add to or subtract from the *basis*.

Adjusted Gross Income (AGI). A line on your tax return and a term used in tax law to represent your gross taxable income less allowable adjustments such as IRA contributions, self-employed tax adjustments, or Keogh contributions. Tax law will often limit other itemized deductions to a percentage of your AGI (for example, medical expenses are limited to two percent of your AGI). See also *Deduction, Itemized deductions*, and *Standard deduction*.

Alternative Depreciation System (ADS). A method of depreciating assets using a straight-line calculation (cost/life in years). Use of this method results in slower recovery of your investment, deduction-wise, and is mandatory for certain assets such as luxury cars, tax-exempt use property, and foreign assets. See also *Straight-Line*, *ACRS*, and *MACRS*.

Alternative Minimum Tax (AMT). An additional tax that you might owe if you take advantage of too many tax havens, which the IRS calls tax-preference items. AMT usually only applies to taxpayers who are in the top tax brackets (30 to 40 percent effective tax rate) and have passive-activity losses, tax credits, or loss carryovers.

Amended return. The tax return form (Form 1040X) that you use to let the IRS know of a change to your originally filed tax return. You have up to three years from the tax return due date to file an amended return.

Amortization. A method (usually straight-line) that allows you to deduct the cost of your investment or spread the cost of the intangible asset over time. Similar to depreciation, but instead used only for an intangible asset. See also *Depreciation*.

Amount realized. A term used to describe the funds received from a transaction, usually sales price less cost of transaction such as commissions, broker fees, and legal fees.

Amount recognized. A term used to describe the taxable gain on a transaction. This amount is not always the same as the *fair market value*.

Annuity. A regular payment of money to a company or an individual. Payments are usually made over a fixed period of time or for the life of the annuity. The taxability of such an annuity depends on what the annuity is for and the other circumstances surrounding the payments. For example, an annuity paid to you from the State Lottery Commission (gambling winnings) is taxable. Whereas an annuity paid on a life insurance policy to the surviving widow is not taxable.

Applicable Federal Rate (AFR). An interest rate set by the U.S. Treasury used to determine imputed interest. See also *Imputed interest*.

Asset. An item with commercial or exchange value (such as a house or a car) that is owned by an individual, an organization, or a company.

Audit. A process where someone—for example, an accountant you hire or a regulatory agency (such as the IRS or a state income tax bureau)—examines your tax return and asks you to provide supporting details as needed. Known to cause ulcers!

B

Bad debt. An overdue amount owed to you that you do not expect to collect.

Balance sheet. An itemized statement that lists each of your assets, liabilities, and equity accounts with their current balance as of a specified date. In a balance sheet, assets minus liabilities must equal the sum in the equity accounts. The amounts given on a balance sheet are generally at historic cost and not at their current value. An exception to this would be assets that are shown net of their respective depreciation and amortization. See also *Asset*, *Depreciation*, and *Amortization*.

Balloon. The final lump sum payment on a loan.

Basis. The cost of an asset. You must know your basis in an asset or property in order to compute depreciation, amortization, and gain or loss on the sale of that asset.

Boot. The cash or its equivalent that you receive in a transaction where property has been exchanged. The tax law treats boot differently, depending on the circumstances surrounding the transaction. For example, if you trade your car to someone for their boat plus $200, the $200 is called "boot." In a tax-free exchange (tax basis of the car equals tax basis of the boat), the boot is taxable income.

C

Calendar year. A 12-month period beginning on January 1 and ending on December 31. Most individual taxpayers must file their tax returns based on a calendar year. See also *Fiscal year.*

Capital asset. Property used for personal use or investment, as opposed to being for business use.

Capital gain or loss. Your net profit or loss from the sale or exchange of a capital asset.

Cash basis. A method of record keeping where you report income when received and expenses when actually paid. Most individual taxpayers use the cash method of accounting. See also *Accrual basis.*

Corporation. A business owned by shareholders and treated as a separate legal and taxable entity. See also *Sole proprietor* and *Partnership.*

D

Deduction. An expense incurred that is allowed by the IRS to be used as a reduction of your taxable income. See also *Adjusted Gross Income (AGI), Itemized deductions,* and *Standard deduction.*

Deferred gain. A gain realized but not recognized by the IRS as being taxable income until a later time.

Dependent. A person supported financially by a taxpayer. If the financial support and relationship meet certain tests, the taxpayer may be able to claim tax benefits (such as additional exemptions).

Depreciation. An expense that represents the wear and tear of tangible property. Tax treatment and calculation of depreciation vary depending on the property type and use.

Dividend. A portion of a corporation's profit paid to its shareholders.

E

Earned income. Compensation for personal services rendered.

Employee. A person who performs work under the control and direction of an employer. See the Appendix B section "Employee or Independent Contractor?" for a list of IRS guidelines.

Exemption. An amount that a taxpayer can use to reduce taxable income based on the number of dependents. The taxpayer and spouse count as dependents for purposes of the exemption allowance calculation.

F

Fair market value (FMV). The price buyers are willing to pay for an object and also the amount the seller is willing to accept.

Fiscal year. A 12-month period ending on the last day of any month other than December. See also *Calendar year.*

401(k) plan. A tax-deferred compensation plan where employees can contribute pretax dollars and earn tax-free income until the money is withdrawn (usually at retirement).

G

Gross income. All of your taxable income prior to subtracting adjustments for adjusted gross income (AGI), deductions, or exemptions.

H

Holding period. The period of time that an asset is owned. For capital assets, the holding period determines whether a sale or an exchange is treated as a short-term or a long-term capital gain or loss.

I

Imputed interest. Interest deemed earned on low-interest rate loans where the stated interest rate is lower than the published applicable IRS federal interest rate.

Independent contractor. A worker who operates under his or her own control and direction and is deemed to be self-employed for tax purposes. See the Appendix B section "Employee or Independent Contractor?" for a list of IRS guidelines.

Individual Retirement Account (IRA). An account that allows taxpayers to save for retirement and realize reduced taxes on that retirement savings. Specific and sometimes complex rules govern contributions to and withdrawals from IRAs.

Internal Revenue Service (IRS). U.S. Treasury division that is responsible for implementing and enforcing the U.S. tax laws passed by Congress, as well as for collecting taxes.

Itemized deductions. Expenses incurred that are allowed by the IRS to be used, in part or in full, as a reduction of your adjusted gross income (AGI). Taxpayers can deduct either their itemized deductions (Schedule A) or the standard deduction but not both. See also *Deduction, Adjusted Gross Income,* and *Standard deduction.*

J

Joint return. A tax return filed by a married couple that reports on the couple's combined income and deductions.

L

Long-term capital gain or loss. A gain or loss on a sale or an exchange of a capital asset held for more than 12 months. See also *Short-term capital gain or loss.*

M

Modified Accelerated Cost Recovery System (MACRS). A method of depreciating an asset (such as a car) to write off the cost over time. MACRS is used for assets placed in service after 1986. MACRS is less favorable than the

previous ACRS system. See also *Accelerated Cost Recovery System (ACRS)* and *Straight-Line.*

Marginal tax rate. The rate at which each additional dollar of income above a specified limit is taxed.

Materially participate. A taxpayer who is involved in a business or venture on a regular, substantial, and continuous basis is said to have materially participated in that business or venture. See also *Passive activity.*

N

Nontaxable exchange. An exchange of property where no taxable gain or loss is recognized.

O

Ordinary income. Income that is not eligible for preferential tax treatment (such as capital assets or depreciable assets).

Original Issue Discount (OID). The amount that is the difference between the face value and the price you pay for debt instruments such as bonds. OID is taxable and must be included in taxable income over the life of the debt instrument.

P

Partnership. An unincorporated business that is owned by more than one person. Partnerships are not taxable entities, so all income, expenses, deductions, and credits pass through to the partners as self-employment income based on the partnership agreement. See also *Sole proprietor* and *Corporation.*

Passive activity. A business or venture in which the taxpayer does not participate materially (that is, on a regular, substantial, and continuous basis). Tax rules are very strict with regard to passive activities in general. Passive-activity losses are limited and may be denied in total. See also *Materially participate.*

Proprietor. A person who is the sole owner of a business.

R

Realized gain or loss. A gain or loss that is recorded in your financial records.

Recognized gain or loss. A realized gain or loss that is reported as a taxable amount on your tax return.

S

S Corporation (S-corp). A small corporation that meets the requirements outlined in Subchapter S of the Internal Revenue Code (IRC). From a tax perspective, S-corps operate like a partnership.

Self-employed. A worker who operates under his or her own control and direction and is deemed to be self-employed for tax purposes. See the Appendix B section "Employee or Independent Contractor?" for a list of IRS guidelines.

Short-term capital gain or loss. A gain or loss on a sale or an exchange of a capital asset held for 12 months or less. See also *Long-term capital gain or loss.*

Sole proprietor. A person who is the sole owner of a business. See also *Partnership* and *Corporation.*

Standard deduction. If you decide not to itemize your deductions, you are entitled to a standard deduction amount as specified by the IRS. The exact amount differs depending on your filing status, age, and vision. See also *Deduction, Adjusted Gross Income,* and *Itemized deductions.*

Straight-Line. A method of depreciating an asset (such as a car), allowing you to deduct the cost over a period of time computed by dividing the cost of the asset by the expected life of the asset. See also *ACRS* and *MACRS.*

Statute of limitations. The date until which the IRS can assess and collect taxes and you can file for a tax refund.

T

Taxable income. Income you receive that is subject to income tax. Also, a line on Form 1040 that roughly computes as your gross income less adjustments, deductions, and exemptions.

W

Wash sales. Occurs when you sell stock at a loss, and within 30 days before or after the sale, you buy the same stock. Seen as a scam by the IRS, wash sales losses are not deductible.

INDEX

automobile expenses
as employee business expense, 205
entering information on, 149-151
medical purposes, miles driven for, 184
mileage/maintenance log, 19
registration fees, deducting, 194
Schedule C, entering on, 145
standard mileage method, 150-151
averages, national, 256, 265-267

B

Back bullet, 52
backing up data, 284-285
Back to Interview button, 172
backup withholding, 108-109
defined, 13
banks
deposit box deduction, 21
foreign bank/financial accounts, 237
Form 1099, filing, 108
Big Five CPA firms, 27
birth date, 79, 80
blind persons
defined, 177
seeing eye dogs, 183
blood relatives, defined, 88
bonds. *See also* broker transactions
original issue discount (OID), 119-120
private activity bonds, 117-118
Bosnia, combat pay from, 80
Boy Scouts, 191
broker transactions
Form 1099, entering income on, 120-125
more-than-18-month holding period, elimination of, 124
statements, 18
business assets
accounting for, 145, 151-153
selling, 153-154
Business Code, 137
business expenses, 144-149
employee business expenses, deducting, 202-204
business income, 136-142
entering, 140-141

business records, 24-25
Buy and Download State feature, 271-272

C

calendar year, defined, 64
California, multiple IRS return-processing centers, 81
capital, defined, 117
capital assets. *See also* business assets
broker transaction income, 121
defined, 117
capital gains and losses, 8
broker transaction income and, 122-124
calculating, 125
defined, 117
more-than-18-month holding period, elimination of, 124
saving taxes on, 34
car expenses. *See* automobile expenses
carryovers, home office deduction and, 158
cash basis, defined, 139
cash disbursements (CD) journal, 24-25
cash transactions, 17
casualty losses, 21
deductions for, 207-209
Form 4684, 208
home office deduction and, 158
insurance coverage of, 208
CD-ROM, CD in, 57
certification of returns, 249
certified public accountants (CPAs), 26-27
audits, representation at, 319
change of address, 80, 238, 247
charitable donations
50 percent limit, 190, 192
as itemized deduction, 188-194
qualified organizations, 191
rules on, 189
timing for, 190
checkbooks
automating, 309-310
reviewing, 17
Child and Dependent Care Tax Credit, 29-30, 230, 231
married filing separate (MFS) filing status and, 85
new rules for, 90-91

TO ORDER BOOKS

Please send me the following items:

Quantity	Title	Unit Price	Total
_____	_____	$_____	$_____
_____	_____	$_____	$_____
_____	_____	$_____	$_____
_____	_____	$_____	$_____
_____	_____	$_____	$_____

	Subtotal	$_____
	Deduct 10% when ordering 3–5 books	$_____
	7.25% Sales Tax (CA only)	$_____
	8.25% Sales Tax (TN only)	$_____
	5.0% Sales Tax (MD and IN only)	$_____
	Shipping and Handling*	$_____
	TOTAL ORDER	$_____

Shipping and Handling depend on Subtotal.

Subtotal	Shipping/Handling
$0.00–$14.99	$3.00
$15.00–29.99	$4.00
$30.00–49.99	$6.00
$50.00–99.99	$10.00
$100.00–199.99	$13.00
$200.00+	call for quote

Foreign and all Priority Request orders:
Call Order Entry department for price quote at 1-
916-632-4400

This chart represents the total retail price of books only
(before applicable discounts are taken).

By telephone: With Visa, Mastercard, or American Express, call 1-800-632-8676. Mon.–Fri. 8:30–4:00 PST.

By Internet e-mail: sales@primapub.com

By mail: Just fill out the information below and send with your remittance to:

PRIMA PUBLISHING

P.O. Box 1260BK

Rocklin, CA 95677-1260

www.primapublishing.com

Name_____ Daytime Telephone_____

Address _____

City _____ State _____ Zip _____

Visa /MC#_____Exp. _____

Check/Money Order enclosed for $_____ Payable to Prima Publishing

Signature _____

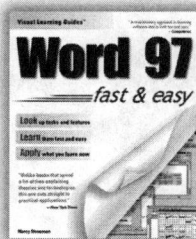

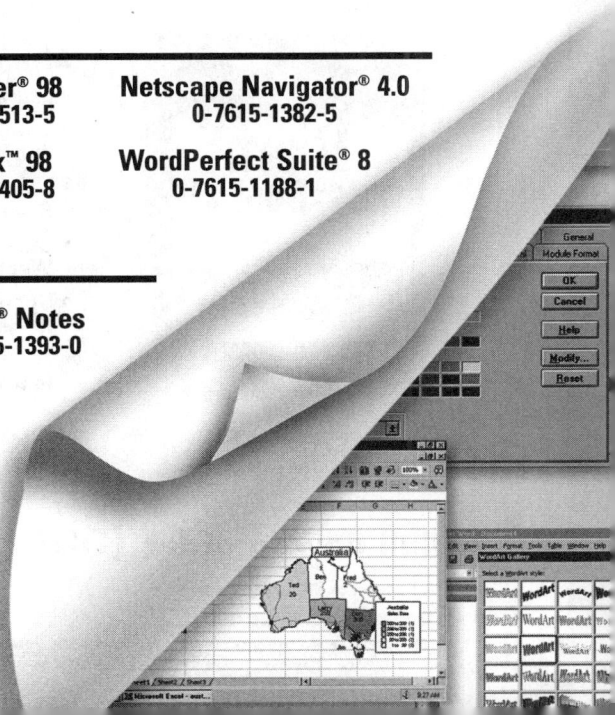

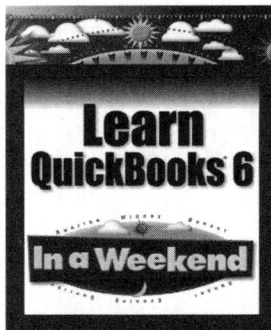